The History of the Galician Division of the Waffen-SS

Volume One

ON THE EASTERN FRONT

The History of the Galician Division of the Waffen-SS

Volume One

ON THE EASTERN FRONT

April 1943 to July 1944

MICHAEL JAMES MELNYK

FONTHILL

Fonthill Media Language Policy

Fonthill Media publishes in the international English language market. One language edition is published worldwide. As there are minor differences in spelling and presentation, especially with regard to American English and British English, a policy is necessary to define which form of English to use. The Fonthill Policy is to use the form of English native to the author. Michael James Melnyk was born and educated in Norwich, England where he currently resides; therefore British English has been adopted in this publication.

The author wishes to hear from readers holding any related material on this subject and can be contacted via the publisher.

Fonthill Media Limited
Fonthill Media LLC
www.fonthillmedia.com
office@fonthillmedia.com

First published in the United Kingdom
and the United States of America 2016

British Library Cataloguing in Publication Data:
A catalogue record for this book is available from the British Library

Copyright © Michael James Melnyk 2016

ISBN 978-1-78155-528-6

The right of Michael James Melnyk to be identified as the author of this work has been asserted by him in accordance with the Copyright, Designs and Patents Act 1988.

Typeset in 10.5pt on 13pt Sabon
Printed and bound in England

Acknowledgements

This book represents the culmination of the contributions of several individuals, none more so than my best friend and mentor Roman Kolisnyk, former officer and veteran of the Galician Division. For decades he devoted himself to the study of the Division and his unsurpassed knowledge and unrivalled network of contacts, was of immeasureable benefit to me and underpinned many areas of my research. I remain sincerely appreciative of his constant support and encouragement, wise counsel and constant enthusiasm. I hope this work will refelect his efforts and contribute to his already formidable legacy.

Other veterans who gave valuable assistance and the benefit of their expertise include;
Myron Scharko, Roman Hawrylak, Volodymyr Motyka, Theo Andruszko and Volodymyr Keczun. I will also remain ever thankful for the support of Ostap Sokolsky, Bohdan Kutny and Eugene Shypailo who, although now deceased, worked tirelessly on my behalf amongst the veteran community. I consider it a privilege to have known and worked with them and I hope that this work will do justice to their unfailing assistance.

My heartfelt thanks also go to my good friend Andrij Zhukevych who very kindly provided me with many photographs from his private collection as well as assisting me with obtaining information and material directly from veterans in Ukraine. Likewise Filip Zierfuss for his artistic skills, photographs and information about the Division in Slovakia and Klemen Luzar and Klemen Kocjancic who made available much useful data pertaining to the Division's activities in Slovenia. Petro Kormylo provided a great deal of important help both from his own father's archive and with the veterans in Great Britain. Author John Moore whose outstanding *Offiziereliste der Waffen-SS*, compiled over the course of many years and whose ongoing projects continue to set a very high bar, never failed to respond to requests for assistance.

I would like to extend my appreciation in equal measure to; Mychailo Klymchuk and his son Andrej Klymchuk both of whom were there from the very start, Horst Wächter, Steve Tyas, Christine Owad, Richard Rygaard, Andrij Usach, Petter Kellander and Ludmila Pekarska, all of whom made noteworthy contributions in providing unique material. My long time friend Andrew Keys who time and again performed minor technical miracles with all aspects of computer technology when all seemed to be lost, deserves my cordial thanks.

Indispensible personal information, documents and photographic material was obtained through interviews and correspondence with the following veterans; Lev Babij, Roman Bilohan, Jaroslav Botiuk, Roman Cholkan, Petro Cisarsky, Roman Chomicky, Julian Chornij, Fedir Cymbaliuk, Stefan Dmytryk, Mychailo Dobriansky, Roman Drazniowsky, Mychailo Duskursky, Jaroslav Hnatkiv, Myron Holowaty, Orest Horodysky, Jaroslav Hunka, Stefan Ilnycky, Roman Jasynsky, Bohdan Kalba, Taras Katzchmarchuk, Walter Keczun, Markian Kohut, Stefan Kosandiak, Mykola Kostiuk, Volodymyr Kudla, Zenon Kuk, Omelan Kulchysky, Jaoroslav Kunysky, Bohdan Kutny, Ewhen Lohaza, Desmond Lusniak, Oleh Lysiak, Myroslav Malecky, Petro Maslij, Ivan Melnyk, Mychailo Mochnaty, Woldymyr Molodecky, Leonid Mucha, Volodymyr Mykula, Ivan Nyzka, Mychailo Ostapiuk, Myron Pasij, Mychailo Paziuk, Petro Pilkiw, Myron Proczak, Mychailo Prymak, Stephan Reskovych, Bohdan Romanovsky, Bohdan Sadiwsky, Michael Sadiwsky, Stefan Sadiwsky, Ivan Sadovey, Myron Scharko, Eugene Shypailo, Vasyl Sirsky, Volodymyr Skilnyk, Orest Slupchynsky, Ostap Sokolsky, Vasyl Tomkiv, Vasyl Veryha, Omelan Wawryk and Julian Wilshynsky.

I trust that these contributors will understand that however grateful I am for their assistance, the pursuit of intellectual honesty and historical accuracy must take priority over personal appreciation in cases of conflicting information or interpretation of the available evidence.

Lastly my mother Rose Melnyk who has lived to see this latest publication, my father's sister Katherine Kushnir and my family in Koropets, Ukraine who have always been a part of our lives.

This book is dedicated to my daughter Anya Melnyk and as always in memory of my father Petro Melnyk.

Contents

Notes on Sources

List of abbreviations
Author's Archive—[AA]
Archives of the Brotherhood of Former Combatants—[ABFC]
Archiwum Panstwowe w Lublinie—[APL]
Arhiv Republike Slovenije—[ARS]
*Bundesarchiv, Koblenz[1]—[BA-KO]
Bundesarchiv-Militärarchiv Freiberg im Breisgau—[BA-MA]
Central State Archives of Supreme Body and Government of Ukraine [TsDAVO of Ukraine]
Horst Wächter, private archive—[HWA]
Imperial War Museum, London—[IWM]
National Archives, Washington DC, USA—[NA]
*National Archives, Kew,[2] London—[NA, PRO, Kew]
Schevchenko Archive, London.—[SA]
Statni ustredni archiv v Praze—[SUAP]
US Holocaust Memorial Museum Archives—[USHMM]

To complete this work I have as far as possible, utilised original source materials. Primary documents relating to the Galician Division can be found at all the institutions cited above and the provenance of each document cited in the text has been carefully referenced in the footnotes.

Supplementary material has been garnered from manuscripts, unpublished memoirs and papers, questionnaires, personal correspondence spanning over twenty five years and extensive notes of interviews conducted with veterans. Among these several deserve special mention including Volodymyr Keczun, Theo Andruszko, Roman Kolisnyk, Roman Hawrylak, Orest Slupchynskyj, Bohdan Maciw, Bohdan Kutny, Ivan Sadovey and Walter Jankiwsky.

Despite extensive efforts over the course of more than 25 Years, it has thus far been impossible to locate the Galician Division's war diaries which it must be fairly concluded have been lost or destroyed. In their absence I have relied heavily upon personal accounts of veterans. These have been reproduced verbatim. Again, to maintain accuracy I have whenever possible made use of those from veterans who kept written accounts or diaries. In instances where diaries were not kept, I have made every effort to independently corroborate information contained therein.

Interviews are indicated by name, date and location, questionnaires are quoted by their numbers which follow numerical sequence (i.e. Q12) and the surname of the individual involved. Further sources of all information and appropriate references can be found in the extensive footnotes. For convenience German technical terms, titles and ranks have been retained.

I am especially indebted to the following for their kind assistance in providing photographic material for use in this publication; The Archives of the Brotherhood of Former Combatants, whose archive is meticulously maintained by Bohdan Maciw, Heinz Stutterecker, Andrij Zhukevich, Petro Kormylo, Andrew Found, Richard Rygaard as well as the Schevchenko Archive in Linden Gardens, London.

It should be noted that several of the pictures selected for inclusion appear to have been altered. These were originally published in various wartime newspapers including the Division's own journals, the prints having first been subjected to artistic treatment by adding lines or shading in order to accentuate certain features, as was the fashion at the time. In such cases the author is often in possession of the original captioned prints (and occasionally original editions of the newspapers in which they were first published) and is satisfied that nothing of importance has been obliterated or added.

All research materials collected for this publication have now been deposited in the hands of the tirelessly enthusiastic and capable curator Ludmila Pekarska, to ensure long term public access. Contact with the archive can be made via its website whose address is http://www.augb.co.uk. A special thanks is offered to Horst Wächter, especially for granting me unrestricted access to his unique family archive which would otherwise have been unobtainable.

Due to several changes in nomenclature, with a few exceptions, I have referred to the formation as 'The Galician Division'/the 'Division' by part or all of the title by which it was officially known at that time. Similarly, following the German occupation, the Galician capital city of L'viv was subsequently renamed 'Lemberg', however I have continued to refer to it as L'viv unless I have quoted directly from period German documents in which case L'viv appears in parenthesis after 'Lemberg' . It should also be noted that the term 'Wehrmacht' when referring to soldiers of the German Army (i.e. Heer) as opposed to those of the Waffen-SS is often incorrectly used in many of the personal accounts of veterans, but as this association was commonly accepted, I have made no attempt to correct it.

For those wishing to obtain more data about the Division, other useful web sites include the official web site of the veterans organisation http://www.infoukes.com/galiciadivision, whilst Petro Kormylo's excellent site http://www.tryzubscotland.com provides lots of useful data about post war internment of Divisional members in Scotland.

Introduction

In June 1944 my father Petro Melnyk was taken at gunpoint from his home village of Koropets in western Ukraine, by retreating German troops and their Hungarian allies, to serve in the '14. Waffen-Grenadier-Division der SS (galizische Nr. 1)'. His elder brother Dymitri was forcibly conscripted by the Soviets into the Red Army, although he managed to esacape and spent the duration of the war in hiding. Both were ardent Ukrainian patriots but due to circumstances beyond their control, they would have found themsleves facing each other on the battlefield. Fortunate to have survivied the conflict, they went on to raise families and live out the remainder of their lives, Dymitri in his home village in Ukraine and Petro in exile in England. Whilst these circumstances were tragic, they were relatively common place in Ukraine and were mirrored in thousands of other Ukrainian families during the Second World War. In the 1980s there was still no 'definitive history' available in the English language of the Division in which my father had served.[1] There were however a number of publications about it which originated in the former Eastern Block countries. These were the products of Soviet and Polish propaganda specialists like Valery Strykul whose remit was self-evident from their fanatical hostility towards the Ukrainian nationalists who had originally supported its formation.

Partly to redress the balance, I embarked on a 15 year research project, culminating in the publication in 2002 of To Battle, The Formation and History of The 14 Galician Division of the Waffen-SS.

Since then other worthy accounts have appeared in the west and gained wide circulation.[2] At the same time the Division's detractors have not been idle with new offerings from the latest generation of anti-Ukrainian zealots.[3] Like their predecessors, most have an agenda which is transparently obvious. Despite the relative wealth of accessible and verifiable material on this unit, their works remain littered with easily disprovable factual inaccuracies and attempts to obfuscate the facts, which do not bear up to even the most cursory scrutiny.[4] Indeed it is the continued appearance of such publications that has caused me to revisit this subject.

In To Battle I concluded that the basis of the cooperation between the Germans and Ukrainians that led to the formation of the Galician Division was as a direct result of both having a mutual common enemy—Soviet Communism. I also deduced that their alliance was fatally compromised by their diametrically opposed agendas; to strengthen the Axis armed forces in their quest for imperialist conquest for the Germans and for the Ukrainians as the nucleus of an independent army—an essential precondition for the establishment and maintenance of a free and independent sovereign state. To this end whilst serving in the Galician Division its personnel fought honourably as soldiers and were subjected at all times to draconian military discipline.

Having already explored the political dimension of the formation of the Galician Division from both the German and Ukrainian perspectives in great detail, I have now elected to focus more on the combat history of the unit. This work should therefore perhaps be considered a companion to my first book.

Despite extensive efforts to locate them, in the absence of any war diaries, for the purposes of this study I have had to rely predominantly on surviving documentation, supplemented by personal accounts from participants. These as always, remain subjective, but nonetheless do add considerably to helping us gain a fuller picture of the events which occurred.

Covering the same subject, inevitably there will be an element of repetition for which the readers indulgence is sought, however to partly mitigate this I have done my best to incorporate as much hitherto unused material as possible.

Michael James Melnyk
Norwich 2016

1

The Crucible of a Nation State

Galicia

The province of Galicia in western Ukraine has always been the traditional centre of Ukrainian Nationalism. After the partitioning of Poland in 1772, Galicia came under the rule of the Austro-Hungarian Empire. As the largest province of that empire the Ukrainian population benefited from the divide and rule nationality policies of the reigning Habsburg Monarchy which ensured that for the next 150 years the Ukrainians enjoyed considerable autonomy and consequently developed a highly distinct national consciousness. In contrast, their eastern Ukrainian countrymen who had been subjected to Russian absolutism and severe cultural and social repression since the middle of the eighteenth century had little opportunity to do so.

At the end of the First World War both east and west were united and a tenuous independent Ukrainian state was maintained from 1918–1920, but unable to fight off its enemies Ukraine was once again split and left to the mercy of its historic adversaries. The far larger Eastern Ukraine was occupied by the Soviets[1] and endured the merciless persecution unleashed by Stalin. This included the forced collectivisation programme and subsequent artificial famine which claimed an estimated 7 million lives,[2] followed by the infamous mass purges of 1937/38.

Galicia was annexed by Poland,[3] whose government began an overt forceful 'Polonization' of the Ukrainian populace introducing Polish settlers and extensive political and social discrimination on the basis of nationality and religion.

The severity of the Polish regime led to the emergence of the 'Organisation of Ukrainian Nationalists'—OUN,[4] which became a powerful focus of the struggle for the restoration of a united Ukrainian state. Germany's mutual anti-Polish sentiment and opposition to the European Status Quo, made her a natural ally for the OUN which sustained a pro-German orientation.[5] The nationalists expectations were raised when in September 1939 Germany invaded Poland, but Hitler handed over Galicia to the Soviet Union where it too experienced Stalin's inhumane policies of extermination, repression and deportation.[6]

The remaining political activists in Galicia centred on the underground network of the OUN which believed that in the event of a war between Germany and the Soviet Union it would mobilise Ukrainian support for the Germans in return for their recognition of an independent Ukraine.

In February 1940, the OUN split and thereafter two rival wings OUN-B (Bandera) and OUN-M (Melnyk) were maintained. The Abwehr (German intelligence service) recruited from both—especially the stronger and more radical OUN-B—and with its approval in April 1941, two battalions[7] were enlisted by the OUN. Roland[8] which trained at Saubersdorf near Vienna and Nachtigall at Neuhammer, Silesia, were regarded by the Ukrainians as the embryo of a future Ukrainian Army. Both were intended to follow a main German attack against the Soviet Union and organise coups in Ukraine.[9]

In contrast to the Abwehr, at this time the Reichsführer-SS Heinrich Himmler rejected an opportunity to utilise 679[10] German-speaking Ukrainians within the rapidly emerging Waffen-SS establishment[11] as he believed it would compromise a racially elite Germanic fighting force.[12]

When Germany invaded the Soviet Union,[13] Roland advanced into Southern Bessarabia and Nachtigall[14] crossed into Galicia with Army Group South. When Nachtigall, entered the Galician capital of L'viv on 30 June 1941,[15] its soldiers found

In their haste to retreat before the German advance, the Soviet OGPU (later NKVD) liquidated thousands of inmates of the prisons in all the major Ukrainian towns and cities. Many of the bodies showed evidence of torture and had been mutilated. In the summer heat the stench of the decomposing corpses was unbearable. The scenes were extensively photographed and given heavy coverage for propaganda purposes. It was not uncommon for Ukrainians who served in the Galician Division to keep copies of these pictures on their person to remind them what they were fighting for, such as this example kept by Volodymyr Gocskyj in his pocket.

the NKVD (Soviet secret police) had fled leaving the main prisons full to overflowing with thousands of tortured and mutilated corpses mostly of Ukrainian political activists and nationalists.[16] There were similar occurrences across the province in towns such as Sambir, Zolochiv, Stanyslaviv, Chortkiv and Ternopil.[17] Julian Chornij recalled:

[...] On 1 of July 1941, after the Soviet troops abandoned the town of Zolochiv I went on my bicycle from Brody to visit the prison in the historic castle. I saw the room where the prisoners were executed. The floor was covered in torn pieces of paper or documents smeared in blood. A window without a frame was used as the place where the prisoner was forced to take a seat facing outside and after being shot in the back of the head, fell down into a pit which at the time of my visit was still full of blood. In the orchard next to the building I saw long rows of corpses about 100 ft long, piled on top of each other 3 -5 (maybe more) corpses high. I tried to check who they were but was forced to abandon the idea because of the repulsive odour.[...][18]

The savage Soviet occupation of 1939–41 later engendered a fanatical hatred of Soviet Communism amongst the Galician Ukrainians which later manifest itself in armed cooperation with the Germans.

With the arrival of Nachtigall, Jaroslav Stetsko[19] seized the opportunity to declare an independent Ukrainian state in the name of the OUN-B.[20] Hoping to exploit it[21] the local German authorities initially allowed it to operate[22] but after only nine days the government was dissolved and Bandera and Stetsko were arrested.[23] Fearing a mutiny, Nachtigall and Roland were disarmed and in early August withdrawn,[24] whereupon after discharging the dissenting element the remaining recruits of both battalions were transported to Frankfurt an der Oder where they were combined and formed into Schützmannschaft 201.[25]

Partly to defeat the Ukrainian nationalists whose centre he correctly recognised to be in Galicia, at a conference on 16 July 1941,[26] Hitler ordered that Galicia be separated from Ukraine. It was to be added to the General Government[27] because of its former 150 year status as a province of the Austro-Hungarian Empire prior to 1918.[28] The remaining Reichskommisariat Ukraine was to be administered by Reichskommissar Erich Koch the barbaric Gauleiter of East Prussia[29] and ruled as a colonial country without political or civil rights.[30] Under his jurisdiction the population in the Reichskommissariat Ukraine, experienced the worst excesses of the Nazi 'New Europe' and its policies of racial extermination and expulsion, mass colonisation and ruthless economic enslavement.[31]

Following their incorporation into the General Government on 1 August 1941, the favoured Galician Ukrainians fared considerably better.[32] Nevertheless although Governorgeneral Hans Frank, permitted the Ukrainians official representation to look after their interests,[33] the province was placed under the Governorship of his friend General der Polizei Karl Lasch who regarded it solely as a labour reservoir for the Reich.[34]

In September to reassert their authority the Germans struck at the cadres of the OUN throughout Galicia and the Reichskommissariat Ukraine with a campaign

Nachtigall and Roland together at Neuhammer 1942. In the centre Roman Shukhevych who lead the Ukrainian underground nationalist partisan movement or UPA (Ukrainska Povstanska Armiya).

The Nachtigall Battalion entered L'viv with the advancing German forces in June 1941. This very rare picture shows the battalion marching on Horodtska Streer, close to Brygidki prison.

of wholesale repression during which thousands were arrested and deported to concentration camps and prisons or secretly liquidated.[35] Some argued these measures were only short term and would improve in time, others were assuaged with the knowledge that the German/Soviet war would be a protracted one. If Germany was to have any hope of winning it, eventually the Germans would have no alternative but jettison their racial ideologies and accept the Ukrainians and other eastern peoples as equal partners.

In November 1941, elements of the German administration in Galicia undertook a local initiative to recruit racially suitable German-speaking volunteers as replacements for front line Waffen-SS formations.[36] This was done on the basis of spurious rumours that a 'Ukrainian Army' was about to be created. Approximately two thousand of the best men with Germanic racial characteristics who volunteered were selected and later dispersed within various Waffen-SS formations at the front.[37] This experiment provided the Galician authorities with an indication of the extent of the potential support they would receive from the Ukrainians for a larger scale undertaking.

By 1942 the myopic German occupation policies that included the feared routine systematic roundups to secure forced labour for work in the Reich[38] and the retention of the loathed kolkhozes' (collective farms) had lost them much of the goodwill of the Ukrainian people.[39] Increasing numbers were turning to active opposition, establishing armed camps in the remote Ukrainian forests and marshlands of Polissya province under the command of Taras Bulba.[40] From these camps the Ukrainian underground nationalist partisan movement or UPA (Ukrainska Povstanska Armiya) emerged, under the leadership of Roman Shukhevych,[41] and began to conduct a series of military operations aimed principally against the Germans.[42]

Without a fundamental revision of the German regime there could be no solid basis for any large scale German/Ukrainian military cooperation in the war against their mutual enemy, Soviet Communism. With the brutal and intransigent colonial mentality of Erich Koch prevailing in the Reichkommisariat Ukraine, only in Galicia—which had escaped the worse excesses—was their any potential for change.

New Governor for Galicia, Dr Otto Wächter

The arrest and subsequent dismissal of Governor Lasch in November 1941,[43] heralded the beginning of a new chapter in the history of the province of Galicia and also led directly to the formation of the 14 Galician Division. Lasch's successor was the former Governor of Cracow, SS-Brigadeführer Dr Otto Gustav Freiherr von Wächter,[44] who was chosen by Hitler himself 'as the best man on the spot'.[45] He took office on 22 January 1942,[46] enthused and determined to follow a more enlightened policy in the province. It was with Dr Wächter that the idea of the 'Galician Division' originated.

Dr Otto Wächter a highly ambitious and effective Governor of Galicia. The architect of the Galician Division, he is seen here at his desk with the rank of SS-Oberführer.

Otto Wächter was born on 8 July 1901 in Vienna and came from a family with a long standing military tradition. His father, General Josef Freiherr von Wächter, (a German Bohemian), had distinguished himself commanding troops of the Austro-Hungarian Army in the war against Tsarist Russia in Galicia. Consequently, in 1918 he had been decorated with the Knight's Cross of the Order of Maria Theresia, which earned him the title of Freiherr (Baron). Later, he was appointed to the post of General und Minister fur Heerwesen (Military Affairs).

A long time member of the Austrian Nazi Party since 1923,[47] Otto Wächter was a lawyer by profession.[48] A keen sportsman and outdoor enthusiast,[49] he was described in his personal SS-officer file as being 'very intelligent' and had 'expansive willpower' to 'implement decisions'.[50] A moderate drinker and non smoker, with a good sense of humour he belonged to a rare breed amongst the National Socialists. Like his fellow Austrian, Alfred Frauenfeld,[51] he was an outstanding intellect and perceptive administrator with far reaching political ambitions.

In the summer of 1934, as political leader, he was one of the main participants in the abortive putsch against the Austrian Chancellor Dollfuss, which resulted in the Chancellor's unplanned death.[52] In conjunction with this, Wächter fled—narrowly escaping arrest and immediate execution—by boarding a Danube freighter bound for the sanctuary of Berlin.

In 1936 he served briefly in a Wehrmacht reserve infantry battalion rising to NCO rank.[53] Following the annexation of Austria by Nazi Germany (Anschluss), from 24 May 1938 until 30 April 1939, Dr Wächter became part of the Viennese

Government under Arthur Seyss-Inquart. As a result of the defeat of Poland in September 1939 and the establishment of the General Government, Seyss-Inquart was duly appointed deputy to Governorgeneral Hans Frank. Dr Wächter in turn became the Governor of Cracow from 7 November that same year and was chairman of the German–Soviet Refugee Exchange Commission. As Governor of Cracow he was frustrated by the severe limitations of his role[54] and was about to resign[55] when he received a new posting as Governor of Galicia. Upon receipt of the notification—which meant a great deal to him—in a letter to his father dated 12 February 1942, he wrote:

> [...] The task is larger and more pleasant and is a prestigious award, but is also more difficult in every respect, politically and economically, because of the two wars in a short period of time and two years of Soviet rule which have had a fundamental impact. The significance of Lemberg [L'viv] as a transit and supply area to the front is imprinting the stamp on this city. The problems there are countless.[...][56]

In recognition of the intrinsic significance of religion to the population he began his tenure as Governor with a demonstration of astonishing acumen. Upon taking up residence in the Governor's mansion he immediately visited the Metropolitan Count Andrej Sheptysky, whereupon having had himself announced and wearing his SS uniform, he proceeded to ask for the Metropolitan's blessing, an act which had a profound and favourable impact on the Metropolitan who had understandably feared the worse.[57]

Wächter believed for reasons of expediency that Galicia, with its Austrian influence, should have its German culture restored and its population—especially the ultra-nationalist Ukrainian youth—turned into an 'active component of German interests'.[58] His former personal secretary, Dr Heinz Georg Neumann, later recalled:

> Although we liked the Poles much more, we [i.e. Wächter's administration] favoured the Ukrainians because of political expediency. Wächter therefore tried to carry out as much as possible the old successful tradition of Austrian policy in Galicia.[59]

As Governor, through the simultaneous introduction of a number of long term initiatives, Wächter endeavoured to promote a greater degree of co-operation between the occupying Germans and the Ukrainians. Foremost among these was a successful attempt to integrate the maximum number of Ukrainians in Galicia into all but the highest level administrative posts in areas of local government. This tactic was complemented by removing many anti-Ukrainian bureaucrats under his command and selecting principal aides for the key posts in his administration[60] all of whom entertained guarded pro-Ukrainian sentiments, notably Otto Bauer,[61] Dr Ludwig Losacker[62] and his military advisor Oberst Alfred Bisanz.

Dr Losacker, who held the post of Chief of Office of the Governor and as such was his 'right hand man' provides an insightful description into Governor Wächter's character:

[...] Wächter was a man of the world with a military appearance. He hid his great energy behind good manners, a pronounced sense of humour and a great flexibility in dealing with people. His method of work was admirable. He was very confident. He very seldom lost his composure. I have however experienced that in disputes with the SS Polizei Führer Katzmann, this noble and restrained man flew into a rage. He then spoke more quietly in a higher tone. Those who knew him, knew that this tone was a sign of danger. In such situations, his logic was a dangerous weapon [against his opponent]. To him the ideologies were suspicious. He was a practical man and possessed the realistic common sense cherished in old Austrian families [...] With the arrival of Wächter [in L'viv] for me, and no less my deputy and friend Otto Bauer [Head of internal administration in the district of Galicia] began a period of excellent, yes friendly cooperation. We formed a kind of triumvirate. Important decisions were henceforth practically made only in triple combination.[...][63]

At a conference of the Governor and the heads of departments in Cracow on 16 February 1944 Wächter stressed the dangers inherent in the German political approach towards the Ukrainians in Galicia which he described as 'extraordinarily confused'. He went on to warn '[...] If an absolutely consistent and positive position regarding Ukraine is not taken soon, dire consequences will result'.[64]

To overcome the growing hostility and to facilitate his desire to harness the population of Galicia to serve German needs, Governor Wächter strove to grant the 'favoured elements' more freedom. Inevitably his method of Governorship, brought him into direct conflict with other senior members of the administration in the province who controlled areas outside his remit. Amongst the most prominent was SS-Brigadeführer and Generalmajor der Polizei Friedrich Katzmann[65] who was stationed in L'viv and responsible for all security matters such as arrests, deportations and execution of Jews, Poles and Ukrainians in the district of Galicia.

Wächter's main adversary, who constantly stymied his efforts to pursue his plans, was Katzmann's chief HSSPF SS-Obergruppenführer Friedrich Wilhelm Krüger who was based in Cracow and with whom he constantly clashed. Relations between the two men came to a head when Governor Wächter attempted to obtain a positive resolution to some of the most unpopular German policies—the foremost of which was the planned large scale resettlement of Germans in Eastern Europe. At the government meeting in Cracow on 17 February 1942 he publically opposed plans to 'Germanise' the city of Lemberg (L'viv) which would have resulted in the expulsion of its entire population stating: 'A German colonization of the east during the war would bring about the collapse of economic production'.

HSSPF Krüger who as Reichskommissar for the establishment of the German Volkstum (ethnicity) was responsible for implementing the resettlement programme, took exception. In a five page letter to Wächter, he referred to the meeting on 17 February and his comments about the resultant projected failure of production. After emphasising that he was Wächters' senior in both age and rank, Krüger reminded him that his recent public pronouncements on this issue were a direct confrontation to the policies of the Reichsführer SS-Himmler. He continued by saying that wearing the uniform of an SS-Brigadeführer has 'certain responsibilities'. Giving vent to his frustration, Krüger wrote in this respect 'I am firstly an SS man whilst you are a politician'.[66]

The vehement disagreement over this issue and Wächter's continued active opposition to Krüger's policies led to a number of open confrontations between them. Ultimately their increasing antipathy was only resolved following the personal intervention of Himmler (who was in charge of all racial re-settlement arrangements). On 17 August 1942, he flew to L'viv to arbitrate and while so doing, Himmler offered Wächter the option of relocating to his hometown of Vienna, which he duly declined, preferring to remain as Governor of Galicia.[67]

Encouraged by the success of his policies in the province, in late 1942, accompanied by his trusted colleagues, Governor Wächter visited the Reichskommissariat Ukraine[68] to witness at first hand the effect of Koch's policies of repression and subjugation in operation. On his return in December 1942, prompted by what he had seen, he took a brave step by sending a contentious secret ten page letter to Martin Bormann[69] in the Führerhauptquartier (Führer Headquarters) in Berlin. In it, he drew attention to the serious errors made in the handling of the Ukrainians and their far reaching ramifications with regard the overall conduct of the war against the Soviet Union. He wrote:

> With growing concern, I am observing the rise of some danger areas, which will, if we are unable to eliminate them, give rise to unforeseeable consequences'[...] 'The Bolsheviks have done useful preparatory work for us. In their own country they are hated and regarded as oppressors. The German soldier is greeted with grateful hearts as a liberator of the enslaved native population. It has probably never been the case that a people have, during the fulfilment of their historical mission, met with such favourable psychological conditions, as we have found in the Soviet Union. Even if we only provide some relief for the population there, in contrast to the terror of the Soviet regime, then we will win them to our side. Unfortunately we are not doing this. The resistance of our enemy in the east hardens in the same degree, as the population in the Soviet Union loses its enthusiasm regarding the German liberation and feels disappointment and defeat with respect to the German measures [...] **We are dependent on the co-operation of the Ukrainians.**[...] (author's emphasis).

Wächter continued with a harsh criticism of the German agrarian policy in Ukraine especially the decision to retain the hated collective farms pointing out that the proper treatment of the Ukrainian population of Galicia had resulted in many successes. He emphasised that these could also be achieved in the Reichskommissariat Ukraine if those responsible (i.e. Koch and his administration) were dismissed assuming that they were unable to follow any promising avenue of co-operation with the Ukrainians. He concluded 'if we show the Ukrainian a task and a place in the battle for the New Order of Europe, then the vast majority of the Ukrainian population will unite on our side and make the battle of the Reich into its own'.[70]

There is no recorded response from Hitler who allowed Koch to retain his office in Ukraine and continued to support his policies, partly out of his comradeship for the Alten Parteikämpfer (old party fighters).

Despite Wächter's unorthodox views, Reichsführer-SS Himmler continued to value him and was determined to keep him in post in Galicia. He had good reason to do so as the presence of a senior SS member helped Himmler to consolidate his power base in the struggle with Hans Frank with whom he was constantly at loggerheads. On 25 February 1943, when HSSPF Krüger sent a teleprinter message to Himmler asking whether SS-Brigadeführer Dr Wächter should be inducted into the Waffen-SS according to the directive for all SS members who were civil servants in the General Government born in 1901,[71] Himmler refused. His teleprinter reply of the same day read: 'The Reichsführer SS had decided that SS-Brigadeführer Dr Wächter is not to be released for service at the front with the Waffen-SS'.[72]

The decision to retain his services was to have far reaching consequences. Governor Wächter had already determined to capitalise on the strong anti-Communist feeling, which was one of the intrinsic characteristics of Ukrainian nationalist movement in Galicia, to support the rapidly deteriorating German war effort.

Despite Hitler's explicit edict that 'none but the Germans shall be allowed to bear arms', by late 1942–43, the Nazi leadership was compelled to modify and dilute this basic principle, to accommodate the acute exhaustion of its manpower reserves. The loss of strategic initiative combined with the increasing partisan activity in the occupied territories, forced the Reichsführer-SS Himmler, whose SS organisation was the torch bearer of Nazi racial doctrine to begin a tactical retreat from his hitherto axiomatic ideologies.

In order to supplement the urgently needed replacements for its depleted front line Waffen-SS divisions, the SS recruitment chief SS-Gruppenführer Gottlob Berger, had extended the term 'Germanic' and the principle of Germanic influence to include the inhabitants of 'ethnically' German areas. The influx of increasing numbers of foreigners had fundamentally changed the profile of the Waffen-SS and paved the way for the raising of divisions from the Baltic States of Latvia and Estonia.

Governor Wächter knew that even in the absence of the critical political factor it had still been possible to recruit anti-Communist Ukrainians,[73] and that by the spring of 1943, approximately 4,000 Ukrainians from the Galician region were serving in Polizei and guard units (Wachformationen) created by various local authorities (Dienststellen).[74] These developments and the success of the previous recruitment action in Galicia in November 1941, convinced Governor Wächter that German/Ukrainian co-operation could assume far greater dimensions.

On Christmas Eve 1942, in a letter to the Reichsführer, he sought a personal meeting. Here at last he could present his ambitious plans and emphasise that his administration policies had created a potential opportunity which could be translated into securing the active military co-operation of the Ukrainians in the fight against the Soviet Union, by setting up an SS formation in Galicia.[75] Himmler's reply dated 18 January1943, read:

The caption of this Kriegsberichter picture describes a Waffen-SS officer decorating a local Ukrainian village militia man with the Ostmedaille with swords for his bravery in the fight against Bolshevism. Governor Wächter recognised the bitter hatred of the Ukrainians and their willingness to fight the Soviets and quickly sought to elevate this local cooperation to the organisation of an entire Galician Waffen-SS Division.

Portrait of Governor Wächter after his promotion to SS-Gruppenführer on 16 May 1944.

[...] I am definitely intending to visit Lemberg [L'viv] during the first part of the year
and [will] then discuss many things with you. Most importantly, at the end of 1942
I would like to affirm one thing: Galicia remained peaceful and orderly. It is greatly
due to your efforts and it is not in the least due to your harmonious work with the
efficient Katzmann. To say impartially, this is the result of the co-operation of the
administration with the SS and Polizei in your district.[76]

Early Plans

At the beginning of March 1943,[77] Governor Wächter met with the Reichsführer-SS
Heinrich Himmler at his field HQ in his train in Hochwald, East Prussia. Wächter
intended to exploit this opportunity to the full and had prepared well in advance.
The agenda for the meeting covered a number of routine matters of concern
including administration breakdowns and the increasing activities of partisan
bands.[78] In addition to these preliminary issues, Wächter sought Himmler's
authorisation for three of his long term political concepts which had far reaching
ramifications.

Firstly he presented a new plan for the administrative structure of the General
Government which envisaged the unification of the two districts of Cracow and
Lemberg (i.e. Galicia) into one 'Greater Galician District' (Grossdistrikt Galizien)
and the merger of the three remaining districts of Radom, Warsaw and Lublin into
two additional districts.[79] The intention here was to both simplify administration
and undermine the solidarity of the Polish resistance movement.

The second was to obtain Himmler's consent to the temporary suspension of
the resettlement of racial Germans in Galicia while the war was still in progress
and the reintroduction of private ownership of land in the province.[80] In the case
of the latter, Wächter knew that a positive resolution to these proposals would be
welcomed by the Ukrainian population of Galicia. Moreover, both were essential
prerequisites for gaining their support for his third and most ambitious project
which involved exploiting the Ukrainian hatred of Bolshevism by organising a
German-sponsored Division[81] from Galician Ukrainians.

The creation of such a unit he argued, would contribute to re-establishing
Galicia's 150 year old Germanic tradition that it had experienced under the rule
of the Austro-Hungarian Empire. It would also raise critically needed additional
manpower for the strengthening of the eastern front. Simultaneously it could be
utilised to help counter the growing Ukrainian underground partisan movement
[UPA] by conscripting the young Ukrainian men into controlled military service.
As an added benefit, it could partially solve the problem of thousands of forced
labourers who had been sent to the Reich but often engaged in sabotage and
escaped. Wächter suggested that they would be granted an amnesty if they were
to enlist, ensuring that this resource was once again working for the Reich.

Himmler promised to give these matters careful consideration, especially the
proposed creation of a Division. He expressed an interest in the basic concept,

provided it met with the Führer's approval but also made it clear that if such an enterprise was to be undertaken, the inhabitants of Galicia would have to provide some of the required matériel. In particular its population and craftsmen would have to supply the necessary horses, carts and winter clothing.

Determined to progress his plans, on 4 March 1943, Wächter despatched a secret letter to Himmler which included a draft text of a planned call to arms to be made to the population of Galicia on the occasion of the promulgation of the proposed division. The appeal to the Ukrainians in Galicia stated that in recognition of their achievements and 'continued pressure to allow them to fight', Hitler had finally given his approval for the formation of the SS-Freiwilligen-Division 'Galizien.' It called on the Galician youth to fight to defend their homes and families against the Bolshevik enemy and for a 'just New Order in Europe'. In order to maintain an erroneous sense of privilege, it also indicated that applications of volunteers whose fathers' had served in the Austro-Hungarian Army would be given preferential treatment.

In his letter Wächter suggested that once the call to arms had been authorised, he would then make the necessary preparations. These would include preparatory discussions with Ukrainian representatives to ensure a favourable reception from the Galician people for the idea of raising the SS Volunteer Division 'Galicia'. He concluded by saying that if Himmler's basic approval was forthcoming, he could begin the technical execution in agreement with SS-Gruppenführer Berger (head of the SS main office) and SS-Obergruppenführer und General der Polizei Krüger[82] in his capacity as the HSSPF in the General Government.[83]

Anticipating official sanction for the project, at the end of March and the beginning of April Oberst Bisanz once again widely disseminated rumours in L'viv about the formation of a 'Ukrainian Army'. Not only did he begin conversations with individual veterans, but according to Kubijovych, he tried to induce the men to volunteer in the as yet non existent formation.[84]

On 20 March Governor Wächter visited SS-Gruppenführer Berger, leaving with him written plans delineating his long term political proposals in detail. Berger duly passed the plans to Himmler's secretary SS-Obersturmbannführer Dr Brandt, with a covering letter which revealed there would be no difficulty in raising the required manpower for a planned 'Polizei Schützen Regiment Galizien':[85]

Regarding.: New District Divisions in the Generalgouvernement
Enclosures.: 2
20 March 1943

Secret!
Dear Doctor!

SS-Brigadeführer Freiherr von Wächter has visited me today and has left the enclosed plans with a letter. I assume that the Reichsführer-SS has spoken to SS-Brigadeführer Wächter with regard to this, and I wish to provide a short briefing.

By 15 April a commission will leave here for Lemberg [L'viv]. 12,000 pre-trained [vorausgebildete,[86]] Ukrainians selected predominantly from the population of the mountain villages, will be presented to us for the formation of the Polizei Schützen Regiment 'Galizien'. Of these 3,000 plus 500 will be selected.[87]

Heil Hitler !

G. Berger
SS-Gruppenführer

Governor Wächter and his aides also began exploratory discussions concerning the use of Galician Ukrainians in a combatant rôle during private meetings with the two chief spokesmen of the Ukrainian Central Committee, Prof. Kubijovych and his deputy Dr Pankivsky. The discussions and commitments at this stage were still vague; nevertheless Wächter was heartened by the positive response. Despite their experiences with the German occupation policies, the Ukrainians were still prepared to support the formation of a military unit to fight against the Soviets in return for ultimate political recognition. To this end, independent of Wächter's proposal, Kubijovych had already broached the idea of raising a Ukrainian military unit on the territory of the General Government to join the Germans against the Soviets in a letter to Governorgeneral Frank which remained unanswered.[88] In so doing, Kubijovych joined other less high profile Ukrainians, who had submitted similar petitions directly to Berlin.[89]

Encouraged by the Ukrainian response, Governor Wächter wrote again to Himmler and Krüger on 24 March 1943, concerning his proposed modification of German agricultural policy in favour of private ownership. Wächter realised the fundamental significance of the abolition of the Soviet collective farms and the introduction of new legislation favouring privatisation which would be welcomed by the Galician Ukrainians. This in turn would facilitate the cultivation of a wider basis of support for his appeal for volunteers especially among the predominantly rural peasant population.[90]

Himmler responded with a secret letter to Wächter dated 28 March 1943, in which he addressed the issues of the abandonment of Soviet collective farms, the re-privatisation of agriculture and the formation of a military unit. He began by informing Wächter that 'The Führer has approved of the formation of the SS-Freiwilligen-Division 'Galicia' in principle'. He then went on to say that he was prepared to reintroduce reprivatisation[91] but only for those farmers who had delivered their quotas in 1941 and 1942 and had satisfactorily cultivated their fields in 1942 and 1943. As for the remainder he wrote, 'Those who are not up to the mark and are lazy will, be reason of their insufficient performance not be reprivatised'. Following this Wächter's summons would be issued to the able-bodied youth of Galicia. He continued: 'In my mind, these men will not be organised in Polizei-battalions but a whole horse-drawn Grenadier-Division'. He reiterated that the necessary horses, supply wagons and winter clothing were to be provided by the inhabitants of Galicia in return for which payment was to be made according to the valid rates for the articles supplied.

In closing he advised Wächter to engage in further discussions with SS-Obergruppenführer Krüger and SS-Gruppenführer Berger[92] and that the staff for the medical examinations would be despatched in good time.

In a second letter of the same date, Himmler revealed he had held further discussions with Krüger on the issue of the resettlement of racial Germans in Galicia and consequently he agreed that he would not demand the resettlement of racial Germans in certain areas near the Galician border 'in view of the political and military situation'.[93]

Not content with Himmler's agreement to limited re-privatisation, Wächter, sent Himmler a telegram dated 3 April 1943, requesting that in order to successfully augment the recruitment drive, the re-privatisation take place without Himmler's demand for prior concessions.[94] This he pointed out, would be interpreted as an anti-Bolshevik move and it was imperative to introduce such an initiative to win the support and active participation of the Galician population as part of 'the anti-Bolshevik defence front' (Antibolschewistische Abwehrfront).[95] In closing Wächter stated that in the next few days he would agree the necessary political measures with Krüger and Berger, and requested an audience with Himmler in the coming week.

Thereafter on this issue Himmler, raised no further objections and accepted the reprivatisation plan without qualification. Wächter was not however granted the meeting he sought.

A New Dimension

Having secured Himmler's conditional consent to the raising of a military unit from Galicia, the implementation of the re-privatisation scheme and some limitations of the resettlement programme, Wächter turned his attention to securing Ukrainian support. His preferred option was the militant OUN both factions of which [OUN Bandera and OUN Melnyk] enjoyed considerable support amongst the Ukrainian population, especially the more radical OUN-B which controlled the UPA. However, previous experiences had already brought the OUN-B into open conflict with the Germans which ruled them out, whilst although the OUN-M was generally more ambivalent, its leadership was divided regarding its support for the idea of the Division.[96]

Therefore on 3 April 1943, Wächter and his vice governor, Dr Otto Bauer, turned once again to Prof. Kubijovych in his capacity as the head of the Ukrainian Central Committee (UCC). During confidential discussions which followed, Kubijovych stressed the willingness of the Ukrainians to fight alongside the Germans against the Bolsheviks. At the same time he warned against undertaking a recruiting drive without a firm political basis of support in the Ukrainian community.[97] Wächter replied that for the time being he had very little latitude in respect of supporting any Ukrainian political developments due to the opposition of certain individuals among the Nazi hierarchy including Hitler and some of his closest associates. For this reason the Ukrainians should not expect to receive any immediate political benefits from enlisting for the Division which was to have a regional (i.e. Galician) and not national (Ukrainian) appearance.

In mitigation Wächter emphasised that the fulfilment of the political aspirations of the Ukrainians in Galicia could only be seen as a consequence of the Division proving itself in battle and not as a premise for its existence. The greater its success in this respect, the greater the amount of political leverage the Ukrainians would have in dealing with the Germans in future. In addition he stressed that since only native Germans could be drafted into regular Wehrmacht units, the Galician Division like those made up of ethnic Germans would be an integral part of the Waffen-SS.

To further induce Ukrainian cooperation, Wächter stated that the UCC would act as the principal representative for the proposed Division before the German and Ukrainian authorities and that a Military Board would be established to be headed by Kubijovych. This would oversee recruitment and assist families and dependants of the volunteers. He also promised the Division would have an evenly divided German\Ukrainian officer corps and that he would work to secure the release of political prisoners (i.e. members of the OUN) from prisons and concentration camps if they agreed to serve. Finally, in acknowledgement of the profound influence of the Church on the deeply religious population he agreed that Greek Catholic priests would be attached to the Division.

Aware that these conditions were still unlikely to meet Ukrainian expectations, Wächter warned Kubijovych that 'Certain consequences would follow for the Ukrainians if a move to raise a division was resisted as the Germans would form such a formation whether the Ukrainians acquiesced and agreed to cooperate or not'.[98]

The Nature of the Beast

On conclusion of his preliminary discussions with the Ukrainian representatives, in compliance with Himmler's instruction, Wächter returned once again to the detailed organisational problems of the formation that he envisaged to be a Polizei Division ('Polizei Schützen Division'). On 4 April 1943, he met SS-Obergruppenführer Krüger in his capacity as the HSSPF, and two days later on 6 April 1943, he met again with SS-Gruppenführer Gottlob Berger.[99] Believing that because of the serious shortages of training instructors and ordnance within the Waffen-SS the unit was to be raised under the auspices of the Ordnungspolizei, Berger reported briefly on developments in a secret letter to Himmler dated 6 April 1943.

6 April 1943

Reichsführer !

SS-Brigadeführer Freiherr von Wächter visited me again today. We agreed that he would approach the Ukrainian population of Galicia with a large scale call to arms.

On the 30.3.1943 the enlistment commission for this new Ukrainian SS-Polizei-Schützen-Division, came into operation. The necessary agreements have been made with SS-Gruf. Winkelmann[100] of the head office (Hauptamt) of the Ordnungspolizei. SS-Brigf. v. Wächter will make sure that we receive the necessary horses from the country. The outcome (of these events) will be reported.[101]

G. Berger
SS-Gruppenführer.

Despite Wächter's considerable efforts, Himmler continued to prevaricate when it came to giving unconditional approval to go ahead with his plan as like Hitler, Himmler remained wary of the Ukrainians whom he never fully trusted. This scepticism was apparent when he was petitioned by one of his best SS generals Felix Steiner[102] to utilise the Ukrainian help in the war against the Soviet Union by granting them political autonomy to secure their support. In his reply Himmler had retorted 'Do not forget that in 1918 these splendid Ukrainians murdered Field Marshal von Eichhorn'.[103]

Although the exigencies of war had already compromised the racial requirements of the SS establishment,[104] Himmler remained deeply distrustful of the Ukrainians and could draw little reassurance from the self deceit of calling them 'Galician's'. Fearful that the new proposed formation would become an instrument for the Ukrainian nationalists (as they intended),[105] on 10 April 1943, his office sent a teleprinter message to Governor Wächter:

10.April 1943

Brigadeführer !

SS-Gruppenführer Berger has reported that you recently visited him and discussed the canvassing and your call to arms with him. The Reichsführer-SS requests that you move slowly with regard to the canvassing and do not yet issue the call to arms. You will receive further information either from SS-Gruppenführer Berger or myself next week.[106]

Heil Hitler

Signed Brandt
SS-Obersturmbannführer

Wächter however had no intention of jeopardising what he had already achieved and continued to drive ahead at a furious pace. On Monday 12 April 1943, he organised a meeting in L'viv, attended by nine locally active SS, Polizei, propaganda department and Nazi party officials.[107] No Ukrainian was in attendance. The objective was to work out a detailed plan covering all the necessary practicalities associated with the organisation of what was clearly planned as a police formation. The conference would endorse a number of key decisions which would then be presented to Himmler for his ratification. These included:

At Wächter's suggestion the title 'SS-Freiwilligen Division Galician' or 'Freiwilligen Division Galician' was to be adopted for the proposed formation. Polizei ranks and uniforms were to be used with a shield on the right upper arm, similar to those of the other European volunteer formations, depicting a traditional Galician emblem 'but nothing symbolic of Ukraine or Ukrainian national aspirations'.

Personnel and material costs were also to be carried by the Ordnungspolizei, however it was agreed that the inclusion of the word 'Polizei' in the title, would be avoided 'on political-psychological grounds'.

The Division was to be a horse-drawn infantry unit with weapons and equipment similar to that of any German infantry division. 2–3,000 draught horses, with the necessary harnesses and carts were to be furnished as far as possible by the Galician population. A musical platoon was to be established. The issues of accommodation, financing, spiritual welfare (the appointment of army chaplains), staff personnel and remuneration all followed. Under section 6, headed 'Training Time' it was noted: 'It will be necessary to allow longer training time to correspond with the nature of the human resource, than is the case with German or Germanic formations'.[108]

It was to have 600 officers, 50 doctors and 20 veterinarians. According to available estimates 300 Ukrainian officers from the Austro-Hungarian Army, about 100 officers from the Polish Army and an unknown number from the Ukrainian intelligentsia who had served in the Polish Army but who for political reasons had not been commissioned, were available. In the case of the latter, after three months service at the front they could be sent to officers schools. The majority of officers from the Ukrainian Galician Army had also served in the Austro-Hungarian Army. In addition 2,000 non commissioned officers would be required to be drawn from former members of the Polish and Austro-Hungarian armies. For the positions of company administrators or 'Spiess' (these were usually the main or regimental Sergeant Major of a company) former members of the Austro-Hungarian Army were to be appointed as they already had command of both languages. Three hundred NCOs from the Netherlands, plus a further three hundred NCOs from Oranienburg were available for cadre personnel along with a regular battalion for the planned 'Polizeiregiment Galizien'.[109]

Once again, to accommodate the 'lower quality human resources' the minimum height requirement for recruits would be reduced to 1.65 m while those born between the years 1908–1925 inclusive would be admitted for voluntary registration.

For recruitment purposes a civilian Military Board (Wehrausschuss) was to be established made up of officers of the former Austro-Hungarian and Ukrainian Armies in conjunction with representatives of the Ukrainian Central Committee

(Hauptauschuss). Its main concern was to be recruitment activity, to be carried out in consultation with German Polizei and administrative authorities.

The last subject matter to be dealt with was establishing a timetable for the recruitment activities and associated festivities. Highlights of the schedule included:

28 April 1943 the opening ceremonial declaration in L'viv, to be attended by county and district chiefs, representatives of the Wehrmacht, the Polizei, the Military Board, the UCC, and the Greek-Catholic priesthood.[110]

29 April every county chief was to hold a regional assembly to introduce recruitment into his county utilising the propaganda materials brought from L'viv.

1 May canvassing commissions to formally take up their duties, to be followed at intervals of a week by the enlistment commissions.

The conference noted special attention should be paid to canvassing among those currently being called up for 'Baudienst' (construction service) while 'the voluntary principle should be fundamentally adhered to in every case'.[111]

So as not to further antagonise Himmler, on the same day Wächter immediately dispatched a teleprinter message to him reporting his recent activities concerning the raising of the SS-Division Galicia and that he would receive a full report via the Chief of the Ordnungspolizei Kurt Daluege. He also repeated his request to be allowed to make a final report to the Reichsführer in person as there 'was still a fundamental political question to resolve'. He then went on to add: 'Prior to your authorisation, the call up will not be made public, nor will canvassing begin' adding diplomatically that 'the starting date for the campaign had not been decided upon but 28 April had been envisaged'.[112]

Himmler's response to Wächter's latest teleprinter message was swift. The next day he spelled out in no uncertain terms that he regarded the 'Galician Division' not as a Polizei formation but as a combat unit to be raised under the auspices of the Waffen-SS. He also stated that 10,000 men would be used to raise separate Polizei regiments for anti-partisan and security duties. The formation in which the individual was to serve would be determined by the religious rite to which they belonged with only the favoured Greek-Catholic Ukrainians from Galicia to be recruited into the 'Galician Division'. The Ukrainians from the Lublin District who were members of the Greek-Orthodox Church were instead to be utilised for the separate Polizei regiments.

To clarify this Himmler's office sent teleprinter messages dated 13 April 1943, to both Wächter and SS-Obergruppenführer Krüger, which stated unequivocally that 'The Ordnungspolizei has nothing to do with the Galician Division'.[113]

The following day on Himmler's instructions, the Chief of the Ordnungspolizei SS-Oberstgruppenführer und Generaloberst der Polizei Kurt Daluege, sent a letter to SS Gruppenführer und Generalleutnant der Polizei Otto Winkelmann, which reiterated the same point and further elucidated on the reason for Himmler's desire to exclude nationalist elements under all circumstances from the formation:

14.4.43

To Generalleutnant Winkelmann

I have spoken with the Reichsführer SS about the mythical 'Polizei-Schützen-Division'. The Reichsführer SS knows nothing of this division and neither does he know of it by its former title. In addition he issues a new order which will contain the following:

A front-line division shall be created for the Waffen-SS and by the Waffen-SS, which will consist of the Greek-Catholic Ukrainians and will probably be called the 'Galician Division'; for these Ukrainians come from Galicia.

The remaining Ukrainians in the Generalgouvernement, including those from the Lublin district, are Greek-Orthodox. These will be made available for the establishment of Polizei regiments with some German leadership; or for the establishment of 3 Battalions comprised solely of these Ukrainians. The use of National Ukrainian intelligence groups,[114] i.e.: Bandera, is absolutely out of the question. The Reichsführer SS forbids this fundamentally. He still recalls very clearly the time during the war (of) 1917–1918, where the German authorities attempted to create an independent Ukraine. The result was that the leading circle—to which Bandera and a great number of his followers belonged[115]—showed their recognition and gratitude by the shooting of German officers and men. I would like to see SS Gruppenführer Berger ascertain as quickly as possible the sizes of the two groups of Ukrainians in the Generalgouvernement, (i.e.; the Greek Catholics of Galicia and the Greek Orthodox of Lublin).[…][116]

On 16 April in a letter to Himmler, HSSPF Krüger sought to clarify the latest edict in view of the respective concerns expressed by Berger and Governor Wächter. In the case of the former, Krüger said that Berger had informed him that the Waffen-SS was not in a position to provide the required training staff for the formation of the 'Freiwilligen Division Galizien'. In the latter case, Krüger wrote Governor Wächter was:

[…] of the opinion that the setting up of the Polizei Regiments in the Lublin district with the powers of the Ordnungspolizei, prior to the formation of the 'Freiwilligen Division Galizien, would not serve the political purpose that was originally intended'. Krüger ended the letter by stating that 'In order to comply with the order of the Reichsführer-SS the formation of the 'Freiwilligen Division Galizien' would have to be provisionally postponed.[117]

Himmler's office responded by immediately sending a teleprinter message to Wächter on the same day instructing him that the Reichsführer could still not fix a specific date for further discussions. He was therefore to wait with the matter of the SS-Freiwilligen Division Galizien until the Reichsführer gave the go ahead.[118]

For the second time in a week Himmler had made a belated attempt to delay Wächter's programme which was rapidly gathering pace. In order to circumvent Himmler's instruction to proceed no further, Wächter turned to SS-Gruppenführer Berger. As an enthusiastic supporter of the Division who also enjoyed the close confidence of the Reichsführer he was a perfect intermediary. In a telegram to Himmler dated 16 April 1943, Berger wrote:

Regarding: Galizien Division   16 April 1943

Reichsführer

In line with orders, I have put myself in contact with those involved [with the Galizien Division] and in doing so have discovered the following:

1. The preparations for the formation of the Division have commenced. Brigadeführer Wächter has in view of the urgency, driven things ahead to such an extent that by 20.4.43[119] the entire population of Galicia will await a call to arms. In view of the severe political unrest, that has at the moment also effected the whole [General] Government, it is possible that the cessation of canvassing for the Division would strengthen resistance activities and would significantly support enemy propaganda.

2. According to Brigadeführer Wächter's communications at least 10,000 men are available at the shortest notice. I fear that the Führungshauptamt [SS Main Operational Office] has neither the necessary instructors nor the necessary weapons for training. If it is to become a division of the Waffen-SS, then I venture to suggest, that the existing training cadres (Ausbildungskadres) be included, if only temporarily, into the Waffen-SS. I request a rapid decision by the Reichsführer-SS.

3. There are several areas in which Catholic Orthodox and Greek Orthodox populations are very mixed. Separation of men into Waffen-SS and Polizei is therefore not really possible.[120]

Signed
SS-Gruppenführer Berger

Three days later on 19 April 1943, Wächter notified Grothmann (Himmler's office chief) by teleprinter that SS-Gruppenführer Berger had confirmed the campaign could be started. In light of this he intended to make the call to arms with a festakt (celebratory decree) on 28 April as proposed.[121] Thereafter he would begin conducting intensive propaganda throughout Galicia with the assistance of the Military Board.[122]

Faced with Wächter's persistence and Berger's arguments, Himmler finally relented and made no further attempt to prevent the call to arms from going ahead as planned.

The Ukrainian Perspective

With the final authorisation for the creation of the Division looking ever more probable, like their German counterparts, the Ukrainians met to formulate their own plans. On 18 April 1943, Prof. Kubijovych assembled several prominent Ukrainians for a meeting in L'viv to discuss the pros and cons of official participation in the creation of a division. The meeting was scheduled to last for four hours with two hours allocated for each of the viewpoints.[123] Among those in attendance were members of various military veterans organisations (who supported the concept), regional chairmen of the UCC and members of the newly formed Military Board.

Kubijovych's main argument in favour was that despite previous setbacks, co-operation with the Germans was as much in Ukrainian interests as it was the Germans, since it afforded an opportunity to form a large disciplined Ukrainian military force. In the event of a German defeat and an ensuing period of turmoil (as had been the case at the end of the First World War), an armed force would be an invaluable asset for the re-assertion of an independent state. In this way the German Army would become a school that would train, arm and equip the Ukrainian youth for a future army. Once established, the Ukrainians could use this to achieve political recognition in the eyes of the outside world. He pointed out that this was especially important since the Germans were already recruiting Ukrainians without using Ukrainian intermediaries into various formations which were in no way connected with Ukrainian political objectives.[124]

In his memoirs, Myroslav Semchyshyn, a former member of the UCC who was present, states that the major argument against at this stage was that no political guarantees were being offered.[125] Other concerns included the certainty of German defeat, how the creation of a Ukrainian formation could complicate relations with the victorious Allies and the untrustworthiness of the Germans in general.

After a lengthy debate, with a few reservations the conference agreed to cooperate with Wächter's proposal and officially endorse the undertaking. Besides the reasons outlined above, the conference acknowledged that active co-operation would enable the Ukrainians to optimise their influence on German policy in Galicia (and to a certain extent in the Reichkommisariat Ukraine), and keep them informed of any new German initiatives. It was also agreed however that as a precondition for the active Ukrainian participation, a number of requests would be put forward as a condition of consent.[126] Foremost among these were:

(1) The Division would be used exclusively against the Bolsheviks (2) its name and markings be Ukrainian (3) its officers be Ukrainians (attached German officers to

act as liaisons with German high command staff) (4) the Division be provided with religious ministration by Ukrainian priests (5) the Division be attached to the Heer (regular army) (6) the Division be considered as the first unit in the creation of the Ukrainian National Army into which it would be eventually incorporated. (7) that all Ukrainian political prisoners in German prisons and concentration camps be released under a general amnesty—including the former officers of Nachtigall (8) that all other Ukrainian military units be dissolved (9) the Division was to be a fully motorised unit possessing a full range of weapons including tanks (10) forced labourers who fled from Germany should be granted an amnesty.[127]

These requests which were presented to the German authorities were not arranged or presented in order of priority. Ultimately points 1 and 4 which coincided with previous German pronouncements were accepted. It was agreed that the unit, when formed, would not be obliged to fight on the western front against the Americans and the British, but exclusively against the Soviets.[128] At the same time, despite the misgivings of many senior Nazi's including Himmler, the Division would have its own Greek Catholic chaplains to serve the spiritual needs of its soldiers. Points 3, 7 and 10 were also partially complied with. Under point 3, Wächter offered a compromise and agreed that it would have a balanced German\ Ukrainian officer corps. Some lesser Ukrainian political prisoners, but not all were released from German prisons and concentration camps. At the same time an amnesty was granted for forced labourers who had escaped, if they registered as for the Division.

As the Germans did not regard them as allies, it was never likely at this stage that they would acquiesce to the remaining requests which suggested Ukrainian political aspirations. This extended to use of the national emblem—the Trident— which was not permitted; instead, at the suggestion of Oberst Bisanz,[129] it was to be the regional Galician symbol consisting of a golden lion (on a blue background) standing on its hind paws with three crowns, two above its head and one beneath the hind paws.[130] Later, Governor Wächter also reneged on his promise that Prof. Kubijovych would head the Military Board, appointing instead one of his senior administrators a German-Galician Oberst Alfred Bisanz in his place.

Unable to obtain a favourable compromise on the remainder of their requests as did other nationalities in similar circumstances,[131] the Ukrainian leaders sacrificed short term form for long term substance. Thus, in the final analysis even before the Division's formation had been officially announced, both sides had adopted diametrically opposed objectives in supporting its creation. This is perhaps best illustrated by Dr Fritz Arlt, one of the leading German personalities dealing with the Ukrainian question, who stated 'the Germans knew that the Ukrainians had their own objectives in the formation of the Division, but this did not matter so long as they would also serve German military needs'.[132]

As a further contingency measure, to this end Governor Wächter issued two important documents. Prepared in advance of the proclamation a secret circular letter dated 28 April 1943, was sent to all local authorities, containing detailed instructions concerning the commencement of the ambitious recruitment programme. In the seven page letter Wächter stated that a Recruitment Commission (Werbekommission) for the Division would be set up for every district to be presided over by the Kreishauptmann of the Landkommissar. This would work in close co-operation with his representative body within the Ukrainian population, the Military Board (Wehrausschuss Galizien). These commissions were to actively support and further the Military Board's propaganda activities. In this way it would be seen as an independent body and maintain the illusion of an equal German Ukrainian partnership. It would also avoid giving the impression that it was 'simply an organ of the German authorities or that it was bound by the decisions of the Ukrainian auxiliary committees and delegations'.[133]

Regarding the procedures, special mention was made indicating that in order to maximise the influence of the clergy and teachers, every consideration was to be given to their utilisation in recruitment activities. As for the actual recruits, to overcome the anticipated difficulties in securing the 20,000[134] men needed to form the Division, it contained a directive that Ukrainians who had escaped from forced labour could be granted an amnesty if they registered by 1 June 1943, as volunteers in the 'SS-Schützen-Division Galizien'. It went on to say enlistment into the Division was to be limited exclusively to volunteers of Ukrainian origin currently resident in Galicia. It also stated that as a matter of principle, service in the Division would take precedence over all other types of employment.[135]

The instructions drew particular attention to the fact that the use of coercion or even moral pressure to obtain volunteers was forbidden, as this would 'destroy the political aim of the undertaking'. Lastly, for propaganda purposes permission was granted to fly blue and yellow flags in the Ukrainian national colours alongside the swastika flag (Hakenkreuzflagge). In closing, attention was drawn to the fact that the use of the Ukrainian Trident was not to be encouraged, instead the regional symbol of the Galician lion was to be employed wherever possible.[136]

Accompanying the circular letter were confidential directives for the Recruiting Commissions which reiterated several of the points in Wächter's circular[137] and secret directives. These included guidelines for the German speakers within the commissions themselves which were not to be seen by Ukrainian members of the commissions and were to be destroyed after the contents had been memorised. They advised speakers 'not to address Ukrainians as allies or give the impression that the Germans are dependant on their help'. Speakers were further instructed with regard to the key issue of political rights that:

Reference to the Galician Ukrainians aspirations for a greater Ukrainian state were to be avoided, or if it was absolutely necessary, it was to be made clear that fulfilment of these desires was dependant on the consequences of the new formation proving its worth in battle and not as a precondition to its existence.[138]

The Opening Ceremony 28 April 1943

On 28 April 1943, as originally planned by Governor Wächter, the formation of the Galician Division was officially announced at a series of large staged rallies in all the larger cities and towns throughout Galicia. The show piece was the grand Festakt (opening ceremony) in the capital L'viv where envoys of the occupying German administration, the Nazi party, the Wehrmacht and the Polizei, convened. Ukrainian delegates and veterans of the Austro-Hungarian Army and the Ukrainian Galician Army were also in attendance and detailed coverage appeared on radio L'viv and in all newspapers throughout the province of Galicia and beyond.[139]

Here, in the Stadthalterpalais, Vice-Governor Bauer began the gala assembly. Governor Wächter then issued a proclamation on behalf of the Germans in which he stressed that having belonged to the Austro-Hungarian Empire for the past 150 years, 'Hitler placed a special importance on bringing Galicia back 'into the lap of Great Germany''. Wächter followed this with his call for volunteers to the SS-Freiwilligen-Division 'Galizien'. In order to maximise the appeal he promised that every soldier of the Division would be placed on an equal footing with his German counterpart in equipment, pay, rations and the provision of social welfare for their immediate dependants. He stated that priests of their confession and nation would attend to pastoral care and emphasized that applications of volunteers whose fathers served in the Austrian RK Army would be given preferential treatment.[140] The manifesto of the Governorgeneral Hans Frank followed, read on his behalf by minister of the interior Dr Ludwig Losacker. It echoed these sentiments adding that the Division would be formed in accordance with the voluntary principle.[141]

On behalf of the Ukrainian delegation, Prof. Kubijovych then spoke to the assembled crowd.[142] He expanded on the theme of a common aim, namely the fight against Bolshevism,[143] as did Mychailo Khronoviat[144] as representative of the military veterans organisations which were to play a key role in the Division's formation.

Thus far, as officially directed, none of the addresses had made any reference to the Galician Ukrainians as 'Allies'. More significantly nothing was said that could be construed as supporting the Ukrainian aspirations for an independent state. This however was about to change.

The 'Sore Tooth'

Official blessing of the Church on the enterprise followed with the conclusion of the opening speeches, at the Cathedral of St George. Here a divine service was held presided over by Rev Dr Joseph Slipyj. Away from pomp and ceremony of the German propaganda machine, the first signs of the Ukrainian nationalist agenda for the Division became evident. The service was conducted in Ukrainian, which few, if any, of the German delegation understood. Consequently to the lasting credit of the Church, the sermon read by Rev Dr Wasyl Laba, ignored the German propaganda theme of fighting together for a 'New Europe'. Instead, unbeknown to the German delegation it openly declared that the Ukrainians should view the formation of the Division as the first step in the re-establishment of a Ukrainian Army:

> The German government, with the permission of the Führer of the German people, has granted the Galician Ukrainians permission to set up their own volunteer Division of riflemen... on this day of celebration, the Ukrainian People's Army is resurrected. The Sich Riflemen return to join the Ukrainian People's Army, to restore the link that was severed twenty years ago. At this decisive time we receive from the German government the weapons that will let us join forces with the renowned German Army and its allies, to take part in the battle against bolshevism.[145]

As a contingency against such occurrences the Germans had taken the precaution of ensuring that audio recordings were made of the sermon. In the weeks that followed these were forwarded by the propaganda department to Berger[146] via Himmler's office[147] with instructions to have them translated and sent back with a written transcript to Himmler's office for assessment. The task completed, Berger returned them with a covering letter in which he suggested that he was confident that the renegade element did not pose a serious threat to German plans. In his view there was no immediate cause for alarm as the necessary steps would be taken to rectify the problem if need be, commenting 'There are certain dangerous expressions included [in the text] but we will remove this rather sore tooth'.[148]

As the last act of the festivities, the first tangible step in the organisation of the Division was taken when Governor Wächter officially confirmed the membership of the Military Board. Once again, to ensure it would serve their interests, Governor Wächter appointed a German-Galician 52-year-old Oberst Alfred Bisanz[149] as its chairman.[150] The executive consisted of 13 men. Another Galician German, Severyn Beigert was the nominated deputy for Bisanz whilst Osyp Navrotskyj acted as the manager assisted by the engineer Evhen Pyndus. The advisor on legal matters was Ivan Rudnytsky, who was in poor health. Stefan Volynets and Mychailo Kushnir were an editor and artist respectively. Spiritual guidance was provided by Reverend Dr Vasyl Laba, the former chaplain of the Austrian Army in the First World War who had been sent by the Metropolitan Sheptytsky. Mychailo Khronoviat and Andrii Palii were prominent leading members of sports and youth organisations the former being responsible for recruitment. Volodymyr Bilozor was responsible for the enlistment of medical staff and Lubomyr Makarushka was a former member of the Polish parliament (Sejm). Jurij Krokhmaliuk was the youngest member and was a professional engineer and author and took on the responsibility for historical archives. Lastly was the former teacher Zenon Zelenyi who dealt with youth affairs.

Wächter considered the Military Board to be a civilian organisation which was to function as an intermediary between the German authorities and the Galician population. As his executive body within the Ukrainian population he intended it to also serve as a useful propaganda tool to assist in the procurement of recruits and as such he sought to limit its authority and independence. This was reflected both in the appointment of Oberst Bisanz, a German-Galician rather than a Ukrainian as its chairman, and in its governing statutes which took the form of a twelve page booklet with bilingual German/Ukrainian text entitled 'Satzungen des Wehrausschusses Galizien'.[151] The statutes defined its purpose vaguely and stated unequivocally that it was to act in an auxiliary capacity under Wächter's personal direction, or that of the head of the relevant authority by agreement with the SS-und Polizeiführer.[152]

The Call to Arms

Immediately after the ceremony in L'viv, on Wächter's instructions an intensive recruitment campaign was conducted across the whole of the province of Galicia under the slogan 'Everyone to the Division.' The campaign was orchestrated by the local German authorities in conjunction with the Military Board, the Ukrainian Central Committee and the subordinate local branches of both organisations in the rural areas. The practical work was undertaken by recruitment commissions whose remit had already been clearly established in its confidential operational directives dated 28 April 1943. Amongst other things, these stipulated that each commission which was to work in two places everyday, was to utilise the active assistance of key members of the local communities including town/village heads, priests and teachers as widely as possible. It was to enrol only Ukrainians from Galicia[153] and only those who had received jail sentences of five years and over, were to be automatically debarred from enlisting.[154] Lastly, the directives contained a tell-tale portent for the seemly arbitrary enrolement which was to follow stating that detailed examinations of the volunteers would not have to be done by the recruitment commissions.[155] This in effect gave the commissions carte blanche to enrol almost anybody in order to boost the recruitment figures and this is precisely what they later did.

As part of the widely publicised recruitment drive, colour posters, placards, leaflets and other propaganda matériels advertising the Division were liberally distributed throughout Galicia. The German propaganda machinery ensured that popular newspapers in the General Government carried detailed coverage of the official proclamation of 28 April. In the weeks that followed they featured numerous articles promoting the Division[156] which, like the rest of the recruitment propaganda deliberately avoided the suggestion that it would be fighting for Hitler and the Third Reich because of the known political sentiments of the population. Instead, appeals were made for the 'active participation of the Galician Ukrainian people in the European fight for freedom against the Soviet Union'[157] and 'to fight for a New Europe in order to earn a proper place among the nations fighting for a New Europe'.

To complement the publicity, individual members of the Military Board visited the larger towns and regional centres in the region to address public meetings and gatherings to urge young men to volunteer.[158] The most popular themes repeated in their speeches were; A Ukrainian military force trained for modern warfare could have a decisive influence in the political re-shaping of eastern Europe; Fighting to defend the Ukrainian fatherland, the natural rights of the Ukrainian people, for the national culture and for the entire European culture; The failure of the European Entente 1918–1920 testified that there was only one nation capable of conquering the USSR—Germany; Taking up arms as a continuation of Ukrainian military tradition particularly that set by the Sichovi Striltsi[159] of the Ukrainian Galician Army; Fighting together with the German Army against the deadliest enemy of Ukraine 'Bolshevism' and the ruin, famine, exile, torture and murder it brought; Avenging the innocent blood of brothers tortured in camps in Siberia and of the millions killed by forced collectivisation.

The Volunteers

The most responsive to these pubic statements were the politically conscious Ukrainians, especially those from urban areas who regarded the Division as the potential nucleus of a future national army that would fight for the liberation of their homeland and in the aftermath of the war, serve a free and independent Ukraine.[160] Many of these university students and secondary school graduates were convinced that its establishment would strengthen the Ukrainian position in Galicia and could ultimately serve to change German policy toward Ukraine. Nationalistic sentiments of this type were propagated at every opportunity by individual Ukrainian speakers involved with recruitment.[161] Arguments such as this provided the inspiration for these highly motivated and nationally conscious individuals[162] who volunteered in the initial period of the recruitment.[163]

One volunteer Theo Andruszko remembered:

> [...] following a talk with a lot of friends the previous Sunday, we decided to go to Stryi and enlist. Stryi is only 4 km from my [home] village of Nezhukhiv. On a Tuesday morning, during the school holidays some 20 of us young idealists, decided to march in a military parade singing some Ukrainian songs as we marched. The enlisting centre was actually next door to my Gymnasium (High school)—almost in the centre of Stryi in the premises of the 'Narodna' School. There were some officials present, Germans and Ukrainians from the 'Viskova Uprava' [Military Board].
>
> We were welcomed and directed to the health examination room where we were measured for height and weight. The acceptance criteria was minimum 18 years of age and height—170 cm. I was 171 cm tall. All the tests went ok for me, hearing, vision, reading and rudimentary maths as well as being right or left handed and if my fingers were capable of squeezing the trigger of a rifle. The final verdict was proclaimed by a German SS military official: 'gratuliere!' (congratulations!) I went

Recruitment of volunteers Rava Russka.

Peremshyl 28 April 1943, gathering place for the recruitment campaign.

Volunteers from Sambir hold placards including one depicting the Ukrainian National symbol, the trident, 13 June 1943.

Volunteers from the Rydky district parade in front of dignitaries from the Military Board including Alfred Bisanz (saluting).

Volunteer with his horse at the parade held in Drohobych on 20 June 1943.

Assembled crowd at Stanislav 11 July 1943.

Stanislav 11 July 1943, mounted Ukrainian Cossacks.

Above: March past before Governor Wächter. Ukrainian carrying the national flag bearing the national symbol of the trident, Stanislav 11 July 1943.

Right: Recruitment poster for the Galician Division. The caption reads 'Join the ranks of the SS Riflemen Galicia for the defence of your homeland in armed fellowship with the best soldiers in the world'.

Recruitment poster for the Galician division comprised of contemporary newspaper cuttings, flyers and propaganda photos of the recruitment rallies held across Galicia.

Volunteers marching Stanislav 11 July 1943.

Volunteers at the parade in Stanislav 11 July1943.

Mounted Ukrainian Cossacks parade before Governor Wächter holding the Ukrainian national flag, Stanislav 11 July 1943.

Mounted Ukrainian Cossacks in traditional Ukrainian dress parade before Governor Wächter, Stanislav 11 July 1943.

outside in terrific spirit, I made it! I was a future soldier of the Ukrainian Division! All my friends were already outside. To my consternation, I learnt that none of the 19 of them passed! All were below the 170 cm mark! Marching back to Nezhukhiv I felt alone and betrayed by my friends. And to add to the case, as I was only 16, I deliberately lied adding 2 years to my age![164]

Recruitment of high school and university students was also aided by teachers and college principals. Like the Ukrainian clergy, many openly supported the concept of the Division as a future Ukrainian force and urged their pupils to enrol, some before they had completed their studies. Another volunteer Roman Kolisnyk recalled: 'I was in the last grade at high school (8). Our teachers and community leaders were for the creation of the Ukrainian Army. All people of the 8 grade with some of the teachers registered for the Division. It was our duty to serve'.[165] Eugene Shypailo, a second year student at the L'viv polytechnic institute recollected:

I attended a student meeting where the speaker was Mr Khronoviat. The main argument was: 'now there is a real chance to get our hands on some military arms and equipment, to get military training, one of the best, and to be ready [for the time] when both superpowers would weaken to the point of chaos. Ukraine's independence can only be achieved with weapons in our hands. As the first Division we were to become the nucleus of a Ukrainian Army.'[166]

Final gathering for speeches in Stanislav 11 July 1943.

11 July 1943, volunteers from the local county town of Tulmatsch (Tovmach).

In a short letter to his parents, he gave his reasons for joining:

L'viv, 6 May 1943

Dear Father and Mother,

I have joined the Division. I trust that you will not object to it, but I have followed my conscience. I want to fulfil my duty to my people. What the outcome will be is unknown, but the moment has arrived and if we lose it, we shouldn't call ourselves a nation.

Around us [i.e.: in L'viv] huge displays took place. The Poles are getting mad. When I get home next week I will tell you everything. Yurko must remain home after I leave and has to take my place. He must repress his eagerness to join the army because he is too young and not too healthy.[...]

Your ever loving

Evhen.[167]

Reporting on the developments of the recruiting campaign, the newspaper Stanislaviske Slovo of 23 May 1943, drew attention to the rising numbers of students enlisting and cited several examples of those who did so under the guidance of their college or school principals.[168]

The leadership of the VSUM—Vykhovni Spilnoty Ukrainskoi Molodi (war-time successor to the Plast[169] Ukrainian Youth Association) was also generally supportive of the Division and encouraged its members to join up. This organisation which was similar to the British Boy Scout movement was a uniformed apolitical national organisation. Highly patriotic, thousands of its members took part in organised outdoor pursuits and sporting activities and were regarded as something of an elite amongst the Ukrainian youth. Between their enlistment in May 1943 and their call up in July many members of this popular movement took part in recruitment rallies. Their presence was a significant contributory factor in persuading many others to join up.[170]

For other civilians like Serhyj Surkiv, the incentive to volunteer originated with their hatred of the Soviets, having directly experienced the loss of family members and friends in the mass deportations and savage policies inflicted by them during their twenty one months of occupation of 1939–41.[171] They enthusiastically embraced the appeals of the Military Board and the other recruiting agencies to fight against 'Bolshevism the deadliest enemy of Ukraine' and to defend the Ukrainian fatherland. The incentive for joining was not therefore belief in a German victory, but rather the disastrous consequences in the event of a German defeat. Encouraged by declarations that the Division would fight only on the eastern front against the Soviets and supported by both the Church[172] and the former veterans especially those of 1917–1921 (many of whom signed up themselves) they too signed up in their thousands.

Some Ukrainians at the time of the announcement of the Division's formation, were already serving in various Schuma or Werkschutz battalions and other units scattered throughout the German armed forces. These were men who had served in non-combatant roles as Hilfswilliger (Hiwis) or helpers in unarmed auxiliary capacities like Mykola Skyba and Roman Hajetzky who had been serving as interpreters (Dolmetscher) in German Army units. Others occupied positions as guides, cooks, orderlies, tailors etc. The applications of such 'experienced' men were often regarded favourably as they had already undergone at least some basic training.[173] The first opportunity to enlist in a Ukrainian formation which offered some kind of national identity was an attractive proposition for men like Ivan Nyzka who was serving as a Luftwaffe auxiliary.[174]

A further category of those who volunteered included former Red Army personnel who had been taken prisoner following the great encirclement battles of the first three months of the war. Men like Volodymyr Kosak, Hennadij Salessky, Serhij Roslyk and Fedyr Baranenko, were all former Red Army lieutenants who had been held captive and in the case of the latter was recruited directly from a POW camp.

There was also a small minority of impressionable Ukrainian youth who were fascinated with somewhat romanticised ideals of military service in a German uniform as Roman Lazurko wrote:

Ergänzungsstelle Warthe (XXI)
der Waffen SS
Nebenstelle Lemberg

Datum des Poststempels.

Einberufungsbefehl A
Gilt als Fahrausweis auf der Eisenbahn.

1. Sie werden hierdurch zum aktiven Wehrdienst einberufen und
   haben sich sofort*) am *19* ten *Juni* 19*44* bis *24* Uhr*)
   bei ~~14. Galiz'sche SS Fraiw. Division~~
   in ~~Neuhammer Schlesien~~ *Übungsplatz*
   Wandern über Frankfurt/Oder
   zu melden.
2. Dieser Einberufungsbefehl ist mitzubringen und bei der Dienststelle, zu der Sie einberufen sind, abzugeben.
3. Bei unentschuldigtem Fernbleiben haben Sie Bestrafung nach
   den Wehrmachtgesetzen zu gewärtigen.
4. Die besonderen Anordnungen auf anhängender Karte sind
   genau zu beachten.

*) Nichtzutreffendes ist zu streichen.

Ergänzungsstelle Warthe (XXI)
der Waffen SS
Nebenstelle Lemberg
SS - Obersturmführer

Доповняюча Варта (XXI)
Установа SS
Станиця Львів

Дата поштової стампілі

Наказ покликання A
Виданий як виказка їзди залізницею.

1. Вас покликають до активної військової служби і маєте
   негайно *) дня *19 серпня SS* 19*44* до год. *) *24*
   при *14. Galiz'sche SS Fraiw. Division*
   у ~~Neuhammer Schlesien~~ *Übungsplatz*
   Wandern über Frankfurt/Oder
   зголоситися.
2. Цей наказ треба принести зі собою і віддати в службовій
   установі, до якої Ви покликані.
3. При неоправданім неявленню, підлягаєте карі після військо-
   вих законів.
4. Звертати пильну увагу на окремі зарядження у залученій карті.

Доповняюча Варта (XXI)
Установа SS
Станиця Львів
SS - Obersturmführer

ВАЖНЕ!   СПЕЦІЯЛЬНІ ЗАРЯДЖЕННЯ   НЕГАЙНО ПРОЧИТАТИ!

1. Від дня сталовища 0,00 год. Ви є зовсім і підлягаєте зовсім, розпорядкам і зарядженням приналежним для вчасн.
2. Якщо Ви до дня сталовища змінете Ваше місце замешкання або Ваше стале місце побуту, то обовязані Ви негайно
   особисто зголоситися до приналежного Крайслявтнякові (Ляндюовісарові). При переселенню до повіту іншого
   Крайслявтнякока (Ляндювісарока) маєте негайно зголоситися до приналежного Крайслявтнякові (Ляндювісарові).
   Предкладайте нижше посилання. Залучене покликання остає в силі.
3. Покликанця маєте зголосити приналежному війську або посадникові і Крайслявтнякові.
4. Цей наказ покликання маєте негайно предложити свому верхньому підприємства, який не має права виключити
   службові умови. Верхну керівникка підприємства не мілько відібрати Вас цього шляху покликання.
5. Якщо Ви в припадку тяжкої хвороби кусте домів, або іна іншої моціякльної причини буди переповідний
   особисто дотиче на означений час, то негайно маєте зголосити що в подачі причина і приблизного часу три-
   вання хвороби приналежному Ляндювісарові. На потвердження хвороби маєте предложити свідоцтво урядового ді-
   кара. Де це вможливо, вистати посвідка літа або посадника.
6. Маєте прихонти, якщо маєте, або розпоряджаєте:
   а) дві сорочки і підштанки, 2 пари шкіль або онуч, одні підшал, два рушники і три хустинки;
   б) миянка, приладдя до миття, до гоління, щітку й гребінь;
   в) ручну валізку або коробку з нами і нитками до нашивання на всяку цивільного убрання;
   г) харч на три дні.
7. Щоби забезпечити Вашу родину на виладок хвороби треба накотити:
   а) обовязані члени законові Касе Хворих (місцеві Касе Хворих і т. д.) мають проєкти свого приналежна, продаж-
      даючи наказ покликання, щоб повідомо про Ваше покликання Касу Хворих;
   б) добровільні чл на законові Касе Хворих і члени неплатних кас, мають зголосити про покликання свій Касу
      Хворих (місцевий Касі Хворих).
8. Ваша родина буде дістаяти родинну допомогу. Родинну допомогу дістається по Вашім покликанню до обовязку
   членам автоматично через уряд для справ начелення і допомоги при Крайслявтнякові.
9. Всякі інші Ваші приналежна є полакні через цей наказ покликання.

Eilige Wehrmachtsache!

SS-Feldpost

Herrn *Krasnyk Iwan*

geb. am 21.5.1917

Przemyśl

Krankenhaus N. 6.

Ergänzungsamt der Waffen - SS
Ergänzungsstelle Warthe (XXI)
Nebenstelle Lemberg
Lemberg 1, Postfach 181

Opposite above: Call up notification for Iwan Krasnyk (Obverse). Call up notification for Iwan Krasnyk (Reverse) SS-Feldpost. Mr Krasnyk, Iwan; Date of birth 21.5.1907, Peremyshl, L Krankenhaus Strasse 6

Ergänzunggsstelle Warthe (XXI) der Waffen-SS Lemberg (L'viv)

Order to report to the Division type "A"
Valid also as a train pass
Translation :
1 You are ordered to active duty in the Wehrdienst (army service) and must appear immediately on *) 19 June 1944 within 24 hours*) at 14 Galizische SS Freiw. Division training camp at Neuhammer/Schlesten (deleted) Wandern near Frankfurt/Oder.
2 You should bring this order with you and return it to the Dienststelle (authority)
3 For an unauthorised non-appearance (Fernbleiben) you will be punished according to military law (Wehrmachtgesetzen).
4 You are responsible for the points listed on this card.
Ergänzungsstelle Warthe (XXI) der Waffen-SS Lemberg, Signed SS-Obersturmführer (signature illegible)

Opposite below: Call up notification for Iwan Krasnyk (Reverse)
1 From the date appearing (O, 00 hour) you are a soldier and fall under military rules.
2 If you change address or move to another location you must personally immediately report to the Kreishauptmann or Landkommissar and show him this order to report. Should you move to another district you must report immediately.
3 You must show this order to report to the village elder or official in your community and the Krieshauptmann.
4 You must report at work to show this order to report to your employer who has no right to change your working agreement and is not allowed to take this order away from you.
5 If you are not able to appear personally because you are bedridden due to a serious illness, you must report immediately to the Landkommissar with an appropriate certificate from a government appointed medical doctor. In case of unavailability, the certificate from the village elder will be acceptable.
6 You are obligated to bring with you (if available)
   a) Two shirts, underwear, three pairs of socks, one jacket, two towels and three handkerchiefs.
   b) Braces, sewing kit, shaving kit, brush, comb
   c) One suitcase or strong box, wrapping paper and string for shipping home your civilian clothing.
   d) Food supplies for three days
7 To provide medical needs for your family in case of an illness you must remember:
   a) Advise your employer of your enlistment and to notify the 'social services'
   b) Advise private insurance
8 Your family will receive medical allowance. Family allowance will be automatically forwarded through government agencies located at the Kreishauptamt.
9 Under this order all previous orders are nullified.

[...] Throughout my war years I had a chance to see uniforms of all great armies of the world. And I have to say out of all of them, our German uniforms were best suited for a soldier. This uniform, from head to toe, turns a boy into a soldier even without any training. This is a very imposing uniform. It lies on a soldier perfectly, gives him sense of meaning and honour. Soldiers steps are hard and heavy, for he is not marching on rubber, but on iron and this creates a feeling in the soldier's soul; here I stand, here I walk, here I march and nothing will stop me.[...][175]

It is also important to note that the publically promised provision of social welfare for dependants[176] was an additional incentive for at least some of those who enlisted.[177] That this was a significant inducement was recognised by the German authorities. In his secret circular dated 28 April Wächter wrote:

Particular emphasis is to be given to the settlement that has now been reached for the care of relatives which, in the framework of the Wehrmacht regulations assure the relatives of the Ukrainian soldiers, the same family maintenance as that given to the relatives of members of the German Wehrmacht. It should be noted that by the term 'relatives' spouse, sisters, brothers, parents, children, grandparents and grandchildren are to be understood.[178]

Several thousand Ukrainians are known to have received and benefited from the social welfare,[179] although what was available was woefully inadequate.[180]

Throughout the recruitment campaign the Ukrainian intelligentsia connected with the Military Board and Ukrainian Central Committee exerted themselves in order to maximise their influence. Anxious to attract as many volunteers as possible a new tactic was adopted whereby to set an example to the impressionable Ukrainian youth, individual members of both organisations volunteered themselves. This symbolic action was merely a token gesture and a propaganda exercise designed to demonstrate mass support for the Division. Unlike those who followed their example, most of the prominent figures who volunteered (including Prof. Kubijovych) actually avoided having to serve. They had their individual cases appealed by local branches of the Central Committee and were classified as being 'unabkoemmlich' (i.e. indispensable for the local administration) and subsequently discharged.[181] The extent to which this occurred can be gauged from the fact that on one day the L'viv committee alone requested 30 individuals who occupied government positions be released from service with the Division.[182]

Compulsion: Rifle or Spade?

Idealism, effective propaganda and successive inducements convinced increasing numbers of Ukrainian youths to report to the enlistment commissions. At the same time, less idealistic incentives and force of circumstance compelled other civilians to do the same. Fear of the returning Red Army was the motivation for many including Volodymyr Keczun:

> [...] I knew that if the Russians came back, there were three possibilities waiting for me; I was old enough to be conscripted into the Red Army and be sent to front, or join the UPA, and live in the forests, or be sent to Siberia and probably never come back.[183]

Mychailo Kormylo was another who feared conscription into the Red Army and all that it entailed:

> [...] My father had told me that it would be better to die with a gun in my hand than a spade. I know what he meant because during the battle of Brody our platoon mowed down a number of Soviets who were attacking us with such primitive weaponry.[...][184]

Then there was the daunting prospect of being drafted for the detested Arbeitsdienst (forced labour in German agriculture or industry). Earlier, in his appeal to the population of Galicia, Governor Wächter had proclaimed that 'An army of Galician workers had shown their gratitude after their liberation by working in the factories and fields to produce weapons and food for victory.' The reality of the situation was somewhat different. Often young Ukrainian males after having been summoned by the German Labour Offices (Arbeitsamter) and given a medical examination, had a choice. Either they could report for registration for the Division whereupon full security would be provided for their families along with automatic exemption from all other duties. Alternatively they could be sent to serve in the Baudienst (construction service and forced labour) where living conditions and treatment for the forced labourers were notoriously bad. Indeed a great many who had escape from Baudienst took advantage of Governor Wächter's amnesty and enlisted.[185]

Choice No More

Regardless of Wächter's pronouncements that the voluntary aspect would be respected in every case and that the use of coercion was forbidden,[186] the German authorities took steps to ensure that the recruitment programme would not fail. A list was circulated to all the recruitment commissions of those categories who were due for compulsory registration and who were obliged to register for a preliminary medical examination. It is therefore evident that from the very start there were those for whom the term 'volunteer' was not applicable. Those for whom there was a mandatory requirement to report were:

> All men born in the years 1920 to 1925 [i.e. those aged eighteen—twenty three];
> All non-commissioned officers up to the age of 40, who had served in any army

whatsoever; All officers and those cadets who had graduated from military academies but had not yet obtained a commission, as well as military officials up to the age of 45; Doctors and veterinary surgeons up to the age of 45.

In the case of university students near the end of their courses the obligation to register was to be deferred until after completion of their course.[187]

Even the mandatory requirement for former officers, NCOs and professionals such as doctors and veterinary surgeons to report for enlistment was insufficient to guarantee the availability of the required numbers. In order to make the prescribed quotas of officers and NCOs, a circular was sent out on 1 July 1943, to all replacements bureaux (SS-Ergänzungsstellen) in Germany asking for the names of any former Ukrainian officers and NCOs while six bureaux were also asked for lists of doctors.[188]

In some cases suitable officer candidates were not released from their employment by the German authorities while other highly qualified men refused to serve, mainly on political grounds.[189] Of those who did enlist a majority had served with the Austro-Hungarian Army of 1914[190] and then with the Ukrainian Galician Army. An examination of their personal files reveals that others had been in the Russian Imperial Army, the Army of the Ukrainian National Republic (UNR) 1918–20, the Polish, Soviet, and Czech armies and even a handful such as Mykola Jurniuk[191] in the Romanian Army. A small number had also served with various German Wehrmacht formations since 1939. In the case of the former officers of the Austro-Hungarian Army, having enlisted, many were subsequently released because of their advanced age[192] and poor physical condition.

The situation with NCOs was only marginally better than with the officers even though veterans of other armies were available, especially the Polish Army. As a direct consequence of foreign occupation of Galicia during the inter-war period which had prevented the maintenance of an indigenous army, the required number of NCOs could simply not be found. Most would therefore have to be trained from scratch. The inability to provide a sufficient number of trained Ukrainian officers and NCOs would not only continue to vex the Division's organisers throughout its existence, but would ultimately compromise its military prowess.

The recruitment of medical doctors caused similar problems. Working in conjunction with the Ukrainian medical association, Dr Volodymyr Bilozor who headed the health department of the Military Board, issued a special appeal for doctors to sign up, but this met with limited success. Although as a result of this appeal 161 reported, very few were suitable, largely due to their age and ultimately only thirty two remained in service with the Division.[193] Unlike their German counterparts the Ukrainian doctors were not given officer rank automatically and were first required to undergo three months of basic training as enlisted men before being given a non commissioned rank. Full officer rank was to have been given pending completion of courses at German medical academies.[194] In practical terms, the German policy of treating the Ukrainian doctors as enlisted men did little to frustrate Dr Bilozor's efforts to recruit qualified medical personnel. The same decisive considerations for enrolling were just as applicable to professionals as they were to the rank and file.[195]

The Sore Tooth Continues to Fester

The recruitment of priests presented a different kind of problem. The prevailing view among senior members of the SS establishment was that the Catholic clergy who would serve as chaplains in the Division were potentially subversive elements. This was clearly evident in a letter dated 28 June 1943, from the Chef der Sicherheitspolizei und des SD, SS-Obergruppenführer Dr Ernst Kaltenbrunner, to Himmler in which he expressed his concern about the numerous voluntary applications of Greek-Catholic priests which had already been received for the SS-Schützen Division Galizien.

In his letter Kaltenbrunner stated that even if the applications were attributed to the enthusiasm the Galicians were showing for the formation of the Division, the deployment of the Greek-Catholic priests as soldiers within it (and thus at the eastern front) could hardly be described as safe, since they would be serving Schepticky's [sic] long standing goal to 'open up the east for the aims of the Vatican'. In light of this Kaltenbrunner requested a decision as to how the voluntary applications of Greek-Catholic priests be dealt with.[196] The reply from Himmler's office dated 16 July acknowledged the danger but went on to say that:

> The Reichsführer-SS wants to exploit the influence of the priests. The best plan would probably be for SS-Obergruppenführer Berger to ask the Metropolitan to come and see him and make it clear to him that as long as the influence of the priests on the troops is good, they can stay. If however, they start to agitate, they will be removed, in which case the Metropolitan will bear the full blame. The Reichsführer-SS is of the opinion that in this way the admission of the priests into the SS-Schützen-Division 'Galizien' can be used to our advantage.[197]

Berger later reported to Himmler that because of ill health the Metropolitan Sheptytsky had been prevented from attending the conference which Himmler had instructed him to arrange. Instead he had sent his representative Dr Laba who had good reason to be apprehensive about the visit knowing that Sheptytsky was hiding hundreds of Jews in his residence and in Greek Catholic monasteries in Galicia. Berger reported that he had informed Laba 'of his duties and those of his clergymen, making him particularly aware of the magnitude of the concession of the Reichsführer- SS in allowing clergymen to be made available to this division'. As regards the priests who would serve in the Division, he went on to add:

> The clergymen—12 in total—will be selected by him and will go to Sennheim[198] from 20.8. to 30.10.1943 for basic military training. [...] The Domherr Dr Laba was most impressed by our discussion, as he had previously thought that the Reichsführer-SS

would resent the deployment of clergymen. He therefore gave me his word of honour that he would do everything to ensure that this experiment for the Galician Division is successful.[199]

By resorting to semantics, Laba left a good impression on Berger cleverly promising that he 'would do everything to ensure the success of the experiment'. However while Berger contented himself that having confronted Rev Dr Laba personally with Himmler's ultimatum, the Church would in future toe the line, Himmler demanded that the position be spelt out unequivocally. In a letter dated 31 July his office informed Berger that 'it be made clear [to the Metropolitan] that the Reichsführer-SS has got no sympathy for even the smallest of experiments involving the creation of a Ukrainian National state or having similar aspirations'.[200]

Much to their chagrin, the Germans never did remove the 'sore tooth' of the influence of the clergy and the Metropolitan Sheptytsky who continued to openly criticise the NAZI regime.[201]

Opposition

No sooner had the formation of the Galician Division been announced than predictably enough opposition emerged from several disparate sources and for a variety of reasons. Amongst the Germans Reichskommissar Erich Koch was the most vocal, claiming that with the commencement of training most of its men were deserting to the nationalist underground partisans.[202] Similar protests emanated from less high profile officials and functionaries belonging to the Polizei establishment and the civilian administration.

Within the Galician population there were also those who objected to the Division, principally because of the brutal nature of German regime in Galicia. They pointed to the indiscriminate confiscation of foodstuffs and livestock, the mass seizures of Ukrainian youth for forced labour in Germany and widespread arrests and many executions of Ukrainian nationalists. Others disapproved of the Division being subordinated to the Waffen-SS, its regional nomenclature and questioned why it should wear German uniform and not a Ukrainian one with Ukrainian insignia (i.e. the Trident).

A further source of opposition originated from both the Communist and Polish underground movements. Traditional animosities meant that both viewed the formation of an armed Ukrainian military unit as a potentially threatening development. Their respective channels were used to circulate anti-Division propaganda via leaflets,[203] the spreading of rumours and occasionally by perpetrating acts of violence against those who had enlisted or their families.[204] The Military Board also encountered attempts to sabotage their activities especially by Polish officials and civil servants in the lower levels of administration. Their efforts were however more of a nuisance and produced negligible results.[205]

The most formidable opposition came from elements within the OUN-B Bandera faction,[206] which after the direct conflict with the Germans in 1941, had rebuilt its organisation around the UPA. Its attitude towards the Division was negative and it continued to exercise a major influence over a large portion of the population especially the young in rural areas. The majority of the OUN-B leadership including Colonel Klym Savur and General Leonid Stupnyckyj initially adopted an anti-Division stance and called for a boycott of recruitment. The essence of their opposition stemmed from their own previous experiences with the Germans. They argued that having exploited Ukraine economically, the Germans now sought to take advantage of the physical strength of the nation by using Ukrainians as cannon fodder. The existence of the Division, they maintained, would result in a loss of prestige for the idea of a Ukrainian state.[207]

Their principal objections were outlined in an article in the Buleten (Bulletin) of the Organisation of Ukrainian Nationalists which argued correctly that the Germans were in a desperate situation and that by creating the Galician Division they wanted to weaken the active underground. It went on to stress that the Germans would occupy the commanding positions and that it would be a 'purely colonial unit'. It acknowledged its supporters believed the Division would be the kernel for the creation of a Ukrainian National Amy that could be used if a similar situation arose as it had after the First World War; however, it dismissed these arguments by stating that it would remain under the control of the Waffen-SS.[208]

To mitigate the UPA's anti-Division activities, both the Military Board and the German authorities held further public meetings where they appealed to Ukrainians to resist the radical elements who would mislead them.[209]

The attitude of the OUN-B leadership gradually became more ambivalent as the recruitment campaign progressed. After several conferences and consultations on the issue of co-operation with the Division's formation, a compromise was eventually reached between its supporters and its opponents. The UPA command decided to oppose the concept of the Division as the natural successor of the Sichovi Striltsi[210] and of the Ukrainian Galician Army, an analogy which was often drawn in the public announcements by members of the Military Board and local recruiting agents. At the same time, following a secret meeting in October 1943, between a representative of the Military Board Roman Krokhmaliuk and Roman Shukhevych, the UPA agreed that the boycott of recruitment would be lifted. As untrained recruits to the UPA were becoming an increasing liability, Shukhevych, determined to use the Division so that UPA members could receive the necessary training that would allow it to become an elite guerrilla force. Consequently he proceeded to order whole groups of men to join.[211] Among those who received personal orders from General Shukhevych to enlist and act as contact officers between the Division and the OUN, were some high profile members of the UPA such as Bohdan Pidhayny, Myroslav Malecky and Swiatoslav Levycky who were sent to the Division to exercise some influence and form a political structure.[212] According to Pidhayny, Shukhevych's plan was to ensure that at least one out of every seven Ukrainian soldiers became a member of OUN.[213]

The Ukrainians who enlisted for service in the 'Galician Division' during the spring and summer of 1943 had varied incentives for so doing. The vast majority who volunteered did so out of patriotism, believing that service with the Germans was a means to an end[214] however the existing circumstances ensured that from the very outset the ardent nationalist element was partly diluted and compromised by those who were compelled to join out of necessity and whose convictions and priorities lay elsewhere. Idealists and patriots, pragmatists and opportunists, all registered, but one thing is certain, not all were volunteers.

An Analysis of Enlistment Figures

In numerical terms there is no doubt that the enlistment figures suggested that recruitment to the Division appeared to be an outstanding success, despite the active opposition. To keep abreast of the campaign's progress Wächter had directed that the number of registrations was to be cabled to him daily by the head of the Werbekommission, along with a short report on 'special impressions'.[215]

In a teleprinter message to Berger HSSPF SS-Obergruppenführer Krüger informed him that Governor Wächter had reported that already by 8 May 1943, the number of registrations had reached 32,000. Of these over 26,000 had been provisionally accepted by the recruiting commissions. In view of the apparent numbers coming forward Krüger proceeded to ask Berger 'What should the total strength of the 'SS-Schützen-Division Galizien be?"[216]

By 14 May the figure had risen to 38,569,[217] and shortly thereafter a euphoric Wächter, who had previously thought because of the extensive labour drafts it would be difficult to obtain 20,000 volunteers,[218] informed Himmler on 17 May that 40,000 men had enrolled.[219] At the same time he invited Himmler to visit Galicia in particular the huge staged propaganda event that was scheduled to take pace in Kolomyia to witness the reception the Division was getting for himself.[220] The day before the region which included the towns of Kolomyia, Horodenka, Kosiv and Sniatyn had registered the second greatest number of volunteers.

In his reply dated 17 May 1943, Himmler said that because of his busy schedule he could not visit Galicia for the time being but suggested that 'When I next visit Lemberg [L'viv] I will be very glad to travel with you through these regions incognito and not in an official capacity, to get an impression myself'.[221]

In Himmler's absence the rally at the Kolomyia stadium took place as planned on a wet Sunday 23 May along with a liturgy on the meadow beside the River Prut conducted by Rev Alexander Rusyn.[222] Transportation from the surrounding area by bus and train was provided free of charge to bolster attendance. The event which became something of a showpiece for the recruiting agencies culminated in a speech delivered personally by SS-Brigadeführer Dr Wächter to the assembled crowd.[223] It also featured prominently in a colour propaganda film made specifically for this purpose which was shown in newsreels throughout the General Government.[224]

As the recruitment drive continued throughout May the number of registrations which were already subjected to serious manipulation increased steadily and was exceeding all expectations. To help maintain the momentum of the early success, the organisers extended the campaign from Galicia to other areas of the General Government including the neighbouring provincial centres of the districts of Cracow and later Lublin.[225]

A report by the Military Board which oversaw the enlistment programme revealed that by 25 May 1943, 67,210 men had registered.[226] By 29 May the total had soared to 73,159, from the districts of Galicia and Cracow.[227]

Finally, on 2 June 1943, less than six weeks after the campaign had begun, the figures for the first stage of the programme were published by the Military Board. By this date a total of 81,999 men had registered, 52,875 of whom 52, 875 had been provisionally accepted. 29,124 had been rejected without even having been called to a medical commission.[228]

The high number of rejects can be traced directly to the instruction given to the recruitment commissions. This stated that:

> [...] detailed examinations of the volunteers would not have to be done by the Recruitment Commissions [as] such examinations would slow down the recruitment process. However attention should be turned to visible diseases or mental instabilities.[229] (author's emphasis).

This allowed them to resort to indiscriminate registration irrespective of eligibility. In this way thousands who were mostly too old for service and near retirement age, were clearly medically unfit, or in reserved occupations were arbitrarily mobilised in order to boost the number of registrations for propaganda purposes.

The worse culprits appear to have been the enlistment authorities in the town of Sianok. Recruitment started here on 15 May when the commission began registering all the men in the town fit for combat. By the end of the first day 300 had been registered of which 250 had been accepted and 50 rejected. As demonstrations of support continued throughout the next two weeks in all the villages of the Sianok district, the commission began to register all the males who supported the Division irrespective of their eligibility. This included a large number of forestry commission workers employed as woodcutters or in the saw mills who reported for enlistment en masse and were later excused from service as their occupations were classified as being essential for the war economy. As a result, a total of 14,446 men had been registered by 31 May 1943, of whom 12,438 were not, and could not be eligible for service in the Division due to their occupation, age, ill health etc. and were subsequently rejected or excused service. Nevertheless despite a rejection rate of 86 per cent, the overall figure was still counted toward the total number of registrations.

Above left: Kolomyia 23 May 1943. On the plains beside the River Prut a field mass to bless the volunteers. In the black cassock is the Greek Catholic priest, vicar of St Michael Church in Kolomyia, Rev Stephen Havryliv.

Above right: Kolomyia 23 May, 1943. In light cassock who greeting Wächter—the parson, Dean of Kolomiysky Greek Catholic Church Rev. Alexander Rusyn.

Kolomyia 23 May, 1943. Kolomyia provide the second largest number of volunteers and featured very heavily in all the German propaganda newsreels.

Above left: Governor Wächter addresses a carefully staged recruitment rally at Kolomyia stadium, 23 May 1943.

Above right: Kolomyia 23 May 1943, Hutsuls with their Carpathian 'Trembitas'.

Another official Kriegsberichter photo by SS KBR Schremmer depicting volunteers registering for service.

In this photo which appeared in contemporary newspapers, Ukrainian volunteers report to the enlistment commission and receive enlistment forms.

Holding their enlistment papers, registered recruits await their turn for examination, in Drohobych.

Ukrainian volunteers seen here being given medicals in Drohobych.

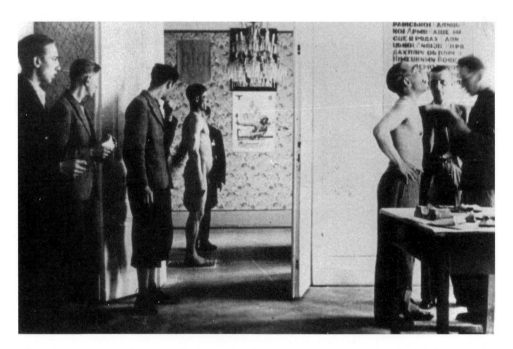

Ukrainian recruits undergo medical examinations. Recruiting posters for the Division can be seen displayed around the rooms.

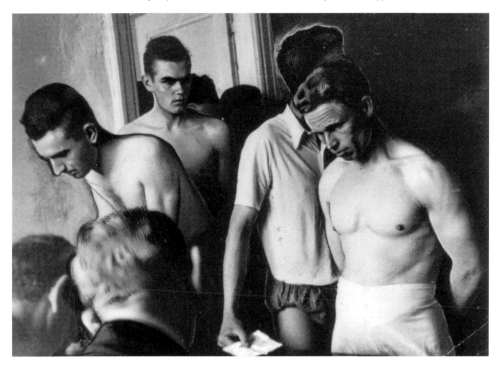

Another picture used extensively in the recruitment propaganda showing recruits reporting for their medical examinations.

May 1943, volunteers undergo a thorough medical examination by German staff. The advanced aged of many is evident from the man at the front awaiting examination.

On 3 June 1943, Berger conveyed the news of the preliminary results to the Reichsführer in a secret progress report which read:

3.6.1943

Reichsführer!

The number of voluntary registrations for the Legion[230] 'Galizien' has risen to approximately 80,000. Of these approximately 50,000 have been provisionally accepted. Of those 50,000, 13,000 have been examined, half of these are k.v. [suitable for combat use] and may be enlisted. Consequently, one may expect after final completion of the examinations, a total of approximately 25,000 suitable individuals measuring at least 165 cm.

I have become convinced that my original plan, to enlist for both the Division and Polizei simultaneously, can for political reasons, not be pursued. It was not previously known to me that approximately 4,000 Ukrainians from the Galician region are to be found in the Polizei and Wachformationen (guard units) created by various local authorities (Dienststellen). Uniformity, in pay and benefits for surviving relatives, has not as yet been established. Undesirable political consequences are therefore to be expected. As far as the Ukrainian population are concerned, these 4,000 men do however count as Polizei, despite the fact that we have no influence whatsoever over this. Hence the decision against [enlisting] the Polizei. Apparently the plan was to enlist 10,000 of these volunteers into Polizei formations for deployment in fighting against partisans. SS-Brigadeführer v. Wächter does not consider this viable. After apprising myself of the situation I have to agree with him. I may refer in this matter to the attached special report.

Since the formation of the Division is at the moment not possible for the known reasons, but since slower progress would cause civil unrest, I venture to suggest the following:

1. The registered officers and NCOs will, after confirmation with the SS-Fuehrungshauptamt, be enlisted as soon as possible in retraining courses and will form the foundation for the planned Division.

2. The Head Office of the Ordnungspolizei, which has at its disposal, the required number of officers and NCOs (Führer and Unterführer) for the training, and which can also provide the necessary weapons, will temporarily transfer training units (Ausbildungskommandos) to the Waffen-SS. These units would later be returned to the Head Office of the Ordnungspolizei, and will be available for the training of the Polizei formations which may be created after the formation of the Division.

In the interim, I will make available to the Head Office of the Ordnungspolizei approx. 1,500 recruits—suitable for combat use in the SS and the army, born 1908 and 1909. A Polizei training for a small fraction of this ethnic group may at a later date become particularly important.

It is possible, if we were to reduce the minimum height to 160 cm, to create a second Division from the Galician region. Most important of all is that the Legion exists prior to the enlistment for the Polizei. After deployment at the front, this Division may be used without difficulty in combating partisans.

I request further orders. The Head of the SS-Fuehrungshauptamptes will receive a copy of this suggestion.[231]

Signed

G. Berger
SS-Gruppenführer

As Berger had noted, the imposition of the minimum height requirement of 165 cm, had a significant effect on the available manpower. To further emphasise the impact of this, Berger notified Himmler that by 21 June the number of those registered who had been medically examined had risen to 26,436 men of which only 3,281 were classified as suitable for service in the Division; while 10,281 were deemed suitable for the army, and 12,874 considered unsuitable for military service altogether (7,139 of which were rejected because of the minimum height requirement of 1.65 cm).[232]

Worse still, as Wächter had feared, access to the remaining suitable manpower was subject to intensive competition from civilian and military agencies including the Luftwaffe which were looking to meet their own needs from the local population.

To inform him of this problem and ensure that Reichsführer had not been misled by the propaganda figures which continued to boast that '80,000 men were available for the Division', on 2 July Berger sent him the following teleprinter message:

Secret! Urgent!

2.7.43

to the Reichsführer-SS und Chef der Deutschen Polizei.[...]
2. Regarding draft status in Galicia, as incorrect numbers have apparently been quoted to the Reichsführer-SS, I wish to report accurately: at our disposal are:

300 officers (including those born 1890)
1,300 NCOs
800 high school graduates
48 medical doctors
20,270 men—of which 3,670 fall into the height range 160–164 cm.

We can expect at least 700 most likely 800 men from the first action, thus around 28,000[233] will be available. In addition to these comes a guard battalion [Wachbattalion] in Debica of about 800 men, who urgently request inclusion, as they were after all the first and would now be disadvantaged if they are not included as part of the Division.

In the interim at least 10,000 volunteers suitable for us have been secured for work in the Reich. Neither the Governor [Wächter] nor I were able to intervene as a direct order from the Führer was shown. If we wait too long then by the 1 October 43, more than 20,000 men will no longer be available, even less [will be available] when the Oberkommand der Luftwaffe [Luftwaffe high command] attempts to take some of these men into the Reich by illegal means for anti-aircraft duties.[234]

der chef des ss-hauptamtes

Signed G. Berger
SS-Obergruppenführer

The reality behind the propaganda pronouncements about the impressive numbers that had responded to the call to arms, became evident when the final results of the first phase of the recruitment programme were announced. This took place at a general meeting of the district representatives of the Military Board held on 30 October 1943. By this time, now that the initial burst of enthusiasm for volunteers had passed, the Germans had established a parallel recruitment agency in L'viv. Its full title was the Ergänzungsamt der Waffen SS Ergänzungsstelle Warthe (XXI) Nebenstelle Lemberg but it was known as the Ergänzungsamt der Waffen SS.[235]

Headed by SS-Hauptsturmführer Karl Schulze it had a staff of approximately 10 all of whom were Germans. In addition to recruitment, it kept registration records and organised the transportation of the recruits. By so doing, it transformed the Military Board into an auxiliary body whose sole remit was confined to propaganda and liaison with the Ukrainian population.[236] At the meeting, Dr Schulze gave a detailed report concerning the results of the enlistment programme based on information collected by the Military Board and his own Erganzungsamt der Waffen-SS. It included the following approximate breakdown of the registrations;

		(* the actual total figure
Volunteered/Registered	80,000	was 81,999.)
Called before the medical commissions	53,000	
Reported to medical commissions	42,000	
Accepted	27,000	
Reclaimed (appealed for release)	1,400	

Received induction notice	25,600
Called up for service	19,047
Actually reported	13,245
Released from training camps as sick	1,487
In training	11,578
Due to be called up Nov 1–13	6,150

It is evident that according to Dr Schulze's figures from the 80,000 men who had registered only 27,000 had been passed as medically fit and of these the best 11,578 reported for and actually began their training. With the exception of 6,150 who were due to be called up in November 62,272 men were unable or unwilling to serve.[237] In addition to those rejected on medical grounds, the report also highlighted the problem of the large number of draft dodgers who signed the enlistment forms and received the summons but declined to report to the drafting boards. Dr Schulze attributed this phenomenon to the fact that the Ukrainians were unwilling to serve in an SS formation and the great influence of the propaganda of the OUN on the youth who preferred to serve in UPA.[238]

The Lion or the Trident?

The ostensible success of the recruitment campaign further polarised the attitudes of the German leadership towards the Galician Division. Its supporters, caught up in the infectious euphoria created by the propaganda figures, saw the potential to further exploit the initiative in the interests of the Reich. This is reflected in a letter from a representative of the propaganda department to State secretary (Staatssekretär) SS-Obergruppenführer Krüger which read:

> The formation of the SS-Schützendivision in Galicia has been achieved with surprising speed. To date 80,000 men have volunteered. If the call up to join the Waffen-SS is reinforced with intensive propaganda aimed at the Ukrainians, then we could, judging by the current position, easily make even more extensive plans. These would result in a measurable reduction of the number of German troops deployed in the east, and a saving of German blood in the battle against Bolshevism.
>
> The propaganda campaign is especially important, in view of the fact that the Ukrainian nationalist partisan leader Taras Bulba occasionally attempts to get able bodied young Ukrainians to join the partisans.[...] The cost of the campaign totals DM 125,000—a figure that does not seem high, when considering the success expected, in view of our previous findings.[...][239]

Simultaneously the inflated enlistment figures were the cause of much concern and suspicion among the Division's many opponents. Their number included the Districtkommissar of Horochow Harter, who voiced his misgivings in writing on 19 June as follows: 'it is generally said these individuals have the same purpose as in 1918, where they accepted weapons only to turn them against the Germans at the appropriate time'.[240] Even more alarming was a disturbing tendency amongst the Ukrainians to perceive the Division and refer to it as 'Ukrainian' and not 'Galician'. On this issue Himmler, knowing Hitler's negative view on Ukrainians in general, remained sensitive to anything which suggested that the formation was thought of as 'Ukrainian'. On 30 June 1943, Himmler sent SS-Sturmbannführer d'Alquen, commander of the SS-Kriegsberichters (SS-War Correspondents) the following teleprinter message:

> [...] 2. In writing about the Galicia Division the words 'The Ukrainian Lion' were used. The word 'Ukrainian' is forbidden, now and for all time. I direct that only [the term] 'Galician' should be used.[241]

> Signed H. Himmler

Other ardent opponents including the HSSPF Ukraine und Russland-Süd, SS-Obergruppenführer und General der Polizei Hans Prützmann,[242] also opposed the use of the term 'Ukrainian'. In a letter to the Reichsführer-SS dated 8 July 1943, he wrote:

> I am taking the liberty to send you the enclosed comment of the Gebietskommisar of Horochow. Since, unfortunately, even in the press of the General-Government [sic], reference is frequently made to the 'Ukrainian SS-Div', I would be grateful for an order from the Reichsführer designating the Division in Galicia as 'Galizische Division' and forbidding the use of the term Ukrainian entirely.[243]

Himmler duly obliged and six days later on 14 July 1943, he issued an order circulated to 'All Department Heads' which read: 'When mentioning the Galician Division I forbid all future mention of a Ukrainian Division or of Ukrainian nationhood'.[244]

Whilst this was reassuring for opponents of the Division, its supporters understood that the order and its implications would be the cause of many difficulties. Now that the necessary numbers had come forward to create a Division, Wächter believed the deceit of calling them 'Galicians' (which he had suggested)[245] had now served its purpose and the pretence could be abandoned. In reply to the order Wächter, wrote a secret report dated 30 July in which he attempted to convince Himmler that it would be advisable for all parties concerned to rescind the order. Wächter began the lengthy memorandum by drawing attention to the fact that the term 'Galicia' described a geographical and territorial concept, not the mixed Galician population of Germans, Poles and Ukrainians. He stressed that any attempt to merge Ukrainians and Poles into 'Galicians', contradicted German literature on the subject. At the same time it conflicted with the previous policy of the German authorities which recognised and officially appointed distinct Ukrainian committees, delegations, Polizei and newspapers. He maintained that the distinction needed to be upheld because the Ukrainians like the Poles were unique in both language and culture and more importantly it was necessary in view of the guidelines issued by Himmler which stated the Division was only open to the Ukrainians of Galicia and not the Poles. He also rejected the use of the alternative term of 'Ruthens' to describe the Galician Ukrainians as inadvisable as this suggested they were pro-Soviet.

He went to emphasise that that in the interests of gaining 10,000 reliable soldiers, the respecting of (Ukrainian) racial identity was imperative. It would also sustain the morale of the population so that a plentiful harvest could be gathered and the supply routes secured for the German armies fighting on the eastern front. In an attempt to put the matter in perspective he concluded that: 'Looking at the position of the Reich, I am of the conviction that the key to victory or failure lies, now as ever, in the East with the Reich's Eastern political activities. I therefore ask you Reichsführer for your understanding perusal'.[246]

Casting around for additional support, at Wächter's instigation a second letter dated 5 August 1943, reiterating all the main points of Wächter's arguments, was sent to Himmler. The unknown author (most probably Alfred Rosenberg) stated that the insistence on making the title 'Galician' obligatory would offend the national pride of the Ukrainians who had responded enthusiastically to the call up for the formation of the SS-Schützendivision Galicia [sic]. Furthermore it could also potentially endanger the whole undertaking and provide propaganda for the Division's critics, especially the Bolsheviks and Bandera adherents.

To assuage Himmler's fear that permitting the Division to be known as 'Ukrainian' would in any way be tantamount to sanctioning the idea of a Ukrainian national state, the letter continued:

> Despite the fact that all organisations of the Ukrainian population of Galicia work under the title 'Ukrainian', this has so far only established ethnic origins and has been in no way connected with thoughts of an independent Ukrainian state or any possibilities of a united-Ukrainian (Gross-Ukrainian) future. In my opinion the concept 'Ukrainian' is of similar value in the SS-Schützendivision Galizien. All call ups to Ukrainians called to the Division, have been geared towards their planned deployment, not for Ukraine or Ukrainian culture, but rather as the contribution of the Ukrainian ethnic group in the battle to defend against Bolshevism and for a new Europe...

The letter ended by saying that refusing to call the Division 'Ukrainian' would have an adverse effect on the morale of its predominantly Ukrainian soldiers and may even encourage some to go over to the Soviet side.[247]

The strength of such arguments however did nothing to remove the veil of self deceit from Himmler who remained defiant. He responded with a circular letter dated 11 August in which he used inconsistencies in Wächter's arguments to reject his long term political ideas for the new administrative structure of the General Government, submitted five months previously. He continued by reminding Wächter how 'magnanimous' he had already been:

> It being my region, I will stand by my order. It is enough that in your area the Galician intelligentsia takes it for granted that we have left them the university of Lemberg, but they, ungrateful and unprincipled, as is the Slav, send out their emissaries into the entire Russian Ukraine to incite.
>
> It goes without saying that if Galicians should refer to themselves as Ukrainians, I will not punish them for this, but I will not let this force me to refer to them as anything other than Galicians.[248]

In his reply Wächter responded by refuting the claim concerning the Galician intelligentsia and stressing that his conception of a 'Galician-Ukrainian' was basically the same as Himmler's.[249] At the same time he reassured Himmler of his loyalty and once again requested an opportunity to report to him in person, which Himmler was either unwilling or unable to accommodate.[250]

For the time being the Division would therefore have to retain its regional identifier. When eventually its title was finally changed to 'Ukrainian' on 12 November 1944, (as noted by the Liaison Officer of the SS to the OKH in the 'Verordnungsblatt der Waffen-SS'),[251] neither Galicia or any other part of Ukraine were in German hands or was likely ever to be again.

To the Training Camps

A handwritten note found amongst Himmler's papers shows how he calculated the numbers of various categories to be called up, based on figures quoted by Berger in his teleprinter message of 2 July.[252] This was translated into a secret circular order dated 5 July 1943 which specified 4,448 officers, NCOs and troops, were to be called up to the SS-Freiwilligen-Division, by the 15.7.1943. These were to be:

1) 300 officers and 48 doctors on courses in the Reich
2) 1,300 NCOs and 800 high school diploma holders for NCO training
3) 2,000 for the Wachbataillon [guard battalion] Heidelager, which would be expanded into the 1. SS-Freiwilligen-Grenadier-Regiment.

It also directed that the 12,000 men who were to be enlisted for the Galician SS-Freiwilligen Regiments 4 to 8, were not as originally specified to be selected according to their religious denomination, instead they were to be drawn from those in the height range 160 cm to 164 cm and those allocated for labour use in the Reich.[253]

Three days later, on Sunday 18 July 1943, the first transport of seven hundred and forty men departed from L'viv for service in the Galician Division. As Berger had already indicated that the Division would be based around those already qualified as officers and NCOs [254] the first transport of recruits included both. Of the remainder, a high proportion were high school graduates and university students designated as suitable officer/NCO candidates.

On that day a crowd of more than 50,000 people had gathered in the city to commemorate the 'Festive Farewell of the first call up of officers, NCOs and riflemen to the SS Schützen Division 'Galicia". Local German and Ukrainian dignitaries were present as well as representatives of military, religious and civil authorities. The event started with a special field mass to bless the recruits, after which they assembled by the opera house to hear speeches by Governor Wächter and other German luminaries. Dr Kost Pankivsky[255] spoke on behalf of the Ukrainians as did a 17 year old Jurij Ferencevych as representative of those who had enlisted. He recalled:

> On July 15, when I came to the offices of the Wehraussuss' D. Paliiv asked me if I was willing to make a speech in the name of the volunteers on 18 July. I agreed to make the speech. Four people were involved in the preparation; D.Paliiv, Michael

L'viv 18 July 1943, ceremonial send off of the first batch of volunteers. Evhen Pobihushtschyi reports to Alfred Bisanz outside L'viv opera house.

L'viv 18 July 1943, a crowd of over 50,000 gathered to mark the ceremonial send off of the first batch of volunteers.

Lviv 18 July 1943, Stavy Pulchynskyh Street, L'viv.

Kushnir (propaganda), Stephan Wolynec and myself. The three gentlemen did most of the talking. At this time there was strong propaganda against the Division by the OUN -B. In my speech we had to say something positive about the Germans but not too much so that the OUN -B could call us collaborators.[256]

His speech below was delivered in both Ukrainian and German:

Governor von Wächter, Colonel Bisanz!

I greet you in the name of the young Ukrainian men who have volunteered to join the ranks of the Grenadier SS Division 'Galizien'. We depart our Fatherland today to begin military training. I assure you that we joined the Division voluntarily, with no hesitation, deeply and sincerely convinced of the justness of this step. We are young, we have no interest in playing politics, we are not diplomats. We believe in the power of our ideals and in the power of a just cause. In the history of Ukraine, it was the military deeds of our ancestors that always impressed us most. We too want to be soldiers. We go to fight the enemies of our people, who are also the enemies of European culture. We understand full well that in joining the disciplined ranks of the mighty German Army we undertake a serious commitment. We will fulfil it.

L'viv 18 July 1943. Members of the Military Board seated in front of the L'viv Opera House. Front row far left: Jurij Ferencevych student representative of the volunteers, second left Volodymyr Bilozor, fifth from left Ivan Tretiak, eighth from left Jurij Krokhmaliuk ninth from left Mychailo Khronoviat and tenth from left Andrij Palii.

And as we leave, Governor von Wächter, we commend to your care our elderly parents, our families, and the Ukrainian people of Galicia,—trusting in the given guarantees and the honour of the German nation.[257]

Alfred Bisanz made the closing speech before the recruits paraded through the city streets carrying placards, flags and banners to be greeted enthusiastically by the Ukrainian citizens of L'viv.[258] Finally a delegation visited Metropolitan Sheptysky which concluded the event.[259]

Proceeding to Chernovetsky railway station, at 1500 hrs the young men boarded freight cars.[260] Zenon Kuk was amongst them:

[...] the boys wrote various slogans like 'L'viv-Kiev' on the cars with chalk; they also drew tryzuby (tridents) on them, which expressed their thoughts and feelings. The Germans were looking at those scenes which were unusual for them, some with surprise, some with indifference but mostly with interest [...].[261]

As per their call up instructions, each man carried provisions to last for three days, and where possible 1 packet of undergarments, 1 sewing kit, 1 knife, a watch and writing equipment.[262]

Late in the afternoon of 18 July 1943, the first transport left L'viv for a transit camp at Brno (Brunn) in Böhmen-Mähren. Zenon Kuk who was on the train remembered the departure:

[...] The train moved very slowly because people were still crowded around it, running alongside it, yelling and waving their hands. Its speed increased and all of them disappeared in the distance. We passed through the suburbs of L'viv, and entered the Peremshyl track. On the stations people were still saying goodbye with flowers.[...][263]

It arrived early in the morning of 19 July at the Waffen-SS training complex called Kuhberg (Kaserne) where the SS-Pz.Gren.Ausb.u.E.Btl. 10 (SS-Panzer Grenadier Training and Replacement Battalion 10) was based.[264]

On arrival at Brno each recruit was required to write a Lebenslauf (Lifecourse) which included personal details,[265] after which medical examinations took place. The next day each man received three sets of uniforms including a field grey Waffen-SS uniform[266] in an approximate size along with other necessary military equipment and Erkennungsmarken, (dog tags) issued from the camps supply store.[267]

Three companies were then formed in which the recruits underwent a general introduction to military service. Five hundred recruits formed the 1 and 2 companies whilst the 3 company consisted of the two hundred and forty former officers. These had qualified while serving in a variety of armies including the Austrian, Ukrainian, Polish, Romanian, Czechoslovak and Soviet armies.[268] The former officers were considerably older than the recruits, for example the age of those who had been in the Austrian Army was generally between 45–55. Their usefulness had previously been discussed at the conference chaired by Wächter on 12 April 1943, when it was noted that:

L'viv 18 July 1943. The first group of volunteers parade before departing for training. Almost all of the first batch of recruits were designated as officer or NCO candidates.

L'viv 18 July 1943, ceremonial send off of the first batch of volunteers. The caption of this Kriegsberichter picture reads 'a wounded Ukrainian volunteer serving with the Wehrmacht is present on the occasion to witness the departure of the first batch of volunteers'.

Parade before assembled dignitaries. L'viv 18 July 1943.

Parade of mounted Ukrainians in national dress before assembled dignitaries. L'viv 18 July 1943.

L'viv 25 July 1943 recruits from Kobaky Kosiv region boarding trains.

Recruits entrain for the training camps. Anti-Soviet messages and symbols were chalked onto the carriages.

An official press photo showing the Ukrainian Trident chalked onto the carriage of the departing recuits.

Group of young recruits pose for pictures with friends and relatives before departing for training.

The former Austrian [army] officers, will as a rule no longer be fit for service at the front because of age. It is therefore suggested that they be used in the replacement units, as on political grounds the active cooperation of this particular element cannot be relinquished.[269]

Less than two weeks after their arrival, the SS-FHA issued a document dated 30 July 1943, that set out the organisational details of the SS Freiw. Div. 'Galizien' and confirmed its formation was to commence at the SS troop training area Heidelager (SS-Tr.Ueb.Pl. Heidelager).[270] Situated near Debica (Dembitsa/Dembica) in the General Government between Cracow and L'viv, this was a former Polish cavalry training ground, which the SS had commandeered for training purposes. It was commanded by SS-Brigadeführer Bernhard Voss.

Consequently two days later on 1 August 1943, at 1400 hrs the Ukrainians left the camp at Brno. The two hundred and forty former officers of the 3 company, had already undergone segregation in respect of their arm of service. Some of these were sent on refresher courses and for further training to various camps according to their qualifications and the Division's requirements,[271] whilst the remainder along with the five hundred recruits were redirected to Heidelager.[272] Here they joined their countrymen from the subsequent transports who had been sent there directly. Mychailo Kormylo was on one of the first transports to leave L'viv on 18 July bound directly for Heidelager:

[...] When we arrived in L'viv, the train bound for Dembica was laden with volunteers. Soon I came across Ivan Humeniuk from Kopychyntsi and Bohdan Tarnawsky from Chortkiw. We made contact then and stayed in touch all through the war and after.[...]
The Germans were in the first and last carriages of the train and when it stopped for any reason they would jump down and run along the line of carriages, always alert to the possibility of attack at any moment. [...] We stopped at a small station and we were fed, which cheered us up. When we continued, our train was constantly pulling into sidings to let others past with wounded going west and weaponry and matériel going east. We were in no hurry but soon we were in Dembica.[...][273]

2

Forging a Fighting Force

Basic Training. 'More sweat at school, less blood in the field'.

Arriving at Heidelager, the first contingent of Ukrainians were incorporated into an SS-Special Purpose Training Battalion known as SS-Ausbildungs -Battalion z.b.V.[1] Commanded by SS-Sturmbannführer Bernhard Bartelt,[2] this unit was responsible for the delivery of basic training and consisted of a staff company and twelve line companies numbered 1–12[3] (9 infantry companies and 3 heavy infantry companies[4]). With a combined strength of approximately 3,600[5] it was closer to the size of an infantry regiment. Thus it was this unit and not Wachbataillon Heidelager as originally intended which formed the nucleus of the Division.[6]

Basic training itself was conducted under the supervision of experienced German and Austrian Waffen-SS instructors temporarily assigned to the unit, many of whom were eastern front veterans holding combat decorations for bravery, who had been wounded and classified as unfit for service at the front.

Facilities at the camp, which was surrounded by mature pine trees, were primitive. Accommodation comprised of single story wooden barracks that accommodated one platoon by squads which consisted of 14–16 men along with a squad führer. The recruits slept on 3 tier wooden beds with straw mattresses, except the squad führer who had a single bed. Each barrack had a washroom with running cold water and a toilet, with hot showers available once per week at a common bathhouse. Each man had a locker that could not be locked as the penalty for theft was death.[7] After arriving at Heidelager, disinfection and enlistment formalities followed. Each day, after morning roll call, the numbers of able bodied, sick and those assigned to 'other duties' were reported after which checks were then made that all equipment was being carried in the recommended way. When everything was in order, the volunteers were marched off to training areas in the field. Volunteer Volodymyr Keczun recorded his arrival and his introduction to military life:

> [...] After another longish stop we arrived at a small station Kochanówka. By the time we got off the train it was already getting dark. As there was only one lorry waiting for

transportation, the front section of our column got on it and rest of us were ordered to march to our training camp that was situated in the forest about 2–3 km's from the station. Later we knew this forest as Dembica [Dembitsa], because there used to be a Polish village of that name there. I was roughly midway in the column so I had to march for some time before I was picked up by the lorry. Just as we neared the forest we noticed some barracks on our right and some soldiers standing there. What a surprise it was for us when they started talking to us in the Ukrainian language. That was a unit of Ukrainian Schützpolizei.[8]

[…] Next morning we were marched to our permanent barracks on Ring 4. We were in them for five months. I will try to describe roughly the layout of Heidelager. There was a road that ran from the railway station to the forest and carried on straight through it. A short distance along the road on the left side, there were still a few derelict houses, remnants of a former village, a canteen and underground bunkers with provisions for the camp. Further on the left there were 2 round forest clearings: Ring 2 and Ring 4. On the right side of the road were three round clearings: opposite the derelict village Ring 1, next Ring 3 and opposite to Ring 4 was Ring 5. After that just countryside—our training grounds. The name 'Ring 4' describes itself.

There was one road circling the ring. On the outside of the ring road there were three separate barracks for each company. Along the main road there was one kitchen building for each company, a large theatre, stores and other utilities. We were taken to the three last barracks furthest from the railway station.

Beyond us was countryside where our shooting ranges and other training facilities were.[…] At first we had instructors for each room including many Austrians. Our Stabsscharführer and real 'boss', was a Volksdeutsch from Silesia who spoke the Polish language fairly well.[…][9]

Within days of arrival uniforms and equipment were issued. Mychailo Kormylo:

[…] The most pleasing episode was when they finally decided to equip us to make us look the part. We were quickly fed up of dressing as civilians and soon we were issued with a whole wardrobe-shoes, belt, underwear, three shirts! socks, braces—the works. This was followed by bayonets and rifles which made us immediately feel like real soldiers. The caps and steel helmet had to have the SS insignia. Blankets, entrenching tools, field utensils, knife fork and spoons. We were also were issued with a toothbrush, paste, shoe brushes, razors, sewing needles and thread. Then there was our 'brotbeutel' (bread bag) and field flask. They dressed us in 'dreliche' (denim) in which we attended field exercises. We had regular grey uniforms for everyday use called 'B Anzug' and a best grey uniform similar to 'B Anzug' for parades and for going out when not on duty called 'A Anzug'.[…][10]

Opposite above: A group of Ukrainian soldiers from 10 company z.b.V, undergoing basic training at Heidelager with their NCO instructor. Kneeling first on right Bohdan Kutny.

Opposite below: A group of Ukrainian soldiers undergoing basic training at Heidelager with their NCO instructor. Back row second from left Mychailo Prymak.

Company from Training Battalion (SS-Ausbildungs-Battalion z.b.V) route marching at Heidelager.

NCO instructors at Heidelager 1943.

The intensive and arduous training course that followed took place in platoons divided into squads. It was conducted under the maxim 'the more sweat at school, the less blood in the field' and lasted until the end of October. The initial period involved long days and covered elementary matters such as learning how to drill, march halt and greet. When these had been mastered, rifles were issued and training began in earnest.

Again Volodymyr Keczun:

[...]The next day we were issued rifles, bayonets, spades and empty pouches for bullets. From then on our life became continuous lessons; how to take a rifle apart, clean it and look after it and how to stick our bayonets into hanging dummies. Before we started seriously, we had to go through inoculation every two days against diseases, like typhus, cholera etc. Left arm, right arm, left breast, right breast and finally two days later, one in the buttock. It did not matter that we were sore all over, we still had to do our marching and exercises.

Then it was found that we had brought civilian lice to the barracks, so we had to go through extensive cleansing. The worst part was when we got to the sanitary barrack. We stripped naked and we were forced to dip a hand into a basin full of vile reeking, biting, fluid and rub it in our armpits and crotches before we were allowed to shower.[...]

Training became more interesting for us when instead of just learning how to aim at targets, we got the chance to shoot blank ammunition cartridges so we could get used to the recoil of the rifle. Blank bullets looked exactly the same as live rounds and sounded the same but their tips were made of hollowed wood.

At last we went to the shooting range. It was explained to us that there was no such thing as a perfect rifle. Each one deviated a bit and we had to find out where to aim to be on target. My rifle had to be aimed slightly up and to the left. Each rifle had a serial number and it was marked in our Soldbuchs. Once we became used to shooting with live ammunition, we started scoring very highly, so our instructors called us 'partisans'.[...][11]

The Waffen-SS published specific guidelines regarding the training programme for its personnel which was reflected in the busy daily timetable which included; Waffenlehre (Weapons instruction), Taktik (Tactics) and Heerswesen (Military Affairs).[12] This ensured all recruits were exposed to a comprehensive and thorough combat training. Instruction covered utilisation and handling of light infantry weapons—rifles (including while wearing gas masks), small arms, hand grenades and light machine guns (for the heavy companies—no's 4, 8 and 12—this was extended to cover heavy machine guns and 8.1 cm mortars); exercises in close combat, night fighting and anti-tank combat; target practice; bayonet practice; lectures on legal matters and conduct on the battlefield; field orientation (map and compass reading); attack and retreat. Drill and field marches in all weathers of up to 40 km at a time to build up stamina also featured prominently. Lastly, all recruits had to perform guard duty on a rota basis. On Sundays the recruits were free giving them an opportunity write letters home, do occasional laundry and attend to other domestic requirements.

Waffenreinigung (weapons cleaning) SS-Ausb.Btl. Z.b.V summer 1943, Heidelager, third from right Eugen Shypailo.

Live ammunition is distributed for target practice.

Unknown training group of Ukrainians from the Division in Heidelager.

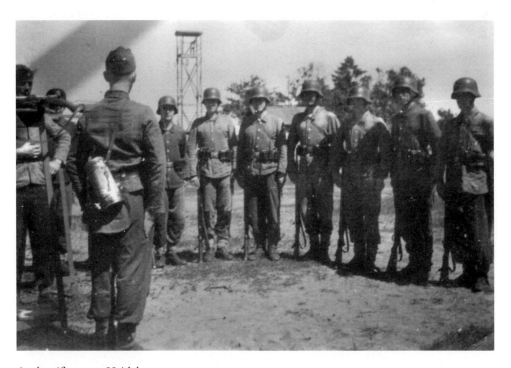

At the rifle range Heidelager.

Ukrainian recruits training with Divisional Kriegsberichter (with camera).

Ukrainian recruits dressed in summer drill fatigues led by their instructor Waffen-Hauptsturmführer Mykola Uhryn Bezhrishnyi.

Above: Free time was limited and put to good use. Here recruits do their laundry at Heidelager summer 1943.

Right: In this photo from the Divisional newspaper 'To Victory' recruits receive letters from home.

The recruits soon acclimatised to the daily routines and duty rotas. Mychailo Kormylo:

Food was initially taken from queues in the kitchen back to the barrack where first back to barracks got to eat at the table while the rest sat and ate on the edge of the bunks. Breakfast and supper always included strong [ersatz] coffee. Meals always seemed to include potatoes with loads of sauce called 'Tunke'. We occasionally got meat—I never asked about its source but just ate it. Life got mischievous with some boys relaying disgusting stories to put their comrades off their food so they could devour it instead. When the weak ones ran outside to be sick we used to laugh but in reality it was a dirty trick to play on friends. Tarnawsky always over salted his food so that no one else would want it. This mischief persisted throughout my whole time in Heidelager.[...][13]

Waffen-Grenadier Volodymyr Keczun:

[...] Our training was getting more demanding. We started to go more often into the countryside to learn about different kinds of warfare. For the beginners course we were taken to a small but dense wood and soft, spongy, ground. Instructors showed us how to camouflage ourselves in natural surroundings: up a tree, behind it, or if you can find a hollow in the ground, how to cover yourself with mulchy soil. Then we were divided into two groups: one to camouflage itself and other to try to find them. It looked like a good game with lots of fun, but it nearly turned into a tragedy. Attackers received three blank bullets and were told to shoot one in the air if they found someone hiding. You could hear shots all over the wood. One soldier could not find anybody but he was itching to use up his blanks so he aimed his rifle at a large bush and fired. Suddenly a horrible shriek! All the instructors suddenly appeared and found one soldier inside the bush with tiny wooden splinters from the bullets tip imbedded in his left cheek.

    Then progress again, my unit received MG 34s and Lafettes[14] for them. Up to then we acted as individuals, now we had to act like a bonded unit: shooter, loader, spare barrels carrier, distance diviner and ammunition carriers had to work like clockwork. Speed to assemble them as a heavy MG was vital. In the countryside the emphasis of our training was more on random and impulsive shooting to get your enemy instead of marksmanship.

    The first time we marched in attacking order through the countryside we were shown how to use terrain to our advantage. When we reached a fairly wide stream which was a few inches deep and too wide to jump across, we were shown how to do it without getting your feet wet, because in winter you can get frostbite and you would not be able to reach and help your friends if they were in a dire situation and relied on your help. The instructor explained that if you put a waterproof wrap around the top of your shoe and the bottom of your trousers, when you put your shoe in water, it displaces the water to the sides and if you take it out quickly the water has no chance of getting into your shoes. We all managed to cross with only few splashes on our trousers but they soon dried from body heat once we started marching again.

The instructor informed us that soon we would reach a small vacant village, the approach to which is defended by 'Papen Kameraden' [soldiers cut out from compressed paper pulp sheets and painted as Red Army men] which would be appearing suddenly from ditches and any other hiding places. We had no ammunition with us, but we were told [to] hold our rifles at our hips aiming forward. When we saw a 'Kamerad
' jump up, we were to try impulsively to aim our rifles at it.[...][15]

It was strictly forbidden for the instructors to physically touch the Ukrainians during training, or indeed for anyone to hit a subordinate. According to his officer file, for striking a private whom he found asleep whilst on guard duty and discharging a firearm (pistol), 43 year old Waffen-Untersturmführer Orest Sahajewitsch received a two year prison sentence (ultimately suspended in favour of two years front probation) and demotion to NCO rank. Consequently as was traditional in all units training in the German Army, there was instead a lot of shouting and verbal abuse in the form of foul language and name calling from the NCOs. Whilst this behaviour offended the more sensitive souls, no exceptions were made and everyone received a verbal onslaught. In line with the strict disciplinary code, severe punishments were meted out even for a badly made bed. This was usually 'Strafübung' which was one hours' repetition of physical exercises in full equipment under the command of a superior. Lesser infringements would result in additional mundane fatigue duties such as cleaning barracks, loss of privileges or additional guard duty.

Whilst undergoing his basic training, another recruit Theo Andruszko recalled how:

On at least two occasions we were ordered to get up from our beds, pull our pants down and had our penises inspected and afterwards asked to swallow a pill for some reason. Some of our knowledgeable fellows assured us the pill was going to suppress our sex drives! (That procedure was popularly called 'Schwantz parade'—parade of the penises!)[16]

The former Ukrainian officers were not required to participate in the training, but were instead sent to individual companies as observers.[17]

Instructions emanating from the SS-Hauptamt (SS head office) directed that the language used for the issuing of orders for the Galician Division was to be German[18] while the language of command was to be 'Galician' [sic] (i.e. Ukrainian).[19] In practice both orders and commands were given in German. At this point few difficulties arose on linguistic grounds because the vast majority of the first batch of inductees had attended or graduated from high school or were university students where the teaching of the German language was mandatory. The former Ukrainian officers and NCOs especially those who had served in the Austro-Hungarian Army also usually knew the German language

Queuing for meals at Heidelager summer 1943.

The 'Gulaschkanone' (field Kitchen) dispenses food during exercises.

well. Occasionally technical terms required those who were fluent in German to interpret. In due course, these men were often appointed as office or administrative workers and their services prized by the German commanders.

Later with the introduction of enlisted men from predominantly rural areas, serious language difficulties occurred which was something the organisers of the Division both German and Ukrainian had overlooked. In some companies this necessitated the use of interpreters by the German instructors to convey the required practical and theoretical skills which proved to be both difficult and time consuming. The significance of this largely went unrecognised which later led to particularly serious ramifications when it was in combat. Many of the frictions which later arose between the Germans and Ukrainians on national or political grounds were also compounded by the existence of the language barrier which was never successfully addressed and remained throughout its existence.

With very few exceptions, almost all of the first contingent of enlisted men were in the 18–30 age bracket,[20] most of whom had come straight from civilian life and had no military experience prior to enlistment. The difficulties of adjusting to the strict discipline and harsh routine of life in the army, especially the Waffen-SS demanded considerable strength and fortitude. This was to a large extent offset by the prevailing high morale and enthusiasm amongst those who believed that they had enlisted into a Division which would eventually become the nucleus of a future Ukrainian Army.[21] One such volunteer was Mychailo Kormylo:

Marksmanship practice with rifle Heidelager autumn 1943.

Photograph from the Divisional paper *To Victory*, taken in October 1943 at the end of the officer retraining course at Leschan. This portrait of a soldier handling light artillery ammunition during a training exercise was taken by Kriesgsberichter Weyer.

Two recuits with the old style Maschinengewehr 08 at Heidelager.

[...] Our initial training in Heidelager was extremely tough, but it was worth it. All those basics made me a disciplined soldier. I wanted to be like those Germans, tough as nails and seasoned. An independent Ukraine would need us well trained soldiers. I was determined to stay and progress while some of the more hot headed nationalists slopped off to join the UPA who would welcome them with open arms. It was pleasing to me when my German instructors referred to me as 'Meine Freiwillige'. The word 'volunteer' had a sort of status both with them and with us. Volunteers usually need no coercing—we were ready to fight for a belief which made us special. [...][22]

A small number of the first contingent had formerly been members of either the Polish or Red Army and were already familiar with the hardships of military discipline. For these men such as Oleksa Horbatsch, Stephan Hulak and Lev Stetkewych the difficulties were alleviated by their experiences while serving with those armies. At the same the former partisans from the Ukrainian Insurgent Army like Stephan Sadiwsky referred to by the Germans as 'Men from the forest', viewed the experience from an entirely different perspective. For months or even years they had fought and lived in remote locations, with improvised facilities, primitive medical care, limited weaponry and little food. For them, the structure, provisions medical facilities and ample supplies of weaponry and ammunition were a comparative luxury they had never experienced.[23]

The rigours and demands of the training schedule designed to acclimatise the soldiers to front line conditions also led to a number of accidents, the most common injuries, ranging from cuts and sprains to broken limbs and wounds from bullets or shrapnel.[24] Julian Chornij:

> [...] I was only injured once by 'friendly fire', from one of my friends during our basic training. Whilst practising a defence on an open field, we were using blank ammunition in our rifles. Previously we had been told by our officer to save the spent cartridges for recycling. I fired my rifle and went to grab the spent cartridge which was lying in front of my friend's rifle. I reached out with my right arm, and exactly at that moment my friend fired his rifle and hit the top of my palm. The skin on my hand was torn to pieces by the explosion and small pieces of the wooden bullet and all the burned material packed into the cartridge was imbedded deep in the flesh on my hand. For two weeks I had my hand in a sling and I was teased by my fellow soldiers who asked me 'where is your medal for heroically fighting the Bolsheviks'? My friend was punished and spent 3 days under arrest for his carelessness.[...][25]

To avoid unnecessary injury, recruits were repeatedly reminded to keep their shins pressed flat to the ground as a lifted leg would be blown clean off by certain types of explosion. Occasionally the consequences of injuries were far more serious and required hospitalisation[26] and later, when live ammunition was issued, there were rare instance of fatalities. Whenever death occurred elaborate funerals took place and internment was accompanied by religious rites and full military honours.

Even the most experienced German officers were still often able to learn much from their Ukrainian counterparts. For example, although they lacked recent technical training they were superior in terrain exploitation. This is acknowledged by the Division's 1a Major Heike who recorded that the Ukrainians 'proved superior in the use of terrain, camouflage, rapid trench digging, building of temporary shelters, establishment of camps and the like'.[27]

The instructions from the SS-Hauptamt stipulated that in conjunction with physical tuition, some form of ideological indoctrination should also be given. Hence in addition to combat exercises and drill, at Heidelager the Ukrainians also received political education known as 'Weltanschauung' (World perception). Taking place once per week in the open air, the sessions lasted between 1–2 hours, and were conducted by company commanders. They were considered to be an integral part of all lessons[28] and were similar in form to the political instruction given by the commissars in the Soviet Army. The themes parroted various aspects of National Socialist ideology such as the invincibility of the Third Reich, an equitable social living order and a New Europe.[29] The sessions were initially regarded as tiresome but eventually became a welcome rest from our gruelling schedules. Theo Andruszko who endured them wrote: 'I enjoyed an hour a week of indoctrination [Weltanschauung] it allowed me to shut my eyes and dream uninterrupted'.[30]

From the very start the Germans did their best to subdue any manifestation of Ukrainian patriotic ardour for example when they were first learning to march the Ukrainians sang their own nationalist songs which were soon changed by the

September 1943, Heidelager, funeral of Josyf Hrytsaykiv. His village priest attended the funeral in Heidelager (he died of natural causes) third from right wearing a leather overcoat SS-Sturmbannführer Bartelt the Battalion commander.

Germans. Phrases like 'Nationalists! One, two, three, young eagles!' were changed to 'We are Ukrainian volunteers!'[31]

This and other attempts at sanitation by the Germans were not however successful. Despite its official prohibition, alongside the Galician lion, photographic evidence shows that the Ukrainians often displayed their national symbol—the Trident. The design appeared in almost every barrack which they occupied and was incorporated into flowerbeds and stone mosaics outside their quarters. Although this irritated the extreme National Socialists amongst the Germans, it could not be stopped.[32]

The first few months passed in this way, in the field, on the ranges and in the 'class room', that is to say the living rooms of the barracks. In addition because Heidelager had a number of temporary storage facilities and vehicle parks, guard duty was also much in evidence. This impacted negatively as it took recruits away from their training. Whilst failure to comply with orders or directives was immediately punished, outstanding individual performance was rewarded often by the granting of additional leave.[33]

It was in late August 1943, when a medical team arrived at the camp and began tattooing the Ukrainian recruits with their blood group under the left arm. This practice, unique to the Waffen-SS and Fallschirmjäger (Parachute) formations, was developed to assist with blood transfusions in the event of a wound being received in combat Mychalio Kormylo:

> [...] I will never forget the day we were taken to the 'revir' [sanitary centre], group by group, to be tattooed under the left armpit with the symbol for our blood group. A,

Above: Practice at the rifle range.

Left: Portrait of a typical Ukrainian Waffen-Grenadier.

First page of the Soldbuch of Iwan Osadtschuk. Many Ukrainians retained pay books and other personal identification papers.

Recruits from Verhniy Luzhok, pose with their mortar out side they barracks at Heidelager.

Squad training at Heidelager photo from *To Victory*.

German commander observes machine gun team in action.

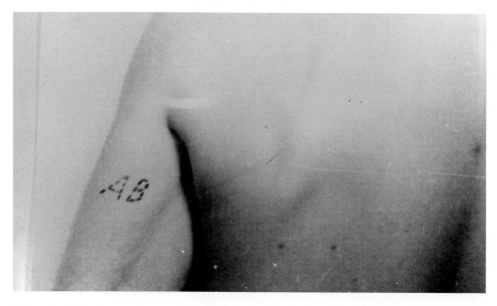

In August 1943, in accordance with a unique practice developed by the SS. The first Ukrainian recruits were tattooed under their left armpit with their blood group. The purpose was to facilitate blood transfusions in case of a wound being received in combat.

AB, B or O. If you ever wondered why the armpit was chosen for tattoos, you would have understood during combat. At the battle of Brody I witnessed the butchery of bullets, shells and grenades as they blew off some of my comrades' limbs so easily, especially hands and arms. I was blood group 'O'.[34]

Swearing In the First Contingent

On Sunday, 29 August 1943, the members of the SS-Ausbildungs-Battalion z.b.V were assembled for the swearing of the oath at Heidelager.[35] Governor Wächter, the camp commander SS-Brigadeführer Voss and the Battalion commander SS-Sturmbannführer Bartelt[36] were present along with members of both the Military Board and the UCC who attended along with some civilian guests who had also been invited. The ceremony which took place in a clearing in the woods started with a field service (Feldgottesdienst) presided over by Rev Dr Laba and accompanied by the choir.[37] Individual companies were paraded in service dress and steel helmets and formed into three sides of a hollow square. On the fourth side of the square facing the assembled recruits, was a decorated podium in front of which were three mortars, two heavy machine guns and twenty one stacked rifles. A German NCO acting as ensign and carrying the Reich's war flag took his place directly opposite the podium. Four members of the Battalion representing their comrades placed their hands on the flag and the Ukrainian soldiers repeated the text of the authorised oath which they had learned by heart: 'I swear before God this holy oath, that in the battle against Bolshevism, I will give absolute obedience to the commander in chief of the German Armed Forces Adolf Hitler, and as a brave soldier I will always be prepared to lay down my life for this oath'.[38]

Governor Wächter addressed the assembled men; then together with SS-Brigadeführer Voss and SS-Sturmbannführer Bartelt, he conducted an inspection. The event was recorded in a special brochure published in newspaper format entitled 'We Are Going Into Battle' (My idemo v biy).[39] In the afternoon, to mark the occasion a Kameradschaftfest (festive celebration) took place in the sports area. Refreshment was available in the form of barrels of a particularly potent Polish beer called Okoc'im, and a programme of entertainment then commenced including dancing, acrobatics and music. The highlight was a performance by the popular Merry L'viv dance and theatre troupe, who were dressed in traditional folk costumes and whose visits were to become a regular feature.[40]

The formality of the oath completed, one hundred and thirty three former Ukrainian officers[41] left Heidelager on 30 August 1943. These men had remained with the recruits as observers and had passed an internal commission for verification of officers' abilities.[42] They were sent for an eight week officer re-training course at the officer school at Leshany.[43] Their return to the Division in late 1943 was scheduled to coincide with the next phase of its organisation.

Something which caused a great deal of consternation to the German authorities at this time was that Heidelager was an 'open' camp which meant that civilians had easy access for the purpose of visitations. With Galicia situated close by, every Sunday when the soldiers were free from military duties trainloads of friends and relatives arrived at the camp. With little more than a cinema, a brothel (the use of which entailed its own hazards) and a crude football pitch[44] for recreation, these weekly visits were a pleasant break in a demanding routine. The visitors came laden with provisions for the men who were able to supplement their rations with the supplies of food and alcohol they brought. These were always shared with those who never had visitors and woe betide anyone trying to hide his 'banquet'. Volodymyr Keczun who being under the age of 21 received additional rations:

> [...] Each month we received 200 cigarettes, a bottle of vodka, bottle of rum, or brandy, small bottle of Sanft [fruit juice] and 5 Marks. Being under 21, I received extra, about 2 kilos of apples and some sweets. Sundays at first were free. Each morning all the companies from our ring gathered outside the ring for a field mass said by Ukrainian padres. Afternoons we usually set up trestle tables behind our barrack and had a party together with visiting families and our instructors. Sometimes we joined together and bought a small keg of beer.[...][45]

However, along with the food parcels, contact with friends and relatives also brought news of continued German defeats at the front and their ruthless administration policies in Galicia. News also arrived of the widespread failure of the German authorities to provide the promised social welfare to the poorer families of the recruits. This was a major concern especially amongst those from rural areas.

On Sunday 29 August 1943, the members of the SS-Ausbildungs-Battalion z.b.V were sworn in at Heidelager. The soldiers of the SS-Ausb.Btl.z.b.V. paraded in a three sided hollow square for the ceremony which began with a Feld Service (Feldgottesdienst) presided over by Waffen SS-Sturmbannführer Rev. Dr Laba. The choir also sang and a visiting German parade unit was present.

Governor Wächter also attended along with the camp commander SS-Brigadeführer Bernhard Voss and the battalion commander SS-Sturmbannführer Bernhard Bartelt, members of the Military Board and invited parents to witness the occasion.

Swearing the oath 29 August 1943, at Heidelager.

The Divisional choir took part in the occasion. *Photo Courtesy Richard Rygaard archive*

The Divisional band conducted by Kapelmeister Andrij Krawchuk also participated in the event. *Photo Courtesy Richard Rygaard archive*

Recruits from SS-Ausbildungs -Battalion z.b.V line up to swear the oath. Heidelager, 29 August 1943.

As part of the programme of entertainment which followed, the Military Board arranged for performances to be given by the "Merry L'viv' dance group as well as musicians and a troupe of acrobats.

Situated close to Galicia, a veritable swarm of friends and family relative descended on the camp to visit every Sunday bringing with them food parcels and news from home. Sitting far left Volodymyr Lutciw.

Recruit Roman Wysockyj receives a visit from his mother at Heidelager.

Another Kriegsberichter picture from To Victory showing relatives and friends visiting Ukrainian volunteers during training.

Worse still from a German standpoint was that Heidelager's proximity to Galicia was also naturally exploited by the OUN/UPA whose propaganda was easily disseminated amongst the soldiers, the vast majority of whom shared its agenda for Ukrainian independence. Ease of access also facilitated the maintenance of contact between the UPA leadership and its own agents who had heavily infiltrated the Division. The enviable result was an increase in desertions which was in danger of becoming widespread. Those who departed frequently took with them weapons and equipment which placed a further burden on the already stretched resources available.[46] Several solutions were sought starting with enforcing restricted access to the camp. Civilians were prohibited from entering the camp compound but this had little effect as the soldiers simply began to meet their relatives in the nearby woods and at Kochanówka station near Debica. Other measures which included spreading a rumour that a typhoid epidemic had broken out in the camp were equally unsuccessful.[47] Ultimately it became evident that it would be necessary to relocate the Division to an established base further afield, preferably in Germany. A shortage of appropriate facilities meant that the transfer could not take place immediately. In the interim the visitations and related problems continued.

New recruits continued to arrive during the autumn months and in September 1943, further personnel arrived at Heidelager who were incorporated into 2 and 5 companies.[48] On the 27th of that month the basic command structure of the battalion was in place. This was:

Battalion commander SS-Stubaf. Bernhard Bartelt.
Btl. Adjutant; SS-Untersturmführer Artur Preuss

The company commanders were:

1. Company Commander: SS-Ostuf. Adolf Hofmann
2. Company Commander: Unoccupied (vice commander: SS-Ustuf. Friedrich Frommelt)
3. Company Commander: SS-Hstuf. Kurt Wawrzik
4. Company Commander: SS-Ostuf. Joachim von Glan
5. Company Commander: Unoccupied (vice commander: SS-Ustuf. Karl Hoffrichter)
6. Company Commander: SS-Ostuf. Olaf Pedersen
7. Company Commander: SS-Hstuf. Heinz Müller
8. Company Commander: SS-Ostuf. Richard Bitzer
9. Company Commander: Unoccupied (vice commander: SS-Ostuf. Alfred Graf zu Dohna)
10. Company Commander: SS-Ostuf. Paul Baldauf
11. Company Commander: SS-Hstuf. Johannes Kleinow[49]
12. Company Commander: Unoccupied; (vice commander: SS-Ustuf. Herbert Schneller)[50]

A strength report for the SS-Ausbildungs Batl.z.b.V. indicated that as of 19 October a total of 3,368 men were undergoing training at Heidelager. Of these 160 were officers and 3,208 were recruits (among them 1,139[51] high school graduates and university students).[52] By 30 October with a constant flow of new recruits in the weeks that followed, in a letter to Himmler Governor Wächter was able to refer to 'the Galician units in which almost 13,000 men were presently under arms'.[53]

At the end of October the '1 Galician Officers [retraining] Course' for the former Ukrainian officers at Leschan concluded.[54] Simultaneously, the Division's command at Heidelager received a report which included suggestions for their employment. Of the successful graduates 11 were classified as being capable of commanding battalions and received the rank of Waffen-Hauptsturmführer;[55] 53 were deemed suitable to command company's and were ranked as Waffen-Obersturmführers; 29 were capable of commanding platoons and ranked as Waffen-Untersturmführers. Finally 8 participants received the non commissioned officer rank of Oberscharführer.[56]

Many of these older Ukrainian officers were First World War veterans not all of whom had come willingly to the Division.[57] For the most part their military bearing and appearance was decidedly inferior to that of their German counterparts, who had the advantage of excellent and modern military schooling. Upon their return to Heidelager, they were frequently treated with scorn and became objects of ridicule amongst the young German trainers and NCOs.[58] One of the younger generation Zenon Kuk wrote:

Graduating class of officers from the Sitchovi Strilci Pikovitz Czech, 30 October 1943. The class included former members of the Red Army as well as Polish, Hungarian and Rumanian armies.

A page from a special edition of the divisional newspaper *Do Peremohy* (*To Victory*) entitled "We are Going into Battle" (*My idemo v biy*), 38, (39) depicting Ukrainian recruits undergoing training at Heidelager.

[...] At first we welcomed our own officers who were returning from their retraining for to tell the truth we had had enough of those Germans. But the great sympathy that we imagined we had for them soon evaporated and turned into antipathy, contempt, disrespect and sometimes even shame. We who had been brought up and trained after the German model were now used to German 'zackigkeit' [snappiness] and precise military behaviour. And now here were our officers who did not fit this model.[...] We were sorry that the German 'corporals' who did not understand our national tragedy namely the lack of continuity of military tradition in modern times—came to laugh at them.[...][59]

There were however some notable exceptions including highly qualified and experienced officers like Volodymyr Kosak, Ivan Rembalovych, Michael Brygidyr, Mykola Palienko, Petro Markevych and Eugen Pobihushtschyi.[60] The mere presence of the older generation also had a positive influence on the ordinary enlisted men as Roman Hawrylak remembered 'They understood our boys and gave them some fatherly love and concern which was highly appreciated by Ukrainian soldiers in foreign uniforms and was a welcome relief and counterbalance against the brutal Prussian discipline'.[61]

At the end of October the first contingent of Ukrainians finally completed their basic training and almost all of the German officers and NCOs [62] were now released to allow the Ukrainian officers to take over. Following this 600 officer and 200 NCO candidates were sent to various schools or specialist Waffenschulen for further training.[63] It is important to note that due to the objections of Waffen Sturmbannführer Mykola Palienko and Waffen Hauptsturmführer Dmytro Ferkuniak, the mandatory requirement that all officer candidates should already have had recent combat experience was waived in this instance because of the urgent need for officers in the Division.[64] A further one hundred recruits were incorporated into the 12 MG-Lehrkompanie (12 heavy machine gun and mortar company) which was unofficially a Non-Commissioned Officers training company in which the recruits undertook short term courses without leaving the Division.[65]

NCO courses lasted four months and were held in various camps throughout the Reich and the occupied territories. The two principle venues for the infantry were Radolfzell and Lauenburg. The remaining principle specialist training grounds for the Ukrainian recruits included:

Glau bei Trebbin: SS-Artillerieschule I
Beneschau (Bohmen): SS-Artillerieschule II
Metz (Lothringen): Nachrichteschule
Prosetschnitz [Kienschlag] (Bohemia): SS-Panz.Gren.Schule Lehrgang I
Teinitz (Bohmen) (panz. gren): SS-Panz.Gren.Schule Lehrgang II
Graz Rosenberggurtel (Austria): Jursiaische Artzte
Bussum (Netherlands): 3.Panz.Jag.Ausb.Abt.2
Pikowitz (Bohemia): SS-Pion.Ausb.Btl.II.Komp 3
Warschau (GG): SS-Kavallerie-Ausb.u.Ers.Btl.

Breslau-Lissa 4 (A): Inf.Gesch.Ausb.u.Ers.Btl.1
Hilversum (Netherlands): 1.Panz.Ausb.Abt.2
Berlin-Zehlendorf
Nurnberg II Zug (SS Kaserne): SS-W-E-Regt
München: SS-Flak Ausb.u.Ers.Btl.
Heidenheim-Brenz: Gal.SS-Freiw.Ers.Btl.
Oranienberg—Berlin: Dolmetscher Schule der Waffen-SS.[66]

In these schools specialised instruction was given, for example fifty four recruits selected for service in the Division's SS-Pioneer Battalion were sent to Pikowitz (Bohemia). Here the tough schedule included route marching, mine-laying and disabling, construction of bridges (temporary and permanent) with varying capacities up to sixty tons in weight, rifle range, machine gun practice, training with explosives, demolition and use of flame-throwers.[67]

The demands of these courses exceeded by some considerable measure the instruction given at Heidelager. Mychailo Kormylo was sent to the school at Radolfzell:

[...] I was assigned to Radolfzell am Bodenzee. My training continued there specialising in using heavy machine guns with Lafette carriages which helped me to make firing a more accurate procedure. These guns also had sights on them which meant we could judge space and distance better. They had quick change belts of bullets and fired ammo with a longer range. [...] We had a really good instructor called Zeiss.

As well as tougher training there was an emphasis on the theory of firing, much familiarity with maps, directions, trajectories and use of a compass. There was a lot of practice firing at the enemy over the heads and flanks of our own soldiers. [...] The training was even tougher in Radolfzell than it was in Heidelager. They put us through long, tiring marching exercises. On some occasions I felt like I was marching asleep. There was a further instance one day during firing when someone let a bullet fly over Zeiss's head. He gathered the company together and gave us a short but sincere explanation as to why training was so tough. It was to prepare us for the hardship and reality of fighting at the front line.

It was not long into the training in Radolfzell when we began to realise that it was a case of the harder the better. There was one training procedure I will not forget easily. It was when we returned to barracks after a long, tiring days training only to be told that within minutes we were to return to the training ground in the dark and set up with weaponry on full alert to prepare for a night attack. At times we wondered if the training was aimed at breaking us. I will never forget those cold and damp training ditches and dugouts even though we were issued with appropriate clothing, 'clothing B' as the autumn turned colder and colder.'[...][68]

The NCO school at Lauenburg in particular which had formerly housed a lunatic asylum, had a reputation of being the toughest in the Waffen-SS.[69] This did not prevent the Ukrainians from twice receiving commendations. Volodymyr Keczun was present on one such occasion:

> [...] Outside our barracks compound there were extensive training grounds. Each company had dugouts on it for MG 42s in case of an air raid. Each time the raid alarm went, we had to rush out with our MGs, Lafettes and ammunition to the dugouts and by extending the Lafettes legs, mount the MG. on it and be ready to fire [we never had to]. From time to time we had assemblies of all the companies for inspection by the school commander. During one such assembly the general announced to our surprise, that the Ukrainian company was always first ready to defend school.[...][70]

Zenon Kuk also took part in one event that led to a commendation being given:

> [...] At Lauenburg we beat the German Army [Heer] record for setting a heavy machine gun into its firing position. The Germans could not believe we had done it, but they were proud that their underlings had beaten the 'Brotbeutels' ['Bread Bags'] which was a derogatory SS term for the Army. I still have the scar on my hand as a memento of that exercise.[71]

On completion of these courses all those who qualified as NCOs returned to the Division in March 1944, and were assigned as commanders of squads or platoons. Before it departed for the front in late June 1944, around two hundred of these men were selected by company or battalion commanders for officer training. This lasted a further four months (for platoon commanders or five months including an additional company commander course) at SS-Waffen-Junkerschulen (SS officers'

Ukrainian NCO candidates addressed by an instructor in the parade ground at the infantry NCO school at Radolfzell an Bodensee 15 November 1943–12 March 1944.

Ukrainian NCO candidates at Radolfzell prior to departure for field exercises.

Ukrainian NCO candidates at the NCO school Radolfzell.

Queuing for food at the NCO school at Breslau Lisa.

Ukrainians receiving instruction at an unknown location.

schools) at Kienschlag bei Prag, Arolsen, Braunschweig, Klagenfurt, Beneschau, Hradischko and Posen-Treskau.[72]

It was because of the exceptionally high standards of these schools, that so many Germans and non-Germans alike failed the intermediate exams or were dismissed from the courses for a variety of reasons. From the original cohort of approximately two hundred Ukrainian candidates who started the five months course at the SS-Junkerschule at Braunschweig in Posen Treskau, only 86 completed it.[73]

The Next Phase

In the interim, new recruits continued to arrive at Heidelager in the late autumn months. The initial flood of volunteers caused by a surge of enthusiasm had now been replaced by a steady trickle and there was a marked difference in the calibre of the recruits. We have already seen that on 30 October 1943, SS-Hauptsturmführer Dr Karl Schulze who headed the Ergänzungsamt der Waffen SS, stated the young men were not willing to enlist in an SS formation. Instead, because of the significant influence of the OUN, most preferred to serve in UPA.[74] Other general negative contributory factors included prevailing conditions in Galicia, the rapid approach of the Red Army and rumours that the so called 'Police Regiments' were fighting in France which caused many to evade enlistment.[75] One solution to the problem suggested by the Military Board was to transfer some 5,000 men who were currently engaged in Baudienst work but whose term of service was about to be completed directly to the Galician Division. In relation to them, the suggestion was made that they be denied home leave to which they were fully entitled before they transferred to the Division in order to prevent many from failing to report for duty.[76]

Jaroslav Wenger enlisted in late 1943 directly from a Baudienst camp where he had been conscripted to perform forced labour:

> [...] On one occasion in the morning, about 120 of us were selected to remain behind while the rest went off to work. We were ordered to our barracks to clean ourselves because we were told an inspection commission was coming to see us. At lunchtime on that memorable day, we noticed a car with German military officers approaching our camp. It halted at the camp office and some soldiers positioned themselves outside the barbed wire around the camp. We became suspicious. Then we heard a whistle and we came out. Some unexpected 'guests'—four officers in SS uniforms came towards us. One had the rank of Waffen-Obersturmführer. He was Savely Yaskevych. He told us that the Military Board had sent them to our camp to recruit volunteers to the Division 'Galicia'. He made a good patriotic speech. He stated that we should acquire military knowledge because Ukraine needed disciplined trained soldiers like those of the Ukrainian Sich Riflemen in the First World War and that

young men should not fear military training. He pointed out how we in the Baudienst were treated very badly and that in the Division we would be treated much better.

What he said was true, but what should we do? We had nobody with whom we could consult, each man had to decide for himself. In general, the situation at that time was critical. We felt great hatred towards the Germans but paradoxically in the Division we would wear their uniform. When it was first announced that the 'Galicia' Division would be formed in Galicia, the propaganda of the Bandera faction of the OUN urged us not to volunteer. There was bad news too for the Germans who had been forced to withdraw to the west. In Volyn, the Ukrainians had created the Insurgent Army (we called them 'Ukrainian guerrillas') and they began to form partisan units in Galicia to combat the Bolshevik partisans which had infiltrated the German lines in order to cause damage in their rear areas. From our village six had volunteered but later two of them changed their minds.

After the talk by Savely Yaskevych, registration started at the camp office. From our village I alone remained as did Benyvy and Zaverukha from the neighbouring village. The others quietly left. It was a decisive moment which is difficult to describe. If I went to the Division it couldn't be worse than this devil's Baudienst, and Yaskevych's speech left an impression on me, especially when he described our dangerous situation in this terrible war. In any case we would not be able to stay at home with our parents.

That day after lunch we were led to the theatre where they showed us a film of the training at the camp Heidelager. After the movie we went back to our camp and were told to remove our belongings from the barracks. About a hundred of us marched to the railway station at Kleparov with the Division's soldiers who had kept watch outside the camp wire. It was getting dark. Near the wagons they gave us food: bread—a loaf between three and a piece of sausage. After supper we boarded the cold cattle wagons. The soldiers had their private wagon. In the corners of the wagons was a little straw for sleeping, but there was no stove. That night a strong cold wind started to blow sleet. Our train was travelling to Heidelager very slowly. We had no winter clothes, only our poor dirty shirts and worn out blue uniforms and shoes on bare feet. Socks in those days were luxury items. We were freezing and our teeth chattered. In such 'comfort' we 'privileged' Ukrainian volunteers rode from the Baudienst camp Levandivka in L'viv to the 'Galicia' Division at the military boot camp Heidelager near the town of Debica in western Poland.

We arrived the next day at eight o'clock in the evening. Immediately they lead us for a shower. A warm shower for us was like healing water. Subsequently, they brought us to beautiful clean and warm barracks. In the middle stood a round stove heated with coal, a table, and on the sides 3-storey beds with sheets and three blankets. Everything was clean. Did we have a meal? I don't remember. Here we were in the training camp Heidelager. I had many thoughts: who made the better decision? We who chose the Division or those from our village who decided to stay at the Baudienst camp in Levandivka? We went to bed and laid on the soft mattresses. The room was warm and we were tired to the limit of endurance by the ride on the train and various thoughts, so we were soon fast asleep. I never experienced such a pleasurable sweet sleep in my life. [...][77]

As regards the newly enlisted recruits, the prevailing shortage of suitable training officers, NCOs and weapons allocated to the Galician Division, meant that a large proportion had to be re-assigned to regular army reserve units. These were based at different locations throughout the Reich[78] for example, on 26 November 1943, one group of 380 volunteers was despatched to Gren. Ers. Regt. 34 at Koblenz where they received their basic recruit training.[79]

Establishing the Korsettstange [German personnel framework]

During the initial training period, because of a shortage of instructors, as a temporary measure the trainees were joined into one regiment which was commanded by the Ukrainian Waffen-Sturmbannführer Evhen Pobihushtschyi.[80] However by September 1943, the organisational framework of the Division in its final form was already beginning to take shape. The man appointed by Himmler to oversee its formation was SS-Brigadeführer und Generalmajor der Waffen-SS Walter Schimana,[81] however his appointment was little more than a paper one and he appears to have had little or no direct involvement with the Division whatsoever. According to his post war interrogation for the entire period that he was 'nominally' in command he was away on training courses:

> [...] I received my transfer to the Waffen-SS. I got the 14 SS Freiwilligen Division 'Galizien'. Apparently at the SS FHA office that order was not very satisfactory. The 14 SS Division was not yet established. That was in summer 1943. I was first sent on training courses, after completion of these courses in October 1943, I was just about to take up my post when I got the call to immediately attend a meeting the HSSPF's in Posen. At the meeting of all the leaders Himmler gave a longer talk. In the course of it he also announced that I would be moved to Greece as the HSSPF and that the Division would be given to someone else.[...][82]

Notwithstanding this, the new Division was formed around a core of three infantry regiments numbered 1, 2 and 3, (each with three battalions). These were supplemented by an Artillery Regiment and various support elements and services which were already in their formative stages. This basic structure did however undergo some modification at an early stage following an order issued by the SS-FHA dated 22 September 1943 which directed that the Freiw.Div. 'Galizien' was to be reorganised as a new 1944 type infantry division.[83] This involved detaching the third battalion of each of the three infantry regiments to provide a field replacement battalion (14.Feld Ersatz Battalion) and an infantry reconnaissance (i.e. Fusilier) battalion.[84] The latter was unique as the battalion accepted only volunteers who were subsequently sent for training to a Wehrmacht ground at Eschweiler near Aachen in Germany. Interestingly, whilst at this camp these recruits were only permitted to wear regular Army (Heer) uniforms, whilst Divisional SS uniforms could only be worn on Sundays and holidays.[85]

Around this time the Division's title also changed following a decision by the S-FHA to renumber all Waffen-SS divisions and their component infantry regiments according to the sequence in which they had been raised. Consequently the '14' which had preceded the formations title almost from the beginning became official. The formation was thus re-titled from SS-Freiw.Div 'Galizien' to 14 Galizisches SS-Freiw.Div.[86] In the coming weeks its infantry regiments were also renumbered as follows:

SS-Freiw.Gren.Rgt 1 became SS-Freiw.Gren.Rgt.29
SS-Freiw.Gren.Rgt 2 became SS-Freiw.Gren.Rgt.30
SS-Freiw.Gren.Rgt 3 became SS-Freiw.Gren.Rgt.31[87]

In the early stages of the Division's organisation, during their formation all three of the embryonic infantry regiments were temporarily nominally commanded by Ukrainians. The first regiment (29) was commanded by 42 year old Waffen-Sturmbannführer Evhen Pobihushtschyi, the second (30) by 55 year old Waffen-Hauptsturmführer Borys Barvinsky[88] and the third (31) by 56 year old Waffen-Hauptsturmführer Stephan Kotyl.[89] Likewise the Artillery Regiment was commanded by 50 year old Waffen-Sturmbannführer Mykola Palienko, the Pioneer Battalion by 46 year old Waffen-Hauptsturmführer Ivan Rembalovych and the Signals Detachment by 50 year old Waffen-Hauptsturmführer Gregory Sosidko,[90] all of whom were Ukrainians.[91]

The Confusion over the Galizische SS-Freiwilligen Regimenter Nos. 4–8'

As early as 14 April 1943, Himmler had issued instructions that in addition to the Galician Division which was to be a combat unit recruited from the Ukrainian Greek Catholic population of Galicia, separate Polizei regiments were to be established. These were to be formed from the remaining Ukrainians in the General Government, that is to say the Greek Orthodox Ukrainians from the predominantly Polish Lublin district.[92] By so doing Himmler intended to ensure that additional Ukrainians could be utilised, while at the same time preserving the fiction of preferential treatment for Ukrainians in the district of Galicia. It seems that the long term goal was to utilise these Polizei units for security duties and deployment in fighting partisans.[93] Following Berger's advice that because the populations were mixed and separation on that basis was not therefore possible,[94] the idea was dropped in this form. Wächter continued to opposed the formation of separate Polizei regiments as did Berger who wrote to Himmler on 3 June 1943, stating:

[…] Apparently the plan was to enlist at least 10,000 of these volunteers [ie for the Galician Division] into Polizei units for deployment in fighting against partisans.

SS-Brigadeführer V. Wächter does not consider this viable. After apprising myself of the situation, I have to agree with him.[...][95]

Himmler however remained unconcerned and on 24 June 1943, he issued an order to all relevant authorities stating that from the Galician volunteers 12,000 be designated for the building of five Polizei-Schützen-Regimenter. The commander of the Ordnungspolizei was to disband one Polizei regiment and its staff were to be distributed amongst the 5 regiments. These were to be armed and supplied by the central bureau of the Waffen-SS (SS Führungshauptamt) in conjunction with the HSSPF Ukraine and the Ordnungspolizei (Orpo) whose chief was also responsible for providing the regiments with 500 officers and NCOs. Acknowledging that the Ukrainians were reluctant to serve in Polizei units of any kind, the order stated that 'These SS-Polizei-Schützen-Regimenter for psychological and political reasons will be designated 'Galizisches SS-Freiwilligen Regiment' with the numbers 4–8', (i.e.: consecutive to the original numbers of the three regiments of the Galician Division).[96]

A circular order followed[97] which announced that a meeting would be held on Monday 28 June 1943, to discus the details associated with the formation of the five Regiments.

The result was an order dated 5 July 1943. In this Himmler specified that during the month of July the manpower required for the Galizischen- SS Freiwilligen-Regimenter 4–8 was to be taken predominantly from two sources, firstly the 10,000 men allocated for labour use in the Reich and secondly from those who were 160–164 cm tall and hence deemed as unsuitable for service in the Galician Division.[98]

Neither the Military Board nor the Ukrainian Central Committee who had supported the formation of the Galician Division, had any knowledge of these plans.

Notwithstanding the revised directive, the new specifications were still not enforced. For example Himmler's stipulated selection criteria which was based on the minimum height requirement or potential non-suitability for the Division was disregarded. Instead, the personnel required were simply taken from the first wave of recruits for the Galician Division, predominantly from the cities of Peremyshl, Yaroslav and Sianok. At the same time, only four of the intended five regiments were ever formed from around 6,500 men, or a little over half the number originally intended. The 8 Regiment which was to have been raised in Maastricht on the basis of personnel from the Pol.Waffenschule IV, was never fully developed.

The remaining four regiments were made up of three battalions, each consisting of four companies.[99] They were trained as separate units at several facilities under the control of the Orpo.[100] Initially the recruits selected for these units were told only their training destination and were unaware that without their knowledge or consent they had been allocated to units under Orpo control, albeit on a temporary basis.[101] When later two of these regiments were deployed on security operations, the consternation and resentment amongst the men who had enlisted to fight the Soviets in a front line combat Division manifest itself in large scale desertions to the UPA as will be seen later.

Despite their temporary secondment to the Orpo, the recruits were issued with standard field grey Waffen-SS uniforms. On these the majority wore either no collar patches [Kragenspiegel] at all, or blank collar patches. Some wore the same collar patch and armshield depicting the Galician lion as their counterparts in the Galician Division,[102] and in a few instances the SS lighting runes. In the case of the latter these were later mostly replaced with blank insignia.[103]

Galizischen SS-Freiwilligen Regiment 4 had a strength of 1,264[104] men and from 20 July 1943, it was commanded by Major der Schutzpolizei Siegfried Binz,[105] an experienced and hardened Polizei officer. Binz's service record indicates that prior to his appointment as commander of the Gal.SS-Freiw.Rgt.4, he had previously commanded Pol.Batl.307, which took part in a number of anti-partisan actions in Weissruthenien (White Russia) in the rear of the Army Group.[106] The 4 Regiment underwent training in the area of Zabern (Alsace), region of France. Its headquarters along with the I. battalion were based at Zabern. The II. battalion was stationed at Saaralben (Saarbrücken) and the III. battalion at a Luftwaffe training ground at Ferschweiler bei Trier.[107] The chaplain (Feldgeistlicher) assigned to the unit was Joseph Karpynsky. According to an order dated 5 July 1943, its German cadre were to be drawn primarily from the Polizei Training Regiment at Oranienburg.[108]

The same order specified that the staff and I battalion of Galizischen SS Freiwilligen Regiment 5 were to be raised in the General Government at the Ordnungspolizei training camp at Adlershorst bei Gotenhafen. Its II. battalion was to be based at the Ordnungspolizei camp at Thorn and the III. battalion at the former resettlement camp at Kösslin. The regiment had a strength of 1,372 men[109] and was commanded by SS-Obersturmbannführer und Oberst der Schutzpolizei Franz Lechthaler, another experienced Polizei officer who had also participated directly in similar actions in the occupied eastern territories in 1941–42 as a member of Polizei bataillon 11.[110] The German training and administrative cadre for this regiment were drawn primarily from the Polizei-Schutz. Rgt. 32.[111] Vsevolod Durbak was appointed as its chaplain.

SS-Freiwilligen Regiment 6 had a strength of 1,800[112] and was commanded by Oberstleutnant der Gendarmerie Werner Kuhn. The recruits for this regiment were drawn mainly from the areas of L'viv and Peremyshl. As of 6 August 1943, the strength and location of its three battalions were:

Regimental staff:

> I. battalion consisting of 700 recruits in training at Sudauen,
> II. battalion consisting of 550 recruits in training at Fichtenwalde and
> III. battalion consisting of 550 recruits in training at Grajewo.[113]

In November 1943, the regiment underwent additional training at Pau and Tarbes in western France at the foot of the Pyrenees. The regimental chaplain was Johann Holojda.

Members of the Galizischen SS-Freiwilligen-Regiment-4 assemble for the oath taking ceremony in the town square Zabern south of France. The proceedings were opened with a Mass to bless the volunteers.

Oath taking ceremony in the town square Zabern south of France. Speeches were made by the senior German commanders.

Swearing the oath—members of Galizischen-SS-Freiwilligen-Regiment-4 Zabern, south of France.

Oath taking ceremony in the town square. The commander of Galizischen-SS-Freiwilligen-Regiment-4, SS-Obersturmbannführer Siegfried Binz inspects the troops at Zabern, south of France.

Members of Galizischen-SS-Freiwilligen-Regiment-4 in training with their NCO instructor.

November 1943, Zabern south of France, members of the 4 Regiment marching to their training ground.

Members of the 4 Regiment undergo training in Zabern south of France.

Members of Galizischen-SS-Freiwilligen-Regiment-4 bivouacked in the field.

Squad from Galizischen SS-Freiwilligen-Regiment-4 with their German NCO instructor.

Part of a training platoon from Galizischen-SS-Freiwilligen-Regiment-4 with two old style Maschinengewehr 08 machine guns. Back far right Mychailo Sergunyk.

Training platoon from Galizischen-SS-Freiwilligen-Regiment-4 second from left Mychailo Sergunyk.

Galizischen-SS-Freiwilligen Regiment-4 marching to exercises.

Galizischen-SS-Freiwilligen-Regiment-5. Adlerhorst, a suburb of Gotenhafen (Gdynia) September 1943, Holy Mass conducted by Rev. V. Durbak prior to swearing of the oath.

German instructors conducting field exercises with a group of Ukrainians from 4 Regiment.

Galizischen SS-Freiwilligen Regiment 7 was also formed and trained in south western France. The regiments' staff along with the I. and III. battalions were based at Salies de Bearn near Bayonne, and the II. battalion at Orthez.[114] Commanded by Oberstleutnant der Sicherheitspolizei Heinrich Huber,[115] it had a strength of 1,671 men. The chaplain serving with the regiment was Danylo Kowaluk.[116]

Contemporary records show that Oberstleutnant der Schutzpolizei Wilhelm Schwertschlager[117] was appointed commander of the planned 8 Regiment as of 1 October 1943, (until 13.1.1944).[118] In his report to the Military Board on 30 October 1943, Dr Schulze stated that the strength of this unit was 1,573 men. Notwithstanding this, and the existence of a complete list of staff appointments[119] it is unlikely that the regiment ever existed except on paper. The personnel who were to have been assigned to it[120] were later allocated to other Polizei units instead.[121]

Galizisches SS-Freiwilligen-Ersatz-Bataillon was established at Heidenheim as a reserve battalion for regiments 4-8. Commanded by Major der Sicherheitspolizei Paul Kärnbach, it consisted of a staff, staff company, signals platoon, pioneer platoon, 1 and 2 rifle companies, and 4 heavy company (with machine gun and mortar platoon).[122] Roman Chomicky was assigned to this unit:

> [...] In late August one of our friends went to the enlistment office asking when he would be called up [to the Galician Division]. The official gave him his enlistment card and a train ticket. We met at Krakivsky market in L'viv, where he told us that he would be departing on the 30 of August. We were jealous and so we also went to the enlistment office. After talking to the official, he issued us with enlistment cards and a transit pass for the train. We were to go to the Galician SS-Freiwillige Ersatz Battalion which was based at Heidenheim in Germany. We left on 30 August at night and arrived at our destination on 1 September in the late afternoon.
>
> When we arrived we were assigned to four different companies. The soldiers were mostly from the Lemko, Peremyshyl and Ternopil regions and the seven of us—'Polish speaking—Lvoviaks'. I was assigned to the 2 company.
>
> After a few days we were issued with old German police uniforms and began drill exercises. Our barracks was situated in a forest. Our weekly programme was as follows: German language classes, religious discussions and songs with the priest, drills and other exercises in a field behind the forest, far away from our barracks. Later we were issued with new uniforms, which had the SS runes on the right collar patch and a blank patch on the left collar.
>
> Every Sunday we all marched singing Ukrainian songs to the church in the city. The civilians looked at us with interest. They couldn't believe that men in SS uniforms were going to church. Some German kids even learned to sing our song 'Rozpriahaite khloptsi koni' (Unleash the horses, lads). Later the SS runes were taken away and replaced by 2 blank collar patches. Throughout the week all of us were helping with building the antiaircraft shelters for civilians.[123]

Significantly, with the exceptions of doctors and priests, none of the officers or NCOs who served in the police regiments were Ukrainian.

Parade of Galizischen-SS-Freiwilligen-Regiment-6.

Galizische- SS-Freiwilligen-Regiment-6 swearing the oath.

Galizischen-SS Freiwilligen-Regiment-6 inspection by regiment commander Oberstleutnant Werner Kuhn (saluting).

Members of Galizischen-SS-Freiwilligen-Regiment-6 undergoing training in western France in autumn 1943.

Published in *To Victory* this picture was taken during a visit by Governor Wächter to the Galizischen-SS-Freiwilligen-Regiment-7 in December 1943 at Salies de Bearn near Bayonne in south of France. The caption reads 'Thousands of young Galicians who have voluntarily reported for military service with the Waffen-SS. In the south of France this group has just been sworn in. After the swearing-in ceremony the commander speaks to his men'. At the podium the regimental commander SS-Obersturmführer Heinrich Huber behind him is the regimental Chaplin Feldgeistlicher Danylo Kowaluk and in the background the Governor of Galicia SS-Brigadeführer Dr Wächter.

The personnel of both the Fourth and Fifth Regiments were given basic infantry training throughout the autumn of 1943. This included instruction based on operations as part of a small combat group, fighting in the immediate proximity of a built up area, safeguarding road, rail, communication and waterway centres and the seizing and securing of industrial and signal installations. Josaphat Konchak from Sambir volunteered for service with the Galician Division and found himself posted to the 5 Regiment. His experiences were typical:

[...] I didn't know where we were going. I was called up to the 5 Regiment. It was stationed at Adlerhorst, a suburb of Gotenhafen (Gdynia). All officers and NCOs were German. Initially I was in the 3 company and then later I was transferred to the 2 company, 3 platoon. I was 17 at the time. At the beginning we were trained to March turn, salute, we also helped in clearing rubble after the bombardment of Gotenhafen [by the Allies]. We had a Ukrainian chaplain [V. Durbak] and participated in Holy Mass every Sunday in the nearby church. The Ukrainian student choir in Vienna gave a concert for us. Once we went to see a Ukrainian show from L'viv in the theatre in Gotenhafen. The daily routine was; 6 a.m.—rising, washing, breakfast, mustering, report to commander, march to exercises. We sang Ukrainian songs, in the field we were trained to dig holes, move stealthily and throw grenades. We returned to the camp at 1200 hrs for dinner. Then it was inspection of hands before going to receive dinner for which we received plastic tokens. In the afternoon we carried out drills, self defence exercises etc. At 1700 hrs we had supper and after that we had free time. There was a canteen where one could buy beer. At 2100 hrs to bed. The soldier on duty in the room reported to the NCO on duty that everything was ok. Of course there were various occasions when we were given punishment i.e. 'lay down!, up! run!' or scrubbing the floor. In the evening we received a piece of bread and usually some sausage for breakfast. The youngsters like me received additional rations. All were required to fulfil a norm for shooting. At Christmas we received parcels from home [i.e. from the Military Board]. In the 3 company a soldier was shot for threatening his NCO.[124]

The Sixth and Seventh Regiments underwent the same standard basic light infantry training as the recruits inducted directly into the 'Galician Division' although according to one veteran this was not as rigid.[125] In respect of the 7 Regiment this appears to have been partly because most of its officers and NCOs were Volksdeutsch Polizei personnel from Silesia and Warthe, few of whom were front line veterans.[126]

Like their counterparts in the Galician Division proper, the families of those enlisted into each of the Galician Polizei Regiments were entitled to social assistance, the responsibility for which was transferred to the Waffen-SS as of 21 December 1943.[127]

Throughout their existence, the additional regiments were temporary seconded to the control of the Orpo for training purposes and ultimately for deployment, consequently, later the 4 and 5 Regiments were despatched to the eastern front for security duties. This was viewed as a breach of trust between Governor Wächter and the Galician representatives and the volunteers who had enlisted explicitly to serve in a frontline combat formation on the eastern front. Once again German interests had prevailed as they continued to for most of the duration of the war.

A New Commander

As the Galician Division was entering its next phase of structural organisation, on 22 October 1943, the Division's nominal commander SS-Brigadeführer und Generalmajor der Waffen-SS Schimana received notification of a new appointment as the HSSPF in Greece, effective from 9 November 1943.[128] The replacement chosen by Himmler was SS-Oberführer Fritz Julius Gottfried Freitag who like his predecessor was also a product of the Ordnungspolizei.[129] He commanded the Division from 20 October until the end of the war.[130]

An ardent National Socialist, Freitag was 49 years old when he took up his post. The son of a railway worker, he abandoned his studies and had joined the German Polizei establishment. He was a decorated First World War veteran, who had served on both the western and eastern fronts being wounded four times during his service and was commissioned as a lieutenant. In 1919 he joined the Freikorps and in 1920 enlisted in the Schützpolizei rapidly rising up through the ranks. His inter-war service included an appointment in 1936 as an instructor in tactics in the police school in Köpenick, Berlin. In September/October 1939 he served as Chief of Staff to the senior police commander in the 14 Army. At the beginning of the German invasion of the Soviet Union in June 1941, he was serving with the command staff of the Reichsführer-SS. He went on to hold the post of I(a) (Operations Officer) with the 1. SS Infanterie Brigade (mot.). This unit, like the 2.SS Infanterie Brigade (mot.) and the 1.SS Kav.Brigade operated separately or alongside the notorious Einsatzgruppen under the direct command of Himmler.[131] As Operations Officer with the rank of Oberstleutnant, Freitag produced the daily activity reports on the units actions for submission directly to the Reichsführer-SS. Reading them, it is evident that its assignment was little more than the ruthless 'pacification'[132] of its area of deployment.[133]

During the following two years he was promoted to the rank of Standartenführer and variously held positions with 8 SS-Kavallerie-Division Florian Geyer,[134] 2.SS Infanterie Brigade, the SS-FHA and briefly with the Lett.SS-Freiw.Legion.

His decorations during his service in the Second World War included both the Iron Cross I. and II. Class (with bars), Deutsches Kreuz in Gold and so called 'Ostmedaille'. By the end of the war he had received a fifth wound in active service and was consequently awarded the Verwundeten-abzeichen in Gold (Wound badge in Gold). His most senior command appointments had been as a regimental commander with the 4 SS-Polizei Panzer-Grenadier Division and in early 1943 he assumed temporary command of the 8 SS-Kavallerie-Division Florian Geyer but gave up the appointment after a short period due to ill health.[135] On 6 August 1943 he was promoted again to the rank of SS-Oberführer.

Having commanded a regiment and a Division (albeit very briefly) on the eastern front, he had gained a substantial amount of combat experience[136] as well as a sound technical knowledge of military tactics. These military attributes would later be of great benefit to the Division and contributed significantly to helping it develop into a disciplined, powerful and effective battle ready unit.

Freitag was not however suited to the command of a Division of non German nationals (i.e. Ukrainians), with whom he had no direct contact[137] and whose psychology he made no attempt to understand. There is no doubt about Freitag's sincerity and commitment to his National Socialist convictions and his Führer Adolf Hitler. To this end, according to his 1a Wolf Dietrich Heike, 'everything he considered necessary for the Ukrainian Division he carried out with vigour and consistency'.[138] However Heike states that 'his desire to achieve personal honours through its successes were merely an extension of his egotism'.[139] Unsurprisingly, the Ukrainians shared neither his Nazi beliefs nor his convictions and could not have cared less for his 'Führer and Fatherland' preferring their own Ukrainian Fatherland and agenda for independence. The resulting unbridgeable chasm between both sides inevitably led to friction and became a permanent obstacle. This sentiment was echoed by Waffen-Hauptsturmführer Dymtro Ferkuniak who was one of the few Ukrainians to serve on the Division's staff. According to him 'Anything that was not German was inferior to him. His conduct towards Ukrainians was hostile and that could be noticed in every way'.[140] Heike summarised his appointment succinctly when he concluded that 'One of the greatest tragedies of the Division was the appointment of such a man as its commander'.[141] His generally negative attitude towards the Ukrainians together with his volatile character and inflexible Prussian approach ensured that his appointment as Divisional commander was ultimately a serious error.[142]

By November 1943, the Division consisted of about six thousand Ukrainians[143] and had reached a critical juncture in its development. The immediate and most important task which confronted Freitag was to supervise the completion of its formation as well as the establishment of its infrastructure. By now the first Ukrainian officers and NCOs who had not been discharged from service by various verification commissions had returned from their retraining courses. A minority returned with their old ranks reinstated, whilst the remainder were given a lower ranks to that which they had previously held. This development,

Oath November 1944. Left to right SS-Brigadeführer Freitag, Waffen-Haupsturmführer Paliiv, Waffen-Sturmbannführer Pobihushtschyi and SS- Sturmbannführer Georgi (Divisional Adjutant).

according to one Ukrainian who trained with them 'did not surprise us as many of the Germans were too proud to take orders from Untermensch.'[144] Now they sought appropriate command postings. Unfortunately, Freitag ignored the long term potential diplomatic role of the 'Galician Division' as envisaged by Governor Wächter. Although Wächter had promised a balanced officer corps, it was apparent that the necessary numbers of Ukrainian officers who had undergone recent tactical training (in all departments) were simply not available. This situation was further exacerbated by Freitag's discriminatory policy which largely excluded those who were available from important posts, (both combat and support) assigning them instead to secondary duties.[145] Freitag also actively blocked opportunities for advancement for these men. A similar problem existed with the NCO corps which would be of vital importance for the effectiveness of the formation.

As a result, virtually all principal positions of command and the greater part of the Divisions' cadre, consisted of German senior and junior officers. Freitag sought to justify his position approximately four weeks after his appointment, when on 19 November 1943, Governor Wächter together with the Military Board arranged a special two day visit for him to L'viv. The itinerary for the visit reflected an effort to introduce him to the local culture of his future charges[146] as well as presenting an excellent opportunity for him to familiarise himself with background information regarding the Division, its long term goals and the role and function of the Military Board in relation to it. At the meeting Dr Lubomyr Makarushka gave a report on the Division's cadre personnel following which another participant Jurij Krokhmaliuk made notes about Freitag's comments. These were as follows:

> Freitag: The soldiers and NCOs make a good impression. The soldiers are very enthusiastic, acquire technical skills extremely fast and learn the German language quickly. There are over 1,100 graduates [in the Division] who are very good, There are 540 NCOs, ergo, enough. Most of the problems are with the [Ukrainian] officers. They have no idea of modern methods. They learn quickly, unfortunately many are dismissed because of old age. Therefore at the outset German officers must come and that's what causes the difficulties. There is an immediate need for 50 young officers. Many companies have nominally one officer. **Asked Himmler to send some German officers because only one of the Ukrainians can be a regiment commander.** [...] (author's emphasis).[147]

Hence in the winter of 1943 and spring of 1944 the departments within its headquarters were staffed almost entirely by Germans with only five token Ukrainians attached to it in secondary roles. The staff appointments were:

Divisional Commander, SS-Oberführer Fritz Freitag
adjutant SS-Sturmbannführer Johannes Georgi[148]

Section Ia (Operations Officer) Major Wolf Dietrich Heike (from Jan. 1944)
adjutant SS-Obersturmführer Rudolph Michel[149]
SS-Obersturmführer Herbert Schaaf[150]

Section Ic (Intelligence/political matters)
SS-Obersturmführer Gunther Mussbach
Waffen-Hauptsturmführer Dmytro Ferkuniak

Section IIa (Divisional records)
SS-Hauptsturmführer Erich Finder[151]
Waffen-Hauptsturmführer Dmytro Paliiv
Ord.Offz 1 SS-Untersturmführer Friedrich Lehnhardt
Ord.Offz 2 SS-Obersturmführer Herbert Oskar Hanel[152]
Kdt.St.Qu. SS-Obersturmführer Ernst Gebhardt

Section III (Military Court)
SS-Sturmbannführer Hans Ziegler[153]
SS-Hauptsturmführer Gerhard Hermann
Waffen-Obersturmführer Dr Ivan Stadnyk
Waffen-Ostuf. Dr jur. Volodymyr Muryovyvh (Beurkundungsführer)

Section IVa (Quartermaster General, supply food and uniforms)
SS-Sturmbannführer Otto Sulzbach[154]

Section IVb (Medical)
SS-Obersturmbannführer Dr Max Specht[155]

Section IVb (Pharmacist)
SS-Hauptsturmführer Werner Beneke[156]

Section IVb (Veterinary)
SS-Sturmbannführer Dr Oskar Kopp[157]

Section IV (Dental)
SS-Obersturmführer Meyer

Section V (Automotive and Mechanical)
SS-Sturmbannführer Heinz Behrendt[158]

Section VI (Spiritual care, Education, Entertainment and information, Recreation)
SS-Hauptsturmführer Karl-Robert Zoglauer[159]
Waffen-Hauptsturmführer Mykola Uhryn-Bezhrishny

(The Divisional chaplain was Reverend Dr Volodymyr Stetsiuk).

In the combat units, Freitag was also understandably opposed to the appointment of officers without recent experience, a policy that inevitably always favoured the German officers.[160] Whereas during the initial organisational stage all of the regimental commanders had been Ukrainian, as soon as he was able, Freitag unceremoniously replaced them with German officers exclusively on the pretext that Hitler had ordered only Germans were to be used as staff officers.[161]

The first to arrive was SS-Sturmbannführer Hans-Boto Forstreuter,[162] a former battalion commander from a Kampfgruppe (Battlegroup) of Freitag's former SS-Pol. Panz.Gren.Div. He was appointed to command the 2 Regiment (30) with effect from 15 November 1943.[163] Three months passed before on 20 February 1944, SS-Obersturmbannführers Friedrich Dern[164] and Paul Herms[165] both of whom had previously served with 6.Geb.Div. 'Nord', arrived to take over command of 1 Regiment (29) and 3 Regiment (31) respectively. In the interim, with effect from 1 January 1944, SS-Obersturmbannführer Friedrich Beyersdorff[166] who like Forstreuter also came from the SS-Pol.Panz.Gren.Div, assumed command of the 14 Artillery Regiment.[167]

Moreover, in the following months, Freitag managed to effect the removal of the majority of the senior ranking Ukrainians all of whom had successfully passed the German verification commissions. These included Waffen Hauptsturmführers' Borys Barvinsky (55 yrs), Mychailo Dawybiba (51 yrs), Stephan Kotyl (57 yrs), Mykola Uhryn-Bezhrishny (60 yrs), Leonid Wasylew and Dr Ivan Stadnyk (the latter two both aged 50+).

Having little confidence in those who remained, he went on to expand the number of German postings to cover all except one of the infantry battalions and all the Divisional sub units.

The first of the German infantry battalion commanders to assume their positions was SS-Hauptsturmführer Siegfried Klocker[168] who became commander of the I./2 Regiment (30) on 6 November 1943.

Of the sub-unit commanders, amongst the earliest to take up their postings were SS-Sturmbannführer Josef Remberger[169] who arrived on 8 November 1943, and became the commander of the 14. Pioneer Battalion. He was followed by SS-Hauptsturmführer Wolfgang Wuttig[170] who was already in place as commander of the Signals Detachment by 8 December 1943. SS-Hauptsturmführer Karl Bristot[171] joined on 15 December 1943, to command the 14 Fusilier Battalion. SS-Hauptsturmführer Hermann Kaschner[172] was appointed to the Anti-tank Detachment as of 5 January 1944, and SS-Obersturmbannführer Franz Magill[173] was posted to head the Supply Section on 2 March 1944.[174]

Thereafter the only Ukrainians who held positions of command at the battalion level or above in combat units were; Waffen-Hauptsturmführer Michael Brygidyr[175] (a former Hauptsturmführer with Schützmannschaft 201) who commanded the I. battalion of the 29 Regiment, Waffen-Hauptsturmführer Mykola Palijenko[176] who commanded a battalion of heavy artillery and Waffen-Sturmbannführer Evhen Pobihushtschyi, who temporally commanded a battalion of the 29 Regiment, until he too was replaced by SS-Hauptsturmführer Wilhelm Allerkamp who joined the Division on 27 March 1944.[177] Other Ukrainian officers took up positions as company, battery or platoon commanders,[178] (the majority of company commanders were Ukrainian) while those who were not considered suitable for use in combatant roles were utilised in the supply and support services.

Many of the Ukrainian officers who had passed the internal German verification commissions were over 50 years of age, however there remained a pool of outstanding younger officers whom Freitag appears to have intentionally overlooked. For example former Red Army lieutenants all with the coveted recent front experience included; Grygorij Bondarenko (aged 26); Fedir Kulibaba (aged 26); Serhij Roslyk (aged 25); Volodymyr Kosak (aged 26); Fedyr Baranenko (aged 40); Mychailo Tchernysh(*); Petro Tyshchenko(*);[179] Vasyl Lychmanenko and the outstanding 23 year old Hennadij Salesskyj, who was described by the commander of WGR 31 SS-Obersturmbannführer Paul Herms, according to his translator Myron Radzykewycz, 'as the best officer in his regiment'.[180]

Despite the decision to raise the Galician Division as a regular front line Waffen-SS combat formation, the consolidation of the German Polizei establishment under the overall umbrella of Himmler's SS empire meant that links inevitably existed between the two. This was reflected in the fact that the majority of the German officers came mainly from the 4 SS-Polizei Panzer-Grenadier Division which had been formed in 1939 from members of the Ordnungspolizei—(uniformed civilian Polizei and Allgemeine-SS reservists) or other Polizei formations. Ultimately at least three of its regimental commanders and a minimum of eight battalion and two battery commanders transferred from the 4.Polizei Division.[181] The regimental commanders included Beyersdorff (artillery), Forstreuter (WGR 30), and later SS-Standartenführer Rudolph Pannier (WGR 31) who joined the Division the following year as a replacement. Amongst the battalion commanders were the commanders of the Signals, (Wuttig and later his successor Heinz), Fusilier, (Bristot); Panzerjäger (Kaschner) and Pioneer (Remberger) Battalions.[182]

The cornerstone of the Division comprised of the three infantry regiments and the artillery regiment and the men chosen to command them were to be pivotal. Freitag's evaluation of them provides a valuable insight into the calibre of commanders with which he surrounded himself.

Like Freitag, the commander of the 29 Regiment SS-Obersturmbannführer Friedrich Dern had previously served in Polizei units, most notably as commander of the 1./14.SS-Inf.Rgt. (Sonder-Battalion zur Verfügung Kommandostab Reichsführer SS).[183] He was a former battalion commander and decorated veteran and holder of the Iron Cross (I. and II. Class) as well as the Order of the Finnish Cross of Liberty (III. Class with Swords).[184] He was exactly the kind of man Freitag wanted in the Division as is indicated by his appraisal of him written some four months into his tenure as regimental commander. It read:

Evaluation, for Dern.

Dern, Regiment Commander—SS Freiw.Gren. Rgt.29
D. has been the Regiment Commander of SS Freiw.Gren. Rgt. 29 since 20.2.44.

D. exhibits his straight and open personality and has a firm and decisive appearance. His physique is robust and fully combat ready.

D. has a solid military knowledge and experience and is leading the regiment to my full satisfaction.

Despite all the difficulties appearing in connection with a unit composed of foreign nationals, D. is trying with untiring effort, to bring his regiment to a high level of training and conduct.

D. is an old National Socialist and is always concerned with the well being of his subordinates.

Because of his conduct and seasoned experience he always sets a good example for all, and he can easily convey his thoughts to his subordinates.

Towards his superiors D. is restrained and tactful. D. is loved amongst his circle of comrades.

D. fulfils his service position well.[185]

A seasoned combat veteran and former battalion commander, SS-Sturmbannführer Hans Botho-Forstreuter was a highly decorated officer, holding the Iron Cross (I. and II. Class), the Infanterie Sturmabzeichen (Infantry Assault Badge), the Nahkampfspange (Close Combat Clasp) in bronze and the celebrated 'Deutsches Kreuz in Gold' (German Cross in Gold).[186] Freitag wrote about the 31 year old commander of WGR 30:

Evaluation, for SS-Sturmbannführer Forstreuter

Forstreuter Regiment Commander SS Freiw.Gren. Rgt.30

F. came from the SS Pol.Panz.Gren.Div. Kampfgruppe where he was subordinated to me as a battalion commander. He was very successful.

F. has led the SS-Freiw.Gren.Rgt.30. since 26.2.1944. F. has mastered outstandingly the difficulties that have arisen with a foreign regiment with untiring eagerness, particularly in its formation and training, where his excellent organizational ability stood out. As a front-experienced battalion commander, F. will provide good leadership of his regiment in combat.

F. has a highstanding decent character and is honest and reserved. In every respect he is an exemplary SS Officer and by his posture, his past, his training and attitude, he understands [how] to instil in his subordinates the capacity to learn and the spirit of the SS.

His high qualities as an organiser, as regiment commander and National Socialist make him worthy of promotion.[187]

The third infantry regiment WGR 31 was commanded by Paul Herms who had the most previous combat experience. His combat decorations included the Iron Cross (I. and II. Class) and the Order of the Finnish Cross of Liberty (III. Class with Swords).[188] Freitag's assessment of him was as follows:

Evaluation for SS-Obersturmbannführer Paul Herms

Herms, Regiment Commander—SS Freiw.Gren. Rgt.31
H.s' character is circumspect otherwise however he is very reliable.
Physically fully efficient
H. is mentally very agile and stands above average.
Even if H. at the beginning had heavy tasks and initial difficulties arising from the formation of a foreign division, over time he overcame them with great effort and untiring diligence. He succeeded in bringing his regiment to a high state of training readiness in a short time. His experience, military knowledge and his good organization talent were of great benefit to him on this occasion.
H. leads his regiment to my satisfaction with much skill and great enthusiasm.
I believe that in combat his men will stand behind H. as regiment commander.
Towards his superiors he is reserved and very much respected amongst his circle of comrades.
To his subordinates Herms is strict but fair.
As a National Socialist his appearance in and out of service sets a good example
Performs well in the position as regiment commander.[189]

The commander of the Artillery Regiment Beyersdorff had also spent time at the front during his military service receiving in the process the Iron Cross (I. and II. Class) as well as the wound badge in black and like the others, he shared the National socialist outlook that Freitag was keen to promote:

Evaluation for SS-Obersturmbannführer Friedrich Beyersdorff

Beyersdorff Regiment Commander—SS Freiw.Art. Rgt.14
B. has since 6.1.44 been utilised as commander of the Artillery Regiment.
B.'s character is of a straight nature, he is open minded, being good natured and confident.
Despite his gastric ailment still arising every now and then, Beyersdorff is extremely fit. Through his hard work and tireless enthusiasm, despite all the difficulties he has succeeded in a short time in bringing the Artillery Regiment to a good state of readiness.
B. has so far very little front experience, but I believe will successfully lead his regiment in combat.
Towards his superiors B. is correct and open. In his circle of comrades [he is] popular.
To his subordinates B. is a fair and helpful superior.
B. has a firm belief grounded in National socialist world perception. In a simple understandable way, Beyersdorff can convey his thoughts well to his subordinates.
B. fulfils his service position well.[190]

The Division's Supply Section was from 2 March 1944, headed by SS-Obersturmbannführer Franz Magill.[191]

Other officers such as SS-Hauptsturmführer Karl Bristot[192] who commanded the Fusilier Battalion possessed qualities and key attributes as well as the combat experience that Freitag felt to be vital in his officer corps. At the time of his appointment, Bristot already held several impressive awards including the Iron Cross both I. and II. Class, Infantry Assault Badge, the Ostmedaille, and the Wound Badge in both black and silver for having been wounded three times in combat. In addition to which he was, like Forstreuter, also a recipient of the highly prestigious Deutsches Kreuz in Gold won whilst participating in the fighting on the Leningrad Front. Possessing in Freitag's words, 'a straight and open personality' he was described by him as having a 'calm and even tempered, demeanour', who 'through his conduct as a National Socialist gives a good example to his men'. This left Freitag to conclude 'I am intending to propose him for promotion at the nearest future opportunity'.[193]

Of the remainder, several had been sent to the Division by the SS-Führungshauptamt (SS inspectorates of headquarters)[194] having first been rejected by other formations. Because of this, in contrast to the attempts by the Military Board to attract the best possible Ukrainian recruits, the Division effectively became a dumping ground for a great many second rate German officers and NCOs as was often the case with many other European Waffen-SS Divisions. Without consideration of their suitability, German cadre personnel were transferred to it from various Polizei, SS and Waffen-SS formations including the 1.Leibstandarte, 2.Das Reich, 3.Totenkopf, 4.Polizei, 5.Wiking, 6.Nord and 16.Reichsführer SS divisions. The service records of personnel who served with the Division, reveal that on rare occasions this extended to former concentration camp personnel such as SS-Untersturmführer Herbert Hanel[195] who served at Majdanek. An eastern Ukrainian Grigorij Osowoy also transferred from the camp at Trawniki, where he had been sent to recuperate from wounds received whilst serving at the front with the 44.Inf.Div. at Stalingrad.[196]

In several cases they received promotions to non-commissioned or even commissioned officers ranks simply because they were fluent in both German and Ukrainian.[197] While some could provide good specialised instruction, few were well enough disposed towards the Ukrainians to establish cordial relations with them. Most remained distant and aloof, firmly convinced of their superiority. More importantly there existed a hard core element of Nazi party members who formed the 'political backbone' of the Division. These men such as Alten Parteikampfer SS-Sturmbannführer Otto Sulzbach and SS-Hauptsturmführer Johannes Kleinow shared Freitag's attitude towards the Ukrainians and harboured prejudices against them and the Division[198] and their presence created a lasting atmosphere of tension.

A few individual German officers were more favourably inclined toward the Ukrainians, the most prominent being an Army Major, Wolf-Dietrich Heike,[199] who arrived at Heidelager on 10 January 1944. A decorated and seasoned veteran who was familiar with the rigours of the eastern front,[200] he was officially 'on assignment' and took up the post of 1a (General Staff/Operations officer).[201] In this position Heike's influence on all matters pertaining to the Division was considerable. Unlike his British or American counterpart, his duties as General

Staff/Operations Officer entailed assisting directly with organisation, training and tactical command. His pragmatic and sympathetic approach to the Ukrainians and the political aspirations which they associated with the formation could perhaps be attributed to his Army background (as opposed to the Polizei background of a large proportion of the other officers). By virtue of his position Heike was able to serve as a moderating influence on Freitag, who was evidently satisfied with his performance describing him in his personal evaluation as having an 'Honest and serious character, strong minded personality', [and a] 'healthy ambition'. 'Slim with an athletic figure', he was a 'good horse rider, [who was] capable of full achievement'. 'Above average intellectually' Freitag acknowledged 'his organisational talent is outstanding' and that he 'fulfilled all responsibilities with industry and diligence, especially in building a foreign division with its occurring difficulties'.[202] Despite this appraisal Freitag never recommended Heike for the promotion which he clearly deserved. According to Jurij Krokhmaliuk this was because Heike always preferred to wear his regular army uniform in preference his SS-Sturmbannführer's uniform, much to the extreme annoyance of Freitag who made quite an issue out of it.[203] SS-Hauptsturmführer Friedrich Wittenmeyer[204] joined the Division on 28 March 1944, as a battalion commander with WGR 30 and later served as a temporary regimental commander with WGR 31. He adopted a similar approach to the Ukrainians, as a result of which he was generally held in very high esteem by those who served under him.

The ethnic German officers, especially the Slovak Volksdeutsche, usually had less difficulty in establishing a good rapport with the Ukrainian recruits. This was partly because their native languages were very similar which necessarily facilitated better communications.

From the cadre of Reichsdeutsch and Volksdeutsche officers, Freitag demanded honesty and dignity (by his own standards) in order that they might set a suitable example to their Ukrainian comrades.[205] On occasion, amongst his own Germanic colleagues, he did not hesitate to punish those whose conduct he did not consider to be appropriate. Equally, as a staunch Nazi, those who shared his political views were often favoured or protected.[206]

The strongest opposition to Freitag's policy of utilising Germans in positions of command wherever possible came from Waffen-Hauptsturmführer Dmytro Paliiv. Forty seven years old in 1943, with a distinct osseous appearance, Paliiv had been an officer in the Ukrainian Sich Riflemen during the First World War, a former journalist, and a member of the Polish parliament.[207] A major proponent of the Division from its inception, he was appointed to Freitag's staff as political adviser on recommendation of Prof. Kubijovych. He also acted as unofficial liaison between the Division, the Ukrainian Central Committee and the Military Board. In this position, as the principle spokesman for the Ukrainians, he made tremendous efforts to maintain Ukrainian interests within the Division which frequently brought him into conflict with Freitag.

Paliiv recognised that failure to create a Ukrainian officer/NCO corps with recent training in a modern army would critically handicap the Division in what the nationalist element saw as its projected role as the nucleus of a future Ukrainian Army. Under the prevailing circumstances, Paliiv chose to pursue a long term solution to the problem by ensuring that as many Ukrainians as possible attended specialised training programmes for officers and NCOs. Thanks to his efforts 600 Ukrainian officer candidates eventually completed their courses and became full officers in the Division. In addition, by the time the war had ended a further two thousand men had successfully finished various specialised programmes for NCOs.[208]

Deceptive Appearances

In supporting the formation of the Galician Division, the Ukrainians had accepted that it was necessary to sacrifice short term form for long term substance. Whereas for their part the Germans relied on cosmetic initiatives to maintain the façade that the Division would exclusively serve their requirements. In reality they did little save for allowing them to preserve symbolic supremacy within it.

Neither the insistence on using 'Galician' for its title nor the adoption of the Galician lion as its symbol were sufficient to conceal its true Ukrainian origins. This was spelled out unequivocally by Waffen-Hauptsturmführer Dmytro Ferkuniak a Ukrainian officer who was assigned to its staff. In an incident recorded in his memoirs, he relates how he and his fellow Ukrainian officers Dr Ivan Stadnyk and Mykola Uhryn-Bezhrishny were invited to a soirée hosted by Sturmbannführer Johann Burkhart. He continues:

[...] The German officers Sturmbannführer Kleinow, Hauptsturmführer Finder and a few others thought that by making Ukrainians drunk they might hear something that would never be said while sober.[...] When political questions were not answered, Kleinow started up about the name 'Galician Division'. I heard Kleinow say that many did not like the name 'Galician Division', preferring [the name] 'Ukrainian Division'. He said that this was impossible and incorrect as Ukrainians lived east of the River Zbruch and most soldiers in the Division were from Galicia. Dr Stadnyk tried to prevent me from talking but to no avail as my patience came to an end. I said to Kleinow 'I feel sorry for you sir since you know so little about Ukraine and its people. According to your statement I should not call you German. I should call you by the name of the province you came from, for instance, Branderburger, Saxonian, or Bavarian etc. All of those provinces combined into one state called Germany and that gives you the right to call yourselves Germans. When this is so then what are the basic obstacles for uniting all Ukrainian provinces into one state called Ukraine and calling its people Ukrainians? I beg of you not to call us Galicians as this suggests you gentlemen wish to follow in the steps of our enemies, the Russians and Poles. Divide and conquer. Since we have began such a discussion I also beg you to understand that the lion with three crowns you gave to our Division is not our coat of arms. The golden lion with three crowns was an occupational coat of arms which belonged to Maria Theresa Archduchess of Austria. Our coat of arms is the 'Trident'. Our host Sturmbannführer Burkhart noticed our discussion was leading to a serious confrontation and he managed to bring our attention to different matters.[...][209]

In much the same way the insistence on subjecting the recruits to the programme of 'political education' designed to promote Nazi ideals was merely a perfunctory gesture. Since the very essence of Nazi ideological doctrine advocated the superiority of the Aryan Herrenvolk (Master race) over the inferior Untermensch (sub-human) Slav, the German instructors had to be careful not to antagonise their Slavic Ukrainian charges. Instead 'the superiority of German arms was always stressed and also our common aim—the defeat of Bolshevism'.[210] Racial theories were limited to eugenics and discussions as to what would happen if black and white rabbits were to be mixed.[211]

Denied an outwardly perceptible Ukrainian appearance, the Ukrainians could still rely on several other factors to ensure the Galician Division remained intrinsically Ukrainian such as the role of the OUN/UPA in relation to it. As well as a host of prominent individuals who served in its ranks, the overwhelming majority of the soldiers were deeply sympathetic to the aims and ideals of the Ukrainian nationalist movement.

Governor Wächter who acknowledged the Ukrainian nationalist partisans as having become 'a considerable factor', argued that it was 'the barricade which keeps the entire youth of Galicia from slipping into a nationalistic hostility to the Reich'. He had anticipated that the formation of the Division would help to cripple the UPA by diverting potential sympathisers into a controlled army unit whereas in practice it offered the insurgents the potential to strengthen their position. Through its supporters within the Division, the UPA was able to obtain limited amounts of weapons, ammunition uniforms and equipment of all types for use against the Germans if need be while at the same time this channel also provided access to first class training for its own personnel. In some instances when soldiers of the Division were granted home leave they were used by the UPA cadres as instructors for their partisans.[212] Others, having received their basic training, were given active assistance via a well established support network, to desert to the UPA.

The Divisions' internal German security struggled to counter these activities, and only occasionally met with success. For example, they apprehended Waffen-Obersturmführer Fedyr Baranenko, a former Red Army lieutenant who commanded 6./I./WGR 30. Together with two men from his company Freiw. SS-Schütze Nikolaus Skyba[213] and Freiw.SS-Schütze Serhi Surkiv,[214] he aided and abetted desertions. The charge sheet went on to state that:

> Within the company Baranenko arranged general plans for desertions. The company führer was the confidant and sponsor. He had full knowledge of it and promoted it. In the company a fake service stamp for travel was held. Several departures were successfully accomplished in B.'s company and he maintained contact with the deserters.[215]

By order of the Reichsführer Baranenko and Surkiv received the death penalty, whilst Skyba received eight years imprisonment in a concentration camp having first been made to attend the executions of his comrades (although Baranenko survived).[216]

It was a similar case with the OUN whose ultimate goal was a free Ukraine. A secret network of known OUN/UPA agents infiltrated the Division at every level. Amongst its confirmed senior members were: Bohdan Pidhayny (chef, 3./ WGR 30), Mychailo Brygidyr (Kdr. I./WGR 29), Myroslav Maletsky (chef, 7./ WGR 30), Mychailo Kaczmar (chef 2./II.Art.Rgt.14),[217] Lubomyr Ortynsky (OO, WGR 29), Bohdan Levycky (Pfarrer, III/Art.Rgt.14), and Dr Volodymyr Kischko (chef, Vet.Kp. 14). Other influential members or sympathisers included the officer corps of the OUN sponsored Roland and Nachtigall Legions whom the Germans had previously imprisoned and then released to serve in the Division. They included: Evhen Pobihushchyi, Roman Bojcun (chef,4./Füs.Btl.14), Myroslav Martynetz, Mychailo Chomiak, Karl Malyj, Myroslav Zharsky, Swiatoslav Levycky, Volodymyr Jarvorsky, Emil Hermann (I./WGR 29.) and Pfarrer Vsevolod Durbak (Pfarrer, Sani.Abt.14). The location of Heidelager close to Galicia further encouraged these activities which the Germans could not successfully suppress.

By far the most serious issue was the almost total absence of Ukrainians from senior positions of command but with a ratio in the Division of approximately nine Ukrainians to every one German, at best the Germans only exercised limited control over the unit which they knew to be heavily infiltrated with UPA members and sympathisers. Even the most committed Nazi and retarded racist among its German cadre realised that to prevent a mutiny, a modus vivendi had to be established which made some allowances for the aspirations and sympathies of their Ukrainian charges.

The Ukrainian Catholic clergy also played a critical part. The appointment of chaplains was one of only two major concessions which the Germans made and kept at the outset. This is even more remarkable since the SS-authorities had developed a deep-rooted distrust of the Ukrainian Catholic Church after Rev Dr Laba's sermon of 28 April 1943, had shown it to be openly supportive of Ukrainian nationalist ideals. For this reason and because the Waffen-SS was predominantly atheist, the chaplains were regarded by the Divisional command as being politically suspect and were forced to operate within the bounds of strict German censorship. Despite the restrictions imposed upon them, they provided vital moral and spiritual support and quickly became both a focal point for the devoutly religious Ukrainians and a centre for their national identity.

Each regiment and independent battalion was assigned a field chaplain who was responsible to Dr Vladimyr Steciuk the senior religious officer and member of the Divisional staff (section VI). Their role and function was defined by Father Mychailo Levenetz who issued basic guide-lines directing the chaplains to make every effort 'towards gaining the trust of the men and getting to know their character and soul in the finest detail, so that he [the chaplain] can, at the decisive moment, have the desired influence on the troops'.[218]

Several prominent members of the Organisation of Ukrainian Nationalists with previous military experience received personal orders from General Shukhevych to join the Division to ensure some 'political muscle' was available. Picture taken during the officer retraining course at Leshany 31 August 1943–1 November 1943. *Left to right:* Bohdan Pidhayny, German instructor, Myroslav Malecky, Dmytro Ferkuniak, Mychailo Kaczmar and Ihor Pospilovsky.

The guidelines listed other duties too such as; assisting with applications for family support made by relatives of the volunteers; ensuring that the daily Wehrmachtbericht (Wehrmacht report) be made available to the men in Ukrainian at least every other day; educating the men regarding conduct towards the civilian population, defending against sabotage, etc and encouraging cultural work i.e. press, choir.[219]

Mass was celebrated in Ukrainian every Sunday and on every major religious holiday in a large clearing in the pine forest at the camp, in all weather. This took the form of a field service with a sermon which since it was delivered without the aid of a microphone and amplification, often left the chaplain hoarse. It was always well attended and presented the priests with a perfect opportunity to thwart the German efforts at political propaganda. Pfarrers' Mychailo Levenetz, Izydor Sydir Nahayewsky, Bohdan Levyckyj and Vsevolod Durbak who were also OUN supporters or sympathisers, propagated Ukrainian ideals as Freitag knew all too well. This is perfectly illustrated in the following account related by Pfarrer Izydor Nahayewsky:

> Several weeks before departure of the Division to the front, General Freitag began writing his 'messages' to the soldiers, in which he strongly condemned the UPA. He already had the Ukrainian text. I was convinced that they were written either by Paliiv or someone in the Military Board in L'viv. But I knew from confidential

conversations, as well as from the confessional that all these measures had the opposite effect. I was asked by our officers to explain to the General [Freitag] this matter and specifically that he get rid of the Gestapo [i.e. Wiens] from the Division because it was hated and was destroying the morale of the troops and that things would get worse at the front. I told the General that I had serious doubts whether under such circumstances the Division would fulfil the responsibilities entrusted to it by the Ukrainian people. Speaking clearly, I said that I thought many soldiers would leave the Division and go to the UPA and that this was not just my opinion, but also that of many Ukrainian officers. And here, surprisingly, General Freitag wanted to know the names of those officers. However, I said that I could not tell him the names because they were revealed to me during confessions and that I was sworn to keep the confessions secret and would reveal nothing even under torture or threats of death. He gave me an incredulous long look and said: 'I was told that you, Herr Feldkurat, in your lectures and discussions with the soldiers and as well in the Sunday sermons continuously speak about Ukraine, but do not forget that without 'the Fuhrer and Reich' the Ukrainians will never attain their goal.[220]

The third contributory element was the existence of the Military Board and its affiliation with the Galician Division.[221] Although Wächter had already taken steps to restrict its influence, this civilian organisation was still able to care for the interests and welfare of its soldiers. It also helped to maintain contact between the soldiers and the population of Galicia.

The Military Board was also responsible for the production and publication of a weekly tabloid-sized Ukrainian language newspaper Do Peremohy (To Victory). Published in L'viv under the capable editorship of the well known writer and poet Mykhailo Ostroverkha, the first issue appeared on 21 December 1943. It contained military news, together with articles about Ukrainian military history and reports about life in the Division by the German and Ukrainian Kriegsberichters who contributed to the journal.[222] All reports submitted for publication were subjected to stringent censorship by the Germans who according to a former Ukrainian Kriegsberichter Oleh Lysiak, 'eliminated anything which smelt of Ukrainian nationalism'.[223] Even the word 'Ukraine' was discouraged as being too nationalistic. Instead the word 'fatherland' was used in its place. The journal also published essays, artwork, and literature contributed by the Ukrainian recruits. Sale of the paper was restricted to members of the Division, however it soon became very popular on the black market. Despite constant German opposition to its editorial policy, publication did not cease until 7 January 1945.[224]

With the coming of Christmas 1943, the Military Board concentrated on conducting very successful fund raising activities[225] and the collection of Christmas gifts for the soldiers of the Division. A sum exceeding 1,000,000 Zloty was raised from money given by the population of Galicia and 20,000 Christmas parcels were packed from the articles donated each weighing two kilos.[226] Dept. VI of the Divisional staff headed by SS-Hauptsturmführer Zoglauer arranged the distribution of the parcels containing 'Christmas comforts' to all Galician volunteers who were undergoing training throughout various camps in Europe. These were distributed in the week before Christmas by truck which called at training establishments and specialist schools at Mielefeld, Osnabrück, Hamm, Verdun, Lübeck, Rallstedt, Hilversum, Oldenburg, Karlstadt, Radolfzell, and Moerchingen amongst others.[227]

The Military Board also presented a gift of 100,000 Reich marks to the Division via its commander SS-Oberführer Freitag, plus 25,000 Reich marks for each of the Galician Volunteer Regiments.[228] The poorer families of the soldiers received parcels containing everyday articles.[229]

These efforts contributed appreciably to the success of the Division's first Christmas which was a great ceremonial event. The culmination of the traditional German Weihnachtsfeier (Christmas festivities) was an evening meal for the senior staff and which SS-Oberführer Freitag spoke on behalf of the Germans as did Waffen-Hauptsturmführer Dmytro Paliiv on behalf of the Ukrainians. The Divisional orchestra then gave a performance. Every Divisional member at Heidelager irrespective of their nationality received a Christmas package, and two bottles of alcohol. The Ukrainians attended their church services. Entertainment was also provided in the form of a performance arranged by the Military Board and staged by the Merry L'viv theatre troop and a Bandura[230] ensemble. On Christmas Eve, traditional Ukrainian dishes including borsch and kutia were served to those in attendance. Keeping in the festive spirit, even though by mid-December the total number of desertions had risen to 184,[231] the Divisional commander agreed to a request to allow leave and on 3 January1944 some 800 men left to join their families for Ukrainian Christmas. [232]

Governor Wächter had already proudly informed Himmler of the Military Board's endeavours in two letters dated 18 and 19 December 1943. In them he pointed out the considerable capacity for sacrifice the donations demonstrated in the Galician people who continued to support the Galician Division. At the same time Wächter kept Himmler abreast of the developments within it and the Galician SS-Volunteer Regiments which he had recently visited in their respective training camps. His party had included his adjutant, Oberst Alfred Bisanz, Dr Makarushka and an entertainment troupe of twelve artists.[233]

In his reply dated 31 December 1943, Himmler congratulated Wächter on his work in Galicia and for the very successful fund raising activities of the Military Board. He also expressed his pleasure with regard to the report on the Galician SS Volunteer Regiments which he promised to provide with some urgently needed footwear. At the same time, Himmler signalled his intention to address a more pressing concern. This was the progress with the formation of the Division. At this juncture it lacked both manpower and several senior officers for key regimental and battalion command positions. Acknowledging the need for action, he concluded by stating that he would 'discuss the problem of the accelerated formation of the Division in the next few days and arrive at a suitable solution'.[234]

November 1943 the Division received a new commander SS-Oberführer Fritz Freitag who addresses the men of his new division while Waffen-Haupsturmführer Paliiv translates.

Unification at Last

The first practical steps had already been taken towards expediting the formation of the Division, when on 11 December 1943, the Reichsführer consented to the disbanding of the Galician Polizei Regiments 6 and 7.[235] Subsequently, Himmler issued an order dated 23 December 1943, which directed that 2,000 volunteers be surrendered to the 14. Galiz.SS-Freiw.-Div. at the Training ground at Heidelager.[236] Of this number 1,200 men were to be drawn from Gal.SS-Freiw.-Rgt.6, 745 from Gal.SS-Freiw.-Rgt.7, and a further 55 men from the Gal.SS-Freiw.Ers.Btl[237] based at Heidenheim. Thereafter 'Galizischen SS-Freiwilligen Regimenter' no's 6 and 7 whose personnel had completed their basic training, were dissolved[238] and on 29 December the first transport left for Heidelager.[239] The German officer cadres of both regiments who were not deemed suitable for combat units were returned to other Polizei formations around 90 per cent of the German NCOs of the 7 being sent to Polizei units in Bozan (Bosnia).[240]

From the remnants of the two regiments one reserve battalion known as 'Galizisches SS-Freiwilligen-Ersatz-Battalion' was formed on 9 March 1944,[241] which was commanded by Major der Sicherheitpolizei Jordan and consisted of four companies with a total strength of around 900 men. The unit remained in south Western France at Tarbes, where its companies performed different duties in rotation, (Jagdkomando, Wachkomando, Einsatzkomando and Bereitschaftskomando). Additionally its personnel were also sent to guard the prison in the Jagerkasserne. These activities continued until it too was transferred to the Division in mid-May 1944.

By 31 December 1943, with the inclusion of the additional 2,000 men, the 'Galician SS-Freiwilligen-Division's' total strength stood at 12,634; including 256 officers, 449 NCOs and 11,929 enlisted men.[242]

Another Reichsführer order dated 22 January1944, was intended to provide the Galician Division with further trained recruits via the incorporation of Schützmannschafts-Batl. 204, (which as Wachbattalion was responsible for security at Heidelager).[243] This order was however not implemented. Although Himmler's original intention had been to expand this battalion into the 1. SS-Freiwilligen-Grenadier-Regiment,[244] it had remained directly subordinate to the Polizei authorities. Moreover HSSPF Koppe, under whose jurisdiction it operated, made no move to comply with the new directive.[245] According to the account of Orest Horodysky who was serving with Schützmannschafts-Batl. 204, a general announcement was made in late January 1944, to its personnel that 'they could ask for a transfer to the [Galician] Division'.[246] As a result 'about 20 men volunteered' whereupon they were assigned to the Nachrichten (signals) section.[247] Once again this left the battalion independent and virtually intact until it was finally dissolved five months later.

Mass in winter 1943 / 44 Heidelager. *Photo Courtesy Richard Rygaard archive*

Left to right: Pobihushtschyi, Freitag SS-Sturmbannführer Johannes Georgi (Divisional Adjutant).

Target practice Heidelager winter 1943.

Oath taking for soldiers who completed their basic training in winter 1943, at Heidelager. Waffen-Haupsturmführer Paliiv translates.

Schutzmannschaft 204 at Heidelager led by their NCOs. Originally intended to be expanded into the 1.SS-Freiwilligen-Grenadier-Regiment which in turn was to be the basis of the Galician Division. Front row centre Andrij Hawirko, behind him partly obscured Orest Horodysky. It was the Wachbattalion responsible for security at Heidelager until it was finally dissolved and integrated into the Division in June 1944.

Funeral Duties for the Ehrencompanie

Since his appointment, the Soviet authorities had become increasingly concerned about the success of Governor Wächter's administration in Galicia and therefore made plans to eliminate him. His assassination did not however take place thanks to a warning he received from the OUN, (for the text of the warning see Appendix 2). Consequently the Soviets sought an easier target and on Wednesday 9 February 1944, Wächter's assistant and deputy Governor of Galicia Otto Bauer[248] and Dr Heinrich Schneider,[249] were simultaneously murdered by the Soviet agent Nikolai Kuznetsov in L'viv.[250]

In response, later on that day the Division's acting command received orders to form an Ehrencompanie (Honour Company) which together with part of the Division's orchestra[251] was to participate in the funeral ceremonies. These were scheduled to take place in L'viv on Saturday 12 February 1944.

On the evening of 9 February the 12 MG-Lehrkompanie was formed from the best forty five men of the 5 company z.b.V. As part of the selection criteria men were chosen who were of good posture, over 1.6 metres in height and whose drill was excellent. The following day, appropriate Galician Divisional uniform insignia was issued. After many long hours practising a parade march, changing formation and giving an honorary gun salute, the men left Heidelager on the morning of 11 February travelling in a convoy of motor vehicles along with members of the Divisional orchestra. The column was lead by two Red Cross ambulances, which also carried live ammunition for the rifles and MGs as well as several cases of grenades. Following the ambulances were twenty Schwimmwagens (open top amphibious jeeps), each containing three soldiers and a driver (who was not a member of the Honour Company). The leading two contained the detachment commander SS-Obersturmführer Herbert Schneller and SS-Obersturmführer Johann Thiessen (the band leader) each of whom was accompanied by three NCOs. Because of the cold weather all occupants wore winter clothing[252] and steel helmets. Bringing up the rear were four trucks covered with tarpaulins which carried the youngest soldiers as well as members of the band with their instruments.

The convoy passed through Dembica, Rzeszow, and Jaroslav before its first stop in Peremyshl. Here the column was informed that as they would now be travelling through the forest between Mostyska and L'viv which was regarded as 'partisan territory' live ammunition would be issued and additional security measures observed. The column arrived in the evening of the same day in L'viv at the former cadet school near Stryj Park without incident.

At 1000 hrs on the morning of Saturday 12 February the detachment proceeded to march through the city's snow covered streets in parade uniforms, along Stryj Avenue to the government building on Charnetsky Avenue. Here at the request of Bauer's widow, the Chaplain Fr Laba, celebrated a Holy Mass and held a memorial service by the flag draped coffin of her late husband. The coffins were placed on horse-drawn gun carriages which led the procession followed immediately by the orchestra conducted by the baton of SS-Obersturmführer Otto Thiessen. Behind them was Obersturmführer Schneller with his sword drawn followed by the Ehrencompanie led by three NCOs. Next came the families of the departed and Governor Wächter and his government officials, representatives of the UCC including Kubijovych and Alfred Bisanz together with the members of Military Board.

The column proceeded to Stryj Park for the funeral where two graves had been dug on the edge of the snow covered, old cemetery. Marching in slow parade steps to the tune of the funeral march by the orchestra was difficult. The streets were icy and slippery and special care had to be taken when stepping on the tram lines. This was only the second public appearance by soldiers of the Division in uniform,[253] who were well received by the cities' inhabitants who lined the route and turned out in large numbers to lend their support.

After the funeral, in the late afternoon Governor Wächter and his entourage visited the company at their quarters where he congratulated its commander on its faultless military bearing and discipline.[254] Wächter was so impressed with the Ukrainian soldiers he selected seven of the men to accompany him on a propaganda tour throughout Galicia to recruit more volunteers. After the funeral, a four hour leave was given for family visitations and sight seeing. One of their number, Volodymyr Keczun recalled a memorable experience in the city:

> [...] I did not know anything about L'viv but Lischynsky used to attend technical college there and knew it inside out and took me sightseeing. We visited a cafe where students used to meet and there we met two of his friends. We had very enjoyable evening. I was warned not to order anything with mince meat in it. Later I learned that this was because during the war the butchers used to mix meat with dog's flesh.[255]

The detachment remained in the city overnight and on the morning of 13 February a parade of the company was held along the streets of L'viv. The orchestra played Ukrainian marches which were greeted by applause from the public and in the afternoon the company was ordered to return post haste to Heidelager reaching Kochanówka station before midnight.

3

First Combat Assignments

First Deployment Kampfgruppe Beyersdorff

The directive to form an Ehrencompanie, at the beginning of February for ceremonial purposes may have been an inconvenience, however its arrival coincided with an additional order which had far more serious connotations.

In the first weeks of 1944, Soviet partisans of the 1 Sydir Kovpak[1] Ukrainian Partisan Division, commanded by Petro Vershigora, successfully penetrated the territory of the General Government. Together with local partisan bands it conducted numerous raids behind the front line, undermining German security in the rear areas and causing fear amongst the civilian population.[2] This area was under the jurisdiction of SS-Obergruppenführer Wilhelm Koppe,[3] the Higher-SS and Polizei Leader in the General Government. Koppe's view was that military units were to be utilised as it was expedient to do so, in order to maintain and secure the remaining German held territory. With no regard for the 'political significance' that either the Ukrainians themselves or Governor Wächter invested in them, he responded to these developments by contacting the Reichsführer-SS directly with an urgent request for additional resources. In so doing he successfully secured Himmler's consent to using a Kampfgruppe (battle group) from the Galician Division to be supplemented with the 4 and 5 Galizischen SS-Freiwilligen Regiments for this purpose.[4] Neither Governor Wächter nor the Division's command, both of whom were sure to have vehemently opposed the prospect of deploying the Ukrainian units in this way, were consulted. Thus it was under such ominous circumstances that the first Ukrainian recruits were to receive their baptism of fire.

For the Ukrainians, the timing could not have been worse. At the beginning of February 1944, all the Divisional sub units were engaged in general training activities at Heidelager. SS-Oberführer Freitag who lacked the requisite experience as a divisional commander, had taken leave from his duties to attend the 9 Divisional Commanders Course which was held in Hirschberg, in the Sudenten

Mountains of Silesia and lasted from 3 February until 1 March 1944.[5] In his absence command of the Division reverted to the senior regimental commander SS-Obersturmbannführer Friedrich Beyersdorff.[6]

A decrypted enigma message in the British National Archives reveals that during Freitag's absence, on the 9 February 1944,[7] HSSPF Koppe, contacted the commander of the Heidelager camp SS-Brigadeführer Voss by telephone. Voss in turn passed on Koppe's order to the acting command of the Galician Division that it was to immediately form a Kampfgruppe for Antipartisaneneinsatz (anti-partisan deployment).

According to the directive, the strength of the Kampfgruppe was to be one infantry regiment and one detachment of light artillery supported by detachments of pioneers and anti-tank grenadiers. The order which was allegedly based on Himmler's personal instructions, further specified that the Kampfgruppe was to be placed under the jurisdiction of SS-Obergruppenführer Koppe in his capacity as the SS and Polizei leader of the General Government. It was to be ready to march within 24 hours.[8]

In a radio communication to the SS Operations HQ, SS-Brigadeführer Voss later recounted receipt of the directive for the formation of the unit and confirmed that no written order to this effect had ever existed. His message read:

> The order given for the operation by a Battle Group was given over the telephone by HSSuPF. OSTLAND, SS Obergruf. KOPPE, who in this matter was completely with the opinion of Chief of SS. Ops. HQ.
> I have forwarded this order to H.Q. of 14 Division.
> All further matters will be [arranged] direct between the HSSuPF and 14 Division.
> At the request of SS Obergruf. KOPPE, I promised over the telephone to strengthen the Battle Group with four Sturmgeschütze (assault guns).[...]
> **There is no written record of either of those matters.**[9] (author's emphasis).

SS-Obersturmbannführer Beyersdorff and his staff were understandably reluctant to comply with the unexpected order which involved temporarily surrendering control of its soldiers to the Polizei authorities for security duties. Having already been required to organise the Ehrencompanie at short notice, it was now to utilise additional personnel who had not yet completed their training. This caused considerable disruption at a critical point in the training schedule, but all efforts to have it rescinded on these grounds were to no avail.

Having been with the Division less than six weeks, the directive placed Beyersdorff in a serious dilemma. After reviewing the available resources and conferring with his senior officers, he contacted Koppe in Cracow and notified him that the Division was not in a position to comply with the order to supply such a large unit at short notice. Instead he proffered a compromise; a smaller battle group would be provided which because of organisational and supply difficulties, would consist of one infantry battalion reinforced with one battery of light field artillery and various support elements. He also indicated clearly that as the officer corps would have to be organised from scratch, forty eight hours grace and not twenty four would be required to oversee its formation. He specified that as the Division had not yet completed its training the proposed battle group would be nowhere near 'combat ready'. Moreover, despite taking command of the unit personally, under the circumstances he could not be held responsible for its performance in action.[10]

Koppe responded by agreeing to a temporary postponement to allow additional time to make the necessary preparations. In the meantime the modified unit was formed by its staff from the best soldiers and officers and readied in anticipation of its imminent deployment. Shortly thereafter,[11] Koppe called again and repeated the order, this time demanding the battle group arrive in the district north west of L'viv within 24 hours to engage Soviet partisans active in that area.

In its final form, the Kampfgruppe was comprised of approximately 2,000 men (from the total of 12,794 men of all ranks listed on the Division's strength return as of 13 February 1943.[12]) It consisted of; one infantry battalion, one light artillery battery (of six artillery pieces), one platoon of pioneers, one anti-tank platoon, a communications section, one supply section and a cavalry reconnaissance unit.[13] Since the majority of the senior German unit commanders within the Division had yet to be appointed, the Kampfgruppe with three exceptions was officered by Ukrainians. The staff of the battle group were as follows:

Commander: SS-Obersturmbannführer Friedrich Beyersdorff
Operations Officer: SS-Hauptsturmführer Johannes Kleinow
Liaison: Waffen-Hauptsturmführer Dmytro Paliiv
Commander (Inf. Bat): SS-Hauptsturmführer Karl Bristot
Adjutant: Waffen-Obersturmführer Michael Kaczmar
Commander (Art battery):[14] Waffen-Hauptsturmführer Mykola Palijenko
Logistics and supplies: Waffen-Obersturmführer Josef Polakiv
Cavalry reconnaissance squad: Waffen-Hauptsturmführer Roman Dolynsky
Veterinary: Waffen-Untersturmführer Dr Volodymyr Kischko
Chaplain: Waffen-Untersturmführer Fr. Vsevolod Durbak
Signals squadron: Waffen-Untersturmführer Adrian Demchuk

Of these, only Beyersdorff and Bristot had recent combat experience.

Having assembled the requisite men, horses and equipment in mid-February 1944,[15] the forces assigned to the Kampfgruppe left Heidelager and entrained at the Kochanówka railway station.[16] As the loading process began, the ad hoc nature of the Kampfgruppe immediately became apparent from the inexperience of most of its personnel. The resulting improvisation which now took place was described by a participant as 'a horrible sight'.[17] In particular, problems arose with the horses tack because it came in several parts which none of the soldiers had experience in assembling. Eventually, after several hours the unit had boarded three troop trains[18] which departed for the Cholmshchyna region situated to the north west of L'viv. This was a highly volatile region where the underground forces of the Polish and Ukrainian populations were locked in bitter conflict.

The four Sturmgeschütze were entrained and together with the artillery moved by rail directly to Lubachev. The infantry transports were diverted through L'viv, because of the destruction of a rail bridge on the direct route.[19] While they were waiting on their trains in the Galician capital, the soldiers were visited by members of the Military Board from whom they received packages of food, cigarettes, newspapers and other items which were distributed by the Women's Auxiliary Board (a subsidiary branch of the Military Board).[20] The unit also marched along the main street of the city in full battle uniforms in order to boost the morale of the inhabitants.[21]

A few days later, after frequent stops at various stations, the infantry units joined the artillery in Lubachev.[22] In this area the Kampfgruppe was to combine with other Army and local Polizei detachments (including elements of Gal. SS-Freiw.Rgt.5) and the armoured support from 4 Sturmgeschütze. Their objective was to eradicate the partisan units which had been active in the Lublin district of the General Government. To achieve this, the Germans planned a three phase encirclement operation co-ordinated by Fieseler Storch light reconnaissance aircraft which would pass on orders directly to the units involved. Kampfgruppe Beyersdorff being the largest of the detachments taking part, was deployed in the southern sector in the areas of Krasnik, Lubachev, Cieszanów, Zamość, Tarnogrod, Bilgoraj and Tomaszow. Julian Chornij was a member of the battlegroup:

I was assigned to the 'Stabswache' which was a guard for our commanding officer SS-Obersturmbannführer Beyersdorff. He chose me to be responsible for his personal belongings and to assist him with some of his activities because I was fluent in German and Polish. Our enemy, the Polish and Soviet partisans were coordinating their actions against us, but most of the time they were trying to avoid a fight with our troops. Usually they retreated and stayed deep in wooded areas. Our unit had three Sturmgeschütze. [four Sturmgeschütze were assigned to the battlegroup but one suffered damage to its tracks from a mine after only one day]. These were in front of our column which consisted of a few light passenger cars, about a dozen heavy trucks and plenty of horse-drawn wagons. One day we were advancing across a wide field on a snow covered road, when the Sturmgeschütze commander stopped his armour. He approached our Swimmwagen and informed us that he suspected that there might be mines on the road and was afraid that a powerful mine might damage one of his vehicles. To avoid the risk, he ordered the driver of our Swimmwagen to ride ahead of the Sturmgeschütze. Apparently the officer was applying a less risky strategy of comparing the loss of one Sturmgeschütze and crew with one Swimmwagen with three soldiers (including myself). We were depressed about the decision but an order is an order so we had to follow it.

We were driving for a while until we spotted some mines on the road which the wind had swept clear of snow. To avoid being blown up we drove in the fields next to the road with the Sturmgeschütze following us. Driving in the fields was strenuous because they had been ploughed and the soil was frozen and rutted. Our car was constantly bumping hard and this caused one of the wheels to break off. There was no way to repair the car so we abandoned it. Now the Sturmgeschütze commander

L'viv, February 1944 members of Kampfgruppe Beyersdorff at the railway station en route to the front received packages of foodstuff and newspapers. Here a soldier reads *L'vivsti Visti* (*L'viv news*).

Right: L'viv, February 1944. Whilst waiting at the railway station en route to the front, part of KGr Beyersdorff was asked to parade through the streets to boost the morale of the residents of the city.

Below: L'viv, February 1944. The same group marching through the streets of L'viv received a warm welcome from the local inhabitants. Their membership of Kampfgruppe Beyersdorff can be ascertained by virtue of the incorrect positioning of the Galician armshield on the lower right arm.

Contemporary photo of Bilgoraj where KGr. Beyersdorff conducted its operations.

told us to climb on the Sturmgeschütze and the column continued to move ahead. The ride was worse than in the car. The day was very frosty and windy and we had no protection sitting on top of the very cold metal with cold hands trying to keep our balance in order not to fall off. In addition some partisans were firing at us from distant woods because we were exposed like sitting ducks. Lucky no one was hit. Half frozen we arrived at a Polish village where we stayed for a couple of days.[...]

While we were stationed in a small town, our staff was located in the town hall on the first floor. I was present when Beyersdorff came to the office in a very agitated state. Then he told us the reason for his excitement. While entering the back seat of his car he was holding his Bergmann automatic machine gun in his hands. While sitting down he hit the butt of the gun on the floor of the car. This caused the loading mechanism of the gun to slide down and then fire a bullet in the chamber. The bullet has missed his head by a fraction of an inch.

Everybody in the room was warned to be very careful with this kind of automatic weapon. In order to demonstrate how the gun had fired, he took it and hit it on the wooden floor and again his gun fired. During the demonstration all of us were standing around him and this time the bullet went into the ceiling. We were astonished and frightened but some of us had to subdue our laughter because the bullet had passed through the ceiling next to a person sitting there at a desk and they started shouting 'the partisans are attacking us![23]

Almost immediately the Kampfgruppe suffered its first casualties. Again Julian Chornij:

[...] Our unit also lost two men by friendly fire. Two of our soldiers while patrolling a village during the night were stopped by the German military police and ordered to drop their rifles because the police had heard them speaking but not in German. The soldiers hesitated to drop their rifles. The German police suspected that they were partisans dressed in military uniforms opened fire and killed both of them. This was a very painful loss for us. The mishap resulted in ordering all German units to stay away from the terrain controlled by our forces.[24]

Shortly thereafter on 27 February Oberstuf. Beyersdorff issued Order No. 2 which laid down explicitly the rules and regulations concerning discipline and the forthcoming combat. It read:

Battle Group Beyersdorff Headquarters,   2/27/1944.

Daily order # 2.
Our group is fighting as the vanguard of our Division. Her good name will cover in glory the Division and all the Ukrainian nation just as shameful deeds will disgrace the Division and the nation. But besides the military successes, the behavior of the Division's elements will also be judged over and above battle action, when they both march and rest.

Therefore I remind you for the last time:

1. The soldiers of the Kampfgruppe must not arrest civilians on their own. Where required by military necessity, the suspects must be apprehended and delivered to the command post.

2. Shooting at civilians is only permitted when they are armed and attempt to use their weapon, or when they are ordered to halt but attempt to flee.

3. It is forbidden to beat and abuse those who have been apprehended.

4. It is strictly forbidden to plunder or to acquire any goods on your own will.

5. During marches and rests it is forbidden to depart from your unit without permission. This will result in very severe consequences for the transgressor. Do not forget that we are in an area which is not favourably disposed to us. Remember too that the bandits, whom we are fighting, may also be dressed in the uniforms of German soldiers, Waffen-SS and German police.
  Unauthorized departure from his unit may cost the volunteer his life, as has unfortunately occurred in two cases. Do not forget with us on our flanks other German units are in action, therefore it is obvious that staying together is even more necessary.

6. On a recent inspection I found that the rifles of some soldiers are so rusty that they are hardly usable in action. Despite my many reminders, some weapons are still not maintained and I will therefore consider unit commanders personally responsible for the state of all weapons.

I expect the officers and NCOs to be hard and demanding toward their responsibilities and equally strict with their soldiers. Do not forget that only strict discipline will lead to great success with least casualties. Lack of discipline will always cause unnecessary loss of lives and be of great advantage to the enemy.[25]

Signed. by Beyersdorff
Obersturmbannführer and Commander

The heavily forested region in which the battlegroup was deployed, favoured the activities of the Soviet-led partisans who received willing support from some elements of the Polish population which provided food, local guides and information about troop activities.

As was noted above, German intelligence had established that the insurgents often wore various items of attire including German Army, Waffen-SS and Polizei uniforms whilst others dressed in civilian clothing and spoke Polish making them indistinguishable from the local civilians. These factors combined with the terrain and the bitterly cold winter weather made the task of combating them extraordinarily difficult. Operating on horseback often in small groups they exploited their mobility using sledges for their light cannons and equipment and always held the initiative. Direct confrontations were avoided and they resorted instead to devious methods, adopting hit and run tactics. After cutting communications lines, they would attack administrative centres, storage and depot facilities and raid towns and villages. To prevent pursuit they would blow up railway lines, mine and block roads and destroy bridges on the main routes which often necessitated lengthy and tiring detours of up to 20 kilometres on poor field roads.

For their part, the Ukrainian soldiers who had been trained for regular combat, had received no instruction in anti-partisan warfare, consequently they were therefore obliged to learn the appropriate tactics in the field. Moreover, some of the soldiers had not been issued with any warm winter clothing at the outset and only received felt boots and winter coats a few days after their arrival in the field.[26]

In the initial stages, units of the Kampfgruppe primarily conducted reconnaissance missions and patrols, led by its cavalry squad which soon proved to be its most effective unit. These undertakings were often confined to marches in freezing weather on icy roads through snow and mud in remote areas with contact limited to occasional skirmishes.[27] Occasionally they discovered evidence of the presence of the evasive insurgents in the form of abandoned positions and deserted towns and villages with burnt houses and heavily barricaded local government buildings. When civilians were present, they were almost always old people and children. Sporadic engagements did take place towards the end of the operation, but did not result in conclusive battles. According to Waffen-Untersturmführer Mychailo Dlaboha

This photograph shows members of the Kampfgruppe who received their issue of winter clothing after arriving in their operations area.

March 1944 Sverzha on the Buh River. Units from the Kampfgruppe in bunker positions.

Left: Portrait of a soldier from the Kampfgruppe (note incorrect position of armshield).

Below: This picture taken from the Divisional newspaper *To Victory* shows elements of the Kampfgruppe conversing with locals civilians.

Unit from the Kampfgruppe patrolling in the Sverkha region.

this was because the German commanders were inexperienced in partisan warfare and Beyersdorff preferred the advice of his operations officer SS-Hauptsturmführer Johannes Kleinow to that of his Ukrainian officers such as Waffen-Hauptsturmführer Ivan Rembolovych (who had participated in two anti-partisan 'winter campaigns' in 1919–1920).[28] This in turn resulted in several heated exchanges and arguments.[29]

Details of the Kampfgruppe's activities during this period can be found in the daily Polizei situation reports for March 1944, by the Operations Officer of the Kommandeur der in the district of Lublin to the Ortskommandantur of the Wehrmacht in Lublin. According to these reports, on 28 February 1944, Kampfgruppe Beyersdorff joined 1./SS-Gend.Batl. (mot), III./SS-Pol.17 and II./Gal.SS-Freiw.Rgt.5. II/SS-Pol.25 which had begun an action on 24 February against 'a large band' of partisans which had gathered in the southern part of the counties of Krasnik, Bilgoraj and Zamość and which planned to attack Janów.[30] With the arrival of these security forces in the area, the partisan group withdrew to the south eastern part of the forest of Bilgoraj, leaving behind strategically placed mines. Here it remained until under pressure from the pursuing units it was forced to retreat to the area of Chmielek, Lukowa and Osuchy. In the vicinity of the village of Chmielek, situated between Bilgoraj and Tarnogrod, at 1530 on 4 March 1944, elements of KGr. Beyersdorff and II./Gal.SS-Freiw. Rgt 5 with a combined strength of 300 men, equipped with heavy weapons, mortars and cannons, together with Gend. Zug (mot.) 72, came into contact and fought a rare large pitched battle with the enemy group.

Approaching from a westerly direction the assault began mid-afternoon. By 1745 hrs, the attacking forces were further strengthened by I./SS-Gend.Batl and one platoon of Sturmgeschütze. These attacked from Babice, outflanking the insurgent group which was reported to be between 400–1,000 men, and which had left in its rear numerous supplies and horses. The fighting near Chmielek with the strong rear guard broke off at 2000 hrs, excessive use of ammunition having been made by both sides. The enemy then retreated at Osuchy eastwards under cover of darkness.[31] During this fighting by Chmielek, KGr. Beyersdorff lost two dead and six wounded including Waffen-Obersturmführer Jurij Cherkashyn, whilst the II./Gal.SS-Freiw. Rgt 5, lost one seriously wounded (by a mine) and three lightly wounded. Enemy losses amounted to 17 counted dead, although the report states that 'many of the killed were taken away by the partisans on carts'. Several Panjewagons, together with a saddle and many submachine gun magazines were captured along with thirteen horses while a further five horses were killed.[32]

On 5 and 6 March Kampfgruppe Beyersdorff together with elements of the I./SS-Pol.4, II./Gal. SS-Freiw. Rgt 5, and I./SS-Gend. Batl. (mot.), supported by two Sturmgeschütze continued to pursue the group and attempted to encircle it. This resulted in a further heavy exchange of fire around midday on 6 March near the village of Kosobudy.[33] Once again, a large group of partisans managed to escape and despite significant casualties continued to undertake further operations in the coming weeks.[34]

Waffen-Schütze Volodymyr Keczun's unit participated in the action with elements of the 5 regiment:

[...] When 5 company arrived back at Heidelager after the funeral in L'viv, other companies were already packed on trains to depart via L'viv to the Lublin region. A few hours later we left camp to join them. On the front of our train was an empty wagon as a precaution in case the railway line was mined. When we arrived our 'Zug' was assigned to a company (I don't remember which) and we started marching, with our transport, from village to village in pursuit of the Soviet 'Kovpak' partisans. Everywhere the snow was very deep. It looked like the partisans were playing with us and having a good laugh at our expense. Each time we got news that partisans were in some village, by the time we marched there they were gone. It seems they had better transport and help from Polish partisans who knew all the short cuts. It was good exercise for us for marching and doing sentry duty in villages. The populace in the villages was mixed: Polish and Ukrainian—Roman Catholic and Orthodox so there was enmity here. That explains some burnt out villages with only chimneys sticking from the ground as we marched through.

Before we reached one village, I think it was called Sul (Salt), some joker sprayed blue powder over the snow on the road, so we felt silly marching along it. We were very well equipped with modern armaments but the biggest mistake was issuing us with special boots for that campaign. They were high boots up to the knee but made of felt. They had leather only on the toe caps and heels. After walking in deep snow they became wet and it was very hard to dry them overnight, because every four hours we had sentry duty outside.

At last warmer weather arrived. Snow could be seen only on high grounds but it was still freezing cold and damp. One early morning orders came to be ready for departure, but without mortars. Instead of marching, trucks arrived to take us to our destination. Late morning we arrived in a narrow valley.

We got two surprises there: first, unknown to us there was already another company here. Among their soldiers I found five lads from my village, who joined the army in July 1943 two months before me. They arrived from a training camp near Gdansk. They were surprised that we already had MG 42s, while their machine guns were ancient water cooled Nol Acht (08), similar to Russian Maksims only more reliable. The second surprise: there was at least one cannon with a long barrel positioned just about 50 metres from us and then it dawned on me that this was not going to be the usual futile exercise, but dangerous and for real.

The other company marched to the left of us to take up position and as we learned later to cover our advance to the village. After a while we marched by the cannons up a slight hill. When we got to the top we could see the other company digging in and then further on the left a forest and in front of us, about three quarters of a kilometre distant, a village. Orders came to spread out as much as possible because we would be advancing down a slope without any cover. On a command (I think it was a very sharp whistle) we went over the rim in scattered formation and started to advance down the hill. Cannon started shooting at the village and a few sputtering shots were fired from the company on our left wing at the village. Then the partisans started shooting at us and at the other company. When I heard the first bullets whistling above my head, I hit the ground in no time. An Unterscharführer came to me and told me to ignore the bullets that I could hear because I would not hear the one destined for me.

After a few shots, the machine guns on our left stopped firing. Later we heard that the cooling water froze and they had seized up. We were lucky that we reached a fairly long embankment about 200 metres from the village. It wasn't very high but enough to hide us from the partisans. It seemed that in that attack our company had at least one soldier wounded because we could hear him yelling from pain.

To give our company better cover in a further advance, we assembled our three MG 42s on carriages [Laffetes], and started firing at the partisan positions over the rim of the embankment. After a while, there were no more shots coming at us so orders came for a slow advance and for us to keep them covered. Once the company occupied the village we dissembled our MGs and joined them. The partisans could not withstand our fire power and decided to retreat through the forest to another village. They left two or three members to hold us up and later rejoin them.

It was getting dark. After about one hours rest and some coffee, we got orders to follow the partisans to the next village and try to corner them there. What happened to the other company and artillery, I don't know. It was dark when we entered the forest and it started raining. Progress was very slow because we had to check for traps. I don't know how long we marched through the forest but it was well after midnight that we emerged from the forest and behold, there was a village, a haven for tired, wet and starving soldiers. Then suddenly orders were issued not to enter the village because there was a typhus epidemic there. Everywhere there were signs in the German language, even on houses, so our unit found a hay stack just outside the village, worked out sentry duty and climbed into the hay to sleep.

What a night! When our uniforms started to dry, heat built up and we started steaming. The lice didn't like it and went on the rampage. All that suffering was for nothing. One inquisitive soldier on sentry duty started snooping around and found out that the 'typhus epidemic' was a sham to keep unwanted visitors out.

We missed the partisans, because about half way to the village they went over a river bridge to the other side and another village. At least we got a very good reception from the villagers (they were Ukrainian speaking) and housewives prepared a very good meal for us. Soon after this episode in our campaign we departed to Neuhammer.[…][35]

A few days later the entire Kampfgruppe was withdrawn from duty and given a week of rest. On 17 March 1944,[36] the first elements entrained at the railway station in the village of Zwierzyniec for the return trip to the Division[37] which in the meantime had relocated to a new training ground at Neuhammer in Silesia. Travelling via Lublin and Kielce, upon arrival at their new camp the soldiers were first quarantined for one week in the wooden barracks of the former POW camp 'Swietoszow' before being re-integrated.[38] During the entire campaign the casualties suffered by the Kampfgruppe were minimal.[39] Among the seriously wounded was a Ukrainian grenadier who lost a leg when he stood on a land mine while crossing a bridge[40] and another casualty Waffen-Schütze Mychailo Mykytiuk whose cause of death was not established.[41]

In recognition of its participation in the operation, in Neuhammer the battle group was paraded one last time for the presentation of decorations by the Divisional commander before being disbanded.[42]

Predictably, HSSPF Koppe was critical of the Kampfgruppe's performance and this negative view gained currency when shortly after its return, two accusations of misconduct by Ukrainian members of the unit were filed with the Divisional command.

The criticisms were largely unfounded and made no allowance for the prevailing circumstances under which it was forced to operate and over which it had no control. According to the Division's 1(a) Major Heike, throughout the campaign the detachment had been subordinated to a Polizei general in Peremyshl. Being 'completely ignorant of military tactics and command', he had not only been responsible for its inept utilisation but for failing to keep the unit adequately supplied.[43] The unfavourable climatic conditions also hampered the performance of the Kampfgruppe which faced experienced and highly mobile partisans. In addition the suggestion has also been made that the Germans showed a marked reluctance to engage the partisans, often declaring an area Partisanen Gebiet (partisan territory) and simply moving round it.[44]

Kampfgruppe Beyersdorff with motorised transport during its operations.

Machine gun team from the Kampfgruppe in action against partisans, March 1944.

Unidentified officer of the Kampfgruppe in Sverzha on the Buh River, March 1944.

March 1944, Kadlubyska in the province of Polissia unidentified German officer and 4 NCOs officiate at the funeral of a Ukrainian member of the Kampfgruppe who originated from the town of Drohobych.

Even so, the undertaking did have some benefits in that it provided the officers and men who took part in the campaign with valuable combat experience. The presence of the battle group also limited the partisans' activities and hindered their infiltration into the neighbouring Ukrainian territory and also brought the first decorations for valour to Ukrainians serving with the Division.

As for the allegations of wrongdoing, in his memoirs Heike maintains that it became apparent to the Divisional command that German units operating in the same area often 'blamed many of their own misdeeds on the non German unit from the Division (i.e. the Kampfgruppe)'.[45]

The first recorded case of misconduct by Ukrainian personnel within the Kampfgruppe concerned the company led by Waffen-Untersturmführer Bohdan Sobolewsky whose soldiers appropriated additional meat from the local population for their field kitchen. Unaware of this Sobolewsky denied the report to his German superior. When he learned from the company cook that livestock had indeed been illegally requisitioned by his men he felt his 'officer's honour' to be at stake and consequently on 13 March 1944, he shot himself.[46] He was buried locally by soldiers from the Kampfgruppe with a priest officiating and a Ukrainian officer from the group command.[47]

The second case involved the alleged mistreatment of a civilian by a soldier from the battlegroup. With no time for a proper investigation Beyersdorff wanted to have the soldier shot in front of the entire battlegroup and the inhabitants of the village as a warning about the consequences of criminal behaviour. It was only because of the intervention of the Ukrainian officers that Beyersdorff was

Award ceremony April 1944, Neuhammer. Freitag addresses the soldiers whilst Palii translates.

Freitag and Paliiv inspect the soldiers.

The first soldiers receive their awards personally from Freitag, April 1944. *Photo Courtesy Richard Rygaard archive*

Waffen-Obersturmführer Roman Levyckyj is decorated April 1944.

finally persuaded to delay his decision and submit him for appropriate trial when the battlegroup returned to its training base.[48] Indeed any cases of proven breaches of discipline by the Division's soldiers however minor, were dealt with by SS-Oberführer Freitag with draconian severity in line with the strict disciplinary code.

Security Duties for 4 and 5 Galizischen SS-Freiwilligen Regiments.

When HSSPF Koppe secured Himmler's approval to form a Kampfgruppe from the Galician Division he simultaneously obtained permission for the 4 and 5 Galician SS-Freiwilligen Regiments to be assigned to him for similar tasks.

The situation with both regiments was identical to that of the Galician Division, in that training had not yet been completed and an ill-advised deployment was likely to jeopardise the progress which had been made. The controlling Ordnungspolizei authority for the 4 Regiment,[49] responded to the plan to utilise it in the east with a secret teleprinter dated 4 February warning that it was 'not ready for deployment'. In justification, the message went on to detail the Regiment's many deficiencies which included the status of the signals company which had not been issued with any radios or communications equipment. It also lacked the necessary light motorised vehicles (with drivers), horses tack and twelve recruits with weapons for the battalions' signals platoons. It went on to state that fifteen recruits were needed to replace 'losses sustained' [cause unspecified] and a replacement for the Regimental doctor who was classified as 'totally unfit for active duty'. Attention was also drawn to the fact that 120 of the newly arrived recruits had only undergone very limited basic training. Matériel shortages identified were four additional riding and ten cart horses and miscellaneous equipment such as wagons, medical packs and equipment for two field kitchens. The document concluded that only when these matters had been addressed would the Regiment would be ready for active deployment. Consequently, a specific date for its readiness could not be given.[50]

The B.d.O. (Befehlshaber der Ordnungspolizei) Danzig which controlled the 5 Regiment, filed a similar report dated 3 February 1944. It too identified shortages of weaponry and matériel, especially wagons and associated gear and two urgently needed motor vehicles. Signals equipment, clothing and various weapons parts were still needed, as were specialist personnel which were listed as; two veterinarians, three German doctors (one for each battalion), one foreign [Ukrainian] doctors assistant, one officer for the signals company, one dental technician and twenty recruits (for unspecified positions). According to the report, the units mobility was compromised as 90 of the regiment's assignment of horses were sick and would not be fit for utilisation until the end of March. Most importantly it stated that the 16 week basic training for recruits was not scheduled to be completed until 5 March 1944, and that 'earlier deployment would not guarantee success'. For the aforementioned reasons it therefore concluded that the regiment would not be combat ready until 15 March 1944.[51]

Disregarding their protests and excuses, on 9 February 1944, the office of the Chef der Ordnungspolizei in Berlin sent a circular to all relevant authorities. It stated that on the orders of the Reichsführer SS, the 4 and 5 regiments were to be transferred at once by train in full strength, to the B.d.O. in Cracow (HSSPF Koppe) who would control their deployment.[52]

Once again Wächter, who felt that using the Ukrainian volunteers in this way would defeat their intended political purpose,[53] was not consulted by either Himmler or Koppe in the matter but despite his misgivings, he was unable to intervene and prevent their utilisation. Faced with a fate accompli he contrived to salvage what he could from the situation.

The public appearance of Ukrainian troops in the Galician capital as the Honour Guard at Otto Bauer's funeral[54] was proving to be a great success. Cognisant of this, Wächter contacted Berger asking him to prevail upon Himmler for authorisation to interrupt the journey of a battalion from one of the regiments[55] en route to its area of operations so that it could be used for propaganda purposes. Berger passed on Wächter's request to Himmler in an urgent secret teleprinter message dated 14 February 1944 for one of the Polizei battalions of the 4. Gal. SS-Freiwilligen-Regiment passing through L'viv, to spend one to two days in the city to take part in a large propaganda demonstration. Subject to the Reichsführer's authorisation, he recommended the 2. btl. of the 4. Regiment be used.[56]

Two days later, Himmler notified Koppe via a secret teleprinter message that he was 'in agreement with any employment of both Galician SS Freiwilligen Regiments', noting 'You have full authority. Consider temporary use in fight against the partisans essential and correct'. The teleprinter message also stated that the decision regarding Wächter's request to use the Galicians for propaganda purposes would be left to Koppe.[57]

Accordingly, in February 1944, on Himmler's authority, Koppe issued instructions for both Regiments to move to the rear areas of the eastern front; the 4 Regiment moved to the Zbarazh region in Galicia[58] and the 5 for the vicinity of Lublin, Hrubeshiv and Cholm (the same area as Kampfgruppe Beyersdorff).

As per Wächter's request, on 25 February the I battalion (not the II as per the original plan) of the 4 Regiment arrived at L'viv station en route to its designated sector, where the soldiers were welcomed enthusiastically by a large crowd of Ukrainian civilians including the women's help service.[59] The battalion then marched to a gathering at the Statthalterpalais where several senior members of the German administration in Galicia and local dignitaries had gathered including the SS-und Polizeiführer in Galicia SS-Brigadeführer Thier, the Amtschef (chief of administration) Dr Brandl, the commander of the 4 Rgt. SS-Obersturmbannführer und Major der Schutzpolizei Siegfried Binz and representatives of the Military Board and the Ukrainian Central Committee.[60]

The battalion was assembled beneath the balcony in the Statthalterpalais where they were addressed in the name of the Military Board by Evhen Pyndus. He urged the soldiers to fight at a time when the Soviet advance on their homeland was coming closer, as worthy successors to their fathers and stressed that the Military Board 'that cared for you so far, will continue to care for you in future'.[61]

Governor Wächter then gave a speech. In contrast to Pyndus, Wächter seized this opportunity to redress the growing influence of the Ukrainian underground movement, by refuting the main opposition arguments against Ukrainians serving in German uniforms. To do this he emphasised that the assembled soldiers had not been enlisted as 'cannon fodder', that would be sent untrained and under-equipped to remote theatres which did not concern the Ukrainians people. Instead as well trained and well equipped soldiers they were being deployed in their homeland in defence of their people. In closing he sought to discredit the strong the influence of the UPA calling on them to reject once and for all the unscrupulous methods employed by the partisans.[62]

Wächter's concern was a harbinger of the inevitability of the events that were to follow. The Ukrainians did not reject the advances of the nationalist partisans (UPA), rather they whole heartedly embraced them as was demonstrated unequivocally when the soldiers of both regiments sought out UPA units at the first opportunity, deserted in droves or clandestinely furnished them with German made weaponry, ammunition and supplies.[63]

With their propaganda activities in L'viv over, the Lemberger Zeitung reported the battalion formed into a column and marched to the station singing, on its way to rejoining its parent 4 Regiment.[64] It was to concentrate its activities in the Brody and Ternopil/Zbarazh districts which were designated as the staging points for actions designed to secure the partisan menaced rear areas of the German Army fighting on the eastern front.

While the 4 Regiment was active in Galicia, the 5 Regiment arrived in the Cholm district where it took over the task of supervising local conscripted labour who were constructing bunkers and defensive fortifications along the Buh River and guarding the positions from attacks by partisans.

Immediately upon arrival in their respective zones, the Germans encountered serious problems with both regiments as the fundamental deficiencies from which both suffered, soon began to manifest themselves.

The Operations of Gal. SS-Freiw. Rgt 4

Commanded by SS-Obersturmbannführer und Major der Schutzpolizei Binz, Gal. SS-Freiw. Rgt 4 was assigned to a sector in the L'viv area, populated by a mixture of Ukrainians and Poles.[65] Here it operated under the overall command of SS-Oberführer Karl Burk who was the senior commander for border protection units and was engaged in security duties and fighting partisans along a front which stretched for 170 kilometres,[66] which drastically undermined its limited capability. It was further hampered by limited manoeuvrability for its personnel and equipment, lack of a heavy company in the II. and III. battalions, effective communications and according to its commander, a 'Ukrainian doctor who was too soft towards the sick'.[67]

Regimental headquarters was based approximately in the centre of its lines at Zolochiv with its three battalions roughly aligned north to south; I. battalion was based in Radechiv, II. battalion in the Koniushkiv[68] and III. battalion closest to the main front in the town of Zbarazh. Here they conducted reconnaissance missions, repaired roads, and carried out routine security operations against partisans leaving more technical work such as clearing mine fields to be undertaken by its specialist units such as the pioneer zug.[69] Indeed it was the pioneer zug of the I battalion which was one of the first units to register desertions to the UPA when ten out of the twelve men did so with their weapons, having first cut the throat of their German Oberscharführer.[70] With an exclusively German complement of officers and NCOs and general dissatisfaction with their assignment, there was inevitable friction between the Ukrainians and their German commanders. Symptomatic of this were the many desertions to the UPA which would become a constant feature of its deployment.

One of the major difficulties facing the 4 Regiment was that its component units were spread out and deployed in isolated pockets close to the front line. Its battalions were therefore subject to ever more concentrated attacks from Soviet and Polish partisans who aimed to disrupt the rear of the German front line prior to an imminent Soviet offensive in the vicinity. As a result of the fluid front, units including those of I. battalion were frequently forced to relocate and short notice. SS-Schütze Myron Lewytskyj was a Kriegsberichter (war reporter) assigned to I. Btl. 4 Gal.SS-Rgt. He gave this account of how he became temporarily detached from his unit:

After the delivery of my report with SS Obscharführer Weyer, on 25.3.1944 I went to Radechiv (I.Batl.4.Gal.SS Frw. Rgt.) and found the Batl. was no longer there as it had moved from this site. While searching for the new battalion headquarters I was taken prisoner by two Ukrainian nationalist partisans. Because they had formerly known me as an artist-painter, they kept me one day and then freed me with my personal documents and weapon. The next morning these partisans showed me the way to the rear guard at Radechiv which I reached the following morning. I waited until 1500 hrs to ride in a truck from Radechiv to Lopatyn. Before I could get my rucksack, the truck drove off without me and then I made my way on foot in the direction of Stojaniw in order to find our bunkers.

The weather was very bad and I got lost and arrived at our front line positions without knowing it, in a snowstorm. I slept in a small farmstead. In the morning I moved on and in the afternoon again I reached a small farm which according to the local residents was already subjected to Bolshevik patrols. I got a ring for my finger and civilian clothes and stowed my uniform and weapon in a bag and hid it. For one day and one night I hid in a barn. To find out about the situation with the population in the areas re-occupied by the Bolsheviks I went further into Volhynia and stayed overnight with a priest. The priest gave me an old cassock with a large cross on it and together we went from farmstead to farmstead to gather information. I always had my Soldbuch with me. I left the priest and I went in civilian clothing to Radechiv

Above left: The caption on this Kriegsberichter picture from *To Victory* reads 'Volunteer [from Galizischen-SS-Freiwilligen Regiment-4] with a Soviet machine gun he won from a Soviet position 300 metres distant'.

Above right: During a lull in the fighting the same volunteer in his dugout preparing his lunch.

where my unit (I Batl.) had arrived and reported back. I had to leave my uniform and weapon behind. On the way back I met no more partisans.[71]

The situation experienced by I battalion was repeated with the II battalion. Military Board member M. Khronoviat visited the 4 Regiment for almost two weeks at the end of February 1944 to see this for himself. Arriving at the regiment's HQ in Zolochiv, he was met by chaplain Karpinsky, who informed him of the general mood amongst the Ukrainians saying that 'the men wanted to shoot Germans!'[72]

Khronoviat went on to take part in an attack on the large Polish village of Huta Peniatska. This village (with approximately 1,000 inhabitants) is openly acknowledged to have become a well fortified armed stronghold and major resistance centre for both Polish and Soviet led partisan groups.[73] These partisans, in addition to harassing German supply columns and disrupting the rear areas of the German Army, also are known to have fought against the UPA as well as terrorising the local Ukrainian population by raiding the surrounding villages.

On 23 February 1944 a patrol which included elements of 2 company with an approximate strength of 60 men was operating in the area. On reaching the village the group encountered significant resistance and despite being armed with heavy machine guns and grenades were unable to take the village. The attack was beaten back resulting in the deaths of two Ukrainian soldiers, Roman Andrichuk and Oleksa Bobak[74] thereby confirming the size of the task confronting them. Their bodies, reported to have been found naked and mutilated, were recovered for burial after a second successful assault made five days later during which between eight—twelve Ukrainians were wounded, including Jurij Hanusiak who died of his wounds.

Having withdrawn, the Germans later brought in additional forces and began a 'pacification action' which ultimately led to the destruction of the village and the liquidation of many of the remaining civilian population.

Mychailo Khronoviat, one of three members of the Military Board, who visited the regiment at the time,[75] witnessed the second attack. In the account that he gave, he described how after the village had finally fallen and the Ukrainians had moved on, a German [Schutzpolizei] unit (unspecified) arrived which destroyed the village, setting fire to the houses (which began exploding because of the ammunition stored in them), and killing many of its inhabitants.[76]

In contrast, as expected several Polish and Soviet sources allege that Ukrainian soldiers from the battalion were present and took part in the pacification action often providing dramatic witness statements in support. These witness statements are often contradictory and confused in respect of dates, times and numbers involved.[77] These inconsistencies fundamentally undermine any credibility that they

Soldiers of Galizischen-SS-Freiwilligen-Regiment-4 with family members form a funeral procession for Roman Andriichuk and Oleska Bobak who were killed by partisans on 23 February 1944 at Huta Peniatska.

may have had. Consequently, despite public posturing by anti-Division elements, in the 70 odd years that have passed since the event, the available evidence has proved insufficient for the Polish authorities to ensure any prosecution or even that any allegation be subjected to due legal process in a court of law.[78]

The III. battalion (also identified as KGr. Mitscherling[79] after its commander) was deployed in the area east of Zbarazh under the overall command of XXXXVII 47 Pz Korps/Pz AOK 4. On 6 March it was subordinated to the battle commandant of Ternopil, General Major Schrepffer.[80] The previous day, on 5 March it was in position east of Lubianky when without warning it came into contact with Soviet tanks which formed the lead elements of the rapidly advancing Red Army which was due to begin an offensive in the area. Attacked by strong armoured forces, the battalion which lack anti-tank weaponry inevitably sustained substantial losses[81] and was forced to retreat to the south. On 7 March it withdrew further to Stupky and the main road Proskuriv-Pidvoloczys'ka-Ternopil and during the following night to Smykivtsi (7 km east of Ternopil). Finally under heavy pressure from the attacking elements of the 336 Soviet Rifle Division it fell back to Ternopil.[82]

By 11 March its strength had been reduced to one hundred and twenty men.[83] It was included in the defence of Festen Platzes Ternopil (Fortress Ternopil) in the northern sector.[84] Together with KGr. Krauss (parts of the II/SS-Inst. Abt. 1 LSSAH),[85] along with a mixed group of approximately 4,500 Wehrmacht troops, the survivors were encircled by Red Army units and virtually wiped out. Less than half a dozen broke out during the night of 16/17 April[86] and eventually returned to the Division.

From 30 April until 10 May the remnants of the Regiment were deployed under the command of 340. Infantry Division/4 Panzer Army (HKGr.Süd) with some success.

In April 1944, Governor Wächter accompanied by SS-Oberführer Karl Burk, together with Oleh Lysiak a Kriegsberichter and Karl Weyer a photographer from the Divisional newspaper Do Peremohy visited one company of the 4 Regiment based in the Kaminka Strumilova district. Here he witnessed the bestowal of the Iron Cross II. Class on twenty four men, twenty German and four Ukrainian of whom Vasyl Biletsky, Vasyl Vyklyuk, and Josyp Yunyk, were decorated for their bravery in combat with Red Army troops in the area.[87] The fourth Ukrainian Grygorij Bobel who the Divisional Newspaper referred to as the 'Hero of the battle for Ternopil', received the Iron Cross II. Class, the Nahkampfspange, (close combat clasp) the Infantry Assault Badge in silver (Infanterie-Sturmabzeichen in Silber) and the Wound Badge (Verwundetenabzeichen). Other individuals who received awards included Ivan Marchuk and Bohdan Hlushko.

In April, 1944 , Oleh Lysiak and Kreigsberichter Weyer visited one company of Galizischen-SS Freiwilligen Regiment-4 at Kaminka Strumilova district to witness the bestowal of the Iron Cross II. Class on 24 men for their bravery in combat with the Red Army. Wasyl Wykluk and Wasyl Bilecky were two of the 4 Ukrainians who received the Iron Cross II. Class as reported in the Divisional newspaper *To Victory.*

The same event, in April, 1944. Governor Wächter (centre left) beside him the regimental commander SS-Obersturmbannführer Siegfried Binz (wearing binoculars) and addressing the troops the commander of the border forces SS-Oberführer Karl Burk, attended the ceremony.

Governor Wächter amidst the four Ukrainians soldiers awarded the Iron Cross II. Class.

The Operations of Gal. SS-Freiw. Rgt 5

Further to the north, Gal.SS-Freiw. Rgt 5, took part in several actions against partisan units (as we have seen partly in conjunction with Kampfgruppe Beyersdorff) for example at the end of March and beginning of April 1944, it fought against a very strong insurgent band in the area near Malkow.[88] In addition, some elements were given the assignment of guarding and supervising the preparation of static defensive positions along the Buh River which entailed working for prolonged periods in the immediate proximity of civilians, among whom were a number of UPA members who promptly sought out the Ukrainian soldiers.[89] The influence of the UPA, dissatisfaction with their assignment and continual pleas from the local inhabitants for protection against ever increasing attacks by the Polish and Soviet partisans also culminated in continual desertion whilst stationed in this sector. This soon threatened to become endemic. 119[90] instances of desertion were documented in the daily Polizei situation reports by the Operations Officer of the Kommandeur der Ordnungspolizei in the district of Lublin to the Ortskommandantur of the Wehrmacht in Lublin. These reports detailed how the soldiers in groups of up to 42 men (identified as either members of Gal.SS-Freiw. Rgt 5, Galician Ukrainian SS-Schützen or simply Ukrainian SS men), took their weapons with them some having first killed their officers and NCOs. For example:

Cholm District. 9.March 1944, During the night of 7.3.44, in the Cholm region, 13 privates from II./Gal SS-Freiw.Rgt 5,(Buh) deserted presumably to the partisans, taking with them rifles overcoats, 2 machine pistols and two revolvers (0.8).[91]

16.March 1944, Cholm, on the early morning of 13.3.44, in the Cholm region, 23 Galician Ukrainian SS-Schützen in field grey uniforms with overcoats, national badges [i.e. Nazi eagle emblem] on left arm SS runes on collar patches, left their Stützpunkt (fortified Station) Stulno, 0 516 (Buh line), with 21 machine guns, 2 machine pistols, 1 light pistol, 19 rifles, 6 pistols and the appropriate ammunition, after having killed two German NCOs, presumably to go over to the partisans.[92]

Gend-Zug Hrubieszow, 17 March 1944,

On 14.3 at 1930 hrs the SS-Schützen below abandoned their posts and deserted:

SS-Schütze Babij, Wasiel

SS-Schütze Bylinski, Wladimier

SS-Schütze Roschtaschuk, Michael

taking with them 3 rifles and 1 pistol 0.8. All 3 SS-Schützen were from Potoschiska in the district of Kolomyia (Galicia).

Security sector Bug, 20 April 1944, In the night of 19.4, all Ukrainian SS men belonging to 5.Gal.-SS-Freiw.Rgt, fled from (Stützpunkt) 12 Hniszo, after killing three German NCOs and wounding one officer. Details not known.[93]

Many other units of squad and even company strength also made unsuccessful plans to desert however their plans were discovered by the Germans who managed to avert a crisis by temporarily disarming the units concerned until they regained control of the troops and restored the situation.[94] Roman Bilohan was a former member of Gal.SS-Freiw. Rgt 5 who deserted along with his comrades in response to repeated requests for help from the local Ukrainian civilians against the Polish partisans active in the area. He recalled:

I was serving with the HQ of the 5 Regiment. In mid-February 1944 we travelled from Leipzig to Kholm. There the battalion was billeted in very large barracks (the ceiling was five/six metres high). We were guarding bunkers, clearing mines and performing security duties in the city of Kholm. Every week we were granted urlaub (leave) and as usual two or three men would go into the city centre. In the centre of Kholm was a big cathedral. We learned from a friendly local Ukrainian policeman that in the cellar was a secret food store. I went there several times with my friends and we took 4 kg of butter, cheese, meat and bread. When we got back to our barracks we shared it with the Germans in our unit by dividing it into portions. The Germans took 50% of their portions to send home for their families.

While we were in Kholm we got to know Ukrainian civilians of our age and they told us stories about how the Polish AK and Kovpak guerrillas were terrorising the Ukrainian community in and around the town of Zamość especially at night, killing educated people and stealing cattle and live stock. The Ukrainian civilians kept coming to us and pleading for our help to fight back. Our German officers understood the problem but they said it was impossible to do anything without orders. They needed evidence and after that it would be possible to 'check' those villages. However the Ukrainians (civilians) returned again and again. Eventually, 38 men from the battalion made the decision to desert and help them so after church on 'wet Monday'[95] we did not return to our barracks. Instead we took our weapons and went to the woods near the town of Hrubeshiv and stayed there waiting until we were contacted by an UPA unit called 'Vovky' (Wolves) commanded by 'Yahoda', who welcomed us. After we joined the UPA we continued to wear the SS insignia on our lapels, however our helmets and gas masks were taken from us. I remained with that unit until August [1944].[96]

Incidents of this nature only served to further undermine the already strained relations between the German and Ukrainian personnel in the regiment and also contributed to an atmosphere of mutual distrust which lasted until its disbandment.

Roman Chomicky, a former member of 11./III. battalion 5 Regiment later wrote about how his plan to desert was thwarted:

[...] In mid-February 1944 we were transported by train to Bila Pidliaska. Before leaving, we were told how to behave (there the soldiers walked around with loaded rifles in hand, ready to fire). We also signed a pledge that we would not communicate with the local population. We spent a week in Bila Pidliaska and continued with our exercises.

We were then entrained again and told that we were bound for Kolomyia. In Krasnestav the German pioneers were repairing the railway bridge which had been damaged by the partisans. We stayed in the train for two days, and then rode via Zamość to Hrubeshiv. We disembarked on Sunday morning and the locals stared at us because we spoke the same language as them. We were quartered at a local school near the road to Kholm.

On Tuesday morning there was an assembly. The commander of the company said goodbye. He departed with the 2 platoon along the Buh River to the village of Matche while the 1 and the 3 platoons were off to Biyalopolia, going in the direction to Kholm. We moved forward in line, keeping a few metres between each other, on both sides of the road.

In Biyalopolia we used peasant sleds which took us towards Dubenka. I asked the coachman where he was taking us. He was silent. But from time to time he glanced at me. There were three of us in the sleds. The German administrator offered us brandy. Then suddenly the coachman began to speak saying that he became speechless after seeing the deaths head insignia on our caps (a skull with two dry bones beneath). The 3 platoon stayed in Dubenka, while the 1 went six kms south of the village of Zahirya. This village, which had about a dozen farmhouses, was located close to the forest. A few hundred metres to the east flowed the Buh River. Between the village and the river was a hill, where the German Ordnungspolizei supervised people who were building four bunkers, surrounded by ditches and barbed wire. About 50 of us were stationed there.

Sunday, March 6. Early in the morning we heard shooting that came from behind the forest where the 2 platoon was stationed, about 2 km from us. All 18 of us were gathered together, armed with rifles with ammunition, helmets on heads. Villagers came out from their houses, some were crying. Just before we entered the forest we mounted bayonets on our rifles. In the forest we moved toward the 2 platoon, taking cover behind trees. On the other side of the river we saw hundreds of people fleeing from the village of Khorytnytsia. Behind them there were two wagons rolling with red banners. Two German planes bombed the village. Later the soldiers told us that one German group commander began shooting at them with a machine gun but his company commander stopped him.

After the German Ordnungspolizei left, we supervised the workers who were fortifying the bunkers. During one lunch break some workers described how they defended their village from an attacking Polish group. I was surprised that they spoke in Polish. They replied proudly, 'We are the Ukrainians from Zamość region'. On quiet evenings we loved to sing. The village people praised our singing.

The frontline was coming closer. Several German companies were stationed in our village. Some Azerbaijani troops arrived with infantry cannons. A watchtower for border guards was situated near the village. One day looking through a telescope from the tower I saw a group of people near the forest. I called the Azerbaijani officer and he ordered to his cannon to shoot at them. Next day we saw many people and some fires on the other bank of the river. The German soldiers and the border guards were leaving the village. Four of us joined them. We met Hungarian troops who combed the forest for partisans. Several Hungarians were wounded. We transported them over the river to the road where waiting wagons took them to a hospital.

Behind Skryhychyn was a bunker, surrounded by barbed wire where twelve of us lived. Every day we ordered a wagon to go to the village of Zahirya to bring food. In Zahirya were some trusted soldiers who planned to join the Ukrainian Insurgent Army (UPA). From time to time we walked in pairs along the river to show our presence.

A German Army battalion was staying in our village. We arranged the date of our desertion at ten o clock on a Thursday in the second half of May 1944. Our group commander was away in the village with the German border guards. All eleven of us waited for a signal. In Zahirya coloured flares were fired. It was now well past ten and nobody from UPA had showed up.

While I was on guard duty, a group of soldiers approached from the village. After the exchange of passwords I discovered that our platoon commander from Zahirya was with them. He told me that we must be disarmed. They took away our weapons and led us to the bunker and told us to lie in beds. After a few days, we were marched away under escort.

We were kept in the barracks at Hrubeshiv. After several days, we were loaded into cattle wagons, 40 man per car, and transported to Frankfurt on the Oder. From there we went to SS-Truppenubungsplatz—Vandern Kirschbaum—Zelencing.[97]

The area in which both KGr. Beyersdorff and the 5 Regiment were deployed in an active mobile role was also one in which the age old Polish/Ukrainian antagonism was strong amongst the mixed but predominantly Polish population. This was largely hostile to the presence of the Ukrainian soldiers. The nature and ferocity of the fighting in which some of its elements were involved is evident from a surviving secret teleprinter report from the representative of the SSPF in Lublin to the HSSPF Ost in Cracow. Although fragmentary, it provides details of actions that took place in its operational sector between 13–16 May 1944. It states that during this period elements of the Gal SS Frei. Rgt 5 were involved in fighting with partisan bands around the villages of Zabuce and Soltysy. Proof that the houses in the villages were used as ammunition dumps by the partisans can be gleaned from the fact that in 16 houses, hand grenades exploded when incendiary ammunition was used. Later the partisans laid mines on the Janów to Krasnik road near the sawmill causing the loss of one armoured vehicle. A small railway bridge between Belzec and Mazila was also blown up by partisans and a locomotive derailed.[98]

During its utilisation, 40 Kriegsverdienstkreuzes II. Class with and without swords, (War Service Crosses—24 with and 16 without swords) were issued to German members of the 5 Regiment. Recipients included SS-Oberscharführer Richard Andersohn, SS-Oberscharführer Rudolf Baronyay, SS-Untersturmführer Emil Weis all members of 3./Gal.SS-Freiw.Regt.5, who were awarded the Kriegsverdienstkreuze (II. Class with Swords) for bravery during the partisan attack which took place on 13 May 1944, described in the above teleprinter message.[99]

The problems which continued to afflict both regiments throughout this period, arose mainly because neither was utilised in an appropriate manner nor sufficiently equipped for its designated task. Such considerations were ignored by HSSPF Koppe. Having been informed of the difficulties, and at a time when both regiments were still active and under his control, he broached the subject in a speech about security questions in the General Government, in Cracow on 15 April 1944. In his view the performance of the Ukrainian Regiments had fallen short of expectations. Conveniently overlooking the fact that he had been responsible for their utilisation in the first place and the obvious causes of their problems, Koppe announced that, 'In this area one had, until now no good experience of the Regiments of this Division'. At the same time, following the numerous desertions which had occurred from Gal.SS-Freiw.Rgt's 4 and 5 and associated deaths of several German officers and NCOs, he stated a great risk was being taken by the arming of the Polish and Ukrainian Polizei.[100]

Notwithstanding this Koppe ignored an order by Himmler dated 22 April 1944, for the disbandment of Galizischen SS-Freiwilligen Regiments 4 and 5 and their transfer to Neuhammer.[101] Nevertheless Koppe continued to denigrate the Ukrainian forces whom he had insisted on deploying. This threatened to jeopardise much of the progress Wächter had made in convincing the higher German authorities of the wisdom of permitting the formation of Ukrainian military units. In the weeks that followed Wächter rigorously defended the Ukrainians who in many quarters were still viewed with considerable suspicion.[102]

4

Final Preparations

Truppenübungsplatz Neuhammer

While Kampfgruppe Beyersdorff and Galizischen SS-Freiwilligen Regiments 4 and 5 were still engaged in the field, the continual requests by the Division's command for transfer to a bigger and better training facility finally yielded results. This was the army facility Truppenübungsplatz Neuhammer (on the River Queis), near Sagan in lower Silesia which had recently been vacated by the 13. SS-Freiwilligen b.h. Division (Kroatien).[1] Relocation which required thirty train loads of men and matériel, began with the despatch of advanced detachments in mid-February 1944,[2] and took a full three weeks to effect.[3]

Unlike Heidelager which had basic wooden barracks and a dearth of permanent facilities such as vehicle parks and supply and storage depots,[4] the main camp at Neuhammer was a well established very large, purpose built, brick camp with modern facilities. The camp layout consisted of a row of several long rectangular squares with asphalted roads running along both sides of the squares, with grassy lawns, flower beds, and occasional trees in between. The squares were flanked by rows of identical red brick buildings, each of which provided quarters for one company so that the buildings surrounding the square were sufficient to accommodate a regiment. One prominent feature was the huge stable block for the horses.

At the southern end of this complex a road went to the east where the large military polygon or training ground extended over a big, slightly undulating wild plain. This was predominantly sandy soil with bracken, some tall grasses, weeds and bushes interspersed with small woods. Farther south the complex was bypassed by the unfinished Berlin–Breslau road which terminated not far from Neuhammer. This section of the well made but unused road was used for parades.

Orest Slupchynsky was part of the Vorkommando (quartermaster group) who were the first to arrive at the camp:

I remember the ride from Heidelager to Neuhammer. I was part of the advance group, which had lots of privileges and advantages. We were riding by cattle train which we didn't mind at all because we were ecstatic just to move, to finally do something and go somewhere and get away from the boring routine of basic training which we knew in every detail. It was also an opportunity to get away from the monotonous landscape of pine trees and sandy soil of Heidelager.

We were in these cattle wagons, very happy and full of expectation for something new. We were fully equipped with uniforms, warm blankets, weapons and most importantly—food. As far as I remember the ride was quite short lasting little more than half a day, but our journey was prolonged because our transport was often rerouted to make way for transports moving to the east (Kriegswichtige Transporten).

In Breslau there were stands with young quite attractive nurses (Schwesters) for all soldiers who wanted fresh and hot soup, not very aromatic smelling [ersatz] coffee and not so bad sandwiches. Also all kinds of ammunition was available in open boxes which you could freely take.

Past Breslau we ran into a heavily wooded area and noticed big herds of deer and bucks. The sight of them made our fingers itchy. Initially we resisted the temptation but we had our Karabiners and plenty of ammunition…

We arrived in Neuhammer through a very high door in a very high brick building (which we later found out was a water tower) in the afternoon and were pleasantly surprised by what we saw. There were no wooden barracks. Instead there were old, solid brick two storey buildings. These were 'alte Kaserne' (old barracks) which smelled of the First World War. Then we were assigned to our building. I took over a room which I shared with three other soldiers who were my friends from the advance team. I remember the long stone covered floors, the rifle stands on the side, and the first rooms as we entered the building for the spies Stabsscharführer and other 'big shots'. In front of our 7 (light) company building was a wide, granite cobbled road, where every morning we ran like crazy for inspection, and most importantly, for a speech of the 'mother' of the company, our 'spies' or Stabsscharführer. He was the 'mother' of the company, and the 'father' was the company führer who at that time was the most distinguished, elegant, and absolutely fair, Waffen-Untersturmführer Tyt Stefaniw.

When you stood outside and faced our building, on the right was the 8 (heavy) company, on the left 6 company and further to the left was the building which housed the staff of 1 battalion, where I got the dream of every soldier in whole world—urlaub (leave).

In front of the 1 battalion was a 200 metre wide wooded area, to the right of which stood the buildings of the 2 battalion. Still further to the right in a little wood was 'Little Red Riding Hood's House', or 'Puff' as we called it, which was a bordello nestled in the small woods. In the middle of Truppenübungsplatz Neuhammer was a swimming pool, and by the entrance to the camp was a kiosk of a photographer which was always closed.[5]

Theo Andruszko whose service with Kgr. Beyersdorff was coming to an end, also found himself at the Division's new base:

[...] After the unexpected recall of Kampfgruppe Beyersdorff in mid-March our train did not stop at Heidelager but kept rolling on to Neuhammer. It was a change to see two levels brick buildings, comfortable beds, and a Soldatenhause with cheap beer devoid of alcohol (you could drink 8 'halbs' (half litres) of beer and never feel tipsy—except for frequent visits to the toilet). The food was bad—very little meat but plenty of turnips! Typical 'Heimat' rationing.[6]

His companion Volodymyr Keczun recalled that following their arrival training began again immediately:

[...] For us Neuhammer looked strange, massive and confusing. Neuhammer consisted of at least three training camps. Central Neuhammer, a brick built camp that looked like a town with tiered houses and all the necessary amenities and two secondary ones with barracks.[...] For daily training we had the same instructor as in Heidelager and he kept us very busy so that we did not get 'rusty', but there was one difference. We had to help the units that used old fashioned water cooled MGs and new recruits to learn how to use modern MG 42s. During training in the field, from time to time our units trained close to each other so they could see how we did it. In the evenings myself and others were sent to their rooms to explain about parts, how they work, how to change the barrel so it did not overheat etc. It was much easier to teach recruits this, than the uses of old fashioned guns.[7]

The move to a new training ground situated further away from Galicia brought with it several practical benefits for the Division. The camp commander General Major Hans Runnebaum[8] was a regular army officer who was not inclined to acquiesce to every demand he received for help from senior ranking officials and was also more supportive towards the Division's needs. He worked closely with it assisting with the procurement of much needed weapons, horses, vehicles and other essential matériel. Also, as an established complex better equipped with fixtures and facilities, fewer men were required to perform guard duty. The new site was also large enough to conduct divisional scale training exercises which expedited progress. In addition, the presence of the River Queis which ran through it, enabled specialist pioneer instruction such as the construction of ferries and bridges of up to twelve tonnes.

Relocation also meant a dramatic fall in the number of desertions which had been a constant concern for its command at Heidelager. Finally accelerated improvement in all areas of training was now possible as being a 'closed' camp, it was no longer subject to the distraction caused by visiting friends and relatives.

Deliveries of regular shipments of new equipment, weapons and supplies, continued until February 1944 when the Division left Heidelager. These included a large consignment of 4,420 rifles (standard carbines 98k model) from army supply depots in Spandau and Breslau on 19 January1944.[9]

It also received additional senior officer personnel for its command staff and field units. In March 1944, two more German officers arrived who assumed positions

The commander of the training facility at Neuhammer General Major Hans Runnebaum.

Above: Freitag (centre saluting) inspects departing troops. In the centre with dark collar on great coat the Division's 1a Major Heike.

Left: The Divisional mascot was an orphan named Anton Zabutsky. In 1943 he was 11 years old. He came from Kypjansk close to Kharkiv. For 8 months he was with German marines in the Black Sea whom he helped to escape encirclement. He withdrew with the German Army to western Ukraine and went to Heidelager.

Anton Zabutsky seen here on a motorcycle, was promoted to the rank of SS-Sturmmann.

Parade and inspection at Neuhammer. *Photo Courtesy Richard Rygaard archive*

Ukrainian recruits take instruction from their officer.

as battalion commanders in infantry units SS-Hauptsturmführers' Allerkamp (kdr II./WGR 29) and Wittenmeyer (kdr II./WGR 30). Another German officer SS-Sturmbannführer Sepp Syr,[10] was appointed to the Division with effect from 10 March 1944.[11] A decorated veteran with extensive experience in reconnaissance units (i.e. Fusilier), Syr had previously served with the 1. Leibstandarte, the SS Kavallerie (i.e. 8) and the 15 Lett.SS-Freiw. Divisions. He was assigned to the Galician Division as a battalion commander for a three month period ending 16 June 1944.[12] His rôle during this period remains ambiguous and he may have assisted with the forming of the Fusilier Battalion but there is no evidence to suggest that he ever took formal command of it.

Soldiers who had undergone specialist training also continued to return from their respective schools for example 61 NCOs and men, who had undergone a course with SS. Signals Training Abt.4, at Mörchingen which concluded on 12 March 1944.[13]

In March the formation of the motorised Air Defence Detachment (SS-Flak Abteilung 14) was at long last completed.[14] With a strength of 860 personnel,[15] it was commanded by SS-Hauptsturmführer Serge von Kuester[16] and consisted of one light battery of 2 cm guns,[17] a medium battery of 3.7 cm guns,[18] and a third heavy battery of four highly prized high velocity 8.8 cm semi-automatic guns.[19] The latter had a sophisticated anti-aircraft rangefinder indicator, the operation of which required a good knowledge of maths hence, most of their crews were university students. The operation of the 8.8 cm batteries never failed to impress and were always a feature or inspections and tours by visitors.

Above: Left to right: Waffen-
Hauptsturmführer Mychailo
Brygider the only Ukrainian
commander of an infantry
battalion, Freitag, Waffen-
Hauptsturmführer Dmytro
Paliiv. *Photo Courtesy Richard
Rygaard archive*

Right: The Division received
a battery of four of the highly
prized 8.8 cm guns, the crews for
which were often drawn from
university graduates because of
their complexity.
Prior to Brody the Division was
very well armed and equipped as
it was intended to be a front line
combat Division.

At the same time the previously established reserve battalion (14. Feld-Ersatz Battalion) was reorganised under the command of SS-Hauptsturmführer Johannes Kleinow. Consisting of four companies, it was expanded to a strength of 800 men.[20] Its purpose was primarily to serve as a source of reserve officers, NCOs and soldiers for all the Division's units as well as being responsible for the retraining and the classification of the ranks of former officers. The unit commander was a poor choice. According to the Division's 1a Major Heike, Freitag ignored the 'continuous complaints about Kleinow that flooded the staff offices'.[21]

Freitag's own estimation of the Division's evolution was summarised briefly in a routine progress report dated 15 March 1944, in which he revealed that the training of artillery, flak abteilung, Panzerjäger company, pioneer unit and signals group was making good progress. The co-ordinated training of the infantry regiments and Fusilier Battalion however could not commence until the arrival of the NCOs from the Waffen SS schools, the reserve army detachments, and those assigned to Kampfgruppe Beyersdorff who were still in the process of returning. Problems highlighted included the lack of suitable German instructors. Morale was said to be 'Good'. In indentifying 'Special difficulties' Freitag showed his continuing bias against the Ukrainian officers when he wrote 'The laziness and unreliability of the mass of Galician officers was impairing the future formation of the Division'. He concluded that the Division was not combat ready as it was still in the process of formation.[22]

As it relied primarily on horse power for its mobility, the most serious of the remaining matériel deficiencies was the number of horses assigned to it. Only 2,996 of the required complement of 4,925 were available leaving a shortfall of 1,929.[23]

At this time, on the request of SS-Oberführer Freitag, a former SD (Sicherheitdienst) officer was transferred to the Division. In late March 1944, Ukrainian born SS-Hauptsturmführer Heinrich Wiens[24] joined a newly created and unique sub-section of Section 1c (Military intelligence) of the Division's staff. Wiens was described by Dmytro Ferkuniak with whom he served as 'A sadist who despised the Ukrainians, especially the Galician Volunteers'.[25] Prior to joining the Galician Division, Wiens had previously served with Einsatzgruppen D (action squad D),[26] a notorious formation charged with the task of hunting down and liquidating Ukrainian patriots, partisans, Jews, and others proscribed by Nazi racial and political policies.[27] The remit of Section Ic/a (counter-intelligence), of which he was in charge covered desertion, censorship of mail and most importantly the elimination of the OUN activists within the Division. Wiens who was a polyglot fluent in Ukrainian, Russian, Polish and German was deemed suitable for the position due to his perfect command of the Ukrainian language and two and a half years experience fighting against partisans on the eastern front. Freitag's evaluation of him read:

SS-Hstuf. Wiens comes from the SD and assumed the post of Ic/A. in the Division. With energy and enthusiasm Wiens carries out his tasks with much success.

Unknown officer in a Divisional Swimmwagen at Neuhammer in summer 1944, on which the Divisional emblem can be seen. The Division received a significant allocation of such vehicles which were amongst the best available at that time.

Neuhammer April 1944, discussion during exercises amongst Ukrainian officers. From left Waffen-Unterscharführer Parfeniuk, Waffen-Unterscharführer Kuchar, Waffen-Unterscharführer Biletchko, Waffen-Hauptsturmführer Evhen Nikitin, Waffen-Untersturmführer Lubomyr Ortynsky, not known.

W. is a man whose training and interests are very much one sided [and therefore] he is not suitable for alternative employment. Neither is he suitable for employment as a representative of Ic. His conduct towards his superiors and within his circle of comrades is appropriate

Wiens performs well in his position.[28]

In this position, Wiens was ideally placed and eminently qualified to help Freitag identify Ukrainian nationalists such as Mychailo Kaczmar and counteract the dominant sentiment which they exemplified.[29] Whatever the motive for his appointment, Freitag evidently thought very highly of him and was pleased with his work which he continued up until he disappeared a few weeks before the end of the war.

The only Ukrainian member of Section Ic, Waffen-Hauptsturmführer Ferkuniak, made an immediate effort to frustrate his work. He advised the principle OUN adherents including Waffen-Obersturmführers Kaczmar, Malecky and Pidhayny to let it be known amongst the soldiers that to avoid serious consequences, the Ukrainians should refrain from expressing their political views in their private letters. This measure met with some success.[30]

The First year

A strength return dated 17 April 1944, clearly demonstrates that at this point, although the unit was 'overmanned' in enlisted men, there was a crippling lack of trained officers and NCOs available. This problem, which had beset the Division from the outset, was especially acute with the NCOs where there was a deficit of 1,765. The figures were:

	should be	is
Führer:	458	291
Unterführer:	2,431	666
Manschaften:	11,110	13,042
davon Hiwi:	2,092	———
Gesamt:	13,999	13,999[31]

As Freitag had already acknowledged, practical consequences of this shortage had impacted negatively on the development of the unit, thus it was only at the beginning of April 1944 that the Division was finally able to commence with full scale battle training which was due to be completed in June. In the following weeks intensified and combined exercises of company, battalion and regimental sized units began, as well as large scale manoeuvres on a divisional scale which took place from dawn until late at night. Special emphasis was placed on the effective interaction between various weapons systems and services and the co-ordination of light and heavy weapons fire using live ammunition. This was supplemented by lengthy forced marches which improved stamina and helped reinforce discipline.

In mid-April 1944, a Training and Reserve Regiment (Ausbildung und Ersatz Regiment 14.Ausb.u.Ers.Rgt.14) was established commanded by SS-Obersturmbannführer Mathias Huber into which all new recruits would be inducted. This regiment was comprised of a command staff, three battalions, (each of four companies[32]), and the 13–15 companies. It also had a Kraftfahr (driver and mechanic) training company, a reserve battalion with staff company (which was responsible for inducting all new recruits), and a Genesenden (convalescent) company.[33] Stationed at Heidelager (from 15 April–15 July 1944), it was directly subordinated to, but independent of the Division.[34] Within two months of its establishment, it had a complement of over 5,000 recruits and was expanding. Its sheer size was a problem in itself for the Divisional command as at that time only forty to fifty qualified German and Ukrainian instructors were available for training. A high proportion of these were unable to take part in practical training because of their wounds.[35] Initially co-operation between the Reserve Regiment and the Division was poor but improved steadily.

In accordance with tradition in the German armed forces on 20 April (the Führer's birthday) promotions in military rank were given (as appropriate) to deserving German and Ukrainian personnel. On this day Fritz Freitag was raised to the rank of SS-Brigadeführer und Generalmajor der Waffen-SS und Polizei.[36] There were also promotions for the younger Ukrainian graduates from the Non Commissioned Officers schools who had recently returned to the Division to assist with the training of new recruits.[37] The month of April 1944, marked the first anniversary of the promulgation of the formation of the Galician Division which was rapidly nearing readiness for deployment. Kriegsberichter Oleh Lysiak recorded in Holos Ukrainski Visti (published in Berlin) that the occasion was marked with a festivity, which included decorating the best soldiers with the Iron Cross II. Class.[38] As the training schedule entered its final stages; regular reports were submitted to the higher German authorities regarding the state of the Division's battle readiness. Governor Wächter and those who sympathised with his views, ensured that these also stressed the political nature of the formation and the relevance of its involvement in military action with regard to Ukrainian interests.[39] Based on these criteria, they included several recommendations regarding its deployment; Because of its inexperience, it was considered advisable to send the Division to a quiet sector of the front to allow it to acclimatise to the rigours of combat; Notwithstanding previous experiences, it was recommended that the venue of its first action be on Ukrainian soil preferably in Galicia. Its staff further proposed an open field engagement as opposed to one in a forested or urban area (for which it was felt the Ukrainians would not be suited); the Division be deployed between two experienced veteran German divisions.

Wächter despatched a copy of a report based on these recommendations to the Commander in Chief of Army Group North Ukraine (AGNU) Generalfeldmarshall Walther Model whose headquarters were based in Galicia,[40] Model, who had previously successfully used Hungarian troops for tactical political purposes,

Funeral of Ivan Ivakhiv from WGR 29, who was killed during a training exercise at Neuhammer. NCO pallbearers from his unit beside the coffin.

The company commander pays his last respects to his comrade. Rev Bohdan Levytsky officiated at the funeral of Ivakhiv who was buried with full military honours.

An Honour Company fired a volley shot as a salute to their fallen comrade.

Ukrainians training with 10.5 cm artillery cannons.

The caption on this Kriegsberichter picture reads "With the smile on the lips and a song our Galician volunteers march through streets of a German town".

Holy Mass was conducted for the soldiers every Sunday, here by Rev. Mychailo Levenetz.

Above: Ukrainian recruits training with a mortar.

Right: The commander 3 company Pioneer Battalion Waffen-Untersturmführer Anton Dyhdalewysch.

Left Bohdan Kutny,
right Waffen-
Untersturmführer
Anton
Dyhdalewysch
on horseback at
Neuhammer.

14 April 1944, commander 3 company pioneer battalion Waffen-Untersturmführer Anton
Dyhdalewysch with his young NCO's. Third from left Jaroslav Benzal, Taras Kaczmarchuk,
Anton Dyhdalewysch, Julian Wilshynsky (partly hidden), at front standing beside Dyhdalewysch,
Bohdan Kutny.

concurred with Wächter's view with regard to the potential significance of a proper deployment for the Galician Division. He showed an enthusiastic interest in the report and promised to actively support its recommendations. To facilitate this, he included the Division in the preparations for his planned operations in this theatre. On a practical level he sent ten experienced Wehrmacht officers and NCOs to the Division. Their task was to acquaint all regiments with the terrain in the proposed area of operations.[41]

At the same time, Governor Wächter who had himself recently conducted an inspection of the Division, sent Himmler a full report on its progress and on the overall situation in Galicia. His lengthy letter dated 3 May 1944, ran to a total of 8 pages. In it, he sought to convince Himmler that from the German perspective, in spite of the initial doubts, the creation of the Galician Division had been a worthwhile venture. It was he stated, the 'barricade which kept the entire youth of Galicia from slipping into a nationalistic hostility to the Reich and at the same time, the point of departure for a European-conscious youth, receptive for the Reich concept'.

He then cited the negative effect of the successive German military setbacks as the impetus for an expediential growth and influence of both the Ukrainian nationalist and Soviet partisan movements on the population of Galicia. Notwithstanding this he went on to say that the 'the bulk of the people still completely rejected Bolshevism' and were still generally welcoming to the German troops as had recently been confirmed by both Generalfeldmarshall Model and SS-Obergruppenführer Hauser who were currently stationed there.

Wächter stressed that to successfully counter the influence of the Ukrainian partisans and to encourage the 'Galician Volunteer Movement':

> The question of a national slogan is of decisive importance [...] It is understandable that young volunteers are more likely to go for a clear and positive political programme than for vague hopes. Many difficulties in the Division and in the [Polizei] regiments can be explained by this fact.

He then reiterated his belief in Himmler's own maxim 'Nothing can be extorted from Adolf Hitler and his German nation, but everything can be gained by proving yourselves to be decent and loyal'. This slogan he went on to say, would appeal directly to the intelligent young people, especially the educated young officer candidates in the Galician Division. These men who had 'stood on the parade ground with other European youths, and ambitiously exert themselves to adopt the impressive style of the Waffen SS' were fully cognisant of its implications. Because of this, they were intended to serve as an example to the other troops:

> I am convinced that this good section will then constitute the nucleus of a growing youth movement in partnership with the Reich. These young men, who in many cases used to be Bandera supporters themselves [i.e. UPA supporters], now find themselves in conflict with the Bandera supporters operating in the woods of their country.

Governor Wächter arrives for a visit April 1944 to be greeted by the Divisional Adjutant SS-Sturmbannführer Johannes Georgi. Standing behind Wächter is his aide-de-camp SS-Obersturmführer Viktor Stiastny, in the back of the car bending over wearing black coat Oberst Alfred Bisanz.

Governor Wächter retained a tremendous interest in the Division the formation of which he had initiated, visiting the Division at both Heidelager and Neuhammer. Here he inspects a signals unit at Neuhammer, April 1944.

Governor Wächter watching field exercises by infantry units, Neuhammer, April 1944.

Inspecting medium calibre 3.7 cm flak gun crew in action.

Wächter's observes a mortar unit in action at Neuhammer, April 1944.

Review of the Division. On horseback saluting Waffen-Untersturmführer. Stephan Karatnysky WGR 31.

Governor Wächter speaks to the officer corps in the officers club at Neuhamer, Paliiv translates.

Governor Wächter addresses the officer corps, *left to right*: Wächter, Paliiv, Freitag, Bisanz not known, Heike (in the corner).

Evening officers meeting—*left to right:* Heike, Pobihushtschyi, Brygider.

Evening concert, commander of Neuhammer General Major Hans Runnebaum, Paliiv, Wächter, Freitag, Bisanz, Heike, Dern.

The Division's Fieseler Storch light reconnaissance aircraft, later used to good effect in anti-partisan operations.

Freitag reviews the Division's artillery during a visit of the parents of the soldiers and the Military Board on 3 June 1944, whilst the Divisional band plays.

When they have experienced the pride of having proved themselves at the front, their contempt for the shirkers and murderous arsonists in the woods will increase.[...]

To counter Koppe's recent public criticisms of the Ukrainian Polizei regiments during their recent deployment in the General Government he continued:

If the various negative events in the Galician Regiments 4 and 5 are held up to refute my optimism, they cannot convince me. By keeping in steady contact with the leaders and troops of the Galician SS regiments and with the Division, I am well acquainted with the situation and have come to the following assessment:

The deployment of the Regiments was extremely ill-omened from the start.
I list the following:

Inadequate armament, this was bound to have serious consequences in the various encounters with Soviet tanks.
The distribution of the troops which were dispersed into tiny bases were easily influenced by nationalist envoys; acting against this was virtually impossible just because they were so dispersed and the communications were so inadequate.
Their deployment (especially in the case of the 5 Regiment) in areas which were totally undermined by the radical Polish—Ukrainian national struggle.
Their deployment at a time of retrogressive front-line development which led to manifestations of disintegration even among the German troops.
A corps of leaders, [i.e.; officers and NCOs] some of whom had no personal experience of the front and only limited military experience.
Last but not least, the lack of a link between troops and leaders who could have motivated the men in their own language with easily understood arguments. The existence of a Galician–Ukrainian corps of Non Commissioned Officers would have had a very positive effect here.

In spite of these considerable disadvantages, some troops of the regiments put up a good performance, especially where the leadership was flawless, and where they had some heavy weapons to back them up at the front. I was told this repeatedly by Wehrmacht officers who were acquainted with the facts.[42]

Many of these disadvantages he added, did not apply the Galician Division which was well trained and equipped and had a good corps of officers and NCOs who had been trained in the academies of the Waffen SS.

Whatever happened, Wächter was determined to ensure a 'politically favourable active deployment' for the Division, preferably against the Soviets in Galicia. To facilitate this he attempted to present Himmler with a fait accompli adding Generalfeldmarshall Model had already expressed an interest in utilising it in conjunction with his Army Group currently located there. Acknowledging the risks involved, Wächter stressed the utilisation of the Division on home territory would be regarded as a demonstration of confidence in the Ukrainians on the part of the Germans.

After commenting on the 'flawless military impression' which the Division had made on him during his recent trip to Neuhammer, Wächter concluded his letter by repeating a request that he be allowed to report to Himmler in person.[43] Undoubtedly, he hoped such a meeting would afford him the opportunity to extract concessions from Himmler in the same way that he had after the two had last met in early March 1943.

Himmler responded positively and a few days later, Wächter received confirmation that his request for a personal audience would finally be granted. More importantly the Reichsführer also indicated that he would be conducting an official inspection of the 14 Galician Division at Neuhammer in the near future.

Himmler Visits the Division

On 16 May 1944, a Focke Wulf Fw.200 condor carrying the Reichsführer-SS landed at Neuhammer. Himmler's diary of official appointments indicates that the scheduled time of arrival was 1700 hrs.[44] On this occasion his entourage included SS Obergruppenführer Oswald Pohl, SS Gruppenführer Hanns Johst and his personal bodyguard SS Hauptsturmführer Josef Kiermaier. Governor Wächter was also present. They were greeted by SS-Brigadeführer Freitag, his 1a, Major Heike and his senior staff officers and driven to the officers' mess. Here formal introductions were made to the assembled regimental and independent battalion commanders and other high ranking members of staff. The visit began with a speech by Himmler to the predominantly German senior officer corps. A surviving audio recording made at the time reveals that for the benefit of the Ukrainian contingent, the speech was repeated sentence by sentence by Waffen-Hauptsturmführer Dmytro Paliiv, in Ukrainian.[45]

Himmler began by addressing the thorny issue of Division's nomenclature. The designation 'Galician' he said, did not reflect an attempt to denationalise the Ukrainians but was merely a means of regional identification. He stated:

> I know that some of you are unhappy about the fact that the Division is called Galician and that you are sometimes or even frequently addressed with the name Galician. I am well aware, of course, that the inhabitants of Galicia, that is to say those of your ilk, are Ukrainians. Just as in Germany the Germans who are at home in Pomerania are called Pomeranians and those who are at home in Bavaria are called Bavarians and call themselves Bavarians, in exactly the same way the designation Galician has been chosen according to the name of your beautiful homeland, of which you can be truly proud.

Interestingly, in so saying he was repeating the arguments which had earlier been advanced by Waffen-Hauptsturmführer Ferkuniak several months earlier.

Himmler flew into Neuhammer on 16 May 1944 in his personal Ju-52.

Himmler greets German staff officers on his arrival.

Himmler greets staff members in the officers club.

Shortly after his arrival Himmler addressed the predominantly German officer corps while Paliiv translated. An audio recording of the speech has survived.

He then went on to emphasise the benefit Galicia had experienced as a result of 150 years of being subjected to German order and justice as part of the Austro-Hungarian empire which ensured 'a proper understanding of the West'.

Next, in reply to the nationalists who accused the Germans of enlisting the Ukrainians as cannon-fodder, he emphasised that the Division had been given a whole year of thorough training and practice in discipline, drill, and weapon craft before being committed to combat.

The absence of Ukrainian officers from senior positions within the Division, presented a more awkward problem especially in light of the official German policy of reserving senior positions of command exclusively to Germans whenever possible. Himmler attempted justify this issue by stating:

> Every position is filled by a man who is capable. **I did not ask, nor did the Division's Kommandeur ask: Is he German or is he Ukrainian?** On the contrary, the only question we asked ourselves was: Does he lead his battalion in such a way that there is no un-necessary loss of blood? Is he a man that can teach his subordinates military virtues and can train them to do their job well? Is he a man who leads his battalion to victory or defeat? Is he a man who buys victory at the expense of far too many lives, or is he such a leader that the dead, the fallen are fewer. (author's emphasis).

To further temper this criticism he drew attention to the 250 men who had already been sent to the Junker schools (officer academies).

In an effort to suppress the strong nationalist sentiments amongst the Ukrainians, Himmler proceeded to forbid the discussing of politics within the Division. He then reverted to a standard theme from one of his many speeches[46] and demanded that his audience uphold a number of cardinal virtues which he considered axiomatic. These were order, loyalty, comradeship and obedience. In the case of the latter he expanded thus:

> There is something I want to tell you: obedience starts the moment you receive an order to do something you find unpleasant. I know if I ordered the Division to exterminate the Poles in this area or that area, I would be a very popular man. But if I tell you or give you the order that the Division is to follow this or that route to the front in full battle order, and fight against the Russians, then that is what will be done, for the Führer will manage to handle the Poles alright—who have ill-treated you in the same way as they have ill-treated our fellow Germans in Poland. You do nothing before the order is given. I expect you, the Führerkorps, whether German or Ukrainian, to set a good example to your men by your exemplary obedience in every, I repeat every, respect.

In closing he indicated that he would be conducting a full inspection of the Division the following day, before it engaged in fight against the enemy Russia and Bolshevism at the front.[47]

According to the testimony of Waffen-Obersturmführer Julian Temnyk who was present, in reply to Himmler's anti-Polish comments Waffen-Hauptsturmführer Dmytro Paliiv acting as the spokesman for the Ukrainian officers said:

> Let it be permissible in your presence, Herr Reichsführer, for me to state that we Ukrainians are not preparing to slaughter the Poles, and that is not why we voluntarily enlisted into the Division Galicia. But after observing German policies in eastern Europe, we cannot fail to cite how you Germans continue to incite us against the Poles and the Poles against us. I feel that it is necessary to inform you that your policies in eastern Europe are not correct and lead to nothing good. Forgive me for such an unpleasant rebuttal, but that is the way it is.[48]

Paliiv's brave comment which was welcomed in some quarters,[49] does not appear to have incurred Himmler's immediate displeasure. However, a few days after his visit to the Division, he issued the following order to the Chief of the security Polizei and SD (Security and intelligence Service) designed to disassociate the Ukrainians from the elite SS establishment once and for all:

> In the criminal report of the Reichssicherheits-Hauptamtes of 26.5.44, reference is made to a Ukrainian SS man under item 2. This should be correctly defined as a Ukrainian serving in the combat units of the SS.
>
> I ask you to ensure that the term 'SS Man', which is so precious and highstanding to us, is avoided in all reports, as well as in all official and non-official announcements concerning the people of foreign race which we today organise under the order of the SS.[50]

Early in the morning of 17 May, Himmler and his entourage together with Wächter, Freitag and Heike set out to conduct a thorough inspection of the Division. The group travelled in staff cars across the moorland and thick forest of the training site, visiting individual sections in different localities and watching demonstrations. Waffen-SS Kriegsberichters Market, Loos and Weyer photographed every stage of the visit for propaganda purposes.[51] The best pictures were selected and made into a beautifully decorated album which Freitag later presented to Himmler as a memento of his visit.[52]

During the course of the day the group observed full scale mock combat assaults involving infantry units supported by artillery batteries attacking dummy enemy positions and emplacements. The group also witnessed heavy infantry weaponry including anti-aircraft batteries (firing against both air and ground targets), and anti-tank guns in action. Major sectional exercises continued and various demonstrations of weapons proficiency were given by infantry support units including mortar teams and machine gunners. Inspections were also made of various sub-units including communications, staff, supply and provisioning services, veterinary, medical, signal, automotive and pioneer units. In order to demonstrate the Divisions capabilities, combat exercises involving all combined forces were conducted under battle conditions. Waffen-Sturmmann Mychailo Kormylo was present during Himmler's visit:

> My personal experience of Himmler was when I was in charge of my heavy MG 42 machine gun group. We were supporting the 3 company on a field exercise. W.Obstuf. Pospilovsky stood behind us and our battalion commander Hauptstuf. Klocker stood right beside us. Both officers had told us that if Himmler approached, not to turn and look at him but to keep focused in on the 3 company dugouts.
>
> Within a few moments someone tapped me on the collar, I looked up and out of the corner of my eye caught sight of a figure looking through binoculars. He then turned to me and asked 'what's your name?' I was amazed that he wanted to know anyone's name. I replied 'SS volunteer Mychailo Kormylo' then he asked me the distance between my machine gun and my proposed target area. I said my bullets are ranged for 700 metres. He then immediately instructed one of his accompanying officers who had with him a large dog, to pace out the distance which he then confirmed was correct. While this was going on, a correspondent from the divisional newspaper asked Himmler if he could take photos of the Reichsführer standing with this group and he agreed. More than a week later our photo appeared in Do Peremohy. I held onto that article for quite sometime as I in intended to show of my friends back home during leave. I kept hold of it religiously and when we where headed for Brody I stored it in my tornister. Unfortunately I left it in the heavy supply lorry that followed us to the front and needless to say I lost a lot when we were encircled and the supply vehicles were bombed.[53]

The day concluded with a review by Himmler and Wächter from the back of an open topped staff car of select units chosen from all sections of the Division. This took place on the unfinished stretch of the Berlin–Breslau road. It began with its band and was followed by the infantry and the cavalry platoons of each infantry regiment. Behind them came the horse-drawn batteries of the artillery regiment including the heavy 150 mm guns. These were followed by the motorised elements amongst which were the light and medium flak batteries, motorised light field howitzers and anti-tank guns. There were also vehicles from the supply and mechanical unit together with Swimmwagens and motorcycles. The parade lasted almost an hour and a half. A closed meeting with Freitag, Wächter and Bisanz concluded the visit at which various issues were discussed connected with the formation including staffing and its imminent deployment.

Throughout his visit, Himmler conversed with many of the men of all ranks, both German and Ukrainian showing a special interest in the younger soldiers with whom he often shook hands. By so doing he had ample opportunity to acquaint himself with the various concerns of the 'Galician Division' at first hand. Evidently he was pleased with Governor Wächter and satisfied with the Division's progress and the level of its training 'repeatedly voicing his complete approval'.[54]

The triumvirate Freitag, Himmler, Wächter.

The following day Himmler inspected many elements of the Division including the artillery.

Himmler observing infantry manoeuvres conducted by WGR 31. *From right:* not known, SS-Obersturmbannführer Paul Herms (Kdr WGR 31), Freitag, Himmler.

Observing large scale exercises.

Right to left: not known, SS-Obersturmbannfüher Viktor Stiastny Wächters aid-de-camp (partly obscured), Wächter (wearing black leather coat), SS-Sturmbannführer Josef Remberger (Kdr. Pioneer Batl), Paliiv (partly hidden), Himmler, SS-Brigadeführer Hanns Johst (partly hidden) Freitag, Heike.

Himmler observes a communication section during his inspection.

Above: Some of the Division's staff with left Freitag (centre wearing light coat and binoculars), Wächter and Himmler.

Left: During his inspection Himmler actively solicited the comments of the Ukrainian soldiers.

Impressed by what had been achieved, in acknowledgement of his considerable efforts on this day Himmler rewarded Wächter by promoting him to the rank of SS-Gruppenführer und Generalleutnant der Polizei.[55] He also ordered nine other promotions as of 17 May 1944, of which two were Germans; Hans-Boto Forstreuter (Kdr. SS-Freiw.Gren.Rgt.30) who was promoted to the rank of SS-Obersturmbannführer and Serge von Kuester (Kdr. SS-Freiw.Flak. Abt 14) was raised in rank to SS-Sturmbannführer. Of the Ukrainians Mykola Palienko (12.9.1896) Abteilungsführer in SS-Freiw.Art.Rgt.14 was advanced in rank to Waffen-Sturmbannführer, whilst an additional six medical doctors were promoted to the rank of Waffen-Untersturmführer.[56] These were Jaroslav Karpewitsch (8.7.1907) Regimentsartz SS-Freiw.Gren.Rgt.30; Volodymyr Lubinetsky (28.10.1913) Regimentsartz SS-Freiw.Gren.Rgt.29; Dionis Dakura (31.12.1904) Regimentsartz SS-Freiw.Gren.Rgt.31; Michael Hryhortschuk (1.6.1906) Regimentsartz SS-Freiw.Art.Rgt.14; Jaromyr Olesnyckyj (27.12.1914) 2./SS-Freiw.San.Abt.14; and Stefan Symko (5.6.1913) 2./SS-Freiw.San.Abt.14. Finally, Himmler also consented to the proposals concerning the critical issue of the venue for the Division's first engagement.

The same evening Himmler left Neuhammer with Governor Wächter and his retinue and flew to L'viv to visit Model's headquarters and confer with the Generalfeldmarshall on the Division's future engagements.[57] Here they discussed Model's planned Operation Schild und Schwert, (Shield and Sword) as outlined in his order dated 17 May 1944 which involved an attack by 1. Panzer Army to

At the culmination of his visit Himmler reviewed a parade of Divisional elements on 17 May 1944.

Himmler reviewing motorised units including Swimmwagens.

Above: Anti-tank artillery, left to right Freitag, Himmler (standing in the staff car, Wächter) SS-Obersturmbannführer Dern (Kdr WGR 29).

Below: The Divisional band played throughout the parade. Initially it was led by Kapelmeister Krawchuk. Later this position was held by SS-Oberscharführer Johannes Thiessen. The Tennermarsch, a traditional arrangement from the old Austro-Hungarian Army, was chosen as the Divisional march.

Himmler reviewing cavalry units. Another picture from the private album of Governor Wächter.

Above: Parade at the culmination of the visit of the Reichsführer SS. This picture was taken from Governor Wächter's personal photo album.

Below: Himmler takes the salute with a very satisfied Governor Wächter behind him. Immediately after the parade Himmler boarded his private JU-52 and flew to Lemberg (L'viv) to discuss the Division's deployment with Feldmarschall Model.

the south of the River Dniester and north of Kolomyia. For this purpose, one option within the order allowed for 1 Hungarian reserve division and the Galician Division to be deployed behind the front of 1 Panzer Army.[58]

The Lynchpin Remains

Five days later on 22 May and following the discussions with Himmler, the Division received its first significant reprieve when the order dated 15 May transferring its 1. General Staff Officer, Major Heike to the 3 Totenkopf Division was finally rescinded.[59] This news must have come as a relief to all concerned as Major Heike was a key asset, and the ramifications of his departure which would have been profound. His military and technical knowledge was indispensible to the Division as a fighting entity and his continued presence preserved the continuity of its command structure for the combat which lay ahead. Even more importantly, Heike understood the psychology of the Ukrainians and was recognised by many including Wächter and Bisanz as the Division's real lynchpin. His understanding and sympathetic attitude towards the Ukrainians, was in sharp contrast with Freitag who remained unpopular and whose suitability as commander had long been in question. Indeed later, Heike would be openly approached by Bisanz as a replacement for Freitag, which he declined.

Now that it was fully formed and deemed operational, on 2 June 1944,[60] a delegation from the Military Board led by Prof. Kubijovych and Alfred Bisanz was also invited to visit the Division at Neuhammer, accompanied by a selected group of fathers' of the soldiers, who came predominantly from urban areas. The visit lasted two full days during which time they too enjoyed watching the Ukrainian soldiers conduct field exercises and demonstrate the results of months of hard training. Waffen-Hauptsturmführer Dmytro Paliiv conducted a guided tour of the training facility for the fathers who were given an opportunity to inspect their living quarters and spend some time with their sons. This public relations exercise raised morale considerably, especially for those whose parents were able to attend and speeches were made by Kubijovych, Bisanz and Dr M. Roslak as a representative of the parents. Later this group proceeded to the reviewing area to watch a parade of all sections of the Division take place to the accompaniment of its orchestra. The visitors returned profoundly impressed having seen a modern and well trained and equipped infantry division which was a credit to its organisers.

The End of the Polizei Regiments and Consolidation

The month of June 1944, also saw the final stages of the implementation of the Division's organisation and the long overdue consolidation of all the remaining affiliated Galician Polizei units, a full eleven months after the first call up had been announced.

The SS-FHA issued an order dated 1 June for the Training and Replacement Regiment (SS-Gren.Ausb.u.Ers Rgt 14/Galiz. Nr.1) at Wandern to provide the necessary personnel for the formation of the missing III battalions of each of the infantry regiments.[61] Earlier on 23 May the Ukrainian soldiers of the Galizisches SS-Freiwilligen-Ersatz-Bataillon Tarbes had arrived at Neuhammer from their base in the south of France following their dissolution of their unit[62] and were transferred to the 14.Feld Ersatz Battalion. While a few remained with it, within days the majority were assigned to the Division's various combat units and the Training and Replacement Regiment where they assumed the role of training assistants.[63]

A further influx of trained Ukrainian soldiers which boosted the formation process of the third battalions came about as the result of the long overdue disbandment of the 4 and 5 Galizischen SS-Freiwilligen Regiments. Repeated petitioning of the Polizei authorities in Berlin by Wächter, the Military Board, the UCC and the soldiers themselves, led to two orders from Himmler for their dissolution. Dated 22 April 1944,[64] the first was ignored by the ORPO authorities, resulting in a second to be issued dated 9 June 1944[65] which directed that both Regiments be released from the Ordnungspolizei and made an integral part of Waffen-SS. Following the second order, their eventual liquidation and transfer to the Galician Division (less the majority of the German officers and NCOs) for which they had originally enlisted, took place. Eight days later on 17 June a report was sent by teleprinter to the Chef der Ordnungspolizei detailing the disbandment arrangements for the German personnel, vehicles and equipment.[66] Having had recent critical combat experience, most of the Ukrainian soldiers in both units were absorbed by the 29, 30 and 31 Regiments and the 14.Feld Ersatz Battalion straight away.[67] Responsibility for those whose training was not yet complete, or who required retraining, was passed onto Waffen-Sturmbannführer Pobihushtschyi.[68]

'Schützmannschafts-Bataillon 204' which was originally intended to be used as a partial basis for the Division, was the last unit to be incorporated into it, following the arrival at Heidelager of Guard Battalion 5 which was sent to relive it. According to a subsequent order dated 20 June 1944, Schutz Batl. 204 was officially dissolved while those men still required by the Kommandeur at Heidelager, were to be temporarily attached to the 5 Wach.Btl. until their final transfer to the 14 Galician Division.[69] This new order brought a further approximately two hundred and fifty German-speaking enlisted men into the Division.[70] The officers and NCOs were however excluded as these were transferred instead to 'Schützmannschafts-Bataillon 207'[71] which was based at Miechow.

As the eastern front continued to move inexorably west, the Ukrainian population especially near the front who knew well what life under the Bolsheviks entailed, continued to enlist for service in the Galician Division. Sensing the possibility that this resource presented, Wächter's long term plans assumed a far more dynamic dimension. On 20 June in a letter to his wife he wrote:

[...] Each week now brings 1,000 SS volunteers [...] We almost do not know what
to do with the men and I have just written to the RFSS (Himmler) with the request
to order the preparation of the second Galician SS Division![...][72]

In mid-June Wächter arranged for Generalfeldmarshall Model to send a
telegram inviting SS-Brigadeführer Freitag, his Operations Officer Major Heike
and adjutants, to the HQ of Army Group North Ukraine for talks on the Galician
Division's future utilisation. Freitag and his retinue left at once for L'viv, arriving
on 19 June. Their first port of call was a meeting with Governor Wächter who
in recent discussions with Fritz Arlt, had already expressed his grave misgivings
about the suitability of the former Polizei general as its commander.[73] In addition
he expressed his anxieties at the shortage of properly motivated German NCOs
within its ranks.[74] Once again Wächter took the opportunity to raise a number
of organisational and political problems concerning the Division at some length.
This was yet another vain attempt to convey to Freitag the potential political
ramifications for the Ukrainians of a successful first combat deployment. On
this issue at this time Wächter wrote 'The troops are all anxious awaiting
their deployment. We are all curious [as to] how it will turn out. This means a
significant political step!'[75]

SS-Standartenführer Gunter d'Alquen[76] was also present[77] and provided details
of Operation Skorpion, a propaganda campaign to be launched under his direction
on the Galician front aimed at encouraging the desertion of Ukrainians serving in
the Red Army. In order to ensure a successful outcome, Freitag was informed that
the Division was to provide a contingent of educated Ukrainians who would play
an active role in the operation. A number of groups were subsequently formed
and employed in this way, evidently with some success.[78]

Leaving Wächter's office, Freitag and his staff officers proceeded to Model's
HQ in Dubliany, a suburb of the city situated directly to the north east, for a
conference and debriefing. Here Freitag provided his evaluation of the Division's
combat readiness, strengths, deficiencies and idiosyncrasies. For example Major
Heike stated 'the Ukrainian soldiers were much more susceptible to heavy
artillery fire than Germans and were easier to flush out of defensive positions.
However they proved superior in counterattacks and almost always regained
lost territory'.[79] Generalfeldmarshall Model listened to his assessment and then
confirmed its allocation to the 1 Panzer Army under the command of General
of Panzer Armies Erhard Raus, located near Berezhany in the Stanyslaviv
region. This proved to be a most appropriate choice and Raus like Model
adopted a very positive and understanding attitude towards the Division.[80]
By now Model's initial plans for Operation Schild und Schwert had been
modified[81] as had the proposed rôle of the Galician Division. By 9 June 1944,
it was assigned for deployment again in a reserve capacity, as part of LIX.
Army Corps, (in the sector of the 371 Infantry Division).[82] In accordance with
this, after further consultations at his regional Army Corps HQ, General Raus
assigned it to secondary positions in LIX. Army Corps sector near the village of

Monastyryska, east of Stanyslaviv. This arrangement was agreeable to all parties as here it would be able to gradually acclimatise to the rigours of frontline combat. Freitag notified Model of the satisfactory outcome of the meeting with General Raus before starting the return journey to Neuhammer to begin the preparations for the transfer (the first echelons of which were due to leave for the front fourteen days later).

In the two remaining weeks before it departed, the Division's equipment was given a final service and its vehicles painted with camouflage colours.[83] As it was now a fully operational frontline formation, it continued with large scale manoeuvres lasting 2–3 days,[84] night exercises and last minute weapon training. In the barracks theoretical tactical revision continued around the sand tables on which were modelled terrain features such as streams, ponds, hills and valleys. Around these geographical features, various forms of attack and defence were discussed and maps and coloured pencils were much in evidence.

Difficulties did however continue to prevail in the vital signals section commanded by SS-Hauptsturmführer Wolfgang Wuttig. There was a shortage of trained German radio and telephone operators, while several of the Ukrainian operators found it difficult to translate military communications from German into Ukrainian.[85] The full impact of this handicap later manifest itself after the Division was fully engaged in combat, impeding its operational capabilities.

As part of the acclimatisation process, on 21 June the final preparations for departure began when all three infantry regiments were given orders to leave their barracks and set up camp in a nearby forest in order to get accustomed to front-line conditions.[86] Shortly before departure ammunition was distributed as well as grenades and new anti-tank weapons including some of the latest automatic weapons and anti-tank weaponry such as Ofenrohrs, Panzerfausts, brand new MG 42 machine guns, mortars and Granatbüchse Modell 39 (GrB 39) anti-tank rifles.[87] Loading (Verladung) officers were appointed to oversee the movement of men and matériel to the front and ammunition was distributed.

Morale was generally good amongst the Ukrainian soldiers and a general air of expectancy prevailed in the camp. Several rumours regarding its destination were in circulation the most popular of which was that it was to be deployed on Ukrainian soil in Galicia around Stanyslaviv or Kolomyia.[88] Many were anxious to return home to defend their families from the Soviets who had already overrun most of Ukraine and parts of eastern Galicia. It should be noted that even amongst the most optimistic men, their enthusiasm was somewhat tempered as in the year which had passed since the Ukrainians had begun their training a great deal had happened. The 'invincible' German Army had suffered several setbacks, the most recent of which was the successful Allied landings which had taken place in Normandy on 6 June and it was becoming increasingly obvious that the strategic initiative had now passed firmly into the hands of the Soviets.

New Orders

On 25 June 1944, an advance party consisting of a group of officers from the Division's general staff, left Neuhammer for the proposed operational area in the Stanyslaviv district to make the necessary arrangements for its arrival.

The following day, unexpectedly its command received notification from the German Army High Command (OKH) of a critical change in the deployment orders. Now it was to be assigned to the 4 Panzer Army which held the front east of L'viv in the centre of the battle lines of Army Group North Ukraine. This was in anticipation of a major Soviet offensive in this area.[89]

A few days earlier on 22 June 1944, which marked the third anniversary of the German invasion of the Soviet Union, the first phase of the Soviet summer offensive known as Operation Bagration[90] had commenced on the eastern front. The offensive, timed to complement the Allied landings in Normandy, which had taken place earlier in the month,[91] had begun in Belorussia with the total destruction of the German Army Group Centre (Heeresgruppe Mitte).[92] Such was the enormity of the forces that they had unleashed in this area, that in a mere twelve days, twenty five German divisions were simply completely annihilated in the worst defeat ever suffered in German military history.[93]

Following the destruction of Army Group Centre, the Soviet High Command (STAVKA) began the second phase, the 'L'viv–Peremyshyl' Operation (later known as the L'viv–Sandomierz Operation, after they had achieved more than they originally planned). The strategic objective was to occupy L'viv the capital of Galicia/western Ukraine and the city of Sandomierz in Poland, in so doing re-occupying the whole of Galicia and the southern part of the General Government.

The Soviet secret report on the operation states that the First Ukrainian Front under Marshal I. S. Konev, which was to undertake this offensive had subordinated to it (including Front operational reserves); 74 rifle divisions (numbering 843,000 troops) grouped together as seven infantry armies, (1, 3 and 5 Guards, 13, 18, 38 and 60 Armies).[94]

Critical armoured and mechanised support for what was the most powerful single Front entity in the Red Army was provided by a total of 2,041 tanks and self-propelled guns. These were grouped together as three tank armies (1 Guards Tank, 3 Guard Tank and 4 Tank) and two independent Calvary Mechanised Groups (named after their commanders Baranov and Sokolov). Between them they consisted of seven tank corps, three mechanised brigades, four separate tank brigades, eighteen tank regiments, and twenty four self-propelled artillery regiments.[95]

Absolutely nothing was to be left to chance as the forces amassed for operational support for the Front consisted of 9,797 guns and mortars (4,887 guns and 4,910 mortars—not including anti-aircraft guns). [96] These were grouped in four artillery divisions, eight gun artillery brigades, one howitzer artillery brigade, 4 howitzer artillery regiments, six anti-tank [destroyer] brigades, thirty six anti-tank artillery regiments, nineteen mortar regiments, one mortar brigade, four guards mortar brigades and fourteen guards mortar regiments.[97]

Disposition of A.Gr. North Ukraine on 12.7.1944

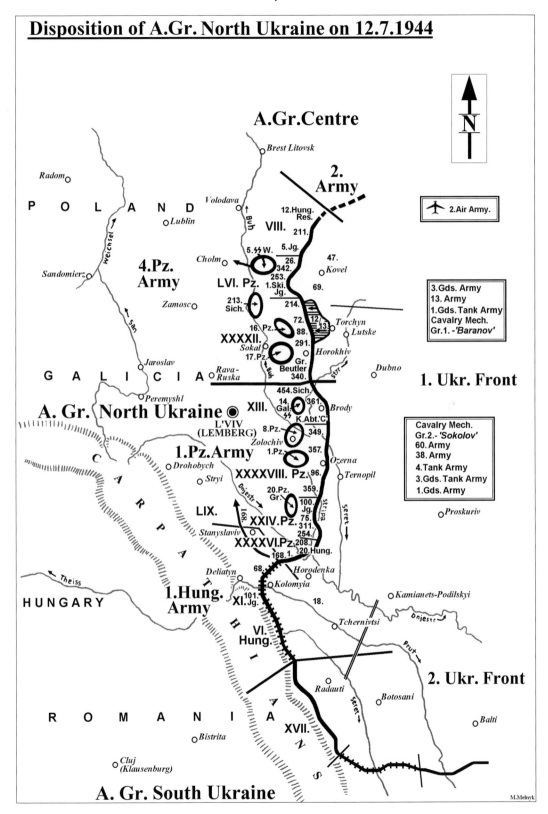

M.Melnyk

Air support was provided by 2 Air Army. It was composed of nine aviation corps, three aviation divisions, four aviation regiments and four separate aviation squadrons. The combined strength of these units amounted to 3,246 aircraft (679 bombers, 1,419 fighters, 1,046 assault [ground attack] aircraft plus 102 reconnaissance and spotter planes).[98]

In his account, Konev's figures concur with those given above except for the fact that he gives the number of men under his command as 1,200,000, i.e. 357,000 more than is stated in the official Soviet General Staff Report.[99]

Opposing this monumental force, was Army Group North Ukraine which after 28 June was under the command of Generaloberst (Colonel-General) Joseph Harpe.[100] It was defending the sector directly opposite the First Ukrainian Front, stretching from the Prypiat marshes to the Carpathian Mountains and comprised of the 4[101] and 1 Panzer Armies[102] and the 1 Hungarian Army. Between them, these amounted to a total of thirty one German divisions (including four panzer) and twelve Hungarian light divisions or brigades. Moreover virtually all of these were under strength, some quite significantly (the average size being between 7–9,000 men).

Army Group North Ukraine had at its disposal approximately one hundred and eighty one tanks,[103] (forty three of the tanks were within 4 Panzer Army), and additional self-propelled guns,[104] and negligible Luftwaffe support (see map 1 for disposition of forces as of 12 July 1944).

Inevitably the fighting strengths of the German forces involved were exaggerated in the previously cited Soviet General Staff report, especially with regard to armour and aircraft. Their calculations were based on full strength paper authorisations for the German units, which in almost every case simply did not exist.[105] Despite this, according to their own calculations the Red Army in this sector enjoyed an huge overall superiority, outnumbering the Germans 1.5/2 to 1, in artillery, tanks and quantity of divisions and by a ratio of 4.5/1 in aircraft, although even these should be regarded as extremely conservative estimates.

Not only were the German forces exhausted after months of hard fighting, but they also had to contend with the considerable impact of the increasing activities of partisan units operating behind their lines which disrupted communications as well as supplies to the frontline units.[106]

Already depleted, Army Group North Ukraine's position had deteriorated significantly since the collapse of Army Group Centre. It had already surrendered three panzer and two infantry divisions to Army Group Centre which constituted most of its tactical reserves.[107] On this basis the decision was taken to divert the Galician Division to reinforce the front in the sector against which the full weight of the Soviet offensive was expected to fall.

Before returning to the HQ of AGNU for new battle orders, its Operations Officer Major Heike, informed Governor Wächter of the hasty decision by the OKH to commit the Galician Division in a different region at short notice. Cognisant of the potential disastrous consequences of the new orders, Wächter agreed to make urgent representations to have the standing orders countermanded.[108]

At the Army Group headquarters, Major Heike was told that the Galician

Division had now been assigned to the XIII Army Corps (hereafter XIII AK) of the 4 Panzer Army. This occupied a position in the Brody district 96 kms east of L'viv. Upon arrival, it was to occupy a secondary defensive line. Further battle training was to continue as prevailing conditions permitted.[109]

The requests to revoke the standing orders met with some sympathy from the Army Group's staff, however, after recent developments on the eastern front they were not prepared to grant the Galician Division any special dispensation. Somewhat short sightedly, the Germans decided that its utilisation in the dire military situation took precedence over any other consideration, including its propaganda value in terms of potential long term political developments. Under these circumstances all attempts by Governor Wächter and the Division's representatives to alter the decision inevitably resulted in failure.

In the meantime, on the 28 June orders were given for the bulk of the newly redesignated 14. Waffen-Grenadier-Division der SS (galizische Nr. 1)[110] to entrain for the eastern front. As it relied heavily on horse draft for its transportation and supply vehicles,[111] the first unit to leave was the veterinary company under the command of SS-Sturmbannführer Dr Oskar Kopp, along with its equipment and a large quantity of fodder.[112] This was followed by other priority units including the anti-aircraft detachment commanded by SS-Sturmbannführer von Kuester and SS-Obersturmbannführer Beyersdorff's Artillery Regiment which proceeded to the Belys military railway station at Neuhammer. Oblivious to the witches cauldron into which they were about to be thrown, these units boarded trains and headed east. Thereafter a further four railway transports left each day.[113] Waffen-Sturmmann Mychailo Kormylo:

> [...] We travelled in the second convoy on the second day towards Ukraine. The 30 Regiment was heading homewards! Waffen-Obersturmführer Pospilovsky of the fourth heavy company saw us on to the wagons where we were to place our heavier weapons on open carriages, dispersed at intervals along the convoy. This was especially for traversing Poland where we were most likely to be ambushed. I had to put my MG 42 at the rear of one wagon while the work companies came and surrounded our position with a small wall of sandbags. At the other end of our wagon was an 82 mm mortar team. Thus forearmed, the convoy proceeded towards L'viv.
>
> As we journeyed through Germany we stopped at various stations. Local Germans welcomed us and asked why we were so happy to be heading to the eastern front. We replied 'Because we are heading to Ukraine! We are Ukrainians and happy to be going there'. They told us that when their German soldiers were assigned to the eastern front they became sad because they believe they would never return home. Our journey through Germany was straightforward but when we approached Poland everyone was on high alert. Luckily the Polish partisans could see we were armed to the teeth so we encountered no resistance as we approached L'viv.
>
> In L'viv our train stopped for two hours while convoys passed through in the opposite direction on their way to Germany. They were hospital convoys laden with wounded Germans. Within half an hour of our departure a convoy came through and

stopped for around twenty minutes. It was a trainload of Ukrainian recruits, some of whom jumped down and ran over to us. They so wanted to come with us but we told them that they had better get all the training possible. Get to Neuhammer and then come and join us!.

As our train continued we received the news that we were not heading for Stanyslaviv but instead north towards Brody. We progressed slowly in the direction of Ozhydiv. On the way, as we passed through people knew that we were heading for the front line and they welcomed us by throwing flowers on to our train. I will never forget the pile of flowers that landed on our machine gun. As we got to the outskirts of Ozhydiv it was time to get all the weaponry ready for action. Pospilovsky instructed us to disembark, leaving our extra baggage to be brought along later.[…][114]

In the wake of the Division's departure, on 15 July 1944, the Training and Reserve Regiment which now consisted of about seven thousand men, was transferred temporarily to the training facility at Wandern near Frankfurt an der Oder.[115] It stayed here one month until 15 August before finally moving to Neuhammer.[116] Here it joined the personnel allocated to form the 3 battalions of the three infantry regiments which had remained behind at the camp and the bulk of the personnel from the Galizischen SS-Freiwilligen Regiments 4 and 5.

To their great disappointment, another group of over two hundred Ukrainian soldiers mostly drawn from those who held administrative positions, also stayed behind. They had been selected to attend a five month unteroffizier (NCO) course at an army run school in Laibach (Slovenia). Amongst this group the desire to join their companions who had left for the front in Galicia was so strong that they had to be kept under guard until the train arrived to transport them to the school.[117]

XIII Army Corps

After a two day rail journey, on 30 June the first echelons arrived in the new district and detrained at the station in the town of Ozhydiv, where XIII AK had its headquarters.[118] Arriving in the evening the soldiers marched through the town, the edge of which had been bombed to find civilians were absent and only dogs remained to greet them, barking from empty houses and yards. The remaining transports followed over the course of the next few days. From Ozhydiv all arriving units proceeded to generally defined assembly areas, for example WGR 30 was based in the villages of Zabolotsi and Sukhodoly and took up position between the main L'viv–Brody road on the right wing of the southern line of Sasiv and Pidhirtsi as far as Sukhodoly.

The unloading of the Division's matériel took place day and night and was interrupted several times by the sudden appearance of Soviet aircraft in the vicinity of the station, seeking a vulnerable target. As a countermeasure, along with two 3.5 cm guns from XIII AKs Flak Rgt. 33 deployed at the station on the wagon platform, the Division's battery of 8.8 cm anti-aircraft guns and several of its 2 cm cannons were installed in, or close to the rail depot. Unloading was then resumed under the protection of the guns which were able to successfully contain most of the attacks, prevent any casualties and keep the level of damage to a minimum.[119]

With the movement orders well underway, Governor Wächter summoned SS-Brigadeführer Freitag to attend a final meeting in L'viv. Now that the Division's deployment was completely beyond his influence, Wächter could only reiterate to Freitag the significance of the forthcoming engagement and remind him that the ultimate responsibility for its performance, was in his hands.[120] As they discussed the ramifications of the new battle orders in L'viv, Major Heike and his adjutant reported to the commander of XIII AK General Artur Hauffe[121] at his HQ in Ozhydiv for a briefing on the overall situation and the new instructions for the Division's tactical deployment. In his memoirs Major Heike states that neither the corps' commander nor his Chief of Staff Colonel Kurt Von Hammerstein knew anything about the as yet un-blooded 14. Waffen-Grenadier-Division der SS (galizische Nr. 1) and both were dubious of its combat capabilities.[122] To make matters worse, in contrast to General Raus, they also proved to be somewhat less inclined to make any allowances for its special needs and idiosyncrasies as a unit made up of foreign nationals.

The prospect of additional reinforcements in their sector was however welcomed especially since all of XIII AKs Wehrmacht infantry divisions were at medium or minimum strength. Added to this the Galician Division was better armed and equipped than the corps other regular army formations, which was a further source of encouragement.[123]

In his assessment of the situation, General Hauffe envisaged a Soviet advance on L'viv, in the event of which XIII AK would be barring the way especially in the area of Zolochiv.[124] Therefore, rather than a direct frontal attack against prepared German positions, the Soviets were expected to employ a pincer movement from the north and south of the corps' area in the event of which the Galician Division would be given the task of preventing any attempt at outflanking the corps. If the front was penetrated, it would be committed to a counterattack to close the resultant gap. Contrary to the standard German practice when confronted with possible encirclement of breaking up divisions into individual units and deploying them as semi-autonomous groups, a special request was tendered that as a non German formation, it should always be deployed as a whole Division and remain directly under its own command.[125] Evidently, the import of this request was not fully realised by the commanding General and his staff, as later events would prove with alarming clarity.

As part of the 4 Panzer Army, XIII AK held a sector of the front that included the town of Brody and the outlying areas immediately to the north, south and east. Having previously been encircled from the end of March until mid-April 1944, the corps had successfully held out until it was relieved by a German counterattack.[126] Since then the Brody sector had remained quiet which gave the Germans the opportunity to recuperate and strengthen their positions. The frontline known as the HKL (Hauptkampflinie—main line of resistance), had been well developed in an engineering sense with defences echeloned to a depth of 6–8 kms. It consisted of three to four trench lines (the first being continuous and full profile) connected by a dense network of communications trenches, several rows of barbed wire entanglements, anti-tank and anti-personnel mine fields and the same obstructions along likely tank axes. Mined obstacles were constructed in forest sectors and key bridges, roads and buildings were also prepared with explosive charges for demolition.[127] More importantly work began on building a static defensive line in its rear area known as the Prinz Eugen Stellung (Prince Eugen defence position). Within it, the Galician Division was ordered to occupy the so called 'Rudolf Position' and having done so, it continued with the construction of the defensive installations and emplacements.[128]

In July 1944, XIII AK consisted of:

> A headquarters unit—based in Ozhydiv with a commanding general and his staff, support, rear echelon and supply services,[129] together with attached corps' artillery group, anti-tank, and pioneer units,[130] [total strength 555[131]] and the following infantry units:
> 454 Security Division: [total strength 5,929][132] commanded by Generalmajor Johannes Nedtwig which was in position on the corps' left flank north of Stanyslavchyk,
> 361 Infantry Division: [total strength 10,131][133] under Knights Cross holder Generalmajor Gerhard Lindemann which was in the centre of the corps' line, west of Brody,
> Korpsabteilung C:[134] [total strength 11,312][135] under the command of General Major Wolfgang Lange composed of the 183, 217, and 339 Division groups, (each at approximately regimental strength) which held the front around Boratyn and Hai Starobridski.

These units were augmented by the assault guns of Sturmgeschütz-Brigade 249, and II./Flak Rgt 33 for anti-aircraft support which was added to the corps' strength at the beginning of July.[136]

Lastly, there were the remaining garrison forces within the city of Brody itself which comprised of the remnants of three infantry battalions with a combined strength of 743 men,[137] Sicherheit Battalion Bauer[138] and elements of the 361 Infantry Division including a Panzerjäger Zug[139] which altogether amounted to a further 1,352 men.

The corps tactical reserve was the 14. Waffen-Grenadier-Division der SS (galizische Nr. 1), which had a strength return of 15,299 men of which approximately 11,000 were actually deployed in the field.[140] XIII AKs total theoretical paper strength therefore stood at approximately 41,000 men.[141]

Originally the 349 Infantry Division [total strength 10,588][142] commanded by Knights Cross holder Generalleutnant Otto Lasch, was part of XXXXVIII PK, and was in place on XIII AKs right flank near Shyshkivtsi. Ultimately, having been cut off from its parent formation during the encirclement it was later formally attached to XIII AK.

On XIII AKs left was XXXXVI Panzer Corps (4 Panzer Army) while on the right was XXXXVIII Panzer Corps (1 Panzer Army) both of which had infantry divisions manning their fronts.

Based on information obtained from reconnaissance reports and the interrogation of Red Army prisoners, XIII AK command anticipated an attack in its sector beginning in mid-July.

No further reinforcements were available to the corps and any attack would have to be repulsed with minimal armoured support since the whole of the 4 Panzer Army had less than fifty operational tanks within its entire sector. Moreover their effectiveness was limited as they suffered from a crippling shortage of fuel.[143] Likewise, critical air support would also be largely absent since much of the Luftwaffe had been diverted from the eastern front to cope with the Allied landings in Normandy we well as having to contend with increasingly heavy British and American bombing raids on German cities and industrial targets.

So as to leave no doubt about the realities of the situation, in his command briefing General Hauffe revealed that the latest intelligence reports indicated massively unequal odds in terms of the known ratio of enemy to friendly forces in the vicinity of his weakened corps and went on to say that this would in all probability render it inadequate for its assigned task.[144]

5

On the Eastern Front

Return to the Homeland

By the end of the first week in July the last rail transports had arrived along with SS-Brigadeführer Freitag, who came to the district by car. Altogether, of the 15,299 men serving with the 14. Waffen-Grenadier-Division der SS (galizische Nr. 1) consisting of 346 officers: 1,131 NCOs, and 13,822 enlisted men[1] approximately 11,000 deployed at Brody. Of the officers, around 150 or less than half were Ukrainian[2] whilst at the time of its deployment it was short of over 100 officers and 1,300 NCOs. Freitag reported the arrival of all the Division's operational and administrative forces to the necessary authorities, after which its general staff allocated positions to individual sections which took up their places and began digging in. Occasionally this necessitated considerable damage to ripe fields of wheat, which despite the proximity of the front some farmers were instinctively continuing to cultivate. This was regretted, especially by those who themselves were sons of farmers, but unavoidable.

The terrain in the sector which XIII AK was defending was mostly flat with the exception of the hills of Iaseniv and Pidhirtsi which were cut with the Seret and Buh River valleys. The soil was mainly rich loam which quickly became soaked during rainy periods and the area was heavily forested with small populated points, many situated in hollows. Punctuated with occasional swampy meadows, the abundance of forests and wooded groves provided ample natural cover especially from the air. The region had the additional benefit of further natural obstacles formed by three rivers; the Seret, the Styr and the lower reaches of the Buh. The road network was well developed, although the predominantly dirt roads became difficult to traverse after rain, especially for wheeled transport.

The Galician Division held a line anywhere between 10–12 kms from the HKL approximately 36 kms in length, running from S/W of Stanyslavchyk in the north to a point S/E of Iaseniv close to the Seret River in the south; (see map 2). Its three infantry regiments were placed in a linear disposition. Waffen-Grenadier-Regiment

Most of the roads in the Brody area were unpaved and became impassable for motorised wheeled vehicles after heavy rain.

31[3] (hereafter WGR 31) supported by the III. artillery battalion was based in the area of Turie and assigned the northern flank. Waffen-Unterscharführer Jurij Ferencevych who was with the staff of 13./WGR 31:

> We (WGR 31) left the railroad station at Ozhydiv and moved north towards the village of Turie. Myself and my messenger were riding horses at the front of the 13 I.G. company. As a precaution, the company commander Waffen-Ustuf. Alexander Olearnyk took off the silver strip on his officers cap so he could not be identified as an officer. As we passed through villages at first the people had serious faces, they did not know who these Germans were - not only Germans but SS. But after we started talking to them and singing Ukrainian songs they started smiling at us, especially the nice young girls and answered our questions. We stayed there about a week working, improving the Prinz Eugen Stellung.[4]

In place covering the centre near the village of Chekhy was WGR 30[5] supported by the II. artillery battalion; while WGR 29[6] supported by I. artillery battalion and elements of the Panzerjäger (anti-tank) company[7] took up position on the southern flank in the vicinity of the village of Iaseniv.

The Division's headquarters was situated in the rear of the three infantry regiments between Sokolivka and Ozhydiv along with its supply and support units. The command post of the artillery regiment was established nearby in the vicinity of the village of Tsishky, a short distance from the IV. heavy artillery battalion.

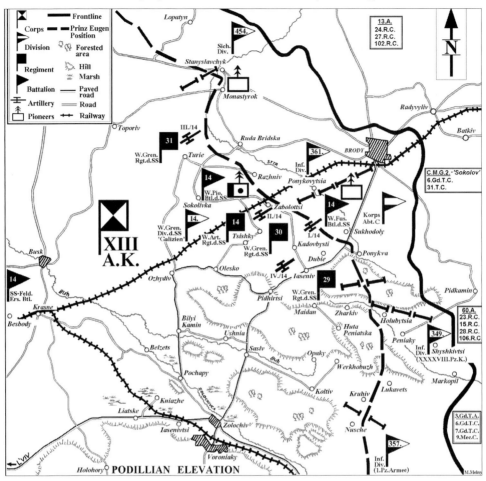

The anti-aircraft batteries were deployed in defence of strategic positions according to the capabilities of their weapons.

The forward-most unit was the Fusilier Battalion commanded by SS-Hauptsturmführer Karl Bristot.[8] It was deployed in front of the Division's main line near Sukhodoly, east of the Styr River where it served as an intelligence unit, establishing observation points to monitor enemy activities.[9] Situated just behind the battalion to provide it with covering support was I. artillery battalion.

Just outside Sokolivka, the Pioneer Battalion was bivouacked in the forest. It was assigned the task of felling trees and preparing the necessary materials for the other sections which had been ordered to build bunkers, trenches, gun positions and fortifications.[10]

The 14.Feld Ersatz Battalion commanded by SS-Hauptsturmführer Kleinow was one of the last units to arrive on 7 July. It was stationed furthest to the rear, some 20 kms behind the Division's positions. Its five companies were located in the proximity of Krasne in the villages of Kutkir, (two companies) Kuduriawci and Bezbrody where they continued with their training with blank ammunition.[11]

Grenadiers with their NCO from the Division's signals Abteilung in the field. The specialist insignia (a lighting bolt design) is visible on the lower left sleeve of all four men. Waffen-Grenadier Roman Kulynycz is on the far left.

A document in the Schevchenko Archive in London, reveals that shortly after the Division's arrival at the front, in an internal circular letter dated 3 July 1944, Freitag attempted to galvanise the Ukrainians under his command for the impending combat. He began by alluding to his pleasure at the good impression made by all members of the Division in on the general command of XIII AK, in the corps' area. With reference to the defensive battles that lay ahead, he stressed that on the eve of a great enemy offensive against the territory of Galicia, it would be up to 'our young Division to absorb and repulse the enemy hordes'. So as to encourage a sense of camaraderie between the Ukrainians and the Germans and instill confidence, he stated that the Division was deployed in the depth of the defensive position and that 'preceding you are the comrades of the German Army hardened in many battles'. He went on to emphasize his trust that the individual Ukrainian members of his Division would, like the German soldiers during the previous 5 years of war, be prepared to fight with their lives and commit themselves fully to protect their families and homeland from the Bolshevik hordes. He ended with the words "Prove that the long and thorough training time has molded you into outstanding and fanatical fighters against the red hordes".

As the Division occupied its sector, its German command staff was confronted by the acknowledged risks associated with using it on home territory. Because of previous experiences with the Ukrainian troops, the possibility of desertion to the ubiquitous UPA units active in the area was considered to be a very real threat especially with the recent Soviet reoccupation of parts of eastern Galicia.[12] There were also concerns about its employment in an area populated by both Ukrainians and Poles.

These anxieties were initially partly obviated by the fact that by order of the corps' command billeting in villages of operational units was strictly forbidden (because of attacks from enemy aircraft) and all units were therefore required to set up quarters and dig fox holes in wooded areas nearby. Waffen-Sturmmann Mychailo Kormylo recalled:

> [...] As the second line reinforcing the German front line we were instructed to dig in and stay in the field regardless of weather—no going to villages for shelter, no sleeping under feather quilts![13]

For the first two or three days contact with the population was also prohibited by later this was relaxed as Unterscharführer Vasyl Veryha a former member of 7./II. WGR 30 recollected:

> There was a great deal of contact [with the civilians]. It was very friendly and amongst themselves the civilian population referred to us as 'our boys'. We were welcomed by almost every family in the village.[14]

The amiable relations with the inhabitants provided an opportunity to augment their rations with foodstuffs willingly given by the villagers. Waffen-Unterscharführer Vasyl Sirsky who was serving with the staff company WGR 29:

> On 2 July 1944 at 11.30 a.m. we entered the village of Iaseniv where I had several friends. The parents of my friend Pawlo Haraniuk invited me to stay with them as long as it was possible. Even a week later when the command post of our stabskompanie was moved to the woods about 1 km east of Iaseniv, Haraniuk's sister Sonia, almost daily, delivered a hot meal to me.[15]

Unfortunately this cordial relationship did not exist between the residents and XIII AKs' German units who in order to fulfil their supply needs formed 'requisitioning detachments'. In exchange for worthless government bonds, these units forcibly procured livestock, fowl, quantities of grain and horses from the local peasants leaving them with little or nothing for themselves. The locals were quick to approach the Ukrainian soldiers who upon learning about the arbitrary seizures often intervened with their weapons on behalf of their countrymen to prevent them from taking place.[16] The Germans were simply unable to grasp that the Ukrainians refused to put German interests before their own and that their priorities naturally lay with their own community and people. With a duplicity that beggars belief, Generalleutnant Lange the commander of KAC, first accused the Ukrainians of 'stealing cherries' (which were in any case given to them freely by their country folk) whilst at the same time criticising their 'lack of discipline' for not permitting the Germans to 'steal' livestock and foodstuffs from their own families. Regarding the Galician Division he wrote:

[...] The small cadre was exclusively German or Austrian; their morale was high and they did the best they could. I received excellent cooperation from the Division staff at all times. Non-commissioned officers and men were almost exclusively young Galicians, mostly sons of First World War soldiers who had served in the Austro-Hungarian Army. Their fresh and youthful appearance pleasantly contrasted with that of the German soldiers who had suffered the hardships of past battles. Their weapons and equipment were excellent and could only be a source of envy among the army units; nothing was missing. However, the lack of discipline was apparent among these young troops. It began with the theft of cherries and finally went so far that young Galician soldiers forcibly prevented supply troops of other divisions from requisitioning cattle for the needs of the troops, so that the live-stock could be retained by the local population in some cases the soldiers' relatives. From this it became apparent how debatable it was to commit the Division, especially in the defence of its homeland.[...][17]

Thereafter, to avoid any repetition of these difficulties, whenever requisitioning had to take place it was undertaken with the assistance of the Galician Division.[18]

Direct contact with the local population did not result in large scale desertions which the Germans had feared[19] however it did assist in the opening of communication links between the local UPA units[20] and almost all the Division's sub sections. The result was a degree of limited unofficial co-operation between the two forces. The local UPA command was often able to provide very accurate intelligence information regarding the strengths, dispositions and activities of the Red Army units in the regions they had occupied. In return, the Division's Ukrainian personnel who were understandably well disposed toward the UPA, began the unauthorised provision of quantities of weapons, ammunition, supplies and uniforms as well as limited weapons training sessions with the insurgent personnel.[21] Waffen-Unterscharführer Roman Drazniowsky who commanded the 3 platoon, 3 company I. bat. WGR 30, experienced this at first hand. He wrote:

During the period from 4–14 July my unit (3 pla. 3 co. 1 btl. WGR 30) was frequently ordered to conduct reconnaissance missions. I used that opportunity to make contact with the UPA. I trained its personnel in the proper use of the Ofenrohr and the Sturmgewehr at Sukhodoly and Holoskovychy. All meetings with UPA soldiers were reported to the company commander Waffen-Obersturmführer Bohdan Pidhaynyj, as was the transfer of weapons and training of their use.[22]

Others recalled the transfer of weapons and supplies. Julian Wilshynsky a Waffen-Unterscharführer of 3 co. Pi.Abtl wrote:

We left Neuhammer in late June. I was a Waffen-Unterscharführer with the 3 'S' [schnell] or 'fast' company which had 182 men, of whom four were German. A regular company had three platoons, but our company had four. Every platoon had three squads but our platoon had two squads, one with heavy machine guns and one with mortars. I was in the heavy machine gun squad. When the company was building a bridge or laying a minefield or doing work we were defending the perimeter. We didn't have rocket launchers but we had flamethrowers and automatic submachine guns. I was equipped with a pistol and an automatic rifle.

Our commanding officer was Waffen. Ustuf. Anton Dydalewytsch. He was an engineer by profession. We had Swimmwagens, motorcycles and bicycles. The horses were attached to infantry wagons for supplies.

Near Sokolivka, the first thing that the company did was to establish a bivouac. The villages were out of bounds because they were being attacked by aircraft so we were bivouacked in the forest. We prepared our defences against all eventualities including attack from aircraft.

The task of 3 company was to prepare materials for fortification. Other units were coming in, picking the material up and taking it away to build the fortifications. We were based there for about a week. There were a couple of houses nearby where we made contact with the UPA. I had a connection with the underground because my family had been involved with it before. I was instrumental in supplying the underground with medical supplies. It [the contact] was well known to the company but the Germans didn't know anything.[23]

It should be noted that this relationship was unknown to the Division's German command staff and on occasion when these activities were discovered it resulted in draconian punishment and death for those actively involved. Waffen-Unterscharführer Jurij Ferencevych who was serving with the staff of 13./WGR 31:

Although I never had any contact with UPA, as I found out later our company Stabscharführer (who took care of the supplies, kitchens etc.), did. He was a veteran of the winter '41 campaign, and he must have been with a German unit before. He gave the UPA some supplies and ammunition. He was caught, placed under 'Feldgericht' and sentenced to death and shot.[24]

For Freitag, any fraternisation which took place was anathema and undermined discipline as was reflected his letter dated 9 July 1944 addressed to the 'Volunteer SS Officers of the Division' in which he wrote:

Our Division has received an exceedingly important job within the corps: to occupy the part of the defensive positions assigned to us. It is one of the most important sectors of the front in the Galician region.

Before us is the HKL [front line] which must withstand the power of the expected major Bolshevik attack. Our lines must finally shatter the enemy attack and if he should succeed in breaking through the lines, he must bleed to death.

The fulfilment of our mission is negated if the Bolsheviks should succeed in overrunning the whole of Galicia annihilating your people.

We know that the enemy has very strong forces (tanks and aircraft) facing us together with conscripts and has the objective of occupying Lemberg [L'viv].

In order to fulfil our mission, the Division must achieve combat readiness to the last man so that the combat value of the Division is assured.

However, I discovered in my inspection trips that neither the SS-Freiw. Officers nor soldiers are aware of the seriousness of the situation or their behaviour and yes, not even training and living in perfect peace and tranquillity.

As your commander I am responsible for the Division and the assigned sector [of the line]. I am personally responsible for the fulfilment of this mission. Just as I, each of you shall be liable to me personally for the fulfilment of this mission with the smallest possible sacrifice in human lives.

This refers primarily to my Freiw.SS-Officers and it is why I write this letter to you, to help you identify the danger that results from the reckless behaviour which I have unfortunately noticed in some company and battery officers.

We can only endure the imminent heavy battle with a force with the best discipline. Do you think, my Freiw.SS-Officers that in quiet training periods, discipline is for nothing? No, in heavy fighting only a disciplined force can exist. If your men cannot maintain upright discipline now, they will not be able to in battle. This is an old soldiers law which also applies to you and your units.

In my driving inspections I have noticed that apparently you and your men believe that you no longer have to follow all the discipline they have learned in recent months. The men do not salute, do not report and appear untidy and make no effort to show soldierly bearing.

Perhaps these things seem insignificant in combat. For me as an old soldier, these are the signs of degradation that I will not tolerate in any case.

Also, I realized that extraordinarily, many men were wandering about in the villages. [This is] A sign that it is still not clear to the men, what is meant by unauthorised absence. Anyone who is half an hour and a few hundred metres away from their unit without orders is committing an offence.

I have given the military police the command to arrest and ruthlessly punish anyone found hanging around pursuant to the application of the field regulations.

In one case, I have encountered the men in a village asking for food from the local population. They claimed to have had no meals in the company for 2 days. I will investigate this case and will proceed with the severest penalties against that negligent officer who in these days ate well while neglecting his troops. For every officer the proper care for his troops must be his foremost duty, but in these hours also requires their sweat.

Positions have to be improved and camouflaged. The Bolshevik attack can begin at any moment in our sector. We must use every hour to complete our defensive system in secrecy out of sight of the enemy. Nevertheless, in some units men are still standing around idly and Freiw.SS Officers watch passively. Or as I found out in one case, the unit leader did not care about the return of his men into the intended positions, but left his unit himself.

Where is the leadership responsibility? Do you have no accountability for the omissions of duty that would cost you and your mens lives?

You can see for yourself how every day the Bolsheviks reconnoitre over the region and it goes without saying also photograph the terrain. So you can act to improve

250   *The History of the Galician Division of the Waffen-SS*

the camouflage on it everyday through the construction phase and educate the men to camouflage themselves.

Another great evil is the treatment of horses. The horse is the most faithful companion of the soldier. To beat the horse and stand idly by as it suffers hunger and thirst is a brutality and a crime against the 'comrade horse'. Educate the men that they have to feed the horse first before they think of themselves. From the picture I saw on my inspection trips I was also able to make a judgment about the responsible unit leaders because the value of a leader can be seen not only in his attitude but also in those of his men. I point out to all volunteers, that for the sake of the Division I will proceed ruthlessly and bring the leaders to justice for the crimes of their men. I will not allow disorder and indiscipline to enter the ranks of the Division which has been set up with such great effort and so many sacrifices.

After re-emphasising the need for the officers to ensure positions were camouflaged, all units were prepared for an attack and that the men saluted, reported and maintained appropriate 'soldierly behaviour' he ended by saying 'Always be aware that a failure of the Division, means your homeland will fall'.[25]

Knowing that the Soviet policy was to conscript all able bodied men in the recently reoccupied territory into the Red Army and immediately commit them to

The caption of this Kriegsberichter photo reads: 'From action [of the] Galician SS on the Eastern Front. Just now, the Division commander has arrived at the main front line where some of the Galician SS volunteers who have come straight from the most advanced trenches report about the latest fighting'.

battle without any training, the Division was able to recruit limited numbers of young men in the locality. An unofficial agreement was reached with the UPA and the local population whereby all young men without any previous military training would join the Division whilst those with military experience would go to the UPA.[26] According to Waffen-Unterscharführer Wasyl Sirsky who served with the staff company of WGR 29: 'On a single day 120 volunteers were registered at the HQ of the 29 Regiment and transported to [the Reserve Battalion at] Krasne for training'.[27]

During the first week in July the Division continued to establish itself within the 'Rudolf Position' which together with the Long Bolt ('Lange-Riegel') position formed part of the Prinz Eugen Position (Prinz Eugen Stellung). In accordance with its anticipated role of defending this static defensive line, all units were allocated a variety of tasks associated with its continued fortification. Anti-tank obstacles were erected and concealed, firing positions for artillery and guns of all sizes and calibres selected and cleared and infantry support weapons sited. With all units entrenched in static positions, the signals units went to work laying telephone lines between regimental, battalion and company HQs'. The Fusilier Battalion built the forward emplacements occasionally drawing enemy fire in the process.[28] Barbed wire barricades were erected by the pioneers who also laid minefields in front of the prepared positions. Supply and ammunition depots were set up and the guard duty that this entailed was conducted in earnest. It seems all such tasks were undertaken with a great deal of enthusiasm as according to Major Heike 'the first practical work in defence of their homeland inspired the Ukrainians'.[29]

The idea that the Division would be able to 'acclimatise to frontline conditions' was however in the opinion of the commander of KAC Generalleutnant Lange debatable as he acknowledged when he wrote:

[...] In many other respects, too, the commitment of that [Galician] Division was an unfortunate choice. The units were deployed in the rear in order to improve positions and to function as reserve in case of an enemy breakthrough. The men were to get used to front line and combat conditions. This conception was wrong. In rear positions, during quiet periods, no unit can become accustomed to combat conditions, yet it would suddenly be exposed to extremely difficult conditions, if any enemy break through should occur. These considerations, which had been discussed in great detail with the commanding officer of the Galician Volunteer Division, were fully confirmed later on.[30]

As often as possible supply work was done under the cover of darkness, to avoid detection by reconnaissance aircraft. Since 6 July the Army Group had expected the Soviet attack to begin and consequently on this day all units of the XIII AK were put on state of alert[31] which gave fresh impetus to the work.

Regular reconnaissance missions were undertaken by small groups from all three infantry regiments including the regimental cavalry units which proved well suited this task.[32] This assisted the Divisional command with establishing the location, strength and intentions of the enemy forces opposite. It also enabled the Ukrainian soldiers to obtain limited battle training under front conditions.

In the vicinity of the town of Brody itself, the heavy artillery battery under the command of Waffen-Sturmbannführer Palienko was briefly brought into action in support of the corp's army units which were holding the frontline.[33] This indispensible experience was later to pay dividends.

To improve their own occupied positions and determine the composition and strength of the German forces, the 1 Ukrainian Front's headquarters planned its own 'Razviedka boem' (reconnaissance in force). By the second week in July this had translated into a noticeable increase in terms of Soviet air reconnaissance and long range artillery fire, activities which augured an imminent offensive. Advance patrols and attack groups infiltrated the German lines, sometimes to a depth of several kilometres which resulted in the outbreak of skirmishes some of which involved the forward most units of the Division.

Within XIII AKs own sector, in the days leading up to the Soviet offensive its Divisions' repeatedly reported to the corp's HQ that their available intelligence reports suggested that they did not expect to find themselves facing the main thrust of the anticipated Soviet assault. Instead they expected a large scale holding attack on their section of the front[34] and the main blows to fall further north and south. Hence, as a pre-emptive measure against the expected southern attack, around midday on 8 July the 14 Galician Division's area of operations was now extended to include the village of Pieniaki, in 349.Infantry Divisions's sector. This in turn was in the area of control of the neighbouring XXXXVIII PzK which bordered XIII AK to the south. In accordance with this directive, whilst the bulk of the Galician Division was to remain established in the Prinz Eugene Stellung, WGR 29 along with its attached artillery and Pak (anti-tank) guns was to be relocated to the village.[35]

The Brody Pocket (Kessel von Brody)

The anticipated Soviet offensive against Army Group North Ukraine began a day early, when unexpectedly, on 13 July Hitler permitted XXXXII Corps of the 4 Panzer Army to make a minor withdrawal from a bulge towards Torchyn, under cover of rearguards. This move which allowed the Germans to shorten their line, was soon detected by Soviet reconnaissance units. With the forward German positions now empty, Marshal Konev ordered the main forces of Gordov's 3 Guards Army and 13 Army's infantry forces to pursue the withdrawing units. The Soviet assault was covered by formations from the 1 Guards and 5 Assault Aviation Corps which on this day flew 664 sorties against the retreating units and various strong points.[36] In the fighting that followed the leading Soviet elements advanced several kilometres but were halted by stubborn resistance from sub units of the 291 and 340 Infantry Divisions which had fallen back to the Prinz Eugen Stellung. In response, following a major artillery bombardment, the second echelon rifle corps prepared their attack in earnest, with armoured and artillery support.[37]

The next day the First Ukrainian Front launched its main offensive. In accordance with Konev's plan, two blows fell in vital sectors either side of XIII AK where the mass of the Red Army infantry, cavalry and mechanised forces were concentrated: to the north near Horokhiv and to the south in the vicinity of Nusche.

The Northern Pincer: Rava Ruska Axis

The objective of the assault in the north was twofold: to deliver an attack along the Stoinaiv/Kaminka Strumilova axis which would envelop the German forces west of Brody from behind; secondly to develop the offensive towards the ultimate objective of the town of Rava Ruska.

Having smashed through the German front near Horokhiv, part of 13 Army's infantry forces, supported by hundreds of tanks and aircraft began to move south west towards the northern perimeter of XIII AK in the general direction of Radekhiv.[38] In this German secondary defensive zone heavy fighting followed. To seal the gap 4 Panzer Army counterattacked with two Panzer divisions hitherto held in reserve—the 16 and 17 Panzer Divisions, which between them had only 43 serviceable tanks, which engaged the Red Army in the Horokhiv and Druzhkopil region.[39] Even with the limited support of German bombers, before they could make any significant headway the counterattack was halted by vastly superior forces. The 3 Guards Army and Putkov's 13 Army shock groups quickly inflicted severe personnel and equipment losses on these panzer units and on the 291 and 340 Infantry Divisions. By the end of 15 July the entire German tactical defence zone had been breached to a depth of 15–30 km.[40] In this period, according to Soviet sources 13 Army alone killed, captured or destroyed 2,450 officers and men, 25 guns, 25 tanks and self-propelled guns and 18 armoured transports.[41]

On the same day in order to continue the Soviet advance and expand on the breach, Lieutenant General Baranov's Cavalry Group was ordered into the penetration sector for action in operational depth. Deployment was effected under the protection of an umbrella of aircraft from 2 Air Army. Its assignment was to capture Kaminka Strumilova, force a crossing of the western Buh and seize and hold a bridgehead on its western bank. The execution of this manoeuvre was intended to block the retreat path of XIII AK, and other German forces west of Brody, while concurrently preventing them from receiving any further reinforcement.

On the morning of 17 July General Katukov's 1 Guards Tank Army was committed for action in the gap which had been created in operational depth,[42] and immediately advanced to the south-west further consolidating the initial gains on the northern flank of XIII AK and successfully developing the offensive.

The Southern Pincer: The L'viv Axis

On 14 July simultaneously with the strike on the northern flank, a second Soviet offensive thrust commenced at the juncture of the 1 and 4 Panzer Armies which threatened to split them apart and encircle XIII AK.

In contrast to the northern flank, the Soviet strike on the southern flank did not go according to plan and was acknowledged by Konev to have been generally more complex and stressful.[43] Continuous Soviet reconnaissance in this area had already established that the foremost well fortified German positions were still occupied in strength, hence, in preparation, an unusually heavy, concentrated and intense artillery barrage took place during the afternoon lasting 1.5 hrs. This was augmented by a massive air strike delivered by 618 bombers and ground attack aircraft of 2 Air Army aimed against the main defensive positions. For 50 minutes between 1540–1630 hrs, there were more than 1,000 aircraft continually above the battlefield in 38 and 60 Armies' penetration sectors.[44]

Although Korpsabteilung C (hereafter abbreviated KAC) managed to effectively repel the direct frontal infantry holding attacks on the 14 July,[45] further to the south the picture was different. Here, General Moskalenko's 38 Army and General Kurochkin's 60 Army, attacked at the weakest point of the front, in the middle of the sector controlled by XIII AK's right hand neighbour XXXXVIII Pz K, at the juncture of the 349 and the 357 Infantry Divisions.[46]

The assault in 60 Army's offensive sector, which was led by the infantry divisions of the 15 and 23 Rifle Corps, fell on XXXXVIII Pz K's 349 Infantry Division, especially its 911 and 913 Regiments. Initially a counterattack by 349 Division's Fusilier Battalion with artillery support managed to push the Soviets back to their starting point, but at a cost of very heavy casualties. However in the early afternoon, its forward positions completely disintegrated under the sheer weight of the Soviet onslaught. Within hours the 913 Regiment had suffered devastating losses in both men and weapons. Its subsequent battle report revealed the extent of its losses, for example its 1./Btl. was reduced to a 'battle group' with a strength of only 26 men.[47] According to the same report its Fusilier Battalion which was entrenched in front of the 913 Regiment was 'totally destroyed'.[48] The report also acknowledged that part of the Division's precious heavy weaponry was lost as its artillery batteries sited in the vicinity were either smashed or had to be abandoned and fell into enemy hands intact.[49] The pitiful remnants of 913 regiment then retreated west to the Prinz Eugen Stellung for reorganisation. By way of explanation for its collapse, the 349 Infantry Division's after action report stated:

Reasons for the breach

1. Intense bombardments, constant heavy air attacks. No action from our own Luftwaffe and meagre quantity of ammunition, much too insufficient for a major counterattack.
2. Far too wide defence front (4–6 km per btl). Consequently; total engagement of all infantry and weapons in the front line, scant reserves.
3. At the outset, immediate severe initial losses in men and heavy weapons
4. Destruction of communications network
5. The right flank was surrounded for hours, so that the positions of the right wing, despite its weak force, had to be re-shaped and lengthened.[50]

By the end of 14 July the Soviet 38 Army and 60 Armies had broken through the prepared German positions and begun moving towards Zolochiv and Sasiv, driving a wedge within XXXXVIII Pz K's lines. Nevertheless because of determined German resistance, progress in this southern sector was slow and Konev was only able to achieve an operational depth of 3–8 kms.[51]

The First Counterattack by WGR 30

In response to the fierce fighting all along the sector of 60 and 38 Armies, the German command took measures to prevent an additional breakthrough, exactly as they had in the north. This involved committing most of its operational tactical reserves. These comprised of one regiment from the 14. Waffen-Grenadier-Division der SS (galizische Nr.1), and all its mobile reserve—the 1 and 8 Panzer Divisions. What followed was a disaster as clearly nobody appreciated the sheer magnitude of the attacking enemy forces and the danger that they were in.

Following the countermanding of a directive to subordinate the whole of the Galician Division to the XXXXVIII Pz K,[52] XIII AK retained control of its infantry reserve. Despite this, in rigid adherence to German military doctrine, its command ordered a single regiment from the 14 Galician Division to reinforce the shattered positions of XXXXVIII Pz K's 349 Infantry Divison. This was against the specific request that as a force made up of foreign nationals, the Galician Division not be broken up and led into battle as individual units and that it should always remain under its own Divisional command.[53] Hence the Division's Waffen-Grenadier-Regiment 30 (hereafter WGR 30) with support[54] from II./artillery battery was split off from its parent Division and subordinated directly to XIII AK's command. Very late in the evening of 13 July[55] it received new orders to leave its prepared reserve position and by 1600 hrs on 15 July move into new positions in the Koltiv area, which was in the neighbouring XXXXVIII Pz K's sector. Here it would assist in halting the penetration to the east of the village.[56] The remainder of the Galician Division was placed on full alert but remained in place.

The urgency of the order and the distance involved in marching there dictated that WGR 30 had no alternative than begin its advance without any of the usual necessary preparation. As the engagement was to take place in the neighbouring corps' operational area, neither the Divisional nor the regimental staff had any time to familiarise themselves with the terrain in the anticipated battle zone.[57] The infantry battalion commanders gathered their officers and gave cursory tactical briefings, before both battalions prepared to move off to the regiment's assigned area. Marching throughout the night on the Zabolotsi/Pidhirtsi road with periodic rest stops, progress was slow. Occasional steep and narrow sections of the road further impeded access for the heavily laden supply and ammunition carts which caused additional delays.

Waffen-Grenadier Orest Slupchynsky from 7 company who was present recalled: 'The march [to the front] was a typical 'army-march', stop and go, more stop than go'.[58]

As 14 July dawned, the meteorological conditions were unfavourable for major Soviet air operations[59] however it went on to become a clear, hot day. Along with the improvement in the weather came Soviet reconnaissance planes which were monitoring troop movements on the main feeder roads to the front, but there were strict orders for the advancing soldiers not to shoot at them.[60]

During the day the difficult marching and increasing thirst was eased when worried villagers especially women, brought the troops delicious curdled milk to drink.[61] Eventually around noon the regiment had reached the dominating heights of Pidhirtsi where it stopped for the troops to rest and have some food. Continuing on in the direction of Sasiv, the road led through open fields then through a forest towards Sasiv where the regiment was once again halted, because the main road was blocked by a panzer division.[62] This information was not imparted to the soldiers who grew increasingly impatient at the delay. Part of I battalion was able to rest in the trees, however further along the point at which II battalion stopped offered little by way of shade. The horse handlers parked the wagons and settled their horses as best they could in the increasing heat, swamped by flies. Only the roadside ditches and small shrubs and bushes offered little respite from the burning July sun. At this point Soviet fighter aircraft appeared and repeatedly attacked the regiment[63] and although the soldiers did their best to disperse and find cover, several supply carts including heavily laden ammunition wagons were hit. In the ensuing turmoil the regiment suffered its first casualties in killed and wounded. With the main road now blocked with dead horses and the debris from destroyed carts, its advance was delayed for several hours.[64]

It was not until the evening and in heavy rain that the road was cleared and the regiment's battalions could set out again towards Sasiv about 10 kms away. It was around this time that the Ukrainians were confronted by the dispiriting sight of retreating veteran German soldiers, first individuals and then in groups. These were mainly from the routed 911 Regiment of the 349 Infantry Division which was in the process of withdrawing to the Prinz Eugen Stellung. A procession of horse-drawn wagons followed, mixed in with vehicles of Sturmgeschütze Brigade 249, a few soldiers on horseback, but mostly soldiers on foot some already having discarded their weapons. The wounded were mixed with the able bodied as they fled in disarray, often looking back in the direction of the front.[65] When the Ukrainians asked how far it was to the front and what was the situation like there, they received the laconic reply 'the front is near and everywhere'.[66] Waffen-Unterscharführer Roman Drazniowsky a platoon commander with the 3./II./WGR 30 wrote:

> We had to plough through German soldiers running away from the front. Some were without weapons, many shouting that the Soviets were not far behind and that we should turn back, some were sitting and staring, some were even crying. This was a very demoralising example especially for our soldiers from the Galician Division who had never seen real fighting and its cruelties.[67]

Counterattack by WGR 30 on 15 July 1944

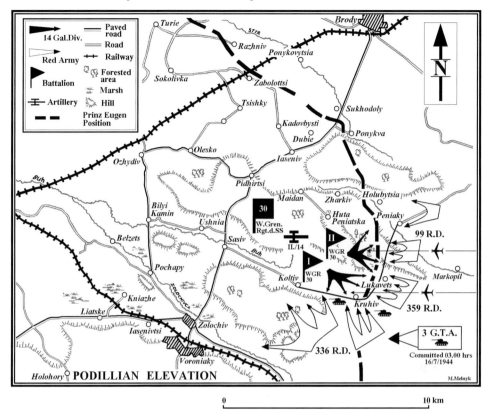

Waffen-Sturmmann Mychailo Kormylo 4./II./WGR 30 who was also present recalled:

> [...] My platoon followed Waffen-Obersturmführer Pidhayny towards the breaks in the line and the retreating Germans. As we advanced to that point at the front line where the Germans had capitulated we met retreating German tanks carrying wounded and dead. Men without weapons, without boots even. They shouted at us 'Where are you going? You don't have the strength to resist them!' When they saw we were not advancing with tanks but with ordinary weaponry, they shouted 'You'll never withstand them! Turn back, turn back!' But we had orders to advance.[68]

As they moved forward the proximity of the front was evident from the smouldering houses in the village of Koltiv and the prostrate corpses of those villagers caught by an earlier Soviet bombardment. II. battalion eventually reached the regiment's exit position late at night on the 14 July but I. battalion was however delayed still further and did not arrive in the designated area until the early morning hours. It was not until 0650 hrs on Saturday 15 July that the hungry, thirsty and tired soldiers of the reinforced WGR 30 were reported to be in place in the forested area stretching from Kruhiv in the south, to Pieniaki in the north a distance of approximately 9 kms.[69]

All 4 companies of Hauptsturmführer Siegfried Klocker's I. battalion were commanded by Ukrainians, these were: 1 company Waffen-Hauptsturmführer Petro Rozanetz, 2 company Waffen-Untersturmführer Leontyj Berezovsky, 3 company Waffen-Obersturmführer Bohdan Pidhayny and 4 company Waffen-Obersturmführer Ihor Pospilovsky.

Similarly, at the time of its deployment the company commanders of Sturmbannführer Friedrich Wittenmeyer's II. battalion were also Ukrainian. These were; 5 company Waffen-Obersturmführer Mykola Jurniuk, 6 company Waffen-Obersturmführer Paul Sumarokiv, 7 company Waffen-Obersturmführer Myroslav Maletsky and 8 company Waffen-Obersturmführer Petro Makarevych.

The staff company was commanded by a German Untersturmführer Rudi Laskowski, whilst 13./WGR 30, was commanded by Waffen-Untersturmführer Andrij Otreschko-Arsky. The 14./company WGR 30[70] commanded by Waffen-Untersturmführer Semen Portuchaj remained under direct Divisional command.[71] Together with various support elements they amounted to approximately 2,000 men[72] and at around 0800 hrs these were in place. In this heavily wooded area they found mostly empty emplacements and only small groups of Germans formed from the remnants of the 349 Infantry Division in the vicinity which with support from a few Sturmgeschütze had retreated and sought to establish temporary blocking positions by using favourable terrain.[73] Notwithstanding their presence the attempt by WGR 30 to close the breach which followed was not coordinated with the remaining elements of the 349 Infantry Division since according to Major Heike apart from isolated instances of direct personal contact, communication between the respective forces was impossible to establish.[74]

As WGR 30 set about its objective of sealing the breach, heavy fighting quickly broke out in its area and before it had even properly deployed it was greeted by fire from the leading Red Army elements[75] which were pressing to infiltrate the already overrun German positions. These were the infantry battalions of the 15 Rifle Corps of 60 Army, under General P. V. Tertyshny, supported by large numbers of Ilyushin fighter planes and armour from 3 Guards Tank Army which included both T34 and heavy Joseph Stalin tanks which had appeared in this sector.[76]

Both battalions were involved in a series of counterattacks, bayonet charges and close combat which lasted throughout the course of the morning until around midday.[77] During this period II. battalion successfully drove back the Soviet attacks and with the intervention of the mortars of the heavy 8 company, individual companies managed to narrow the breach and force a temporary local retreat.

As the day wore on, the Soviet attacks became harder to repel as they concentrated on the areas either side of WGR 30's positions and threatened to outflank it.[78] It became progressively more difficult to deploy the integral heavy infantry support weapons such as mortars and artillery because of the constantly overlapping front line. The unit of light artillery did manage to maintain its position for short periods but was continually forced to change its position.[79]

The proximity of the forward positions in wooded terrain meant observers found it difficult to locate targets and when cannons were unable to withdraw, they were forced to simply shoot straight ahead.

From the moment that combat began, the regiment which was operating in an unknown and unreconnoitred area, was beset by exactly the same problems that the 349 Infantry Division had experienced the previous day. In particular the essential communications links between the regimental headquarters and battalion commanders were virtually non-existent and those that were available were only usable for a short period.[80] This meant messengers and despatch riders had to be used and that unit commanders had to react to local developments with whatever resources they could muster; worse still, during the fierce fighting the regimental HQ near Koltiv[81] came under direct attack and was destroyed. Athough the staff escaped, the abandonment of the regimental command post caused a further loss of critical coordinated central direction. Mychailo Kormylo was a member of 4 company I. battalion which took part in the initial counter attack:

[...] We followed Waffen-Obersturmführer Pidhayny as far forward as possible. Finally we saw the positions—nobody was there. Quickly we dug in all the heavy machine guns, placed them on their lafettes and waited. Soon I heard the sound of an MG far to my left flank. Then I saw lots of Bolsheviks in our positions. Everything was happening so fast. Some of our men were fighting at close quarters, while others were feeding bullets into the MG's. Our company commander Waffen-Obersturmführer Pospilovsky told me to run and help with my MG to hold that left sector because the situation there was critical. As soon as possible I instructed my guns to start firing. I could see on my left that other platoons had done this but were now all out of ammunition and were fighting furiously hand to hand. I opened fire, then W.Ostuf. Pospilovsky arrived and gave our group orders to retreat. All the while there was hand to hand fighting and screaming in the dugouts and our boys were being overwhelmed by [sheer] numbers. My group, retreated, turned, fired, retreated, turned, and fired and so on. We managed to retreat across a road into a mature wood and set up firing positions again. I couldn't open fire because our men were fighting in close quarters and I would have killed them and the enemy.

After a couple of hours the planes returned and started bombing us again. They were destroying the road upon which the Germans were trying to retreat. The carnage was awful and all we could do was watch it from our dugout and be ready for the Bolsheviks. My group managed to move the machine guns onto the backs of burned out lorries at the road's edge so that we could get an angle for firing at the low flying planes.

My friend Wasyl Samson, from the artillery section, was set up on the hill above us and he was giving them all he had. He was using flare shells as well as his normal ammunition firing at the planes—but there were so many of them you would have thought the sky was black. Planes fell again and again, left and right. I counted nine planes down in that episode. Later on my boys brought down two low flying fighter planes. This helped boost our morale. Shortly afterwards they stopped attacking us until the next day.

When we ran out of ammunition the first thing was to use the weapons that had been left by our dead, and dead Bolsheviks. There were plenty of weapons lying around them. When my automatic eventually ran out of bullets I managed to get hold of a Russian 'finky'[82] just in case. I also managed to pick up a decent rifle from underneath the body of one of ours. There were bullet belts lying around as well. I still had my bayonet, my knife and my pistol and three refills for that. At Brody I was never without weapons. The German instructors had taught me that I could throw away my food but never my weapons.[...][83]

The intense fighting eventually died down at dusk on the evening of 15 July which allowed the supply sections to retreat from the vicinity of Koltiv through the fiercely burning village of Ruda Koltovska in the direction of Pidhirtsi. Here, WGR 30 had re-established its regimental HQ and a temporary clearing station for the many wounded in the castle.

By the end of the combat on the first day the regiment's losses included over half of all the company commanders killed, wounded, captured or missing. These included 2 company W.Ustuf. Leontyi Berezovsky (kia), 3 company W.Ostuf. Bohdan Pidhayny (wounded and evacuated), 5 company Ostuf. Mykola Iuryniak (Mia), 6 company W.Ostuf. Paul Sumarokiv (wounded but remained in place after treatment), 7 company W.Ostuf. Myroslav Maletsky (wounded and evacuated) and 8 company W.Obstuf. Peter Makarewytsch (captured). The critical loss of so many Ukrainian company commanders in such a short space of time had a major impact on the fighting. To continue to withhold the enemy advances in several instances it had been necessary to place the remnants of the companies under platoon commanders or even senior NCOs.[84] A number of the regiments infantry support weapons had also been lost including mortars and artillery pieces.

During the night, of 15/16 July both sides sought to reorganise and consolidate their positions. Periodic skirmishes continued to erupt illuminated by burning buildings and punctuated with the firing of recognition flares and tracer bullets. In the darkness Red Army infantry managed to infiltrate the extended wooded sector between the villages of Lukavets and Kruhiv where elements of WGR 30 were deployed and by the morning of 16 July the enemy had reached the eastern edge of the forest clearing, 2 kms east of Werkobuzh.[85]

Committing WGR 30 against the breakthrough on the 15 July had relieved the pressure on the weakened 349 Infantry Division, however conservatively outnumbered three to one[86] and without any additional armoured or air support it was inevitably unable to stem the breach. The reasons for the failure were virtually a carbon copy of those given by the 349 Infantry Division the previous day namely: early losses of over half its key Ukrainian company commanders killed, wounded or captured; Concentrated and immense artillery bombardments and unrelenting air attacks which resulted in significant losses in men and matériel. The attacks also shredded the vital telephone wires causing severe difficulties with the essential communications links between regimental and battalion HQ's forcing company commanders and their deputies to act independently. The extended length of the regiment's position caused its individual companies to be spread out too thinly which undermined their effectiveness. Deployment in an un-reconnoitred heavily wooded area—which the Division's command had advised against—and which was outside of XIII AKs operation sector was also a major problem. The lack of heavy weapons support and sufficient anti-tank weaponry meant they were unable to deal with the vast number of Soviet tanks. The fluid front line and proximity of the enemy forces severely curtailed the effectiveness of the supporting light artillery coupled with the inexperience of the Ukrainian troops unaccustomed to such heavy fighting in such difficult conditions. Despite all of these problems, to the credit of SS-Obersturmbannführer Forstreuter and his unit commanders, some individual companies—although heavily depleted—did at least manage to narrow the gap in some sectors.[87]

The counterattack by WGR 30 was later maligned in an after action report by the Chief Operations Officer of the veteran 349 Infantry Division which had itself earlier been completely routed and forced to abandon some of its artillery. In it, reference is made to the 'Galicians' who 'represented a burden for our infantry' and who 'with only a few exceptions, were unable to withstand any Russian attacks'. The same report does however go on to concede:

It must however be taken into account that this was a newly established non-German unit, not battle hardened, which was first deployed during a retreat and was therefore particularly vulnerable to the material superiority of the Russians [Soviets] in this area.[88]

In contrast, their Soviet adversaries recorded that on this day in this area the forward battalions were only able to capture individual sectors in the first and second trenches[89] and that they 'encountered stubborn fire resistance and counterattacks'.[90]

Failure of the Counterattack by 1 and 8 Panzer Divisions.

At the same time, in conjunction with the attack by WGR 30, 1 Panzer Army ordered the whole of its mobile tactical reserve to strike at the Soviet spearhead. This force comprised of the veteran 1 and 8 Panzer Divisions, which the German command believed could halt the enemy breakthrough and restore contact with XIII AK.

As planned, the adept and skilful counterattack by General Major Werner Marcks' 1 Panzer Division successfully penetrated the left flank of the 38 Army near Oliiv and temporarily drove back its leading combat formations 2–4 kms in several sectors.[91]

Further to the west however, only a small part of the 8 Panzer Division actually engaged the enemy in the region of Kruhiv before being forced into XIII AK's area.[92] Soviet air reconnaissance had revealed the concentration area of the approaching German armour and to counteract this threat and to prevent any further incursions into 38 Army's flank, Marshal Konev reacted quickly and unleashed the 2 Air Army. Its commander Colonel General S. A. Krasovsky was ordered 'to destroy the enemy tank grouping by large scale attacks from bombers and assault aircraft'.[93] 2 Air Army immediately delivered massed bombing and ground attacks against the panzer divisions located north and north east of Zborov. 1,848 sorties were completed during the afternoon of 15 July during which 17,200 bombs of different types were dropped and 1,700 rocket missiles and 83,000 conventional missiles were launched a total of 716 tons on the German armour concentrated in an area of only 7 square kilometres.[94] As a result of this 1 Panzer Division sustained considerable losses in both tanks and personnel and was forced to disengage from the fighting to withdraw and reorganise. The brunt of the 8 Panzer Division fared far worse. The experienced commander of this Division General Major Werner Friebe, ignored his explicit instructions to advance on a carefully reconnoitred route through a wooded area and instead, to save time he moved his forces along the main road Zolochiv–Zborov road, which he had been expressly forbidden to do. Exposed to the onslaught of Soviet aircraft in transit on an open road, it suffered what were described as 'devastating losses'.[95] The attack was halted as long columns of tanks and lorries burst into flames before the remnants were forced to withdraw ending all hopes of closing the gap in the front at the first attempt.[96]

Following the combat on 14–15 July in the southern sector the Soviets had achieved a small but decisive breakthrough which the Front Commander Marshal Konev was determined to exploit. His strong armoured vanguards and mechanised units followed by the infantry pushed through the villages of Harbuziv, Perepelnyky, Iwaczow, Nushche and Trostianets Malyi,[97] until they reached the main paved road at Pluhiv, from where they continued to energetically pursue their advance towards the town of Zolochiv.[98] As they did so they formed a narrow corridor approximately 16 kms long and 6 kms wide between XIII AKs southern flank and the hastily restored defensive positions on the northern flank of XXXXVIII PzKs.

At the end of the 15 July XIII AK was isolated from its neighbouring corps to both the north and south. Cut off with it were sizeable parts of the 340 Infantry Division and all the remainder of the 349 Infantry Division which had become separated from their respective parent corps, along with an element of 8 Panzer Division.[99] Despite the introduction of most of the tactical reserves, their counterattacks designed to prevent a Soviet breakthrough had failed and German offensive capabilities were from this point on severely impeded.

The 'Koltiv Corridor'

By the morning of Sunday 16 July the Soviet Front command had shifted the main weight of the attack to the southern sector. Here the progress of their offensive had been slower, especially in the area of 38 Army where German resistance had 'succeeded in upsetting 38 Army's offensive and extremely complicating its operations on subsequent days'.[100] To accelerate the penetration of the German defensive positions, Konev had already begun moving substantial fresh veteran armoured and infantry reinforcements into what became known as the 'Koltiv corridor' which was constantly being expanded in a west and north-westerly direction.[101] The main forces of General Pavlo Rybalko's elite 3 Guards[102] Tank Army, (6 and 7 Guards Tank Corps and 9 Mechanised Corps) were now committed into the corridor between Koltiv and Trostianets Malyi (ultimately over 1,000 Soviet tanks and self-propelled guns were to pass through it). The narrow sector and lack of roads forced the army's formations to move westwards along a single route in a continuous compact column in the general direction of Krasne. This placed them in an extremely vulnerable position, as the long narrow corridor was susceptible to German artillery fire from both sides. The danger in this respect was however largely offset by large Soviet fighter formations which supported the insertion of the mobile forces into the existing penetration area.

Too Little, too Late

Hoping to capitalise on the Soviet situation and fearing the arrival of large tank and mechanised forces in its rear areas, the German command continued to counterattack throughout the day in a futile attempt to cut the spearhead.

Threatened with the prospect of complete encirclement, XIII AK began by strengthening the precarious position on its right flank by belatedly committing the last of its tactical infantry reserve comprising of the Galician Division's two remaining regiments (WGR's 29 and 31) together with their artillery support units and other combat elements. Under the direct command of XIII AKs staff, on the night of 15 July,[103] first WGR 31 then later WGR 29 received orders to abandon some 50 km's of previously prepared defensive positions,[104] proceed to the south by forced march to join the battered remains of WGR 30 in the field, and attack the existing penetration and sever the Soviet spearhead.[105] In the first stage, the units furthest away were to move to their assembly area to the south of Pidhirtsi, marching at night after which they were to advance towards the front.[106] The Galician Division would then occupy the difficult heavily wooded terrain in the sector from the tip of the forest 1.5 km south east of Wolochy in the north, across the Iaseniv Valley to the east to Pieniaki, then to Werkobuzh and Koltiv in the south. This was adjacent to KAC's southern flank and overlapped the northern flank of 349 Infantry Division.

As an added contingency measure, that same morning, because of the rapidly worsening situation in this sector, XIII AK, also ordered the creation of a blocking force composed of elements of the KAC.[107] This blocking force commanded by Major Lawatsch, was given the task of securing the line Pobich–Maidan Pieniacky–Zharkiv,[108] due east of the Sasiv–Pidhirtsi road. At the same time the KAC's Fusilier Battalion relocated to the area south west of Pidhirtsi where it would be available for immediate response.[109]

At first light at 0500 hrs on 16 July the Soviets began another heavy bombardment of the German front line positions as a precursor for the inevitable renewed ground assault.[110] With the coming of another warm and sunny day, the ever present dive bombers and fighter planes also appeared and continued to attack all traffic on main roads, intersections, and bridges. In daylight, any troop movements towards the front became ever more difficult as the main roads became heavily congested with supply and support units heading in the opposite direction. Intermixed with them were fearful civilians, some with wagons, others driving their livestock ahead of them, fleeing from the battle zone which made rewarding targets for the swarms of assault aviation aircraft of 2 Air Army as did those units of the Galician Division which were still advancing. These attacks which resulted in further casualties in killed and wounded also prevented movement for extended periods. The Division's heavy artillery battalion was particularly vulnerable as it moved along the Ozhydiv–Olesko–Pidhirtsi road. Its long exposed columns of horses and vehicles could not easily disperse and seek cover in the trees when attacked by aircraft, in addition to which it had to negotiate hilly terrain and poor road conditions. Together these took their toll on the draught horses, several of which were killed and many others left exhausted by the time the battalion had eventually moved into position close to Iaseniv.

WGR 31 under its commander SS-Obersturmbannführer Paul Herms, had the furthest to move. It comprised of I./WGR under Hauptsturmführer Heinz Kurzbach and II./WGR 31 commanded by Hauptsturmführer Hans Salzinger together with III artillery battalion. The regiment was ordered to occupy the line Huta Werkobuzka–Huta Peniatska–Hutysko Peniatske,[111] in front of the Lawatsch blocking force and relocated its HQ east of Huta Peniatska.

As before, upon reaching this staging area, the Galician units found little evidence of the 349 Infantry Division's 912 and 911 Regiments which were still supposed to be holding the main front. Often, individual elements of this army unit had, contrary to their explicit orders, rather expeditiously already started to leave their rudimentary emplacements a few hours before and retire westwards.[112] Consequently, on reaching their new, unfinished positions, the Galician units immediately began widening any existing trenches, digging foxholes and hastily constructing additional emplacements and fire points on approach roads and likely axis's of advance. The gradual retreat of the German forces from the front, soon exposed the newly occupied Ukrainian positions which meant that during the morning II./WGR 31 found itself in embroiled in combat with the leading Red Army forces in the vicinity of the village of Zharkiv.[113] It also quickly lost contact with Divisional HQ forcing the use of runners and despatch riders to pass on orders to the regiment's units. Waffen-Unterscharführer Jurij Ferencevych who was with 13 (I.G–Infanterie Geschütz[114]) company WGR 31:

> [...] After a few days, I remember it was a Sunday, the whole of WGR 31 was relocated. Our company command post was situated in the woods near the village of Zharkiv. I heard artillery activity and Soviet planes were flying overhead. The four I.G. platoons of our company were near the front line supporting our infantry units. During the first two days our company commander Waffen-Untersturmführer Olearnyk was visiting regimental headquarters in his Swimmwagen and reporting on the situation at the front line and the location of our platoons. When the Soviets

broke through the first defence line, there was chaos. It was very depressing for us to see Wehrmacht units retreating in small groups through our second defence line.[115]

SS-Standartenführer Friedrich Dern's WGR 29, which of the Galician Division's 3 infantry regiments had the highest ratio of Ukrainian officers,[116] was originally entrenched in secondary positions on both sides of the Brody–Zolochiv road. I./WGR 29 commanded by Waffen-Hauptsturmführer Mychailo Brygidyr was in the village of Dubie and like WGR 30, all its line company commanders were Ukrainian. These were; 1 company Waffen-Obersturmführer Ivan Witushynsky; 2 company Waffen-Obersturmführer Emil Hermann; 3 company Waffen-Obersturmführer Mychailo Lischtschynsky and 4 company Waffen-Untersturmführer Volodymyr Kosak.

II./WGR 29 commanded by Hauptsturmführer Wilhelm Allerkamp was situated in Hayi Dubecki. This comprised 5 company commanded by Waffen-Untersturmführer Serhij Ruditschew; 6 company Waffen-Untersturmführer Volodymyr Witoschynsky; 7 company Waffen-Obersturmführer Dmytro Danylyschyn and 8 company Waffen-Obersturmführer Savely Yaskevych. The 13./ company was commanded by Waffen-Obersturmführer Roman Tschaikowskyj whilst 14./WGR 29 commanded by Waffen-Obersturmführer Ostap Czuczkewycz remained directly under the control of the Divisional HQ. The regiment's staff company was commanded by Obersturmführer Gunter Weiss.

The regiment moved a short distance and occupied new positions to the south east from the forest near Wolochy in the north, to south east of the village of Zharkiv situated in the centre of the Iaseniv Valley. I. artillery battalion was deployed nearby and regimental HQ was near Iaseniv. Its forward positions were occupied by I. battalion which placed its anti-tank weaponry in the valley beside the road in anticipation of an advance by Soviet armour. Apart from Soviet planes dropping bombs and strafing the fields behind II. battalion's positions there appears to have been very limited contact with the enemy during the morning.[117]

Before all the Galician units were in place, by midday on 16 July it had already become apparent to XIII AK command that because of the enemy's immense superiority and the rapidity of the advance its tactical manoeuvres would not contain the thrust in the south.[118] With the Soviets now close to the town of Zolochiv, it was clear that a large scale retreat would be necessary if XIII AK was to have any hope of avoiding complete encirclement. Thus the units on the corp's left flank (454 Security Division, 361 Infantry Division, and KAC), received orders to withdraw to the unmanned Prinz Eugen Stellung. The orders specified unequivocally that the withdrawal was not to begin until 2400 hrs on the night of the 16/17 July by which time Major Lawatschs' blocking force and the remainder of the Galician Division would be in position.[119] The heavy weapons and rear echelon and supply units were to relocate several km's east to the woods south of Ozhydiv, to be followed by combat elements and the rearguard which were to conduct a fighting withdrawal only when they were under severe enemy pressure.[120]

The remnants of the 349 Infantry Division which had been unable to hold the Prinz Eugen Stellung in its sector, was also instructed to disengage from the enemy and withdraw to the general line Koltiv–Opaky–Werkhobuzh.[121] The principal strategic intention behind this move by XIII AK's command was to narrow the front, create reserve positions and to free up part of its forces which could then be re-grouped and deployed in accordance with the demands of the developing situation.

Withdrawal to the section of the Prinz Eugen Stellung stretching from Stanislavchyk to Wolochy by the 361 Infantry Division, 454 Security Division and KAC went according to plan.[122] In so doing this left the positions to the west of the main Brody–Zolochiv road near to the positions of I./WGR 29 open, so that 5 company WGR 29 now formed the extreme left flank of the Galician Division.[123]

XIII AK, then ordered the 361 Infantry Division to form a Kampfgruppe from its reserve battalion (Kampfgruppe Haid[124]) for immediate despatch by truck to the area east of Sasiv and then to Koltiv to assist the 349 Infantry Division in an attack scheduled for the following morning.[125]

Further to the south, a reorganisation of the Soviet forces in the Koltiv sector meant this area was quiet in comparison with the initial ferocity of the fighting of the previous two days and had begun to stabilise.[126] During a temporary lull in the fighting, the two surviving regiments (911 and 912) of the 349 Infantry Division, along with the remnants of its other sub-units and their remaining heavy weapons, abandoned their positions and pulled back to its new line without significant difficulty.[127]

In the interim, in the afternoon of the 16 July sporadic contact between the Galician units and the enemy continued. The staff company WGR 31 which was manning trenches beside some open fields to the south of the regiment's positions was bombarded and attacked from the woods on the other side of the open ground. The company managed to beat off the attacks with heavy machine gun fire until it was relieved by the Division's Fusilier Battalion a few hours later.[128]

Later, the forward elements of WGR 29 including I./WGR 29 were also forced to defend themselves after coming under fire and sustaining casualties amongst whom was the commander of the 1 company Waffen-Obersturmführer, Ivan Witushynsky who was killed.[129]

During the day news had spread throughout the remainder of the Division of the hard fighting that WGR 30 had endured. On 16 July having lost almost half of its total strength[130] in its first engagement including all but one of its Ukrainian company commanders killed, wounded or missing,[131] the regiment was withdrawn. Temporarily no longer effective as a cohesive fighting unit, during the day it was pulled back to Ruda Koltovska before ultimately relocating to Pidhirtsi where one of its last fully combat fit company commanders Waffen-Obersturmführer Igor Pospilovsky (4 CO) was killed. The remnants were then formed into smaller battle groups which in addition to being used as the Divisional reserve were assigned the task of clearing the surrounding woods of the enemy infiltrations which continued to occur and securing the main Koltiv–Sasiv road. Waffen-Sturmmann Mychailo Kormylo 4./II./WGR 30 was amongst the survivors:

> [...] we went to Pidhirtsi, there I saw our battalion commander Hauptsturmführer Klocker, Waffen-Obersturmführer Pospilovsky and Baranovsky—he was a good man.

A group of soldiers in typical terrain at Brody, July 1944.

Destroyed Soviet tank at Brody.

Machine gun team from the Galician Division in action in the Brody pocket, July 1944.

The retreat path was marked by burning villages, July 1944.

I positioned my MG and some mortars close to the road because we knew that the Soviets might attack with T-34's. Later Pospilovsky told me to go to the hospital in Pidhirtsi to help put our wounded soldiers in the trucks. I said 'ok' and told him to take care of my MG.

I saw a lot of wounded men. I told them I had come to help them. One of them told me to leave them all there. I also saw 2 nurses. One said that she would return with me but the other nurse said that she would stay with the wounded and if the Bolsheviks killed the wounded soldiers they could kill her too. So I left them with two trucks. I don't know what happened to them after that. When I returned to my position I noticed my MG had been crushed and there was lots of blood but nobody around, only Pospilovsky's body. Then I saw a soldier who told me what had happened. They had seen a group of Bolsheviks and Pospilovsky had told them to put their hands up but one of them had a hidden gun and shot Pospilovsky. Baranovsky killed that Bolshevik and two others that were standing close to him. Then I left to look for Baranovsky and the others.[...][132]

By the evening of 16 July the front had stabilised to a degree. All elements of WGR 29 and WGR 31 were finally in their preparation areas and moved out separately towards the Soviet lines.[133]

17 July In the Front Line

By dawn on 17 July XIII AK, had moved into its new position and re-grouped its forces. KAC now occupied the centre of XIII AKs' lines facing north east. To its left was the 361 Infantry Division (less Kampfgruppe Haid) at the railway line 1.5 km north-east of Zabolotsi. To its right the Galician Division at the forest tip, 1.5 km south-west of Wolochy.[134] While two of the KACs Divisional groups held the front, Div. Gr.339 with artillery support,[135] was withdrawn and received the order to reconnoitre in a southward direction over Bilyi Kamin for an attack on Pochapy and Zhulychi. For this the Lawatsch blocking force was dissolved.[136]

Around midday on the 17 July KAC was also ordered to move its Fusilier Battalion into the vicinity of Iaseniv, to secure the main Brody—Zolochiv road and counter a renewed powerful Soviet strike by 23 Rifle Corps with armoured support towards Maidan Pieniacky.[137]

Facing this attack were the Galician Division's WGR 29 and WGR 31 which now occupied the front line. Deployed on the right flank of KAC, Waffen-Hauptsturmführer Michael Brygidyr's I./WGR 29 occupied the foremost positions with its companies positioned in the wooded hills forward of, and either side of the village of Zharkiv. By mid-morning in this sector, large concentrations of Red Army infantry units from 23 Rifle Corps with armoured support had begun to move forward to attack and at around 1030 hrs these were spotted by the commander of the 3 battery I./artillery battalion Waffen-Untersturmführer Mykola Dlaboha from his observation point on a hillside. The timely intervention of his battery deprived these Red Army units of the element of surprise, alerted the infantry to the enemy advance and dispersed the attacking forces.[138] After regrouping, to reinforce the infantry attacks, 23 Rifle Corps[139] proceeded to bring forward heavy weapons which included heavy artillery, Katyusha rocket launchers and anti-tank guns with additional ammunition supplies which moved along the roads to Ponykva, Wolochy and Hutysko Brodskyj. Once again by targeting their fire onto these approach routes the batteries of I. artillery battalion successfully destroyed 6 artillery guns and 3 anti-tank guns, temporarily delaying the offensive in WGR 29's sector.[140]

The Soviets responded by subjecting II. battalion's positions to a ferocious preparatory bombardment by artillery and Katyusha rocket launchers. Masterfully seeking out the juncture between divisions, an infantry force in the strength of a battalion attacked the positions of 5 company which formed the Galician Division's left wing.[141] Despite being wounded, its commander Waffen-Untersturmführer Serhij Ruditschew, courageously led the soldiers in a successful counterattack, disregarding the hail of bullets and continuous explosions of grenades but later died of his wounds.[142] Clearing the breakthrough and driving the enemy back brought a temporary respite for the hard pressed battalion which was then able to regroup, organise ammunition supplies and evacuate the wounded.

South of WGR 29, both battalions of WGR 31 were embroiled in fierce combat in the densely wooded areas around Maidan Pieniacky, Huta Peniatska and Hucysko Pieniakie. In this area, in addition to battling the Red Army there were also a number of villages where the local Polish population was, as had been anticipated, hostile to the Ukrainian soldiers.[143] This is evidenced in the account of Waffen-Unterscharführer Wolodomyr Molodecky,[144] a former member of the Division's independent Panzerjäger [anti-tank] company[145] whose group experienced serious difficulties at first hand in the village of Maidan Pieniacky.[146]

As well as the frontal attacks, WGR 31 came under increasing pressure from the enemy who had crossed a stream and were gradually advancing from the forested area to the south. Despite the regiment commander SS-Obersturmbannführer Paul Herms's order to 'hold to the last man' periodically local break-ins supported by enemy tanks began.[147] On the right wing the Soviet tanks drove into Huta Peniatska where Waffen-Hauptsturmführer Hennadij Salessky, a former Red Army officer, demonstrated exceptional bravery personally destroying several of them with bundles of grenades tied together.[148] After regrouping the regiment entrenched for the remainder of the day, repulsing repeated attacks. A new regimental HQ was established further to the rear in Pidhirtsi where, based in the forest 300 metres west of the village[149] the operational part of the Galician Division's HQ endeavoured to co-ordinate all actions of its individual elements in what was later described as 'the most difficult and most unclear frontal sector of the Corps'.[150]

To strengthen weak points and localities in which the Soviet assaults were particularly heavy, the Division's command committed critical reinforcements comprising of the Division's Fusilier Battalion and independent Panzerjäger company (which was fully mechanised) which on the morning of the 17 deployed to the empty and destroyed village of Huta Peniatska.[151] The Pioneer Battalion which was originally encamped near Sokolivka also marched to this area as recollected by Waffen-Unterscharführer Julian Wilshynsky, a member of 3 co. 14. Pi.Abtl.:

[...] On Sunday there was an alarm and we proceeded by forced march to the town of Pidhirtsi where we stopped for two or three hours. We marched all night in the darkness. Then we marched to Maidan Pieniacky and on through Huta Peniatska where we entered the battle zone. We didn't know where we were going but when it started to get light we saw a lot of wreckage in the forest and broken trees. A German unit was supposed to be there but all we found was a lot of dead Russian soldiers.

We occupied the trenches and picked up some of their equipment and maxim machine guns. During the afternoon the Soviets attacked but we managed to beat them back with our machine guns. Late in the afternoon we got the order to pull back to Huta Peniatska. In Huta Peniatska we dug in with 1 anti-tank gun that was attached to our company. We stayed here two days. The gun commander had sixteen rounds, eight anti-tank and eight anti-infantry and asked us 'what should I do? should I fire on them or hold off?[...][152]

To the rear, the Division's artillery batteries continued to provide fire support for the infantry but struggled to relocate to new firing positions on the earth roads which, already badly damaged by bombardments, were transformed into mud by heavy rain which began on the night of 16/17 July.

The supply and medical units experienced the same difficulties as they persevered to maintain ammunition supplies and evacuate the constant stream of wounded to temporary casualty clearing stations on roads where motor vehicles and horse-drawn supply carts sank up to their axles and fatigued the horses.[153]

In the same area on 17 July KACs Fusilier Battalion received fresh orders from XIII AK, to advance from its assembly area south of Maidan Pieniacky and with the support of two Sturmgeschütze, retake the village of Werkhobuzkh.[154] On its right flank was a unit from the Galician Division, whose combat units were by now heavily immersed in trying to gain control of the forested area and trying to eliminate the numerous infiltrations with local counterattacks. Its left flank was open.

While combing the extremely dense woodland south of Maidan Pieniacky, contact between the Fusilier Battalion of KAC and elements of the Galician Division on its immediate right was lost.[155] The battered units of the Galician Division which had now re-committed the remnants of WGR 30, had been unable to make significant headway against the overwhelming enemy forces in this operational area. These included elements of 23 Rifle Corps' 99 Rifle Division, 359 Rifle Division, and the 68 Guards Rifle Division, together with the 336 Rifle Division from 15 Rifle Corps.[156] These were supplemented by armoured support from 4 Guards Tank Corps from the Front Reserve and a portion of 4 Tank Army deployed in an infantry support role.[157]

Confronted by an enemy equipped with liberal quantities of tanks and heavy weapons of all types and following bitter close combat with heavy losses, the Galician units were forced to retreat to their preparation area.[158]

The Fusilier Battalion of KAC now came under very heavy fire on both open flanks, and finding itself in an untenable position, entrenched and waited until nightfall before it too fell back to its assembly area of Maidan Pieniacky.[159]

Generalleutnant Lange the commander of KAC later summarised these developments writing:

> When the enemy had penetrated the woods west of Pieniaki counterattacks were executed with insufficient forces by KAC and later by the Galician SS Volunteer Division; these had some success but failed to make contact with the 349 Infantry Division[160] which was attacking from the south.[161]

Elsewhere in the south on 17 July the 349 Infantry Division reinforced with Kampfgruppe Haid had been ordered to attack to retake the Prinz Eugen Stellung in the vicinity of Kruhiv-Peniaky. The attack began as planned but quickly ran into strong Soviet defensive positions supported by heavy JS-2 [Joseph Stalin-2] tanks.[162] Although some progress was made, with only local reinforcement and minimal armoured backing from a handful of Sturmgeschütze and tanks[163] the infantry units found themselves in an identical situation to the Ukrainians and were quickly pinned down and unable to move. A strong Soviet counter-thrust captured Huta Werkobuzka which the 349 Infantry Division was unable to retake, and when darkness fell on 17 July the attack ground to a halt.[164]

Once again, XIII AK's command had overestimated the capabilities of its forces, none of which had been able to achieve their objectives in this difficult sector where the course of the front line was in a constant state of flux.

Following the failure of the attempt to retake control of the south-eastern most part of the corps' area, during the night of the 17/18 July KACs' Divisional Gruppe 339 reinforced with artillery and six Sturmgeschütze, was given fresh instructions to make a renewed effort to seal off the area of enemy penetration in the south. Divisional Gruppe 339 was ordered to march south until it reached Ruda Koltovska where it was to attach itself to the 349 Infantry Division. Both units were then to attack to the south to take the village of Obertasiv where they were to join with the 8 Panzer Division which had reorganised and was still incorrectly assumed to be striking northward, to re-establish a solid front.

Although Divisional Gruppe 339 and elements of the 349 Infantry Division managed to achieve their objective and reach their destination—the high ground north of Obertasiv, on the morning of 18 July the attack by the 8 Panzer Division had to be aborted again.[165] Placed under the command of Major-General von Mellenthin, for the second time direct orders were disobeyed, this time by the commander of the Panzer Regiment, thereby preventing it from reaching the target area.[166]

Against manifestly unequal odds, XIII AKs last attempt to seal the gap created by the Soviet advance in the south and link up with the relief forces, had failed. As a result the Prinz Eugen Stellung had to be abandoned and XIII AKs left wing had to be bent back to form a front facing north.

The Galician Division which had been badly mauled in its initial engagements received fresh orders. WGR 30 was given the assignment of clearing the neighbouring woods of the remaining enemy force while the rest of the Division was to set up a blockade of the Iaseniv and Sasiv Valleys which were suitable for Soviet penetrations and not allow the enemy passage into the vast surrounding woodlands and XIII AKs rear.[167]

Despite the day's events, the commander of XIII AK General Hauffe still did not appreciate the full danger or the radically worsening operational situation. As prisoners subsequently revealed 'Many officers reported to General Hauffe (XIII AK commander) about his forces' situation and expressed the opinion that he should withdraw, but the general demanded that they hold out in the hope that help would arrive'.[168]

Encirclement

As this was taking place, the Galician Division's HQ received further alarming reports. Its supply and reserve units stationed about 15 kms to the rear, had come under attack from the leading elements of the Soviet assault forces near Krasne and were therefore retreating westwards. The 14. Feld Ersatz Battalion managed to disengage with minimal casualties and hurriedly escaped ahead of the approaching tanks after abandoning most of its equipment.[169] Taking little interest in the fate of his unit, its commander SS-Hauptsturmführer Johannes Kleinow fled leaving the soldiers to fend for themselves.[170] A former member of the 5 company 14 Feld Ersatz Batl Waffen-Schütze Petro Maslij wrote:

German tanks move from the south to support the breakout attempt.

Our company was stationed in the village of Bezbrody, close to Krasne, where we were allocated a stable which was to serve as our dormitory and training place. Every day the company carried out rifle and machine gun training. On Monday 17 July it was raining. We heard artillery fire, our company commander SS-Obersturmführer Schneller ran outside to see what was happening but soon came back saying that he thought it was the Wehrmacht practising and we continued with our training. After a while intensified artillery fire began. Once again, SS-Obersturmführer Schneller left the barn and returned saying that there must be partisans nearby and the Wehrmacht units were shooting at them with artillery. He ordered the company to leave the barn and assemble outside. We could see swarms of refugees and retreating soldiers through binoculars. In the distance we saw Red Army tanks approaching. SS-Obersturmführer Schneller ordered us to set up machine gun posts and defensive positions. Even though some men did not have ammunition for their rifles, he refused to permit us to withdraw because he had no orders to do so. With a few machine guns and a couple of Panzerfausts we could not repulse an attack by tanks and despite Schneller's threats we decided to withdraw with or without orders. At that moment some UPA officers rode up on horseback and told us that our position was hopeless and that we would soon be completely overrun by the tanks. As the main road in the direction of L'viv was blocked by columns which were being attacked by Soviet planes they offered to lead our group through the woods. We abandoned our positions and followed them.[...][171]

Several of XIII AKs other supply and support units situated furthest to the rear also withdrew quickly after only brief contact with the enemy thereby avoiding encirclement too.[172] Their comrades further to the east were not however so fortunate.

By the end of 17 July Lieutenant General Baranov's Cavalry Mechanised Group of the northern pincer had captured Kaminka-Strumilova, deep in the rear of XIII AK. Having dispersed an attack by two German infantry divisions—20 Panzer Grenadier Division and 100 Jäger Divisions in the area,[173] it went on to throw a detachment forward to the Derevliany region. Here, on the 18 July the 2 Guards Cavalry Division (from Baranov's Group) linked up with the 71 Mechanised Brigade of the 3 Tank Army in the south, whose forces had occupied the important road junction at Busk at noon on the same day.[174] Before maintaining its westward advance, the latter left part of its forces (71 Mechanised Brigade, 50 Motorcycle Regiment and the 91 Separate Tank Brigade) in a strong screen along the northern bank of the Buh River from Sasiv to Derevliany facing north and north-east. Small sub units from these formations then occupied all of the river crossings, the important villages and towns and blocked all the roads. In so doing they cut off the withdrawal route of the German forces which by now had committed all their reserves.

Six days after their main offensive had begun, the complete operational encirclement of what was collectively referred to in the Soviet battle reports as the 'Brody Grouping' had been achieved. Along with a variety of smaller units[175] the greater part of six divisions have been confirmed as having been trapped in the 'Kessel von Brody' (Brody pocket).[176] These were—454 Security Division, 361 Infantry Division, 349 Infantry Division, 340 Infantry Division, Korps Abteilung C and the 14. Waffen-

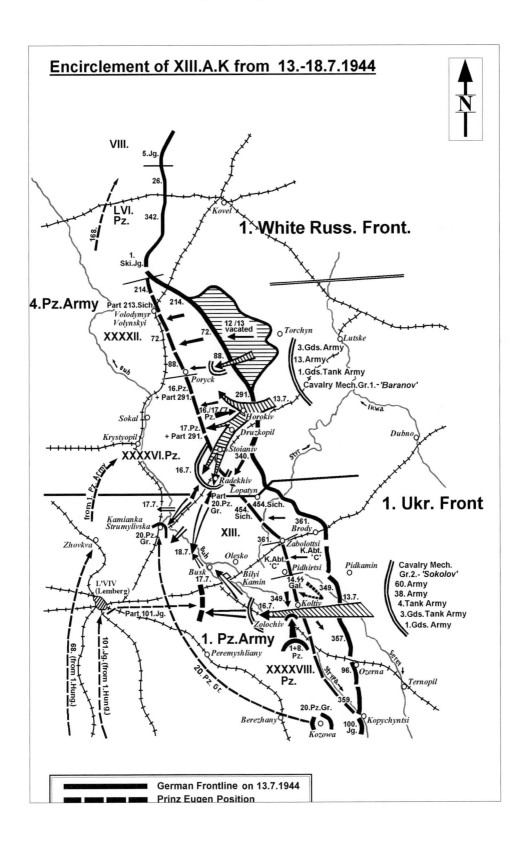

Encirclement of XIII.A.K from 13.-18.7.1944

N

German Frontline on 13.7.1944
Prinz Eugen Position

Grenadier-Division der SS (galizische Nr. 1). The external boundary of the pocket ran along the general line: Toporiv, Busk, Sasiv, Koltiv, Opaky and Kadovbysti.[177]

The first objective of Marshal Konev's plan had succeeded. The next day in Moscow, Stalin greeted the news of the operational encirclement of XIII AK by ordering twenty shots to be fired from 224 cannons in celebration.[178]

18 July: Trapped

Following the successful completion of the operational encirclement and isolation of the Brody grouping from the rest of the German forces west of the Buh, Marshal Konev ordered his mobile formations to push on towards their strategic objectives which were Rava Russka on the northern axis and L'viv on the southern axis.[179] Simultaneously, to facilitate the maintenance of the offensive on the Galician capital, the 1 Ukrainian Front undertook the immediate commencement of the swift liquidation of the entrapped German forces. One of the main factors which dictated this mission was that the presence of the group, which was surrounded over a sizeable area, required large numbers of Soviet troops to contain it.[180] It also compromised the manoeuvrability of the Front's combat formations along the L'viv axis.[181] Moreover, the possibility could not be excluded that the Brody grouping could still link up with the remaining German tank formations south of Zolochiv, thereby severing the base of the Soviet spearhead in the south.

The task of dismembering and eliminating the Brody group was allocated to 60 Army reinforced by the 4 Guards Tank Corps from the Front reserve in co-operation with a portion of the 4 Tank and 13 Armies'.[182] To accomplish this, they directed their main effort at first chopping the main grouping into a series of smaller groups isolated from one another; secondly depriving the Germans of the opportunity to manoeuvre their forces freely and prevent them from concentrating along the most important axes; thirdly repelling attempts by the encircled units to penetrate the encirclement ring.[183]

Surrounded in an oval shaped area covering a distance of approximately 40 kms on its north-west/south-east axis by 24 kms on its east-west axis, XIII AK, was now subjected to a barrage of artillery fire and air strikes by close support aircraft from all directions. The intensive shellfire wrecked the field telephone installations and shredded telephone wires. This severely disrupted internal communication facilities on both the corps and divisional level, making it appreciably harder to maintain centralised command and preserve order.[184]

With all its overland supply routes severed and its retreat path to the west blocked, the only hope of XIII AK avoiding complete destruction was to break out of the encirclement. Only now, having already delayed his decision too long, did General Hauffe finally agree to do so. Following advice from a westward reconnaissance against an attempt in that direction, on the afternoon of 18 July, XIII AK command elected to try to join with the XXXXVIII PzK via a thrust to the south roughly level with the main L'viv/Zolochiv road.[185]

To accomplish this, preliminary orders were issued for XIII AKs strongest unit, KAC, to initially take up positions on the Zahirtsi–Tsishky–Chekhy ridge north-east of Khvativ, during the night 18/19 July. Its two remaining divisional groups (183 and 311) were to hold that line until being relieved from the front by the 361 Infantry Division and the Galician Division respectively. The component units of the KAC were then to gather in the woodland either side of the road to Bilyi Kamin and in the Havarechyna/Horishnia area on 19 July in preparation for the breakout attempt which it was to lead.[186]

Having reverted to the command of its own staff, on 18 July the Galician Division's area of operations extended from 1.5 km's south west of Wolochy in the north to Koltiv in the south.[187] Here, on the east and south-eastern edge of the pocket all three of its severely depleted infantry regiments and other weakened combat units were involved in a gruelling series of defensive engagements. Consequently, heavy concentrations of well equipped and fresh Red Army infantry began intermittent massed attacks against its positions from three sides.

Soviet intelligence had quickly indentified the presence of the Galician Division in the pocket by virtue of the unique Waffen-SS camouflage clothing and Galician insignia worn by its personnel[188] and having done so the Red Army units set about attempting to annihilate it.

In the vicinity of Iaseniv where WGR 29 was deployed, at 1300 hrs the enemy attacked from its staging area south of Wolochy.[189] Moving through the forest, three battalions of Soviet infantry attacked 6 company forcing it to retreat after heavy fighting and in the process tearing open a gap between I. and II. battalions. Information from prisoners revealed that their local objective was to capture 2 artillery observation positions (which had caused them so much difficulty), hit the HQ of WGR 29 and II. battalion's positions and move into the forest behind the remnants of WGR 31 rolling up its positions from behind.[190]

The positions of I. battalion were also penetrated, forcing it to retreat back into the lines of the II./WGR 29.[191] Leading the attack was a Red Army penal battalion whose men, primed with extra vodka rations,[192] were driven like cattle in front of NKVD officers who shot anyone who tried to turn back.

SS-Standertenführer Friedrich Dern immediately ordered the II. battalion commander Hauptsturmführer Wilhelm Allerkamp to counterattack 'regardless of the losses'.[193] 8.II./WGR 29 led by Waffen-Obersturmführer Savely Yaskevych supported by the staff company WGR 29 under Obersturmführer Gunter Weiss took part in this action.[194] Waffen-Unterscharführer Wasyl Sirsky of the staff company WGR 29:

[...] At 1300 hrs an alarm was raised. The company commander SS-Obersturmführer Weiss described the overall situation at the front: 'The enemy has managed to penetrate the positions of our I battalion. Our company's orders are to clear the breaches. We leave in 10 minutes'.[...] We were armed with MG 42s, rifles, hand-grenades and Panzerfausts. We marched through Hayi Dubecki in an easterly direction. On the way we came across wagons loaded with dead and wounded.[...] before we arrived at I battalion's positions the Soviets had advanced right up to II battalion's HQ.

This critical situation was saved by Waffen-Obersturmführer Yaskevych who at the head of 8 company forced back the enemy advance. Before our eyes the enemy was hastily retreating to the east. We continued to march towards the south east and took over the defensive positions of I battalion.

After we had occupied the trenches, Obersturmführer Weiss ordered Waffen-Unterscharführer Osyp Levko to take command of the company and taking 22 men with him headed for Zharkiv. Having covered over a kilometre through thick bushes we heard heavy firing. Within 10 minutes we got to the edge of a wood where a small unit of the I battalion was holding out under attack and heavily outnumbered by two companies of Soviets. From our concealed position we watched them attack, against all military training in tight formation stumbling and shouting obscenities. With cries of U-r-r-a! the drunken ranks were advancing one after the other not even bothering to fall to the ground and take cover. We waited in silence until they got to within 100 metres of us and then opened fire from the flank with seven MG 42s. They were taken completely by surprise and within minutes the remaining Soviets were fleeing in panic into the woods leaving some fifty corpses on the battlefield. We advanced another 200 metres or so and tried to make contact with the unit which had been holding out.[...] Our fighting unit had secured the defensive positions of the I. battalion.[...][195]

With the Regiment's lines temporarily stabilised, the commander of I. battalion Waffen-Hauptsturmführer Brygidyr sent an urgent request to the Divisional command for additional officers as replacements for those already lost. These included the commanders of its 1 company Waffen-Obersturmführer Ivan Witushynskyj who had been killed and 3 company Waffen-Obersturmführer Mychailo Lischtschynsky who was badly wounded in the left arm, which later had to be amputated. None were forthcoming.[196] In the attack, I. battalion had taken heavy casualties especially 3 company and now faced the threat of encirclement, principally the anti-tank platoon in the valley to the right of 2 company. With the telephone wires cut, Waffen-Hauptsturmführer Brygidyr sent word via the Ordonnanz Offizier Waffen-Untersturmführer Lubomyr Ortynsky to the regimental commander SS-Standartenführer Dern that it was essential to withdraw about 3 km's to the rear to new positions to avoid being surrounded.

When he arrived at regimental HQ in Iaseniv, a meeting of the Divisional commander with his regimental commanders was coming to an end. Freitag had already informed those present of the planned withdrawal by WGR 29 to a new line during the night of 18/19 July in order to take over from elements of KAC and that the general assembly area for the remainder of the Division was to be the elevated area behind Zahirtsi around Khvativ/Hucisko Oleskie. Waffen-Untersturmführer Ortynsky wrote:

[...] Dern told me to describe briefly the events in I./29.The atmosphere was grim, even depressing. Everyone knew that the enemy ring around the German units and our Division was closed, and the prospects were not good. After Freitag and the commanders had left, Dern described the situation. We [WGR 29] had until 0600

The caption on this Kriegsberichter picture reads 'The Divisional commander Freitag studies a map during the fighting at Brody'. The picture is dated July 1944.

Machine gun team from the Galician Division fighting in the Brody pocket.

hrs [19 July] to man the line Pidhirtsi–Zahirtsi line. The adjutant wrote the orders to the battalion commanders..[…][197]

Meanwhile the remnants of WGR 31 were now deployed on the east side of the pocket around villages such as Ruda Koltovska, Opaky and Maidan Pieniacky where sustained Soviet assaults resulted in bitter fighting. At the same time elements of WGR 30 were defending the area around Ushnia and were dug in on the main road running from Sasiv to Koltiv, which formed the southern perimeter of the pocket.[198] Here they faced 3 entire divisions of 60 Army's 23 Rifle Corps,[199] 1 Division of 15 Rifle Corps[200] and the 91 and 93 Independent Tank Brigades (from 3 Guards Tank Army and 4 Tank Army respectively).[201]

The Fusilier Battalion, Panzerjäger and Pioneer battalion continued to be used to support the infantry. Waffen-Unterscharführer W. Molodecky was a former member of the independent Panzerjäger company:

> […] The whole company retreated south from Iaseniv in the direction of Zolochiv. Everyone said if we could get there we would be saved.
>
> Our column of vehicles travelled slowly on the road and after a couple of hours we passed through a forest into open fields. I noticed piles of hay in the fields which I thought was quite normal in July but my driver who was brought up on a farm was perplexed and could not understand why there were piles of hay between the forests. Suddenly the piles of hay started firing at us. Our column had been ambushed by Russian T34's that had been covered with hay and well camouflaged. Luckily they had no infantry support.
>
> Under heavy fire from the tanks we deployed our anti-tank guns as quickly as possible. With shells bursting all around us there was no time to get to cover or help the wounded. At last our guns opened fire. The shells and ammunition in our burning vehicles began exploding causing more casualties. I was standing close to a gun when it took a direct hit from a T34. The explosion pierced the gun shield and forced part of the gunner's helmet into his head killing him and forcing part of his brain out of his skull. I moved forward to take his place. The tanks were moving towards us and several burst into flames as we hit them. At the critical moment some German Sturmgeschütze appeared which had heard the noise of the battle. They attacked the tanks forcing them to retreat. Without their help we would have been annihilated.
>
> The entire engagement lasted 10–15 minutes but during that time the company was completely destroyed. Of 150 men about 30 survived while out of the twelve guns only three remained. We put the wounded on the last remaining serviceable Raupenschlepper [caterpillar tractor] and hitched the best gun to it. The two remaining guns had to be destroyed because we had no way of moving them. From this time there was no longer a Panzerjäger company and we had to fight as regular infantry.[…][202]

Throughout the day positions were lost and then regained again following vicious counterattacks. The difficulties in retaining any ground were compounded by the need to constantly shift regimental/battalion command posts. Indeed, some measure of the intensity of the combat in this area can be gauged from the fact that in the period from 17–19 July the forces defending the village of Koltiv came under attack twelve times by Soviet infantry in regimental strength with each attack supported by heavy artillery and numerous tanks, in one case thirty five.[203] Similarly, Sasiv where groups of Ukrainian troops were also deployed was repeatedly assaulted by infantry in battalion and regimental strength on eight separate occasions.[204] The aircraft from 2 Air Army were also of great assistance to the Soviet ground forces during the fighting from 16–18 July flying 10,289 sorties during this period of which bombers and assault aircraft conducted more than 5,000.[205]

The Galician Division's Artillery Regiment, gave its full support to the infantry throughout all engagements reinforcing all local counterattacks and providing cover during retreats. Its batteries were so busily engaged that the frequent changes of position were accomplished without the assistance of horses, so that the crews had to manhandle the guns themselves. When the artillery ran out of ammunition the guns were disabled by removing and burying the breech blocks, leaving the gun crews to fight as infantry often in hand to hand combat with the enemy.

By this stage even the Division's Kriegsberichter platoon was caught up in the combat as recalled by technical assistant Jurij Kopystansky, who reported:

> On 18 July at 1600 hrs I returned with the German commander of the platoon from the Divisional HQ to Havarechchyna where the platoon was stationed. The commander was very depressed and chain smoked. He told us the bad news that the Division was encircled. Everybody was to take with them their guns, ammunition and backpack.
>
> We blew up the truck along with other [unnecessary] materials using two bundles of grenades and he told us to go in the direction of Bilyi Kamin. (Some members of the platoon were away on assignments in the units of the Division). Myself, Misko Furman (also a 'technical assistant') and the commander got into an Opel car and drove to Bilyi Kamin. After two nights we stopped in a village where the car was destroyed by enemy gunfire. We left the platoon commander there and we both went to break out with other Ukrainian and German soldiers.[...][206]

In the course of the fighting the Galician Division's soldiers found themselves responsible for a number of prisoners. Tragically, some of the older captives (aged 40–45) were found to have been fighting against their own sons.[207] Although often equipped with automatic weapons, apart from ammunition, most carried little or nothing else and seldom had any food except corn seeds.[208] Whenever possible those who had been forcibly conscripted into the Red Army from the local population (known as 'booty Ukrainians'),[209] were disarmed, released and allowed to return home or simply left behind untouched.[210] The rest were taken to regimental or battalion command posts where, as circumstances permitted they were passed on to the custody of the Division's military police unit for interrogation.[211] Some implored their Ukrainian captors to be allowed to remain under their protection fearing their fate (and often not without good reason) if they were to be handed over to

Germans. Waffen-Unterscharführer Veryha serving with 9./II./WGR 30 and Waffen-Unterscharführer Ferencevych 13./WGR 31 were two of several veterans who reported witnessing the execution of Red Army prisoners by German soldiers.[212]

A New Line, 19 July 1944
'Only psychopaths don't have fear'—German officer to Waffen-Unterscharführer W. Molodecky

During the night of the 18/19 July the first stage of the preparations for the breakout began which involved the replacement of the elements of KAC, which was to act as the spearhead, so that they could withdraw to their assembly areas. This operation coincided with renewed efforts by the Soviet forces to reduce the already compressed and constantly shrinking area via a series of concentric attacks.

On receipt of the new orders, the Galician Division began to pull back to its new positions. In the early morning hours of 19 July the remnants of WGR 31, the Fusilier Battalion, Panzerjäger Battalion and the Pioneer Battalion began to retire at night to the west in the general direction of Olesko. In so doing, several previously heavily contested villages such as Maidan Pieniacky, Huta Peniatska and Iaseniv were abandoned one by one. The Red Army units noticed the movement and followed in close pursuit harassing the retreating units. In their haste, to lighten their loads as they marched some of the very tired soldiers panicked and threw away ammunition and weapons, despite warnings from their commanders.[213] Passing through Maidan Pieniacky the Fusilier Battalion reached the assembly point—the forest near Khvativ/Hucisko Oleskie, where in a half kilometre sector the remnants of WGR 31 and the Fusilier Battalion assembled and were ordered to dig in. By now it was apparent that the situation was catastrophic. When an officer asked where the enemy was, the commander of WGR 31 SS-Obersturmbannführer Herms pointed in one direction, whilst the commander of the Pioneer Battalion Sturmbannführer Remberger denied it and pointed in the opposite direction.[214] Shooting could be heard from all around which some attributed to partisans (Polish and Soviet partisans were known to be operating in the area), others—the Red Army.

To the north, both battalions of WGR 29 also disengaged and commenced their withdrawal to the Pidhirtsi–Zahirtsi line under cover of darkness. In the process some men got lost having become separated from their units and not all of them found their way back with some taking the opportunity to desert—mostly to the UPA. In an attempt to delay the advance of enemy armour, smaller bridges on the main roads were mined and blown up.

In the early morning of the 19 July the last elements of WGR 29 were taking up their new positions as ordered. As they did, the first Soviet tanks advancing in open ground on the main paved Brody/Olesko road, reached the recently evacuated and now burning village of Iaseniv. Waffen-Obersturmführer Lubomyr Ortynsky from WGR 29, recalled the handover and how from their elevated vantage point, the leading Soviet tanks began firing at distance into the rearmost ranks of WGR 29:

[...] Near the church in Zahirtsi we were met by a young German lieutenant and we could see that he was in a hurry. On the map he showed the positions that he had held since last night as a second line of defence and then he hastily departed. The commander [Dern] and myself looked over the terrain and saw no sign of any positions except two deep holes that a peasant probably dug for keeping potatoes for the winter. But that was no surprise, his troop was here for just 12 hours and the soldiers were too exhausted [for building positions] and fell asleep.

The commander of I./WGR 29 arrived. We read the map and SS-Standartenführer Dern assigned Waffen-Hauptsturmführer Brygidyr the sector for I./WGR 29. Suddenly we heard loud shots from the road: Tanks! We all looked towards Iaseniv. Bolshevik tanks could be seen breaking into the last ranks of the column of II./WGR 29. On one hill we could see around 10 tanks firing on the road and the column of I.WGR 29, while the Soviet infantry were advancing like a swarm of bees.[...][215]

As the Galician Division continued to move into and consolidate its new line, on the morning of 19 July at XIII AK HQ, General Hauffe's Chief of Staff Oberst von Hammerstein issued the detailed orders for the breakout plan to the divisional 1a's of all the corps' units.[216] The plan was expected to take three days. According to it, at 0300 hrs on 20 July KAC would spearhead an attack from its position at Bilyi Kamin in a south westerly direction over the Buh River towards the Podillian Elevation.[217] For this purpose the 249 Assault Gun Brigade and a battalion of the 361 Infantry Division, would be attached to it. This route involved the crossing of two rivers (Buh and Zolochivka) as well as very large stretches of marshy ground before negotiating a steep incline covered in thick brush. Consequently, it was thought to be the area in which an attack would least be expected and therefore offer the best chances of success.[218]

The 349 Infantry Division was to provide flank protection as the attack force moved southwards while the Galician Division, along with the 361 and 454 Divisions were to form the rearguard. These divisions which were located furthest to the north were ordered to remain in place and await orders to fall back. Their task was to defend their positions as long as possible and prevent any serious breach of the perimeter which would not only have effectively terminated any chance of a breakout but lead to the destruction of the entire corps.[219]

To assist the breakout, elements of XXXXVIII Panzer Corps which was wrongly assumed to be holding a solid front five kilometres south of the main L'viv–Zolochiv road[220] would simultaneously strike north towards the beleaguered corps from the outside. Only when the breakthrough had succeeded and a suitable corridor established would the corp's wounded, supply services and remaining heavy weapons be evacuated. These were to be followed by the three divisions which formed the rearguard.

In his secret after-action battle report, the commander of KAC General Lange, gave his account of the handover. His comments suggest an intrinsic prejudice against the 'foreign' Galician Division which unlike the corp's battle hardened regular army units was undergoing its first experience of combat:

[...] 19 July 1944. The relieving of the Div.Gr 183 [by the 361 Infantry Division] proceeded according to plan. The Divisional Gruppe with its attached units, had by midday [on 19] reached the woods south of Ozhydiv. At that time, the Gren.Rgt. Gr.311 first handed over [the positions] to the 14.SS.Freiw.Div-Galizien, so that the covering of the withdrawal could be carried out under pressure from the enemy which in the interim had also moved in tanks on the main Lemberg [L'viv]–Brody road. The increased enemy activity at this point was made more critical for the XIII Army Korps when the enemy met with only minimal resistance. The 14.SS-Freiw-Div.-Galizien had during its first deployments shown an unusually low ability for holding position. As was anticipated, the Galicians in no way showed themselves to be the fanatical defenders of their homeland against Bolshevism, therefore their superior armament and equipment, could barely be brought to effect and consequently this armament found itself in the hands of a totally undisciplined, disordered mob over whom the minimal German leadership, despite their upmost efforts, could have little effect.[221]

As we have already seen, XIII AKs regular German Army units were not adverse to overlooking their own failings and casting aspersions against the Ukrainians who unlike them, were wearing Waffen-SS uniforms. Indeed, Lange's negative evaluation stands in marked contrast to that of the Galician Division's 1a Major Heike who unlike Lange, was fully cognisant of the difficulties under which it was operating when he wrote 'More could not be expected of them [the Ukrainians] as many German units had panicked as well'.[222]

For the remainder of the 19 July events continued to cruelly conspire against the Ukrainian soldiers who were under orders to hold the Pidhirtsi–Zahirtsi line to enable the breakout preparations to progress. Entrenched in their positions, they now faced the unabated fury of strong infantry attacks by fresh Red Army formations (some of which included women).[223] With the weakening of the perimeter area, the already hard pressed rearguard units had to absorb additional pressure primarily from 102 Rifle Corps's 162, 172 Rifle and 117 Guards Rifle Divisions, along the northern and north-eastern edges. On the pocket's eastern and south-eastern sides they faced 23 Rifle Corps' 68 Guards, 99 and 359 Rifle Divisions.

During the heavy fighting the headquarters of WGR 31 came under direct attack and was completely overrun. In the turmoil that followed the regiment commander SS-Obersturmbannführer Herms and almost the entire regimental staff of WGR 31 were killed in bitter hand to hand fighting north of Sasiv.[224] There were only two survivors, Hauptsturmführer Helmut Funk and Unterscharführer Kohlheimer.[225]

Communication difficulties ensured that the news of the death of SS-Obersturmbannführer Herms and his staff took several hours to disseminate. Waffen-Unterscharführer Jurij Ferencevych:

[...] In the evening of 19 July the company commander Waffen-Unterscharführer Alexander Olearnyk sent me a message to bring my company staff unit [13./WGR 31] to Pidhirtsi where WGR 31 [now] had its headquarters. We marched all night passing a battery of our artillery. On 20 July we approached the village of Pidhirtsi, looking for the company commander. Passing by a farm a Ukrainian NCO in charge of regimental communication Waffen-Oberscharführer Ewhen Harasunchuk came to the front gate and told me that the regiment commander and his chief of staff had been killed. I was in a hurry looking for my unit so didn't bother to ask for any details. I eventually found our commander Waffen-Untersturmführer Olearnyk and two of our platoons in position, giving fire support to our retreating units of the 31 regiment. He told me to go towards Bilyi Kamin, and we marked on our maps the location where we were going to meet. We set out with 4 Panjewagens some telephone and radio equipment and our personal belongings.[...][226]

Because of the high attrition rate among its units, the Galician Division was now increasingly forced to improvise and rely upon the placement of minefields in front of its forward positions.[227] Any such additional fortification work was however, rendered virtually impossible during daylight because of the proximity of the enemy lines and constant threat from Soviet aircraft. A limited amount of such work could be undertaken at night but this did little to deflect the full force of the attacks. Individual breaches when they occurred, could only be contained by the desperate expedient of transferring soldiers from the Division's supply and support units to emergency battle groups or scratch companies of mixed German/ Ukrainian composition.[228] The fighting was especially ferocious in the vicinity of the villages of Khvativ and Pidhirtsi with its dominating heights[229] where the Galician forces included 1 company of the Fusilier Battalion which had orders to recapture the castle.[230] Remarkably, to their credit the Ukrainians from the Division previously described by Lange as 'a totally undisciplined, disordered mob' were still able to retake both and clear their own lines without additional German infantry support as his report acknowledges:

[...] In the afternoon the [Galician] Division also lost Pidhirtsi and Khvativ. To counter the danger within the encirclement the 311 Grenadier Regiment and the KACs Fusilier Battalion were sent to consolidate the position under orders of the XIII AK. **In the event they did not encounter any action. The SS-Freiwi.Div.Galizien** [sic] **retook Khvativ and Pidhirtsi with support from self-propelled guns.** (author's emphasis).[231]

Over the course of this day and the next, Pidhirtsi continued to change hands resulting in house to house fighting as each side sought to gain possession from the other. On the approaches to the castle four enemy tanks were destroyed by the Fusiliers.[232] Waffen-Unterscharführer Julian Wilshynsky of the Pioneer Battalion was also involved in the fighting here:

[...] From Huta Peniatska we pulled out to Maidan Pieniacky on the road and straightened out our line. That is where our company suffered its heaviest losses. For some periods of time the cannonade—from artillery and mortars—was so heavy we

Machine gun team in action at Brody.

Wreckage of burning trucks which blocked many roads in the pocket paralysing all movement.

did not know if it was day or night. There wasn't a square yard that was not covered with explosions. Our company lost around 70 men here in one single attack.

After that we pulled back to the road from Maidan Pieniacky to Pidhirtsi where the company commander Waffen-Untersturmführer Anton Dydalewytsch told us to dig in on both sides of the road because we didn't know where the Soviets would come from. There were about 80 men left [of 182] from our company including 2 NCOs and the company commander. We stayed there for 1 day and from there we pulled out to Pidhirtsi. Here we were part of a makeshift force of about 250 men. We had some infantry support guns (Infantrie Geschutze) and one anti-aircraft gun. We were in a battle here that lasted over 24 hrs. Pidhirtsi changed hands about 4 or 5 times. The tanks were attacking from the flat land and they overwhelmed us with artillery. Our patrols had some successes because they captured some heavy Soviet mortars. At that time is was raining but when it started to get bright there were hundreds of planes dropping bombs and strafing us. We did not know that we were surrounded.[233]

As part of the rearguard, the Galician Division now held a section of the northern perimeter which ran along the line of Adamy–Stolpin–Perevolochna–Sokolivka, over the Brody–Krasne rail line to Tsishky.[234] North of Olesko, between Sokolivka and Tsishky, units of 162 and 172 Rifle Divisions of 102 Rifle Corps, supported by large formations of Soviet T-34 tanks joined up with other units coming from the west near Busk. Attacking from north to south the armour crossed the rail line and made a concentrated attack towards Olesko which was situated in the centre of the Galician Division's lines and several kilometres behind its easternmost positions. To counter this outflanking manoeuvre, the Division's command hurriedly despatched the remnants of the Fusiliers, Pioneers and Panzerjäger to the vicinity. Alongside them were hastily reorganised scratch infantry companies comprising of soldiers from all branches of services. Armed with the last remaining anti-tank guns and carrying Panzerfausts, they had orders to hold at all costs. The Panzerjägers, together with the infantry destroyed several of the tanks at close range and drove off the rest, preventing a major breakthrough and temporarily averting a potential disaster.[235] Waffen-Unterscharführer W. Molodecky from the independent Panzerjäger company:

[...] We reached a village where the remains of our Panzerjäger company were organised into groups. From here we were sent with two or three infantry companies to Olesko and Ohyzdiv where we were to hold a very important railway junction. I heard that there had been a breakout from the encirclement and that we had to hold the Soviets for a couple of days so we could move our wounded out. We were formed into an infantry unit under the command of an east Ukrainian Waffen-Untersturmführer Simon Owtscharenko and dug trenches just outside Olesko. Again we were attacked by Soviet tanks but managed to fight them off before we retreated. The same day we reached a village where German and Ukrainian units were regrouping. At that time they were still trying to keep German and Ukrainian units separate. We were no longer receiving regular supplies but when we entered a village with our wounded the villagers tried to help us and immediately brought out any food—bread, milk—anything they had to us which reminded us that we were fighting for our country.

In another village south west of Olesko I met another Ukrainian Untersturmführer who tried to organise what was left of our Panzerjäger detachments. So far all he had found apart from myself was two other men and a 7.5 cm gun which he asked me to take command of. I agreed but said that I needed more men and he replied that he would try and find some. We were exhausted and tried to get some rest for the next couple of hours while we waited for him to return. Without any warning the Soviets opened fire on the village with Katyushas. The village was completely destroyed and I never saw that officer again. One of the men who was with me was badly wounded. I saw a German officer talking to another soldier nearby and I called to him to help me with my friend. He just got in a car and drove off.

We left the gun and the two of us that were left buried our comrade and began to walk towards the south west. On the way I met a group of Ukrainians who had found a box of hand grenades which they were busy putting detonators in. They invited me to take a few which I did. I recognised one of them as my friend from high school Nestor Zhoubrit. He told me a little bit further in the next village there was a German Army major who was trying to organise a breakthrough group. This German major started organising groups into platoons of about 50 men and for the first time he didn't bother separating Germans and Ukrainians, he simply counted them off in groups. When he found an officer whether he was a German or a Ukrainian he placed the officer in command. Then he divided the groups into ten and I was given command of one of those groups of ten men. He wore the Iron Cross I. Class and when I asked him he told me that he had won it at Stalingrad. I said to him that this battle must seem like childs play in comparison. He laughed and said to me 'when you are being killed it does not make any difference if you are at Brody or Stalingrad'. I replied 'it must be nice to have no fear' and he looked at me and said 'now look young man, only psychopaths don't have fear, normal people are always afraid and courage means only that you can control that fear and do your duty'. These words which I could still clearly recall years later made a profound impression on me.[…][236]

Pioneer Waffen-Unterscharführer Julian Wilshynsky was also fighting in this area:

[…] From Pidhirtsi they took what was left of our company to Olesko. Here we beat back an attack by Soviet tanks but the route to the west was closed by the remnants of the Soviet tanks. Soon after that our commander was wounded in the right hand from a piece of shrapnel.

Near Olesko I met a man who I knew as a recruit and he asked me 'is the road to L'viv still open?'. I replied 'I don't know' and he said 'we are surrounded'. Our commander said to us 'well boys that's it, save yourselves'. From there we started to retreat. We saw all the equipment our companies had left behind strung over the fields that they we marching on, laying in the fields wrecked. When we returned to our company command post near Pidhirtsi it had been attacked by Soviet partisans. That's when we lost the last of our heavy equipment.[237]

With food, fuel and ammunition supplies already in very short supply, the defensive fighting in the pocket was becoming progressively more difficult. Noticeable by its absence throughout the entire battle, the Luftwaffe did manage to parachute in token air-drops of less than a dozen tons of fuel, ammunition and food for which the recipients were extremely grateful. Waffen-Unterscharführer Wasyl Sirsky: 'In the village of Voluiky (part of Olesko) my friend offered me some food but I stayed there only a few minutes expecting an attack of Russian paratroopers. Luckily for us the Luftwaffe delivered to us some food and ammunition'.[238]

Further brutal battles were fought around the villages of Kadovbytsi and Chekhy by the fatigued remains of WGR's 29 and 30. As the situation demanded, the Galician Division's command was obliged to further disperse its forces and shift individual battalions which still had less than five days battle experience, to cover weak spots in other sectors including the village of Opaky where veteran German units were constantly struggling to contain Soviet attacks and having to retreat.[239] With its units scattered over a wide area, its dependence on field radios to transmit and receive orders and reports was all the more acute but these were in short supply and those which were available began to overload or could not be used at all because of the nature of the terrain.[240] The difficulties in this respect were exacerbated by virtue of the Ukrainian communications personnel having an insufficient command of the German language to interpret or pass on instructions to other units. In the absence of fresh orders, individual units which had lost contact with regimental, battalion and company commands were forced to work independently causing the Division to lose its cohesion. In several instances soldiers sent to unit command posts in the rear to receive new orders arrived only to discover that they had been abandoned and overwhelmed by marauding groups of Soviet tanks and infantry which had penetrated the Division's lines.[241]

By now all three of the Galician Division's infantry regiments had suffered very heavy losses and the artillery regiment had lost most of its guns. Perhaps the worst affected was WGR 31 which following the death of its commander SS-Obersturmbannführer Paul Herms and most of his regimental staff[242] had begin to splinter.

Denied the use of their aircraft because of the heavy rain and mist on this day, the Soviets constantly bombarded the Division's positions with artillery, heavy mortars and the lethal Katyusha rockets[243] which wrought terrible destruction, obliterating entire villages within minutes and shattering the morale of the soldiers in their target area.[244]

Most of the Galician Division's companies had gone into battle with only one Ukrainian officer and as long as the officers were alive and there were clear orders, they fought courageously and held their positions. However with the loss of the telephones and radios and with the messengers often unable to get through to deliver the orders, each unit was left to fend for itself. The particularly heavy casualties amongst the Ukrainian officers also had an exceptionally deleterious effect as without a Ukrainian officer in command, some units which up until that point had fought bravely, lost their discipline and abandoned their positions as self preservation took over.[245] The commander of the SS-Kriegsberichter (war reporter) platoon attached to the Division, Oberscharführer Erich Mekat was tried after the battle for leaving the battlefield without permission. In his trial statement he wrote:

> Since 2/7/1944 the SS-KB-Zug 'Galizien' was with the 14.-Galizien SS-Inf. Div. in the deployment area of Brody. After the Division had taken up its defensive positions just west of Brody, the entire front was stable until mid-July. Since Sunday the 16 July the Soviets began attempts to break through south and north of Brody. In the end near Busk, on the road to Lemberg [L'viv] the Soviets managed to cut us off from the supply routes to the west. Simultaneously, [enemy] forces managed to break into the position of a Wehrmacht infantry division situated south of Brody. The 30 Regiment was used in support. Still, as they pressed forward they met the advancing Soviets. These attacked strongly outside the established position[s of] the troops of the 30 regiment, resulting in great confusion, (at this time.) Immediately leaving behind almost all their possessions [weapons] the regiment splintered. This was the first phase of the collapse of the front at Brody. When the Wehrmacht saw this they reported 'The Waffen-SS are running away!' (outwardly all [Galician] units present were identifiable as SS because they wore a camouflage suit without the Galician Lion).
>
> The effect on the morale of the remaining units was inevitable and everywhere there was a noticeable great unrest. The German SS officers succeeded in hastily gathering the scattered parts of the regiment to use again at the seriously threatened places. Meanwhile, however, the Soviets had infiltrated in several further places and had now completely closed the ring. This was the case a day later on 17 July. It was now for everyone only to maintain and improve the current position. In the next 2 days nothing essential changed. Then the pressure increased and from now on with the stronger involvement of the Soviet Air Force the constriction of the encirclement began. I followed the developments through the daily briefings of [our] Ia and found out that in many cases ever new parts of the Division had left their positions despite strict instructions to remain. The 29 regiment was partially fragmented and without some of their weapons flooded back inside the pocket.[...][246]

At this time the Divisional headquarters began receiving reports from some surviving unit commanders that their positions had become untenable.[247] For over 78 hours its units had been engaged in combat without rest, against vastly unequal odds and plagued by communications problems. Having lost many of its Ukrainian officers, without regular rations and with ammunition in short supply because of the excessive expenditure caused by the constant defensive actions, the Galician Division began to show signs of collapse.

A delegation from the UPA arrived at the Division's HQ at this time to offer assistance but this was declined in the interests of both parties.[248] Even had it been accepted it is unlikely to have made any appreciable difference to its overall condition which was deteriorating rapidly. The UPA did however continue to assist individuals and small groups throughout the battle.

By the evening of 19 July the diameter of the pocket had shrunk to approximately fifteen to twenty km's and had its centre near the village of Olesko.[249] Shortly before the breakout was due to commence, the situation in the Galician Division's sector had become critical. Units of the 172 Rifle and 117 Guards Rifle Divisions made a number of serious penetrations around Olesko, Khvativ, and Zahirtsi. Unable to stabilise the front with its own internal resources, the Division had to call upon the help of remnants other units principally from the 361 Infantry Division. With enormous difficulty these were successfully contained and local counterattacks organised to regain lost or strategically important ground.

The Division's commander SS-Brigadeführer Freitag, received the news of these developments with growing consternation. Although many Ukrainian company commanders had been killed, wounded or captured, at this stage the Division's command structure was still largely intact. Almost all of the senior German commanders were still alive and in post. Having lost only one of his regimental commanders killed (Herms WGR 31), and one lightly injured (Dern WGR 29) but requiring treatment, Freitag now lost his nerve. At this critical juncture, irrespective of any other consideration, he promptly resigned his command. The Division's 1a Major Heike who overheard the conversation was astounded. He wrote in his memoirs:

> [...] by evening, however when withdrawal was about to begin, enemy units penetrated the Ukrainian Division's [sic] sector. The situation was critical and the Division was only able to stabilise it with the help of other units. Right at that moment the Corps commander telephoned Freitag and asked for a situation report. The latter replied that he was not in a position to give such a report because he believed that the Division was no longer under his control. I could hardly believe my ears. Why had Freitag not given any indication of his opinion to his closest fellow tactical officer? He had arrived at this conclusion entirely on his own, in haste and without due deliberation, under the influence of threatening conditions and in a critical situation and had announced it to his superiors.[250]

By so doing Freitag not only disassociated himself from the Galician Division (and hence part responsibility for the rearguard), but as later events would prove, he almost certainly increased his own personal chances of survival.

General Hauffe accepted Freitag's abdication, and called him in for duty with his staff. The remains of the Galician Division were placed under the brave and very capable commander of the 361 Infantry Division and Knights Cross holder, Generalmajor Gerhard Lindemann who took control over all units in the Division's sector.[251]

From this point on, although some larger groups were still functional, the Galician Division could no longer be considered as a unified whole. From the remnants of the individual and identifiable combat and support units which no longer existed, special battle groups were established (as they had been by all the Corps' divisions). By subordinating these groups to neighbouring units and utilising his own local reserves, with considerable skill Generalmajor Lindemann managed to restore the front which was an essential prerequisite for the successful prosecution of the breakout which was to follow.

The day's events were recorded by Waffen-Untersturmführer Ivan Polulach from WGR 29:

Wednesday, 19 July. In the sky, the lead filled clouds weighted down on us. The air smelled of thunder and uncertainty. Slowly, tired, after two-days hammering by Bolshevik attacks, my soldiers marched heavily, dragging carts of Ofenrohr rockets. We were an advanced guard of II./WGR 29s. The houses were burning.

On the left of the horizon smoke was rising over the burning castle in Pidhirtsi. On the right and in front of us we could hear grenades exploding. After a short break the exhausted boys headed in the direction of Skole, 2–3 km beyond Iaseniv. Here we met the regiment commander SS-Standartenführer Dern with his adjutant Ordonnanz Offizier Waffen-Untersturmführer Ortynsky. Dern indicated the previously prepared trenches which were to be occupied by 29 Regiment. Slowly the I./battalion arrived under the command of Waffen-Hauptsturmführer Brygidyr, followed by the II./ battalion. It was apparent that the regiment had suffered so many casualties that there was barely enough left to form a single battalion. Waffen-Hauptsturmführer Brygidyr assumed command of the remnants which took up position on the hill, left of the main Brody–Olesko road. Since we had abandoned Iaseniv rumours spread that the Bolsheviks would send in their tanks. There would be a job for the tank hunters. All our anti-tank guns had to be left behind with broken breechblocks or blown barrels. Our only defence was the two weary Ofenrohr platoons under my command. I reviewed the situation and decided on a 'forward deployment' on the slant of the hill. This option seemed suitable, but also the most risky. The lads were already in position, in a big pit smoking, waiting for the Bolsheviks. Here were Waffen-Hauptsturmführer Brygidyr, Waffen-Untersturmführer Johann Jaremych, Waffen-Untersturmführer Josef Rudakevych and me.

Dern's adjutant and the former commander of the annihilated regimental staff company, Obersturmführer Weiss came running towards us. 'Order of the regiment commander for Waffen-Hauptsturmführer Brygidyr! Immediately withdraw from the occupied trenches, cross the road and support the Wehrmacht units in defending access to Skole!' Waffen-Hauptsturmführer Brygidyr passed the order to his officers. The first to leave with his [2] company was Waffen-Obersturmführer Hermann who moved up the hill which was obstructing our field of view. In the meantime we went towards Khvastiv with the intention of joining the battle from there.

Meanwhile, a communication came from Dern asking why the battalion had left its previous positions, when the order was for only one company to move. It turned out that Weiss had given the wrong order. If it had been a Ukrainian, he would probably have been shot for such a mistake. Brygidyr insisted on returning to the old positions but I proposed to take up new positions in the ditches beside the road. Finally Brygidyr ordered me to gather the men and return to our former location. We got together in short order and went. After a few hundred metres we were met by Dern, Ortynsky, Czuczkewycz, Chaplain Fr. Levenets and Waffen-Hauptsturmführer

Allerkamp. Dern asked Brygidyr 'where are you going Haupsturmfuhrer—to our former positions? Too late!' Despair and a sense of hopelessness could be seen in the eyes of the commander. Brygidyr replied 'Its not too late! Occupy a position here on the hill. We can still dig in. I will defend the main road and the meadow with Ofenrohrs from a possible tank attack. Let the infantry occupy the top of the hill. This is especially important because behind us are three 10-cm guns'. 'Good' said Dern. 'Let's do it'. Then he ordered Allerkamp, to take over the command.

The commander departed to the village. Here he summoned the officers. From the whole [29] regiment, only ten remained: myself, Fr. Levenets, Ortynsky, Czuczkewycz, Rudakevych, Jaremych, Weiss, Ditze, Brygidyr and Allerkamp. Later Waffen-Untersturmführer Dlaboha, the commander of an artillery battery joined us. Nearby sat Waffen-Sturmmann Dyderchuk with his 7.5 cm anti-tank gun.

'Gentlemen' began Dern, 'the situation is extremely serious. We are surrounded. Today a German Panzer Division begins an attack from the outside, which has to break through the encirclement near Zolochiv. It may happen tomorrow. Our mission: we must hold our position until tomorrow (Thursday, 20.07.44) until 1200 hrs. Clear?' 'Yes!' we replied. 'To your positions!'

I went to my Panzerjägers and checked again the number of Ofenrohr rockets and showed the positions to each team. One platoon I put in a zigzag pattern on both sides of the road, while the second closed the passage to the meadow. To the left and right were hills which prevented the possibility of tank attacks. I issued orders: 'One machine gun with a senior messenger and two men take up a position with me on the slope above the cliff, the second machine gun would give support to the infantry'. I cannot recall the name of the Waffen-Unterscharführer who commanded the first platoon. The second was commanded by Waffen-Unterscharführer Forma whose machine guns and riflemen were to shoot only at the infantry. I ordered Forma's men to adopt the following tactic: if a large number of tanks approached, he would let the first tanks pass and shoot at the last tanks, the middle positions would take out the tanks in the middle and the last positions would take care of the first tanks. 'Is that clear?' I asked, 'clear!' they replied.

I went back to Dern. There was a group of officers on top of the hill, Allerkamp tried to guide the scattered troops to the positions. I reported to Dern: 'Standartenführer Dern, my men are in position. I am going to Hstuf. Allerkamp'. Dern nodded his head. Ortynsky and Father Levenets came with me. Later, the others followed. Below remained only the adjutant Ditze. Waffen-Untersturmführer Czuczkewycz and Waffen-Untersturmführer Josef Rudakevych who was already succumbing to stress. On the next day his nerves could not hold and he shot himself.

Hstuf. Allerkamp gave each officer a position and some troops who dug in, while father Levenets went from one soldier to the next to boost their spirits. You could see in him both the priest and the soldier. Somewhere near 1800 hrs news came from behind the lines that the Bolsheviks had concentrated 24, T-34 tanks against us. The attack was to be expected at dawn. The night was calm. It was obvious that the Bolsheviks were gathering their forces. Despite this we managed to sleep.

The next morning we were awoken by shooting. The Bolsheviks approached the edge of the village. Our infantry opened up with furious fire and the Bolsheviks retreated. It was the first reconnaissance. I looked at my watch: it was 0730 hrs. A cloudy day. Noise of aircraft could be heard. They were flying over us very low. They turned around Olesko and flew over us again. 20–30 minutes later we received very heavy artillery fire. The Bolshevik shells landed behind us, they probably missed because of the hills. Jaremych was standing next to me. The old warrior was not even lying down, just occasionally hiding behind an apple tree. The artillery barrage stopped. At 0830 hrs we heard the noise of tank engines. A quiet rumbling at first which grew louder.

I looked through binoculars. In a minute I passed the order to the communication officer. 'Wasiunec, there are two T-34s heading our way. They are scouts, we should allow them to reach our positions and only then shoot them'. 'Yes' he replied. The order was passed to the radioman and he passed it to the platoon commander. Enemy tanks were quickly approaching and were already between our Ofenrors. I gave the order to the platoon commanders. 'Fire!' The air was filled with sudden explosions of anti-tank missiles. Both tanks quickly passed between our positions. 'Sir, it didn't work!'

'Hell!' I swore and ran to my mens' positions, grabbed an Ofenror and loaded it with a rocket. Meanwhile, the T-34's had driven towards Olesko, which lay to the left behind us, fired a few shots and headed back again in our direction. 'Do not shoot!' I commanded. The first tank had already passed us. The second approached our position. A shot and a violent explosion. In an instant, the tank turned into a flaming stain of fuel with an undamaged iron barrel. Cheers went up across the infantry in the trenches. I came back from the road smiling. It would have been horrible if our new, untested weapons had not been working!

We could hear the roar of engines in the distance. I looked through my binoculars. There were more of them! They wanted to avenge their loss. One, two, three ... eight, nine tanks with infantry riding on them. I repeated the same order to Wasiunec. Machine guns started to fire. The artillery started to fire again, but this time it fired on us. I asked Jaremych to open up machine gun fire on the infantry sitting on the tanks. A T-34 crashed into our positions. 'Fire!' I ordered. 'Fire at the infantry!' Yaremych shouted to his boys. The first tank was ablaze and had blocked the road for the others—it had stopped in front of our line and opened up with its machine gun. Insane shooting erupted. Explosion! One, then a second enemy tank was in flames and a third followed. This was the work of Bachynskyi and Zakala.[252] One T-34 was disabled. I checked my Ofenrohr, aimed and then there was another detonation. I hit the fuel tank. The turret lid swung open and a Red Army soldier climbed out. Wasiunec shot him with a Sturmgewehr 44 and a moment later his tank was enveloped in flames. Of nine tanks, only four made it. Three drove to Olesko and opened fire on the town. The fourth was fired on by Waffen-Unterscharführer Hrybovych's 7.5 cm anti-tank gun. Although he was already wounded in the lower jaw he continued to fire. After a long duel, it had to flee damaged. In the heat of the battle, I was informed of one more T-34 on our right wing. We immediately dispatched Forma with an Ofenrohr. Some time later, he returned to inform us that the tank had been destroyed, but our infantry had left their positions 10 minutes previously, and the Bolsheviks were approaching from the side.

I looked my watch: it was 1215 hrs. I gave the order to retreat towards the village. We were the last ones to leave. Myself and Weiss left under fire of Bolshevik maxims. Along the way we met another NCO and two soldiers, who attended to one of my wounded soldiers. We laid the wounded on Zeltbahns and brought them to the village. It turned out that the whole staff of our Division was in this village. In the courtyard of a house we met Sturmbannführer Kaschner, the commander of the division's Panzerjäger battalion. I informed him of the battle. Kaschner listened silently and shook my hand. He thanked me, congratulated me on my success and said he would inform the Division commander right away.

Shooting and explosions in nearby Olesko became increasingly frequent. Taking an Ofenror on my shoulder and two men with five rockets, I jumped the fence and headed through the gardens for Skole. One of the men was a young hutsul named Sharoburchak. Two of the tanks, which broke through to Olesko were destroyed. The third could not be finished off because seven more arrived.[253]

20 July 1944, A Fateful Day

In the early hours of 20 July 1944, the breakout finally got underway. Originally scheduled to begin at 0330 hrs the time assigned for preparation was exceeded because of road congestion mainly caused by the horse-drawn vehicles of the Galician Division and because the smaller tracks had become flooded due to the rain.[254] One and a half hours later than originally planned, at 0500 hrs, the three assault groups formed from KAC finally switched to the offensive.

The start of the attack began with the launching of signal flares from the command post of the corps' HQ. Initially the three assault groups made good progress and by the afternoon had secured their initial objectives. The group on the right wing penetrated the first inner Soviet ring, crossed the Buh River and reached the outskirts of the enemy occupied village of Belzets. The centre group ran into unexpectedly heavy resistance from self-propelled anti-tank guns and tanks several of which were captured during the fighting intact. By early afternoon elements of KAC which formed the third armoured group, had crossed the bridge over the Zolochivka River and continued to push in a southerly direction,[255] dislodging units of the 336 Rifle Division (15 Rifle Corps) in the process.[256]

Behind the leading elements were the long columns of the corps' motorised and horse-drawn train and supply vehicles and ambulances loaded with wounded. Together with the remaining heavy weaponry and other war matériel which the orders stipulated were to be saved, they too were completely dependant on the main Ozhydiv road leading south and set out on the same route. Confined to the main paved road because of the steep slopes in the east and for fear of becoming bogged down and stuck in the marshy terrain to the west,[257] their movement betrayed German intentions to 2 Air Army's reconnaissance aircraft. In his after action report General Lange once again sought to place the blame squarely on the Ukrainians who were now under the command of Generalmajor Lindemann when he wrote:

'[...] In an inexcusable way, the numerous horse-drawn vehicles belonging to the 14.SS.Freiwi.Div-Galizien [sic] moved in the direction of Bilyi Kamin in broad daylight. Thus they revealed to the Soviets—as confirmed by s.Qu [Staff Headquarters]—the direction of the breakout and blocked all roads and paths so that all decisive troop movements were significantly hindered.'[258]

In his report, General Lange conspicuously neglected to mention that by now for the most part the Galician supply units were operating without orders as Waffen-Grenadier Svyatoslav Wasylko who served with 1 company Nachschubtruppe recalled:

Having received no previous order to withdraw beforehand, on the night of 19/20 July the commander of the 1 company Waffen-Hauptsturmführer Roman Dolynsky gave the order on his own initiative for the horse-drawn vehicles to proceed to Bilyi Kamin, the only available road at that time, under the command of Waffen-Obersturmführer Jurij Mitzowskyj. He [Mitzowskyj] was lost together with the whole group under his command.[259]

As regards the Division's motorised elements, many, sometimes fatal accidents occurred amongst the inexperienced Ukrainian drivers. Having received only four weeks instruction sufficient for driving light personnel cars, they had subsequently been given three and five ton trucks[260] fully loaded with men, equipment and ammunition to drive under battle conditions.[261]

Traffic control quickly deteriorated as there were insufficient numbers of military police available to enforce road discipline, consequently the road itself as well as the surrounding areas came to resemble an enormous car park rather than the main approach road to the assembly area for a force about to launch a surprise attack.[262] Once the direction of the planned breakout had been established, on this clear summer's day, 2 Air Army promptly sent large assault aviation and bomber forces against the personnel and transport massing in the Bilyi Kamin/Sasiv regions. Their objective was to contain the breakout, prevent the concentration of German forces and weapons at critical points and to destroy the remaining encircled group.[263] The most recently released post war Soviet account later estimated that between 19 and the 22 July the 2 Air Army's formations conducted a total of 2,340 sorties (of which bombers accounted for 402, assault aircraft 1,136, and 802 by fighters) against the German positions at Brody.[264] At regular intervals the main roads, access roads, battery positions and bottlenecks such as intersections and bridges came under constant bombardment from Soviet aircraft, virtually unopposed by the Luftwaffe.[265]

Waffen-Hauptsturmführer Dmytro Ferkuniak was amongst the stalled columns caught up on that road on 20 July. In his memoirs he recorded these events:

[...] The road towards Bilyi Kamin was congested with slow moving ambulances with red crosses on them, filled with wounded men. About 0700 hrs the first escadrilles of between 40–50 enemy planes appeared bombing and machine gunning the column and masses of defenceless men in the open fields who were trying to get to Bilyi Kamin on their own, without leadership. There were no words to describe this scene of carnage. It could be properly said it was hell. Every half hour, new planes arrived. It seemed as if they were competing to see who could deliver the most bombs and cause the most destruction. Not even one German plane showed up to try to paralyse that slaughter [...]

Through the roaring motors of the planes, exploding bombs, crying wounded men and neighing wounded horses, we made it about 1100 hrs to Bilyi Kamin which had partially been taken by our leading forces. Here again we had to wait as enemy fortification in the village of Popivci on the River Buh was not so easy to conquer. Enemy planes took the advantage of our situation and caused us a lot of damage. We were informed by 1400 hrs that the enemy fortification on the Buh had been overrun by our forces and the village of Popivci was in our hands. Bilyi Kamin 'White-Stone' should really have been called 'Krovavy-Kamin' 'Bloody-Stone'.

To move by car from Bilyi Kamin was impossible as the road was blocked by columns of smouldering ambulances with burned men inside. The vehicles and horse wagons on that road were nothing but hunks of twisted metal and chunks of wood mixed with human and horse flesh and blood. The road had to be cleared of all obstructions before we could proceed to our destination.[...][266]

In the vicinity of Bilyi Kamin and Pochapy, the few operational flak batteries did their best to defend the retreating columns. One battery of the Galician Division's anti-aircraft unit hit an estimated 27 planes on this day until it too was put out of action,[267] and several bombers and fighter aircraft flying at altitudes as low as 100 metres, were also brought down by rifle fire.[268] Some crashed amongst the troops, injuring some and killing others.[269] After each attack the wreckage of burning vehicles, destroyed equipment, dead horses, smashed carts and abandoned weapons rendered whole sections of roads impassable, paralysing all movement. Further casualties were caused by exploding ammunition on the trucks. General Lange himself later acknowledged that if at an early stage all vehicles and equipment had been pushed clear of the tracks and abandoned, it would have improved the chances of survival considerably.[270] The blocked roads created chaos among the disengaging rearward portions of XIII AK, as they fell back fighting from Sasiv and Olesko towards Ushnia and Bilyi Kamin, putting an end to their last hope of conducting an orderly retreat. In the ensuing turmoil, a number of the larger units fractured into groups of varying sizes,[271] which in the absence of any definite orders or directions sought to save themselves by breaking out on their own.

Hit equally as hard by the air strikes, the leading groups from KAC which had already experienced difficulties with the broken terrain along the breakout route also encountered stronger resistance from Soviet ground forces. On the morning of 20 July one mixed group managed to break out, storming their way past sub units of 15 Rifle Corps (336 I.D.) and cross to the southern bank of the Buh River at Bilyi Kamin.[272]

To thwart the breakout, Colonel General Kurochkin the commander of 60 Army, moved the 8 Anti-Tank Artillery Brigade, the 107 Rifle Division and other rifle and artillery units forward to the Belzets/Bilyi Kamin region. Simultaneously, Lieutenant General Pluboiarov's 4 Guards Tank Corps (1 Guards Army) was directed to the Kniaze/Pochapy area, to spoil the escape attempt.[273] Larger aviation and bomber forces were also sent against the German forces massing in the Sasiv/Bilyi Kamin region.[274] One group which was unexpectedly able to cross the river without using a bridge reached the village of Chylchytsi, where its sudden appearance caused panic amongst the Red Army units in the area. Waffen-Unterscharführer Myron Radzykewych who served with the staff company WGR 31 wrote:

> [...] In the morning I woke up and went into the fields where 4 cannons were ready to fire on Bilyi Kamin. The officers told us to attack the village. They opened up with a cannonade and so did we. There were about 200 of us. We left Bilyi Kamin and went in the direction of Pochapy. All the time we were under fire from planes, artillery, mortars, Katyushas and infantry. One German fighter plane appeared but that was chased away by two Soviet planes.
>
> Suddenly I heard roaring engines coming from Bilyi Kamin. There was a column of about 15–20 Schwimwagens. I managed to jump on one as did some others from our Division. Near Pochapy they crossed the river and drove to Chylchytsi. This was enemy territory. The Soviet soldiers were so surprised and stunned that they just threw away their weapons and raised their hands or ran away. They even left behind armoured vehicles. In one to my delight I found a big jug of sour milk. The Schwimwagens spread out in the village and I went to look for our soldiers.[...][275]

With the introduction of the additional Soviet forces, by around 1600 hrs on 20 July the advance had lost momentum and come to a temporary halt.[276] Several of the remaining German tanks and armour from the Sturmgeschütze battalion which continued to provide critical support were gradually lost one by one as they were destroyed by enemy fire, ran out of ammunition or got stuck and had to be abandoned or rendered useless by their crews.[277] Those that were left did their best to intervene but their effectiveness was compromised by the shortage of fuel.[278] As he moved south in the chaos of Waffen-Grenadier Ivan Nyzka recalled 'I asked a German tank commander why he didn't help and he replied 'how can I move without any fuel?'[279]

The same day, the first news arrived of the attempted assassination [Attentat] of Hitler. A German soldier serving with the Galician Division's Pioneer Battalion later described the impact of the announcement as made to his unit and how:

> The news struck us like a bomb [Die Nachricht schlug wie eine Bombe bei uns ein.] We received no orders to attack, nor any orders for any other deployment. We were also lacking reliable information regarding the status of our neighbours. My unit was separated from the Pioneer Battalion. In a Wehrmacht unit I tried to get a clear picture of the situation, but even here nobody knew the course of the HKL [front line] and the extent of the encirclement.[...][280]

In such a confused situation and with few communication channels still functioning, the news was not immediately disseminated on a large scale.[281] Nevertheless not all the Germans who learned of the event retained the same equanimity and their conduct and fighting morale suffered accordingly as Waffen-Unterscharführer Roman Drazniowsky recollected:[282] 'After the attempt was made known some German personnel became despondent, threw away their weapons and simply waited to be taken prisoner. This [in turn] had a bad affect on the morale of the Ukrainian soldiers'.[283]

Predictably, on this and the following days, wild rumours about Hitler's death quickly began to circulate. Waffen-Grenadier Ivan Nyzka later said that 'News of the attempt on Hitler's life caused panic amongst the Germans and their morale collapsed but this was not so for the Ukrainians'.[284] Waffen-Unterscharführer Jurij Ferencevych also remembered hearing such morale-sapping rumours from German soldiers who repeated 'Men, go home, the Führer is dead, the war has ended'.[285]

On the evening of 20 July XIII AKs staff re-assessed the situation and despite the setbacks, decided to continue with the original plan. Encouraged by the breakout of one group earlier that day,[286] orders were given to resume the attempt in the direction of Liatske and Zolochiv at 0100 hrs on 21 July whatever the cost.[287]

The reality of the situation, however, now meant that the chances of the corps breaking out as a unit were now negligible at best. At this stage for the most part its command had to resort to the use of couriers equipped with cars, motorcycles, horses or bicycles to transmit orders[288] and ultimately, when these failed it was necessary to send messengers on foot. Contact with the commanders of the leading, flanking and rearguard units could only be maintained in the same unreliable and time-consuming way. This, and the fact that the breakout was due to recommence in darkness, further reduced the possibility of a concentrated attack which was vital under the circumstances. Moreover, there was no sign of the link up with the relief forces which should have been advancing towards the surrounded corps, but had in fact been brought to a standstill by strong well dug in Soviet infantry and anti-tank positions.[289]

Friday 21 July 1944

Under such adverse conditions, on 21 July the battle groups of KAC made a renewed but unsuccessful effort to escape from the encirclement. In the early hours of the morning one large group of around 3,000 men from XIII AKs Army units and approximately 400 men from the Galician Division, did manage to get out via a temporary opening created by a battle group from the 1 Panzer Division near Liatske.[290] Later, a few small groups also succeeded in slipping unnoticed through the Soviet ring which was already echeloned in depth, via a few short-lived breaches.[291] Waffen-Hauptsturmführer Dmytro Ferkuniak's group had fought its way to the last enemy line in the vicinity of the village of Iasenivtsi. He wrote in his memoirs:

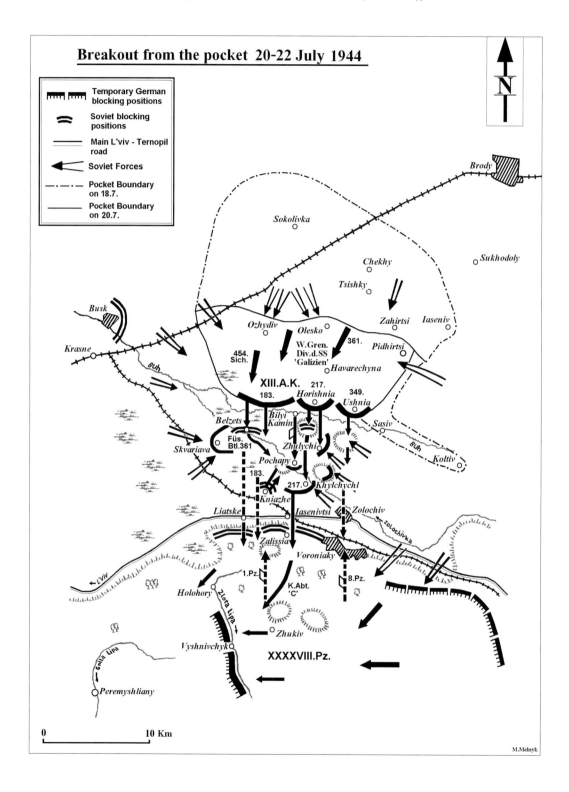

Breakout from the pocket 20-22 July 1944

[...] The escape route was still closed by the third enemy line of encirclement which followed the L'viv/Zolochiv railway to the village of Iasenivtsi and from there to hill 412, south of the village. After a while our units advanced and captured the villages of Hylchytsi, Poniatychi and Kniaze from the enemy. The village of Poniatychi was about 3 kms from the L'viv/Zolochiv railway line and approximately 4–5 kms west of Zolochiv.

We reached Poniatychi by nightfall. The commander of the assault battalion gave the order to rest until 0330 hrs on 21 July. During the night more troops arrived along with Waffen-Obersturmführers Czuczkewycz and Karatnycky and Sturmbannführer Ziegler. Until 2400 hrs, the officers present gathered the men and divided them into formations. To form companies or battalions was out of the question as there were not enough officers to command them so we formed groups of 200–300 men each. For the consciousness of our [Ukrainian] youth who had thrown away their rucksacks with their clothing and had kept their machine guns and ammunition instead, we thanked them. Four units were formed; Czuczkewycz's group with 9 machine guns, my group with 9 machine guns, Karatnycky's group with 7 machine guns, and Ziegler's group with 5 machine guns. Altogether there were approximately 1,000 men from our Division with 30 machine guns.

The attack began at 0330 hrs on 21 July as was ordered, supported by one tank, one battery of light infantry artillery and two anti-tank guns. Our assault in the direction of the village of Kniaze/Liatske was repelled by enemy armoured units reinforced by infantry units, which had arrived during the night. There was only one thing left to do; a direct attack on the village of Iasenivtsi and hill 412. To do that we had to cross a marsh. About 3 kms of marshland separated us from the railway, then there was 300 m of flat land from the railway to the main L'viv/Zolochiv road. We had to drive the enemy from the village of Iasenivtsi and hill 412, which were in the hands of the 'Komsomol' [fanatical Communist youth] who fought to the death and then get to the forest beyond hill 412 where there were yet more Soviet troops. There was no other way other than to go for the breakout and pray to God for luck, or get killed in the marshland.

The Soviets attacked our rear units from the direction of the village of Kniaze in the west, breaking our line between the villages of Popivtsi and Poniatychi and concentrated heavy mortar fire on the rear of the troops advancing on Iasenivtsi. In fierce fighting Czuczkewycz's group crossed the railway embankment (between 3–4m high) and reached the flat land between the railway and the main road. With losses amounting to about 50%, there he took up a defensive position. At that time my unit came out of the marsh, took up position on the escarpment and opened fire with all my nine machine guns on the village of Iasenivtsi. Under the protection of my group's machine gun fire, Waffen-Obersturmführer Karatnycky on the right wing, crossed the railway and managed to get to the outskirts of the village from the west, setting a barn on fire. Then under the cover of the smoke entered Iasenivtsi, inflicting heavy losses on the enemy. Sturmbannführer Ziegler's rearguard group sustained the greatest losses from the heavy mortar fire from the village of Poniatychi. At approximately 1900 hours the third line was broken and those who remained alive got out past village Iasenivtsi and hill 412 into the forest.[...][292]

The fighting around the breakout points especially the villages of Kniaze, Pochapy and Zhulychi was particularly ferocious. Waffen-Unterscharführer Wasyl Sirsky also escaped from the pocket on this day:

> During the sunrise on Friday morning 21 July 1944, with my 7 men, I reached the village of Pochapy. It was a beautiful summer's morning. There I met the remnants of the flak [Abtl.] most of whom I knew from the 2 company SS-Ausbildungs Batl. z.b.V. I was given an MG 42 and hearing the command 'machine guns to the front!' ran about 150 metres and started to shoot at the Soviets who quickly disappeared in a field of wheat. A distance of about 1 km divided the village of Pochapy from the village of Kniaze. My detachment which eventually grew to about 100 men, attacked the outskirts of Kniaze. From the railway embankment I shot from my MG 42 at the Soviet positions. Eventually we captured the eastern part of Kniaze—the rest of the village remained in Soviet hands. They bombarded us with heavy mortars. There we suffered heavy losses.[...][293]

All those who managed to break through the third and final Soviet ring and cross the railway and the road were confronted with an additional obstacle—the Podillian elevation, a steep, pathless incline covered in thick brush which was under fire from machine guns, heavy mortars and light artillery[294] which resulted in heavy casualties. Anyone attempting to scale it also had to contend with well concealed and very experienced snipers.[295] Negotiating it meant that nothing but essential portable weaponry could be carried, so the last remaining vehicles and any heavy weapons which had miraculously reached the break out point, were put out of commission and had to be abandoned.

The bulk of the leading groups of KAC were unable to make a decisive break through on 21 July and repulsed by the enemy armour and artillery and the stubborn opposition from the infantry—sustained heavy losses. Brutal fighting broke out for the villages of Pochapy, Khylchytsi, Kniaze and Zhulychi as 60 Army's formations quickly moved to seal the gaps that had been made. To the north, elements of 13 Army continued to press in on the bulk of the assault forces and rear echelon units which were still trapped in the encirclement, the radius of which no longer exceeded four kilometres.[296] By the end of the day enemy units of the 172 Rifle Division (of 13 Army's 102 Rifle Corps) had captured Sokolivka and burst into the northern outskirts of Bilyi Kamin.[297]

Following the failure of the previous day's attempt, the corps' command was becoming progressively more pessimistic. With increasing pressure on the pocket's northern and eastern perimeter, during the night of 21/22 July it again issued orders for another night attack.[298] The remaining troops were to breakout on a broad front but in the prevailing chaos it is unlikely that the orders got through. Thereafter, there was no more co-ordination or contact between the fast disintegrating units, many of which were already trying to break out on their own and it was now every man for himself. Waffen-Unterscharführer Jurij Ferencevych:

[...] Before we reached Bilyi Kamin we met a group of approx 20–30 soldiers hiding at the side of the road. Waffen-Hptstuf. Dmytro Paliiv was trying to organise these soldiers who had become separated from their units. He came to me. Although I had my communication men and radios with me, we could not get the radios to work. He asked me to join him with my group of soldiers, but after I told him of my assignment to meet my company commander he let us go. This was the last time I saw Paliiv.

When we reached our destination we met some soldiers and a group of officers including Waffen-Sturmbannführer Palienko, but there were no organised units and I couldn't find my company commander. It was different with the Army units. I saw more Army units—some with commanders, and artillery units in position firing. I found out later that there were also units from our Division that fought to the last moment, but there was no coordination. By this time it was clear that we were encircled. The road was completely blocked with wagons, carts and soldiers.

The biggest problem was the Soviet planes flying almost continuously over our heads, strafing us and dropping bombs. On 21 July in the afternoon, after one of those attacks near the village of Pochapy, I lost all my men from the staff company. I never met them again and none came back to Neuhammer.

I was on my own, with no idea of which way to go or where the enemy was. While I was hiding from bombarding Soviet planes, I met a group of around 80 soldiers from our Division following a young medical officer. Amongst them was my friend and we volunteered to go ahead to check if we could get through in a south-westerly direction. By now it was night and the rest of the group agreed to wait at the edge of the forest for our return. We set out towards the south-west but soon we received strong fire from machine guns and light mortars and so we turned back. We returned to the edge of the forest but found nobody there. It was quiet and both of us fell asleep as we were exhausted and had not slept for several nights.[...][299]

On this day, the commander of the 14. Feld Ersatz Battalion, SS-Hauptsturmführer Kleinow reported by radio the presence of the largest contingent from the Galician Division which had gathered thus far outside the pocket minus most of its equipment, to the SS-FHA in Berlin:

To SS Führungshauptamt Berlin,
The troops from various units from the 14 Gal. SS Div. are dispersed. Vet. comp. 4/18/113, butcher comp. 35 PLOZ, mechanics [repair] comp. combat strength unknown. Connection to the Div. not possible. According to directive of the battle commander the assembly point SAMBOR [sic] was arranged. Further present is the Felders.batl.14, 11/56/954, but without any orders. Recruits are in the first and second week of training. Equipment five per cent.

From Kdr. Felders.batl.14.[300]

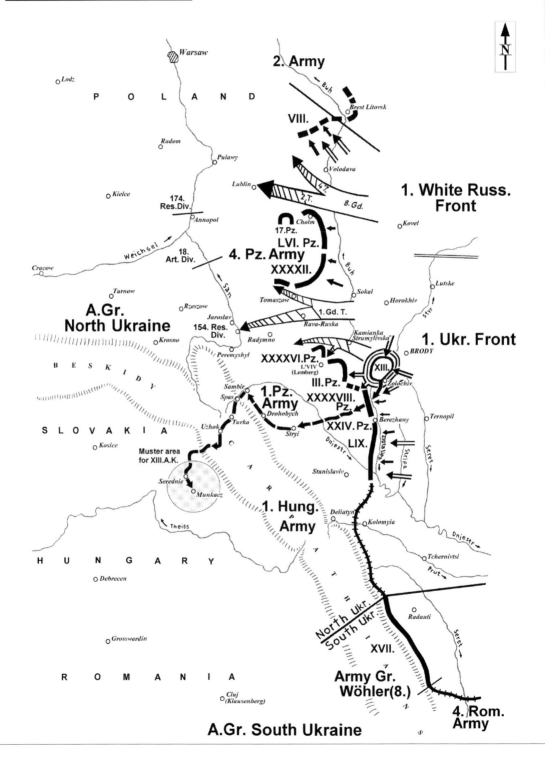

Position of Army Group North Ukraine on 22.7.1944 and retreat of XIII.A.K.

Warsaw

Lodz

P   O   L   A   N   D

2. Army

Buh

Brest Litovsk

VIII.

Radom

Pulawy

Volodava

Kielce

174.
Res.Div.

Lublin

Annopol

Chelm

Kovel

1. White Russ.
Front

4.7

2.T.

8.Gd.

17.Pz.

LVI. Pz.

Weichsel

18.
Art. Div.

4. Pz. Army

XXXXII.

Cracow

San

Buh

Sokal

Horokhiv

Lutske

Tarnow

Rzeszow

Tomaszow

1.Gd. T.

Skyr

A.Gr.
North Ukraine

Jaroslav

Rava-Ruska

Kamianka
Strumylivska

Krosno

154. Res.
Div.

Radymno

Peremyshyl

BRODY

1. Ukr. Front

B   E   S   K   I   D   Y

Sambir

XXXXVI.Pz.

L'VIV
(Lemberg)

XIII.

Zolochiv

III.Pz.

Spas

1.Pz.
Army

XXXXVIII.
Pz.

S   L   O   V   A   K   I   A

Drohobych

Berezhany

Ternopil

Uzhok

Turka

XXIV.Pz.

Kosice

Stryi

LIX.

Dniestr

Zbtuliv

Stripa

Seret

Muster area
for XIII.A.K.

Stanislaviv

Serednie

Munkacz

1. Hung.
Army

Deliatyn

Kolomyia

Dniestr

Theiss

Tchernivtsi

H   U   N   G   A   R   Y

Prut

Debrecen

Radauti

Grosswardin

North Ukr.
South Ukr.

XVII.

Seret

R   O   M   A   N   I   A

Cluj
(Klausenberg)

Army Gr.
Wöhler(8.)

4. Rom.
Army

A.Gr. South Ukraine

N

22 July: Liquidation

In the early hours of the 22 July three mixed groups comprising of the remnants of the units which spearheaded the breakout forces, assembled at the railway embankment south of Boniszyn. Led by Generals Lasch and Lange,[301] at 0300 hrs under cover of darkness they began their last desperate effort to fight their way over the embankment, across the open ground to the main Zolochiv–L'viv road and storm the last Soviet positions at the edge of the forest between Liatske and Woroniaky.

As soon as the advance began, the Red Army units unleashed a hail of fire from well prepared positions. Artillery, tanks, anti-tank guns, anti-aircraft guns, mortars and machine guns swept the front, flanks and the rear of the soldiers attempting to escape. Oblivious to the heavy casualties, the advancing soldiers broke through the enemy positions and thrust forward to the main road. Several blocking tanks were eliminated in close combat by determined individuals and the way ahead across the main road was cleared. The badly wounded, or those who couldn't walk had to be left where they fell to the mercy of the captors. Many preferred suicide rather than burden their comrades.[302]

The fighting continued until eventually a narrow breach was made between the villages of Kniaze and Iasenivtsi.[303] This breach, which was initially only 150–200 metres wide, was subjected to continuous and well-directed fire from weapons of all calibres.[304] Beyond it, the troops could see the rising slopes of the Podillian heights. Minimal protection was afforded by four Sturmgeschütze of the 8 Panzer Division which had fought their way to this point from the outside but did not manage to penetrate the pocket.[305] After violent hand to hand combat, about 0500 hrs Iasenivtsi had been taken, as well as the heights to the south and south-west of the village. Elements of the XIII AK merged with soldiers from the '14. Waffen-Grenadier-Division der SS (galizische Nr. 1)', then escaped through the temporary gap which was only later widened and reached the comparative safety of the edge of the forest south of Zalissya.[306] Waffen-Unterscharführer Jurij Ferencevych:

[…] Early in the morning of 22 July we were awoken by heavy artillery fire. We saw a large group of soldiers, mostly Wehrmacht running towards the hills. We joined this group. I did not see any officers amongst them. Under heavy fire, after getting past the village of Kniaze, we crossed the railway track and the road on which there were 2 destroyed Soviet tanks then moved forwards and climbed up the hill though thick bushes.[…][307]

Waffen-Grenadier Jurij Kopystansky, from the Galician Division's Kriegsberichter platoon was with one of these groups. He wrote:

[…] We were told that the gathering place for the breakout was south-west of the village of Pochapy and they added that the first attempt to breakout had failed. Farther down we met one of our Divisional officers who gave us packages of biscuits for which we were grateful, not having eaten for three days. We reached the outskirts of Kniaze and from a field a Lieutenant Colonel came towards us, covered in medals. We asked him where the gathering place was. His answer was short: 'shit, we won't come out of this'. A few minutes later he was dead having shot himself.

Here were remnants of various Ukrainian and German units lying on the ground. From 1400–1600 hrs Soviet artillery was shelling continuously. Experts were telling us that it was a minimum of twenty five batteries firing. We noted several officers not far away lying down talking. We approached them and my friend Misko Furman asked why they were not trying to breakout. Misko said it was better to die trying than die doing nothing. One of the Army majors asked if there were many like Misko who wanted to try and breakout. We replied there were. The major gave the order to prepare to breakout. He looked at his map and said we would breakout between Kniaze and Iasenivtsi and that 500 metres from here were three light tanks. Someone had to go and order them here. A lieutenant volunteered to do so. He said that another three Tiger tanks were 8 kms away on the hill of Woroniaky but they could not be of any use as the hill was too steep for them to negotiate and below was marshland in which they would sink because they were too heavy.

We formed a battle line of about 1,500 men. No one wanted to surrender. As I knew, all Ukrainians kept a bullet aside for themselves just in case. We had three light tanks, a few submachine guns, rifles, pistols, and grenades. That was all. The tanks moved forward and we followed. Below the hill in the valley stood four T-34s. Our tanks moved up the hill stopped and engaged in a fight with the Soviet tanks. One of our tanks destroyed a Soviet tank with a direct hit. After an additional three shots another Soviet tank was destroyed. The Soviets managed to destroy two of our tanks. We thrust forward with a loud 'Hurrah!', shooting at will and creating panic among the Soviet troops. They started to retreat. Our last remaining tank moved forward and shot the third Soviet T-34 tank. The last one started to retreat when it too was hit by our tank and blew up. This gave us more confidence in ourselves and with vigour we pushed as hard as we could. Soviet machine guns and mortars were thinning our line fast. To get out of this bloodbath we had to reach the hill at Woroniaky where our tanks were supposed to be. I was close by the major who was commanding the breakout. I liked his tactics. The Soviets were retreating and we were in pursuit shooting at them and shouting 'Hurrah!' at the top of our voices. We had the Soviets on the run.

The hill of Woroniaky was approx. 2 kms away and our line was getting thinner by the minute. The Soviets were hitting us with everything they had. We reached the railway but getting over was not easy as the embankment was 3–4 metres in height. The Soviets machine guns were shooting along the railway line continuously. We were desperate and those who tried to cross over died. We saw a dead solider lying over an MG 42 machine gun. We promptly took that gun which saved some lives. I started to shoot in the direction of a Soviet machine gun and silenced it for a while. At that time a lot of men leapt over the railway line. I had my chance. Those of us who made it pushed forward to the main Zolochiv/L'viv road. Past the main road lay a meadow covered with lots of bushes. Only another 600–700 metres to the hill at Woroniaky. It would be easy if it wasn't for the carnage.

'What now?' I asked the major. He calmly said to wait. Abruptly the Soviets stopped firing. The major remarked that it would be bad now and that the Soviets would be attacking us. He ordered us to move forward and we started to run. The Soviets began a heavy bombardment with their mortars and machine guns. A T-34 came from the village of Iasenivtsi, shooting at us from its turret. Men were falling dead and wounded, crying out in agony and pleading for help. No one paid attention to their pleas. The hill was getting closer and the bombardment was dreadful. I saw the major fall dead. I felt a sharp pain in my right foot. My shoe was full of blood. I crawled towards the hill without stopping and kept on crawling until I reached the top of the hill where there were two Tiger tanks. Two crewmen ran to me with water and helped me closer to the tanks. I did not see anyone come after me to the top of the hill. Out of 1,500 men that had tried to breakout only 46 reached their goal alive.[308]

For those yet to breakout, the railway embankment came under such heavy and continual machine gun fire, that crossing it was no longer possible without suffering massive casualties. Numerous scratch groups of varying sizes which followed the same path, tried to disperse to lessen the effect of the fire but having endured appalling losses in their attempt to cross the 'Valley of Death' were turned back.[309] Some of the survivors found culverts through which they were able to crawl to the other side.[310] As Waffen-Sturmmann Mychailo Kormylo did so, he witnessed how his former Divisional commander SS-Brigadeführer Freitag, who had become detached from XIII AKs staff, escaped not at the head of his troops but rather crawling to safety with his chauffer:

[…] As I was attempting to cross a marsh about 7 metres in front of me a car drove into the same spot. When I saw whose car it was I was dumbfounded. It was our Divisional commander Freitag. The Soviets guessed that this figure was a 'big fish' and began firing at him. He and his chauffer jumped from the vehicle. The Germans crawling beside me on their hands, knees and stomachs began shouting at him and to the others—'get down and crawl on your stomach towards the heights, or the Soviets will finish us off!' Freitag did exactly as he was advised as he too wanted to live. He and his chauffer were soon crawling well ahead of us.

I was shattered after crawling so far for so long—all this after having no real sleep for three nights. We had come through three days and three nights of attacks and alarms. There was still 200 metres to go to reach the brow of the hill, 200 metres which I thought almost unachievable as I was so exhausted from elbowing along on my stomach. I managed to crawl round bodies into the culvert running under the railway line. In the culvert almost blocking my progress, lay the corpse of a huge muscovite with a bayonet through him. On top of him lay one of our men clutching that bayonet, but there was blood coming from his back where another Muscovite had obviously killed our man in turn.

Once through the culvert a strange thing happened. Three metres in front of me sat a large hare. As I inched forward so did the hare, always stopping to look at me. As if he was leading and protecting me, this hare preceded my every move as I made my way slowly uphill. Just as I was about to reach the ridge itself the hare stared at me then lopped off into a patch of potatoes.

I reached the top of the ridge and its line of thick bushes. In the bushes I encountered three Germans lying immobile and badly wounded. They began to beg me for water. I showed them my water flask and rattled it to prove it was empty. I could do nothing for them and continued crawling over the ridge. Just on the cusp of the ridge I came across another German drenched in blood who beckoned me. He lay on his front as the whole of his back had been torn off by an explosion. I could do nothing to help him. He had not long to live.

I turned and felt for my binoculars looking back down to where I had scrambled from. There were hordes of our men and Germans down there on their knees and stomachs making their way as I had done. I turned my binoculars to the right and witnessed eight of our men now through the culvert off their knees, making a run for it up the hill. A mortar shell later and three of them lay dead. The others made it over the ridge.[…][311]

Later that day, the 60 Army's formations including parts of the 359, 336 and 107 Rifle Division's among others, closed the breaches and re-established their encircling ring once and for all. The bulk of XIII AK remained trapped in broad daylight crowded together in the midst of the wreckage of burning villages and under ceaseless bombardment in an even smaller area from which there was little hope of escape. With neither food nor ammunition and no effective command or control, everyone was acting individually. Some assertive and resolute officers gathered groups of soldiers and organised successful breakouts. Waffen-Grenadier Ivan Nyzka recalled encountering one such SS-Hauptsturmführer from the Galician Division who gathered a group of 12-15 and told them 'Do as I say or I will shoot you!'[312]

Further uncoordinated makeshift groups and individuals continued trying to break out from Pochapy towards the forested heights in the south for the remainder of the day. Amidst a cacophony of screaming wounded men, exploding shells and gunfire, they charged with reckless abandon at the enemy positions in a frantic effort to escape. Time after time the Red Army units forced back the repeated charges and very few were able to get through as the casualties continued to mount hour by hour. For the encircled forces resistance could not continue very long in such as state. Eventually, demoralised and completely exhausted by the uninterrupted combat and the absence of food and sleep, the Germans began to capitulate.

Often amongst those who fought to the bitter end were many of the Ukrainians who were under no illusions about their fate in the event of their being taken prisoner. No one wanted to be captured and face the prospect of brutal interrogations, mass executions or being condemned to life in a Soviet Gulag. Waffen-Unterscharführer Julian Wilshynsky later wrote:

[…] Some of the Germans whose spirit was broken, surrendered to the Soviets. Some units fought on but most did not give a damn. Our fellows [Ukrainians] knew

Drawing by a Ukrainian who was captured at Brody depicting the treatment of prisoners by their Soviet captors.

that if we fell into the hands of the Red Army that would be the end because we had recovered some bodies of our officers near Huta Peniatska that the Soviets had captured. Their eyes had been gouged out and they had been stripped of everything—watches, personal belongings, boots, so we knew if we fell in their hands the same would happen to us.[313]

Inevitably some were taken prisoner. Often wounded, dazed and both physically and mentally exhausted, their fate was often determined by the arbitrary conduct of their captors.[314] In one instance Waffen-Grenadier Zenon Wrublevsky, a driver with the Pioneer Battalion, had a lucky escape when he was taken prisoner by a sympathetic Red Army officer of Ukrainian origin who cut off his Galician lion insignia to save him from being shot.[315]

Frequently the severely wounded or those unable to walk were simply shot out of hand, whilst others were gathered up without being harmed. In the case of the latter they included both enlisted men and even some officers such as Waffen-Hauptsturmführer Arsen Melnytchuk, Waffen-Obersturmführer Mychailo Kaczmar (wounded), Waffen-Obersturmführers Petro Makarevych (wounded), Dr Wolodomyr Prokopowytsch and Waffen-Untersturmführer Serhij Roslyk.

During the battle, or in the immediate aftermath when the opportunity arose a significant number of Ukrainians deserted to the UPA, which the Germans had always feared would become widespread. Of these, some of the notable officers included: Waffen-Obersturmführers Roman Dybko, Roman Kosak, Swietoslav

Above left: Roman Shumsky was a
Waffen-Unterscharführer with the Division
who served with the Nachrichten (signals)
Abteilung.

Above right: Shumsky deserted at Brody
and joined the UPA serving under the
alias 'Kachalka' he was later captured and
convicted.

Left: Roman Shumsky received a 15 year
sentence in forced labour in Norilsk and a
second 10 year term in Tajshet.

Levycky, Petro Skobelsk, Dr Jaromyr Olesnycky and the commander of 13./WGR 29 Waffen-Obersturmführer Roman Tschaikowskyj; Waffen-Untersturmführers Bohdan Hwosdesky, Petro Ilnytsky, Zenon Lokatsch, Alexander Magowsky, Stefan Symko, Myron Tarnawsky, Volodymyr Fedyniak and Wilhelm Choma. However not all of them joined the partisans, for example Waffen-Untersturmführer Ivan Polulach deserted and managed to obtain civilian clothing locally before eventually finding his way to Germany where he registered as a worker.[316]

The Ukrainian soldiers also took advantage of the friendly population who often concealed their own country men sometimes for many months.[317]

By the evening of 22 July first individual German soldiers and small groups, then bigger units began to discard their weapons,[318] and started to surrender in large numbers.[319] Local fighting continued for the next day or so, but to all intents and purposes by the end of the 22 July the liquidation of the encircled units of XIII AK had been completed.[320]

Over the next few days a slow trickle of determined groups and individuals continued to filter through the Soviet lines, but the bulk of XIII AK remained trapped. The declassified Soviet General Staff report on the battle states that the corps' commander General Hauffe was captured and taken prisoner along with his staff.[321] The next day, during his transportation to captivity the vehicle in which he was travelling ran over a mine and Hauffe was killed.

A large proportion of the rearguard units who were sacrificed to allow their comrades to escape, were also taken prisoner including their commanders— Generalmajors Gerhard Lindemann (361 Infantry Division) who was wounded and 50 year old Johannes Nedtwig (454 Security Division) who had sustained a serious head wound.[322] Both were to spend the next 10 years in Soviet captivity before eventually being released in October 1955.

In the immediate aftermath of the battle, in the July heat the stench of the decomposing bodies of soldiers and horses alike quickly became unbearable so that the Soviets were compelled to dig mass graves with bulldozers. These were filled in with the decomposing cadavers from which there was a high risk of infection, along with the wreckage of destroyed vehicles and equipment before being covered over with chemicals and soil.[323]

6

The Final Reckoning

Sammelstelle, Stary Sambir (assembly point Stary Sambir)

Many of those who had successfully run the gauntlet of the breakout and the exposed heights initially congregated in clearings at the top. Everyone was mistakenly convinced that the worse was now over. Hungry, exhausted from their exertions and thirsty from the burning heat of the summer, there was only a brief opportunity to rest. Troops were separated according to their divisions and the officers present soon issued instructions to keep moving as the entire area was teeming with elements of the Red Army. Waffen-Unterscharführer Jurij Ferencevych:

> [...] We moved forwards and climbed up the hill though thick bushes. At the top was a clearing in which there as a group of around 3 to 4 hundred soldiers, mainly from Army units. Here I met Obersturmführer Michel from our Division.
>
> In the clearing was a wagon with one horse and on it were 3 wounded Red Army soldiers. Two of them were sitting bundled up on this wagon in black jackets and one young man was in regular uniform. I went over to them and we started talking. He was a Ukrainian from Kamianec Podilsky. When the Soviets came back to Kamanec Podilsky he was drafted and now he was lightly wounded. We talked for a while like two Ukrainian friends. I asked him for the red star from his cap and he gave it to me. I had this for a long time. There were some lightly wounded German soldiers and they wanted to use the wagon but I wouldn't let them take it. Suddenly a voice called 'Galizische Division sammeln!' ('Galician Division assemble!'). There were about 80 of us. Obersturmführer Michel asked if there were any officers and nobody answered. Then he asked for NCOs. Three of us raised our hands. He then split our group into three parts and said—'general direction south-west'. I took my group and we went. At that moment I heard three shots. The Germans had killed the three soldiers.[...][1]

Elsewhere, having extricated themselves from the pocket, the two largest groups of German and Ukrainian soldiers from the Galician Division which had gathered around SS-Brigadeführer Freitag and Major Heike respectively, reunited. This mixed group which included men from other XIII AK units, had an approximate strength of eight hundred men.[2] In the absence of the captured Generalmajor Lindemann under whose command the Galician Division had been placed, SS-Brigadeführer Freitag assumed overall command.[3]

Moving to the south-west, this group organised itself into 3 sections; the advance guard, main body and rearguard and followed those who had fought their way before them through various blocking positions, passing corpses from both sides and the debris of recent violent battles. The course of the front line was impossible to establish as the retreat route to safety for the remnants of XIII AK cut through no mans land between the German lines situated to the west and the rear areas of the advancing enemy to the east, roughly level with the Red Army artillery positions.

After about 10 kms in the vicinity of Holohory on the Zolota Lypa River, Freitag's group made contact with the retiring rearguards of the XXXXVIII Pz K, in the form of some tanks and armoured personnel carriers of the 8 Panzer Division.[4] Here at last was an opportunity for the wounded men to obtain rudimentary medical assistance and some respite by riding on their tanks or halftracks but later, in this exposed position further casualties occurred when they periodically came under fire from enemy forces in the vicinity.[5] The tank commanders also had radio sets which brought the first reliable news about developments and current enemy positions.

With the help of many signals, the Galician Division's command was able to reassert control over its dispersed personnel and lead the Ukrainian and German soldiers once again. To assist with this, the 8 Panzer Division loaned SS-Brigadeführer Freitag a car for transportation.

1 Panzer Army's command, which as of 23 July estimated the number of XIII survivors (from the corps' 349.I.D., 454. I.D. and SS Div. Galizien) as being 8–10,000 men,[6] issued orders for designated gathering points for the remnants of all the corps' divisions. The Galician Division was to gather at Stary Sambir and this information was passed on by the Division's command. Under Freitag's leadership and led by him in a borrowed motor vehicle, this group then resumed its retreat, initially under the protection of the German tanks, and moving at a continuous forced march because of the speed of the enemy advance. Their route took them through several villages such as Chemeryntsi, Vypysjy, Tuchne and Strilychi. Here and elsewhere, Red Army units had established defensive emplacements occasionally reinforced with two or three tanks, at road junctions, intersections and river crossings along the main retreat route. Timely reconnaissance allowed some to be bypassed whilst others had to be cleared in short but violent skirmishes, before continuing on.[7] Waffen-Sturmmann Mychailo Kormylo followed the same path:

[...] I moved on realising there were other breakthrough lines yet to encounter. To my left were more Germans trudging slowly in the same direction. They were being led by a bootless officer in his stocking feet and using a branch as a walking stick. There was one among them dressed in our uniform. I shouted over in Ukrainian 'which unit are you from?' he replied that he was from the Divisional artillery and had been supporting our breakthrough until they ran out of ammunition. They had then destroyed their own cannons and fled. I joined them and we merged into the flow heading for the next crossing point. We passed over and around numerous dead bodies, Soviets, Germans and Ukrainians.

Meeting no resistance at this time we approached another breakthrough point past a destroyed Soviet field kitchen littered with dead Soviets and dead horses. About three hundred metres beyond this, I once again scoured the horizon with my field glasses. I spotted a village, I forget the name, and could see men scattered all around it. There were many wounded lying around, both Germans and Ukrainians. Beyond the village I counted eight tanks with black crosses—our help—but they had halted. They obviously could not traverse the deep marsh ahead of them and the bridge across the river looked too feeble to support them. Nevertheless they were the help that we needed.

I turned my eyes filled with tears to heaven and thanked God for such a beautiful sight. I gave my binoculars to the German officer for him to survey the scene. He turned to his men and said 'kameraden, eight of our panzers await us, thank God for this help!' The German gave me back my binoculars and thanked me that he could see with his own eyes that we were nearing the village. As we headed there our mood lifted.

On reaching the village we came across Germans and Ukrainians, many of them badly wounded. Amongst them were villagers helping with wounds and giving them food. I was given some bread and soup and immediately felt revived. I wandered further through the village and recognised two of ours—Lischynsky and Dyakivsky. They had been at Unteroffizierschule at the same time as me but we had attended different training schools. As we sat down to discuss each other's tragic events we suddenly heard an approaching whoosh and recognised it—in seconds we hit the ground just as their Katyushas went into action. The Soviets had reconnoitred and were bombarding us—their shells falling around and between the tanks. We jumped to our feet and Lischynsky told us that Freitag had ordered 'Sammelstelle' in Stary Sambir so we set off in that direction. We were going to go to Turka but the villagers informed us that although some of our men had gone there, most had made for Sambir.

On the way, we were passed by four retreating squads of heavy cannons being towed by tracked vehicles. They halted and asked where we were headed. Lischynsky shouted 'Stary Sambir' and they shouted 'Stary Sambir' and we were invited to jump aboard.[...][8]

Taking advantage of the cover afforded by the dense growth and the uneven terrain, the dispersed groups of various sizes consisting of remnants of the various units moved along different routes but in the same general direction towards the south east. Trying to avoid contact with the enemy, lengthy detours had to be made by the groups which initially moved cautiously through forested areas on field roads and tracks, as the main roads were still subject to attack from Soviet aircraft.[9] With the constant threat of ambush, there were few opportunities to rest and it was necessary to stay alert and be ready to move immediately at all times.

Groups constantly fluctuated in strength because of losses and as small groups and individuals became separated and left, whilst others accidentally encountered, joined. The percentage of wounded men who dragged themselves along increased steadily. Gradually officers began to stick together and the Germans too often separated from the Ukrainians. Passing small settlements, local villagers passed on directions or information by word of mouth about muster points and where others soldiers that had passed through were heading as hardly anyone had a map. The famished soldiers also went looking for food. But despite the generosity of many of the villagers, some Germans were not adverse to taking what they wanted. As had happened previously with the arbitrary seizure of livestock, upon witnessing the disrespectful treatment of their country folk, the Ukrainian soldiers occasionally intervened with weapons in hand. Waffen-Unterscharführer Jurij Ferencevych later wrote:

[...] I came across a woman with a small child who was standing in front of her house. A German soldier was pointing his rifle towards this woman and was saying 'baba mleko' ('Woman, milk'). I drew a pistol, pointed it towards him and asked him to move. He left. Later two or three times I saw Ukrainian villagers had killed a cow, cooked the meat and were distributing it to the passing soldiers. There were more German Army soldiers walking on the road. I did not meet any German officers or NCOs from our Division, they did not mix with us.[...][10]

The occasional sound of cannons and gunfire in the distance alerted groups to the presence of enemy positions which could then be bypassed, however, intermittent encounters and casualties continued throughout this period.[11] Waffen-Unterscharführer Wasyl Sirsky wrote:

[...] We retreated in the direction of the village of Zhukiv. Mostly we marched through the woods. In the morning for a while we fought a light skirmish with Red Army paratroopers in the vicinity of the village of Dunaiv and were forced to retreat to the village of Bile.

A local lady invited me for breakfast telling me that her son was also serving in the ranks of the Division. I accepted her invitation and then asked her about the Soviets. She answered 'they are digging trenches behind my farm!' Of course I ran from the house and on the nearest street I met a German Panzerwagen. I was given an MG 42 and from behind the turret I shot at the Soviets [...] Around 1600–1700 hrs in the afternoon, we met Standartenführer Dern (Commander WGR 29) and his aide-de-camp SS-Hauptsturmführer Hans Ditze. We marched through the woods thinking it was much safer than sticking to the roads.[12]

Unexpected encounters with the enemy frequently caused groups to scatter and head off in different directions causing some Ukrainian soldiers to attach themselves to other units from the 1 Panzer Army as well as a Kampfgruppe from the 18. SS-Freiwilligen Panzergrenadier-Division Horst Wessel which was also passing through the same area while falling back to the west.[13]

Meeting with Bisanz

The column led by Freitag, who was accompanied by approximately 30–35 German officers[14] passed Pidkamin, crossed the Dniester River and reached the town of Stryi. After a brief rest, it moved on to the appointed muster area about 48 km's away at Staryi Sambir or rather the village of Spas on the northern slopes of the Carpathian Mountains.[15]

En route, arriving at the town of Drohobych, Freitag met the head of the Military Board, Oberst Bisanz to whom he gave a biased summary of the Division's failure in battle, denigrating the moral and soldierly fortitude of the Ukrainian soldiers in the harshest terms. Freitag and his 1(a) Major Heike, then left the group to report the departure of the remainder of the Division to the commander of the 1 Panzer Army General Raus at his HQ.[16] Bisanz then contacted Dr Wächter to inform him about his conversation with Freitag and the disaster which had befallen the Division at Brody. In the interim, the column left Drohobych and arrived in Sambir, followed by mixed groups of varying sizes made up of XIII AK stragglers who continued to arrive in the vicinity. Waffen-Sturmmann Mychailo Kormylo:

> [...] When we got to Sambir things were looking better. We were told to individually approach houses and ask for food. I remember approaching a house where a woman was standing in the doorway crying her eyes out. She said a German had not only taken bread and meat but was making off with her cow. I found out later that she had two sons at Brody who were flak gunners and were missing without a trace. He was not long gone when I spotted him and ran after him. He said he had been ordered to requisition the cow. I told him that this was not going to happen as this cow was her only beast. I ordered him to turn round and take the cow back. He refused and began shouting at me. I told him to give me the cow or I would shoot him like a dog accusing him of being no honest German but a thieving bastard. He started back at me so I took out my pistol 38 and fired a round past his face. He took fright and ran off.
>
> When I returned to the old woman she kissed my hands. The woman then ran into her house and reappeared with a large loaf and a cup of milk for me—the man who chased off the German. I took the loaf and broke it in half giving her half back while I devoured mine. It was a loaf just like my mother used to make back home in Khorostkiv. Having polished off the loaf I told her I had very little time and had to head for Stariy Sambir. I said that I hoped God would return her sons safely to her. We three met up again behind the houses as agreed and once on the road again

I related the incident with the German to Lischynskyj and Dyakivsky. They had the opposite experience and had met decent people.[...][17]

Since breaking out of the pocket, the opportunity to desert had been readily available, more so for those who had been recruited locally and were now passing through areas they knew well which may explain why some Ukrainians were intercepted and disarmed by the remnants of other XIII AK units in the area.[18] Waffen-Unterscharführer Jurij Ferencevych:

[...] Our group of soldiers (mostly Army) began walking in a south-westerly direction towards Khodoriv. On the way I met an elderly Ukrainian officer wearing high officer boots. He was very tired and he asked me if I could carry his machine pistol (MP 40) which I took. A few kilometres later on this road Wehrmacht soldiers were taking away our weapons. I told an Army NCO that this MP 40 belonged to an officer. He did not attempt to take it from me.[...][19]

There were of course those Ukrainian soldiers who were accustomed to the discipline of a formal structured unit and preferred to remain in the Division's ranks.[20] For some Ukrainians however there was now no immediate incentive to continue to fight on the German side. UPA units were active across this entire region and many of the retreating soldiers came into contact and received assistance from them.[21] The insurgent bands which controlled the mountain passes frequently relieved the German soldiers of their weapons but spared their own countrymen, instead attempting to persuade them to defect to their ranks.[22] Guided by their conscience, some like Bohdan Delenko and many others slipped away from the retreating troops and joined them. During the retreat Waffen-Grenadier Bohdan Chambul (III.Art.Rgt) also encountered the insurgents:

[...] We spent the night in Peremyshliany, but near dawn we heard the clattering of a Soviet 'Maxim' (machine gun), fairly close by. We gathered our things and made our way to Khodorov where the Galician Division had an assembly point. Here we also met up with the Ukrainian Insurgent Army and with their assistance headed toward Stryj and Skolje.
   In Skolje we spent the night at the house of an UPA runner and in the morning it was expected that we would join up with a unit of the UPA in the forest. However I was of the opinion that we should head west. We discussed this matter during the night and in the morning went to the train station where we found a train filled with wounded German soldiers. We managed to get a ride on this train and took it all the way to Lavochne. We noticed that the rail lines were being blown up by the Germans which meant ours was the last train out of Skolje.[...][23]

Although they empathised with their aims, the decision to defect to the UPA was not necessarily straightforward as was the case with the group in which Waffen-Unterscharführer Roman Drazniowsky was travelling. He later recounted:

My group of about 60 men broke out of the encirclement on 22 July. We were one of the last groups to break out. Our route which took us through Pochapy, Kniaze, Stryi, and Drohobych, followed in the wake of the remnants of the Division. Around the 25 July the group which I was leading was resting on the outskirts of the vicinity of the town of Sambir. I was awoken by sentries who told me that UPA people had arrived. These were two young men who insisted that we hand over our weapons to them. I refused and told them that if we did and were later caught by the Germans with no weapons, we would be shot as deserters. I told them if they wanted weapons they should go and look fifty kilometres away at Brody, where they could find artillery, machine guns and all the weapons they wanted. I asked them to take me to their commander. They agreed and together with two other men from my group we were taken to meet him. I asked him why we should give them our weapons and in reply he suggested that our group join forces with his. I returned to my group and asked them whether they wanted to join or go back to the Division. The response was a unanimous decision in favour of joining.

For six days we stayed with the UPA unit during which time we were treated more like prisoners. The UPA group were local men who knew the area, but we did not so I repeatedly asked for a map so that I could get my bearings—but this was never provided. On the sixth day a girl came to our group which was resting at the edge of a wood and told us that German and Hungarian soldiers were in the village nearby. The UPA men wanted to avoid a confrontation. I asked for a map so that we could split into three groups but they still refused to give me one. We started to receive heavy artillery fire from the German and Hungarian troops in the village. During the attack the UPA men fled leaving our group alone to fend for itself without any idea of where we were. We decided to surrender to the German units in the village. We made white flags and approached the village shouting 'don't shoot'. The Germans recognised our uniforms and held their fire. I asked to be taken to a German officer. Our group was disarmed and debriefed. We said that we had been marching in the woods since we broke out and had not had any contact with anyone from the Division or any Ukrainian or Polish partisans since. After sometime we were taken away on lorries to rejoin our Division.[24]

The King Without a Country, the Commander Without a Division.

On 26 July 1944, the man who had been the driving force behind the Galician Division from the outset, Governor Wächter, flew to the picturesque village of Spas in a Fieseler Storch light reconnaissance aircraft where he met with Freitag and saw at first hand what had become of the Galician Division. Governor Wächter was nonplussed by the sheer speed and unexpected success of the continuing Soviet offensive which had reached the San River and which had both devastated the Division and occupied most of his province leaving him to refer to himself as 'A king without a country'.[25] In a letter to his wife the following day he described his journey:

Krakow 27.7. 44

My Dearest Hümmchen!

Now my project regarding Galicia is over again. The day before yesterday I rode by car to Tarnow and got stuck there, as the Sanok-Sambir road was very congested and the Soviets had advanced south-west of Peremyshl. In Tarnow the commander of the Army Group kindly offered me his Storch. In it I flew yesterday morning along the Tarnow-Jaslo-Sanok road on the edge of the Carpathians to Sambir into what was left of my Galicia. Below me [spread] the beautiful country and on the roads the dense columns of retreating troops. East of the San [River] were the densely departing trains. Near Sambir the enemy had put out reconnaissance at the edge of the town. At Stary Sambir we landed on a lawn in the loop of the rails and soon my brave Dr Weteka who works nearby, came on a bicycle. Then we went to the staff of the Galician Division, 2 km south, near Spas, and I visited the Commander Freitag,—the king without a country, the commander without a division, on the last corner of the Galician country. Freitag was slightly wounded, the Division was surrounded twice, fought hard, but lost all its heavy weapons and most of the men. Now she assembles at the foot of Carpathian mountains. I spoke to the German and Ukrainian officers who were naturally despondent, and comforted them as much as I could. I reported to the chief of the Army Group General Harpe (Model has long been transferred to the central sector!) about the situation. It was good that I came to them in this difficult situation. They lost everything even their personal possessions.[...][26]

Waffen-Hauptsturmführer Dmytro Ferkuniak who was present at the time remarked:

[...] It was 26 July,[27] when I arrived to Stary-Sambir and was directed to the village Spas where the gathering of the Division actually took place. Ninety per cent of the German officers from our Divisional command and 17 Ukrainian officers were present upon my arrival. On that day Governor Dr Wächter arrived. I was asked by the Governor to gather all the Ukrainian officers as he wished to meet them. When they had gathered the Governor came to meet them. He shook the hand of every Ukrainian officer and then said to them: 'You gentlemen have lived through a savage battle and proved that you know how to fight and how to die for the freedom of your nation. The German people will honour their word and your dreams will come true'.[...][28]

Governor Wächter then held a meeting with Freitag who went on to give his wholly negative account of the Division's participation in the battle, emphasising only the worse aspects of its performance, and berating the Ukrainian soldiers whom he accused of cowardice while at the same time blaming them for the Division's near annihilation. There was no mention of the fact that at the critical point in the battle when strong and decisive leadership was needed more than ever, he had neither kept his nerve nor resolution. According to his 1a Major Heike, in a show of blatant egotism in acrimonious tones Freitag went on to 'express the belief that he had lost all face before his superiors, and that his career was finished, all because of the Ukrainians'.[29]

Having devoted himself tirelessly to the Division for almost the last year and a half and done everything possible to ensure its success, Wächter must have found this unwarranted outburst galling. Nonetheless he kept his composure sufficiently to retort that in Berlin the office of the German High Command was fully cognisant of the adverse conditions under which the battle had been fought and of the part which the Galician Division had played; after all the Soviet military superiority had been so great that virtually the whole of Galicia had been seized from the Germans.[30] He continued by stating that in contrast to Freitag's account, the Division's performance during the battle had been viewed positively, and especially in light of the fact that it was its first engagement, the general opinion was that the Ukrainians had fought well.[31]

After the meeting Wächter returned to Cracow. Here, as a pre-emptive measure against Freitag's vehement defamation of the Ukrainians, he contacted Himmler's office to convince the Reichsführer of the viability and political importance of rebuilding the Division.[32] A mere six weeks earlier Wächter had already written to Himmler with a proposal to form a second division because of the excess availability of recruits before the battle,[33] so finding the requisite numbers required would not therefore be an issue. He undoubtedly also advised against allowing Freitag to continue in his role as Divisional commander in the interests of all parties.

As regards his own position, with his Governorship now lost Wächter complained to Himmler that Governorgeneral Frank had denied his appeal to be released from his administrative obligations in the General Government, so that he could request an appointment in the Waffen-SS.[34] With one eye on post-war developments, Himmler was not about to assign such a valuable asset as Wächter to the Waffen-SS. In a secret teleprinter message dated 1 August Himmler replied that he had ordered SS-Obergruppenführers Kaltenbrunner and Stuckart to request his release. He was then to assume a new commission as head of Military Administration in Italy under SS-Obergruppenführer Karl Wolff, commenting 'You would be of immense use in this equally interesting and difficult field'.[35]

Following his departure, Freitag, whose mood was probably somewhat tempered by Wächter's comments, assembled his fellow officers both German and Ukrainian, and sought to vindicate himself for his behaviour. According to Waffen-Hauptsturmführer Ferkuniak's account, Freitag gave a short address which began by admitting that initially all three infantry regiments had fought well. With extraordinary logic he then gave all the credit for the successful breakout to the German officers, (90 per cent of whom were present in Serednje), whom he stated had stayed and fought courageously, whilst simultaneously claiming that the Ukrainian officers had run away from the battle despite the fact that over 70 per cent lay dead on the battlefield. Freitag used this as the basis for an attempt to justify why he had relinquished his command during the battle. He then singled out the Division's only surviving Ukrainian battalion commander, Waffen-Hauptsturmführer Brygidyr whom he criticised for his tactical deployment of his battalion (I./WGR 29) and which he claimed had led directly to its collapse.[36] This occurrence and the events which followed, he continued:

> [...] showed that the Ukrainians did not have the will to fight and started to disperse. This is what caused my resignation as commander of the Division. Only German soldiers, NCOs and officers rallied around their commander and by their own force got out of the encirclement.[37]

Freitag's injudicious remarks understandably gave rise to feelings of resentment amongst the Ukrainians who believed, and not without some justification, that they were being made scapegoats to preserve their commander's reputation.[38] This was further aggravated by Freitag's failure even to acknowledge the fact that he had only escaped due to the bravery and fighting spirit of his Ukrainian escort, (two of whom had had to literally drag their exhausted commander up hills with an ad hoc harness fashioned from two belts, because he was physically unfit).[39]

In his memoirs Waffen-Sturmmann Mychailo Kormylo aptly summarises the feelings of the Ukrainians towards their commander when he wrote:

> [...] Most of us never rated Freitag as a leader. He was typical of the arrogant Nazi stereotype that we despised. What kind of man abandons his troops in the heat of battle when the odds are down? He was unpopular with us before the battle but from now on he would be hated. And he was![40]

As a result of Freitag's allegations, some of the senior German officers developed an inimical attitude towards the Ukrainians, so much so that according Waffen-Hauptsturmführer Dmytro Ferkuniak 'During this period the Ukrainians were isolated and treated as [if they were] prisoners of war'.[41]

Leaving Spas, the remnants of the unit together with additional survivors who had found their way there, began the last stage of their journey across the Carpathians and the Hunyadi Stellung[42] to the Mukachiv district in Hungary.[43] This was the officially allocated collecting point for all XIII AK units.[44] A marching column of 864 men[45] was formed and placed under the command of SS-Sturmbannführer Remberger the commander of the Pioneer Battalion, who travelled at its head in a car with two German NCOs. Following behind on foot were mostly Ukrainian officers, NCOs and soldiers while bringing up the rear were three German officers on horseback. Under such an 'escort' the column proceeded down the ravine road through Turka to the village of Uzhok where they slept the night.

The next day the troops boarded a freight train which arrived on 29 July at the final assembly area, the town of Serednje, or more specifically a satellite village of Lintsi situated between Uzhgorod and Mukachiv in the foothills of the

The long retreat toward Hungary. The caption of this contemporary newspaper reads 'Ukrainian troops in the Carpathian mountains'.

Carpathians. During the next two weeks the group was joined by a slow trickle of survivors known as Rückkämpfer (retreating fighters) many of whom had successfully fought their way back to the German lines either in groups or singly.

Muster Point Serednje

In Serednje the group finally began to assume a recognisable appearance as a fighting formation. Groups were split up and each soldier returned to his former company as finally an attempt was made to re-establish identifiable elements and all units were billeted in private houses in the town itself or villages close by. For the first time since the breakout the soldiers had access to limited facilities and services and the opportunity to recuperate from the recent traumatic events. Some replacement items of uniform were provided for those who were in urgent needed of them and hot food (often heavily spiced with paprika) was available from field kitchens. The Ukrainian soldiers who had received back pay in Hungarian currency (pengos), were also able to purchase a few other essential necessities, provisions and even luxury items,[46] initially at least.

The prevailing atmosphere however remained sour as was noted by a German platoon commander SS-Oberscharführer Erich Kernmayr who joined the Division at this time:

[...] In Serednje I found the Division's interception point and reported to the commander. The general mood was as might be expected, the German officers rivalling each other in cursing the Galician volunteers—probably for not doing what they themselves should have done.[...][47]

Kriegsberichter Alexander Lutsky remembered the arrival of Kernmayr and the real purpose of his visit:

[...] the Austrian SS-Oberscharführer Erich Kernmayr together with Kriegsberichter Marian Sheremta arrived from Berlin at Serednje, the assembly area for the Division after Brody. He met with me and Myron Levitskyj and told us that he had a special order to verify the report of SS-Brigadeführer Freitag who accused the Ukrainians of the Division of treason and recommended that the Division be disbanded. He ordered us to gather true information about Brody from the Ukrainian officers, NCOs and soldiers including the actions and behaviour of the Germans.[...][48]

Waffen-Unterscharführer Jurij Ferencevych recalled how he rejoined the Division at Serednje:

[...] Next day we were told to go to Stryj and report there. My group of Ukrainian soldiers walked to Stryj. Here we met a German cook in the first floor window of a building. He gave us some food. We were told that the collection point of our Division soldiers had moved to Stary Sambir.

After breaking out of the pocket, burial of soldiers from the Galician Division in Serednie.

We spent the entire night at the railroad station. There was a train with wounded soldiers and some empty cattle wagons. A small Soviet plane which was circling the station dropped some small bombs but none hit the train.

In the morning a military train came from the east. It was returning to Germany carrying military equipment, wagons, and horses which were in a very poor state. Our group of about fourteen, got on the train. I fell asleep and woke up as we reached the railroad station at Sambir. In an hour or so the train moved west but about 2 miles west of the town we received enemy fire. The whole transport unloaded and we walked to Stary Sambir and arrived there at night. We slept in a barn on straw with three German soldiers who were already in the house. The owner gave us some food.

The next day we found an office and some Army soldiers told us that our Divisional soldiers had already left and gone to a small town called Turka. We walked and arrived in Turka late at night. We found a military office, woke up a Army NCO and he directed us to a building where we found double beds and slept there.

The next day we went to the railway station and a train arrived with open carriages full of artillery shells. We climbed on and disembarked in a field before reaching the town of Uzhorod. There were two officers with us, one of whom was Waffen-Hptstuf. Nikitin who went to the town. They returned late and we walked to the town of Serednje. There were about 70–80 of us.

We arrived at midnight. They asked for NCOs from different units. I was the only one from the 31 regiment and I was told to find some accommodation for the soldiers of the 31 regiment. Next day we walked to the village of Lintsi where we stayed for about 3 weeks before we went back by train via Budapest and Vienna to Neuhammer. This was the largest group of Division solders that I met. Later there were more soldiers coming in groups of two–three.

One day, two German NCOs gathered all the Ukrainian soldiers, and started to conduct drill exercises with them. I joined them and started doing field drill, run, fall, run, fall, run up the hill etc. I did everything with my soldiers. I think that the two German NCOs of my rank were not so sure of themselves because I was with my soldiers. It never happed again. There were a few German officers, who stayed by themselves and in general they did not bother us.

In the first few days we were able to go to Serednje. I went almost every second day. There were some nice coffee houses, we had some Hungarian money and enjoyed good coffee and sweets, maybe a shot of cognac. But after about one week we Ukrainians were not allowed to go to Serednje. There were no restrictions for Germans.[49]

At this time for one group of about a dozen men who had recently graduated from an NCO course at Lauenburg and returned to the Division in Serednje, it was a very sobering experience. Finding all their comrades had gone, they were grateful that they had been spared the battle as Volodymyr Keczun recalled:

[...] When we reached headquarters, each of us was sent to his former company. The remnants of my 5 company were billeted in the loft of a barn of a large farm. There were 12 of them and I did not know any of them, because they were horse grooms assigned to our company from transport.[...]⁵⁰

Another of the arrivals Theodor Andruszko wrote:

[...] We were redirected via Breslau–Vienna–Budapest–Chop and Khust in Carpatho-Ukraine, finally walking all the way to village of Lintsi near Serednje, where we found the remnants of 8 company of 30 regiment.[...] We found 10 survivors of our 10 company with a lot of horror stories from all of them about Red Army bombardment, encirclement and miracle escapes. Of course many more made it to Neuhammer but not via the Carpathian mountains.

There were three Ukrainian civilians there who joined our soldiers and I was instructed to teach them military drill. We spent some 10 days in Lintsi before being transported by trucks to Serednje and then by train via Budapest, Vienna and Breslau to Neuhammer.⁵¹

The Divisional command now began the process of preparing detailed reports about its actions and of the current status and strength of its remnants as did XIII AKs other units. As all papers had been lost in the pocket, several survivors of each regiment or independent battalion were selected to recreate their units' war diary from memory. In the village of Lintsi in the first days of August 1944, Waffen-Unterscharführer Jurij Ferencevych was amongst a team of three men selected for this purpose:

[...] A German officer, an Untersturmführer from the 14./31, an older German NCO—a Hauptscharführer from the staff of II./WGR 31 and myself, an Unterscharführer from the 13./3 spent several hours trying to prepare a 'Kriegstagebuch'—day by day history—of the 31 Regiment. The Hauptscharführer was taking notes. We only met once. At this meeting they took my topographical map, which I had taken from a Red Army officer when we had a skirmish with a small enemy unit after breaking from the encirclement. It was a Soviet topographical map of the area of the battles which was much more precise than the old Austrian maps that we were using in the Division. It was taken from me at this meeting as it was better than the old Austrian maps we had.[...]⁵²

Simultaneously, Waffen-Unterscharführers' W. Sirsky and Roman Shirko who were assigned the task of registering the survivors⁵³ accounted for a total of 2,807 men from all the Galician Divisions' units. This included approximately 1,190 men reported earlier by SS-Hauptsturmführer Kleinow from the supply and support units such as the veterinary and technical supply companies and from the 14. Feld Ersatz Bataillon which had mostly escaped encirclement and therefore had minimal losses.⁵⁴

To this figure possibly as many as an additional 800 personnel can be added, these being men who had either been wounded and evacuated prior to the encirclement, or had reached the west and had been assimilated back into other

German units,[55] and were expected to rejoin the Division. This brought the total number of returnees to as many as approximately 3,600 men.

After only ten days in battle, the remaining 7,400 men of the approximately 11,000 who had deployed at Brody, were classified as 'missing in action'.[56] For the few Ukrainians with families or relatives, who having fled were now resident outside of Galicia, official notification to this effect was sent to the next of kin by the information office of war casualties (Auskunftstelle fur Kriegerverluste der Waffen SS).[57]

Predictably, the combat units sustained the greatest losses. To cite a few typical examples; from 1,903 men of WGR 30 who deployed at Brody,[58] 29 were recorded as having been killed and 1,442 missing, leaving a total of 432 returnees, whilst of the 900 men of the Fusilier Battalion only 53 came back.[59] From the initial strength of 275 personnel of the staff company of WGR 29, only 7 were accounted for after Brody.[60] Likewise of the 205 men from 13 company from WGR 31, a mere 17 reappeared at Neuhammer.[61] Similarly from an original strength of 182 men of the 3 company of the Pioneer Battalion, no officers, 2 NCOs and 7 men survived the battle and returned to Neuhammer.[62] Indeed no individual unit escaped unscathed. From the 780 men who deployed with the Division's supply troops, only 78 gathered in Serednje.[63]

Even the Division's Kriegsberichter platoon recorded 9 men from a total of 24 as missing. These were: Waffen-Schütze Wolodar Ratysch, Waffen-Schütze Dmytro Dziuban, Waffen-Schütze Jurij Plynetz, Waffen-Schütze Eustachy Fedeniak, Waffen-Schütze Roman Dmytrowytsch, Waffen-Schütze Volodymyr Surowetzkyj, Waffen-Schütze Mychailo Onyschko, Waffen-Schütze Bohdan Kushnir and Waffen-Schütze Mychailo Fedan.[64]

Four of the highest ranking Ukrainians who deployed at Brody and were known fatalities included Waffen-Sturmbannführer Mykola Palienko (CO heavy artillery battalion) and Waffen-Hauptsturmführers; Dmytro Paliiv, Peter Roschanetz, and Basil Sajatz. Another Waffen-Hauptsturmführer Arsen Melnytschuk who was posted as 'missing in action' had in fact been taken prisoner whilst a sixth, Ivan Rembalovych, deserted to the UPA. Amongst these men it is perhaps the experienced Paliiv's absence which was the most acutely felt in the coming months. According to Waffen-Hauptsturmführer Ferkuniak, Paliiv 'was the only one who had a strong influence over the divisional commander. He knew how to convince the commander to put his ideas across and sometimes would almost terrorize him to do the things he wanted his way.'[65]

Equally as significant, several of the prominent OUN members were either killed or deserted including Swiatoslav Levycky (deserted to the UPA), Emil Herman, (missing presumed killed) Pfarrer Vsevolod Durbak (missing presumed killed) and Mychailo Kaczmar (Chef 2./II.Art.Rgt.14) who was wounded in the leg and captured.[66]

From the Ukrainian perspective it was the loss of leadership in terms of both key individuals and sheer numbers of officers and NCOs which was a real body blow. The Division had gone into battle already short of over 130 officers and

1,400 NCOs whilst over half of the Ukrainian officers that did deploy and did not return to the Division and were classified as either killed or missing in action.

One contributory factor which helped to reduce its losses was the fact that an element of its personnel had been recruited from the Brody area. These soldiers in turn were able to assist their comrades, both German and Ukrainian to escape as acknowledged by a former German member of the Pioneer Battalion who wrote:

> [...] What saved us was the fact that our Ukrainian comrades knew the area. This enabled us to avoid the purely Polish villages where assaults from the population would have been likely.[67]

It should however be noted that to this day its casualty figures have never been appraised with degree of certainty.[68]

Ultimately of those categorized as 'missing in action', the total number who deserted remains unknown. It is possible that as many as 1,000–1,500 elected to join the UPA,[69] either through choice or force of circumstances, rather than return to the Division.[70] There is no doubt that the influx of soldiers from the Galician Division during July 1944 added immeasurably to the UPA's structure. They introduced a degree of order and discipline hitherto unknown and those who defected later became the backbone of many of its elite units.[71]

Of the remainder, those men who had served for less than two months (i.e. those in the Feld Ersatz Battalion) and had not been tattooed with their blood group under their left armpit, were not readily identifiable as having served in the Division. Their sudden reappearance in their local village did not necessarily arouse suspicion and they were able to re-assimilate into the civilian population.

In addition to the huge loss of manpower, the inventory of lost war matériel was of equal concern. Aside from hand-held portable armament, virtually the entire complement of the Division's heavy weaponry of all calibres was lost including artillery pieces, Pak guns, anti-aircraft guns (including the prized battery of 4 × 88 mm guns) mortars and heavy machine guns. Likewise, virtually all equipment, supplies, motorised vehicles and horses and wagons had been left behind on the battlefield at Brody or had to be abandoned during the breakout.

The other battle-hardened German units which had formed XIII AK produced similar reports. In the region of 5,000 men of Korpsabteilung C which formed the spearhead of the breakout forces escaped the encirclement with side arms and without vehicles, horses and other weapons supplies and equipment.[72] A total of 73 officers and 4,059 NCOs and men were listed as killed or missing.[73]

By comparison, the 361 Infantry Division which deployed fewer troops at the beginning of the battle than the Galician Division and together with it formed the rearguard, suffered losses that equated directly with it. In the period between 16–22 July it sustained almost as many casualties with total losses amounting to 6,310 officers and men (dead, missing or wounded).[74] The necessary manpower required to rebuild this and the other German formations was not available and they were subsequently disbanded and the survivors incorporated into other divisions.

A significant number of soldiers deserted to the UPA during the battle as is evident from the Divisional uniforms amongst his group in the picture taken in August 1944.

As for XIII AK, the final report of the corp's liquidation commission (applicable to its regular army units only) recorded 21,766 killed or missing in action.[75] Together with the approximately 7,400 killed or missing men from the Galician Division, this brings the total lost to around 29,000, a figure which corresponds with General Lange's own estimate of a total of 25–30,000 lost in the encirclement.[76] On the other hand the declassified secret Soviet General Staff report states that during the course of the battle their forces destroyed more than 30,000 soldiers and officers, 85 tanks and self-propelled guns, over 500 guns of various calibres, 476 mortars, 705 machine guns, 12,000 rifles and submachine guns, 5,843 vehicles, 183 tractors and trailers and 2,430 motorcycles and bicycles. It also claims that over 17,000 soldiers and officers were taken prisoner.[77] In addition 28 tanks and self-propelled guns were captured, as were over 500 guns of various calibres, more than 600 mortars, 483 machine guns, 11,000 rifles and sub-machine guns, over 1,500 vehicles, 98 tractors and trailers, 376 motorcycles and bicycles, in excess of 3,000 horses and 28 warehouses full of military goods.[78]

An estimated total number of survivors of all XIII AK units has been given by the adjutant of the 349 Infantry Division as 15,000 officers and men[79] while a slightly lower figure of 12,000 was subsequently given by Oberst Wilck.[80] In any event, it too ceased to exist and its remaining staff were called in for reassignment to other army units.

Endnotes

Notes on Sources

1. The German military archive formerly held at Koblenz has transferred all its Third Reich material to the archive at Berlin-Lichterfelde. The files deposited here retained their original references.
2. Formerly known as the Public Records Office, Kew, to avoid confusion with the National Archive in Washington USA reference to documents from this source is given as NA, PRO, Kew.

Introduction

1. The best available account was the memoir of Wolf Dietrich Heike, the Division's German former 1a (Operations Officer) (see bibliography).
2. For example Hunczak, Verhya, Logusz, Cabalerro (see bibliography).
3. Prominent amongst their number are David Cesarani, Edward Prus and Begliar Navguzov.
4. For example on page 74 of his book *Pure Soldiers or Sinister Legionnaires*, he writes about *Kampfgruppe* Beyersdorff: 'On 23 November 1943, the Beyersdorff detachment along with other police units is reported to have raided the village of Kokhanivka. 11 villagers were shot, 7 hanged and 15 beaten and tortured to death. On 13 July a raid on the Olesko district resulted in the deaths of 162 residents by gun, rope and club while gas vans accounted for another 120'. This sub unit from the Galician Division was in fact only active from 27 February 1944—17 March 1944. The unit commander SS-Obersturmbannführer Friedrich Beyersdorff did not join the Galician Division until 1 January 1944.

1   The Crucible of a Nation State

1. Eastern Ukraine had 41.9 million inhabitants.
2. The famine killed over 7 million Ukrainian peasants. See Robert Conquest The Harvest of Sorrow: Soviet Collectivisation and the Terror Famine, Hutchinson, London, 1986.
3. Consigning 6 million Ukrainians to Polish rule (4.5 million in Galicia).
4. The OUN had its origins in a union between the 'Ukrainian Military Organization' and smaller radical groups of Ukrainian nationalists and intellectuals. In 1929 these emerged into what became known as The Organisation of Ukrainian Nationalists (Orhanizacija Ukrainskych Nacionalistiv—

5   In the summer of 1939, the Abwehr was able to create the Nationalist Military Detachments (Viis'kovi viddily natsionalistiv) to facilitate the advance of the German troops in the planned invasion of Poland. The unit commanded by a German, Colonel Erwin Stolze comprised of two under strength infantry battalions with a combined strength of approximately 600 men and operated under the name of Bergbauern-Hilfe (BBH–Mountain Peasant Helpers). Formed in Austria from members of the OUN living in Germany and former soldiers of the Carpathian Sich it was organised by Colonel Roman Sushko Encyclopaedia Ukraine, *op cit*.; vol. V, St-Z, pp. 114-115.

OUN) and developed into the most important Ukrainian force which continued to lead the armed struggle for the independence and sovereignty of a united Ukraine.

6   The secret 'Molotov–Ribbentrop pact' brought together the two hitherto bitterly antagonistic regimes with a declaration of non-aggression, friendship and co-operation as well as a trade agreement. By surrendering Galicia to Stalin Hitler meant to appease him. Hans W. Neulen, An deutscher Seite. Internationale Freiwillige von Wehrmacht und Waffen-SS, p. 306, München, 1985.

7   Formed without the knowledge of the Nazi leadership, they were camouflaged as 'State Labour Units within the Reichsarbeitsdienst (RAD) so as not to arouse suspicion from Germany's Soviet ally. In addition both factions of the OUN also formed expeditionary groups, which were sent to Eastern Ukraine to organise civil governments at the lower level and were arrested and persecuted by the German authorities. Some were executed. See Lev Shankovsky, Pokhidni hrupy OUN: prychynky do istorii pokhidnykh hrup OUN na tsentralnykh i skhidnikh zemliakh Ukrainy v 1941–1943, rr, Munich, 1958.

8   Roland had a strength of about 280 men and was commanded by Major Pobihushtschyi (its de facto commander was an Austrian—Colonel Riko Jary). It had a more pronounced Ukrainian character than Nachtigall and wore blue and yellow insignia and the Ukrainian Trident on their caps.

9   To ensure co-operation, the Abwehr made several concessions which recognised Ukrainian national identity and guaranteed the units a degree of independence namely; neither would be required to swear an oath to Hitler but instead to Ukraine, the OUN and its leader and that they would be used exclusively against the Soviets. Myroslav Kalba, Druzhyny Ukrainskyh Nationalistiv u 1941–1942 rocac, München, 1953, p. 23.

10   The breakdown was given as follows: 64 racially suitable (kv.F. and gv.F.) and 615 racially unsuitable inspected (kv.F. and gv.F.). See Berger to Himmler 28.4.1941: CdSSHA/Be/We. Tgb. Nr 358/41 geh, National Archives, Washington DC, (hereafter abbreviated NA) T-175, roll 110, frame 2634861.

11   The Waffen-SS was the fully militarised combat element distinct from the Allgemeine-SS which formed the general body of the SS and comprised of both full and part time, inactive and honorary members. SS-Gruppenführer Gottlob Berger the recruitment chief of the Waffen-SS, had as the result of wartime mobilisation, instigated a rapid expansion programme for the Waffen-SS in order to create an army that would rival the Wehrmacht. By the spring of 1941, four full divisions and one brigade, and the first major non-German formation the so called 5. Wiking Division had been raised.

12   The response to the Waffen-SS recruitment chief Berger read: 'I have informed the Reichsführer-SS of your letter dated 28.4.1941 regarding the Ukrainians. The Reichsführer-SS is not willing at this stage to take any action regarding the combat training of these men.' Himmler's reply to Berger 31.4.1941: Tgb.Nr.945/41/geh. Be/Schb. Betr.: Ukrainer. NA, T175 roll 110, frame 2634860.

13   According to Hitler's political testimony Mein Kampf this was to be an 'ideological crusade' in which the racially superior Aryans (i.e.: those of Germanic descent) were destined to eliminate

the Untermensch or Sub-humans, (that is Slavic peoples such as Ukrainians) and establish a 'New Order' in Europe.

14 Nachtigall was deployed with the 1 Brandenburg Battalion which was attached to the 1 Gebrigs Division. Letter to author M. Kalba, 16 November 1992. It carried a written authority for their convoy to take precedence over all units. See article in World War II Investigator, Vol. 1, Nr. 2, May 1988, London, England, entitled 'The Mysterious Death of Lieutenant Herzner', p. 28.

15 This took place at 0500 hrs. According to a former member of the battalion, Nachtigall's entry into L'viv was greeted by the population 'With great ecstasy and tears of joy'. Letter to author M. Kalba 16 November 1992.

16 Brygidky, Yaniwska and Lontsky prisons were surrounded by terror-stricken civilians and in the heat of the Ukrainian summer 'the air was full of the stench of decomposing bodies'. Interview M. Dobrainsky, London, 15 October 1992. German propagandists were quick to exploit the evidence of the atrocities committed during the Soviet occupation. The bodies were photographed and the pictures published in propaganda publications and widely exhibited in shop windows in L'viv.

17 For figures see Ukraine During World War II, *op cit.*; pp. 12-13.

18 Julian Chornij, unpublished memoir p. 14.

19 Individual officers from Nachtigall including Roman Shukhevych and from other Wehrmacht/units were present and even participated in the proclamation. Letter to author M. Kalba, 16 November 1992.

20 To lend it authority a statement of support from Metropolitan Sheptysky, the head of the Uniate Church, was obtained and shortly thereafter Stetsko broadcast the proclamation from the city's radio station.

21 The Germans sought to take advantage of the situation by distributing phonograph recordings of the proclamation to be played through loudspeakers at the frontline to encourage Ukrainians serving in the Red Army to desert. These recordings were given to Ukrainian interpreters serving with the Wehrmacht and their use met with significant success. Interview M. Dobriansky, London, 15 October 1992.

22 Indeed Stetsko promptly sent a letter dated 3 July 1941, to Hitler in Berlin, in the name of the Ukrainian people and its government in liberated Lemberg (L'viv). The letter applauded the 'heroic German Army which had won new glory in conflict with Europe's greatest enemy Muscovite Bolshevism'. It went on to say 'The victory of German arms will give you the opportunity to extend your projected construction of a new Europe to its eastern part. In this way you have also enabled the Ukrainian people to play its part in the realisation of this great plan, as one of the fully fledged, free members of the European family of nations, in its Ukrainian sovereign state'. A copy of this letter was published in Luxemburger Wort, 11 December 1986.

23 This caused a rift between the Germans and the OUN-B which eventually ended in open opposition. The leadership of the more conservative OUN-M which believed that through its reckless actions the Bandera faction had brought its misfortune on itself, had not experienced the same kind of confrontation. It still hoped to reach its goal of a sovereign Ukrainian state by evolutionary means and through close conformity to the Germans. Consequently, it continued to assign many of its adherents as interpreters with regular Wehrmacht units and to aid the local administration in Eastern Ukraine where they continued to promote the nationalist cause. Bandera and Stetsko were deported to Berlin and placed under house arrest for two months. *Ibid.*, Documents 23 and 24, p. 53.

24 The commanding officer of Nachtigall, Lieutenant Herzner noted in his unit's war diary 'The Ukrainians were shocked. Hardly had their fight for freedom commenced and now its all over'. World War II Investigator, vol. 1, Nr. 1, April 1988, London, p. 8.

25   After re-training Schutzmannschaft 201, which had a strength of around 650 men, was transported to Belorussia in March 1942, and deployed to guard transports and fight partisans. Letter to author M. Kalba, 16 November 1992.

26   Göring, Lammers, Keitel, and Bormann were present as was the party ideologue Alfred Rosenberg (1893–1946)— a Baltic German who headed the Ostministerium (Eastern Ministry) from April 1941 and supporter of autonomous Ukrainian state; 'Ukrainian nationalism must be given every encouragement, Ukrainian writers scholars and political leaders must be given the task of reviving the Ukrainian national consciousness'. At the same conference Hitler rejected the help of Slavic peoples stating; 'It must always remain a cast iron principle that none but the Germans shall be allowed to bear arms. Even when it might seem expedient to summon foreign peoples to arms one day it would prove our absolute and irretrievable undoing. Only the German must be permitted to bear arms, not the Slav, nor the Czech, nor the Cossack, nor the Ukrainian'.

27   Galicia became the fifth district of the General Government along with Cracow, Lublin, Radom and Warsaw.

28   This move was also intended to weaken Ukraine as a whole.

29   Koch's single objective was to run a slave state which would be an indispensable source of supply for German war industry while the sub-human Ukrainian population, fit only for slavery, would provide an enormous pool of slave labour for the Third Reich. To show his contempt for the idea of a Ukrainian state he moved the capital of the Reichskommissariat from Kiev to the small provincial town of Rivne. A leading apostle of the Untermensch policy, his appointment ushered in an era of terror and oppression and his name became the symbol of German brutality and stupidity in the East. More than anyone else he succeeded in alienating the population of Eastern Ukraine from the Germans.

30   On the model of British rule in India. Ilnytsky, 'Deutschland...', *op cit.*; 'Aktenvermerk 16:7:41', p. 315.

31   From approximately 2,800,000 Ostarbeiter conscripted for work in Germany, 2,300,000 came from Ukraine. Having promised liberal inducements which failed to materialise, the German authorities resorted to the employment of press gangs to secure the necessary labour.

32   At this time several former Ukrainian high ranking officers had expressed an interest in establishing a Ukrainian military unit within the German Army to fight against Bolshevism. For details see Taras Hunczak: On the Horns of a Dilemma, The story of the Ukrainian Division Halychyna, University Press of America, 4720 Boston Way, Lanham, MD, 2000, pp. 5-6. Likewise representatives of the Ukrainian veterans' organisations also requested that the Ukrainians be permitted to join the German-sponsored legions of Europe for the same purpose. All such appeals went unheeded. Svoboda, Jersey City, NJ, Nr. 215, 18 September 1941 and Kost Pankivsky, Roky nimetskoi okupatsii (Newark, NJ, 1965), pp. 218-219.

33   This was the 'Ukrainian Central Committee' (UCC). Similar representation was also granted to the Polish and Jewish populations. Although the Ukrainian committee had no political standing and very limited authority, it provided help with food distribution and social amenities i.e.: medical care, educational services, and assistance for refugees during the winter of 1941–42.

34   Numerous petitions and protests requesting the curbing of the worst abuses perpetrated on the local civilian population by the German occupational forces were repeatedly ignored, regardless of the detrimental impact they were having, such as the public striking of Ukrainian peasants by Germans. Physical abuse is overwhelmingly reported to have been one of the major stimuli to anti-German feeling in the occupied eastern territories. Interview M. Dobriansky, London, 15 March 1991.

35   The German security police known as the *Sicherheitspolizei* (SD) ordered the arrest of all members
      of the OUN-B and gave instructions that 'After thorough interrogation (they were) to be secretly
      liquidated as brigands'. See Einsatzkommando C/5 of the security police and the SD—kdo—Tgb
      Nr. 12432 25 November, 1941, in The Third Reich and the Ukrainian Question, Documents
      1934–1944, W. Kosyk, p. 14, Document Nr. 59. Among them were Bandera and Stetsko were
      confined to the political bunker of the Sachsenhausen concentration camp on 15 September 1941,
      where they were to remain until their release three years later.

36   Especially from the regions of Podilla, Pokuttia, and the Carpathian Mountains, Ereignismeldung
      UdSSR Nr. 79, 10 September 1941, p. 8, R58/217, BA. Hunczak, 'Ukrainian...', *op cit.*; p. 1.5.
      According to Alfred Bisanz, the UCC was directly supervised by Abwehrstelle Cracow headed by
      Major Hans Dehmel. Amongst them was Kost Pankivsky, the cousin of the deputy head of the
      UCC. Kost Pankivsky: Roky nimetskoi okupatsii. (Years of the German Occupation) New York:
      Kliuchi, 1965. 2nd ed. New York: Naukove tovarystvo im. Shevchenka, 1983, p. 220.

37   These included the 1 SS-Mot. Brigade and SS-Regiment. Letters to author R. Kolisnyk, 28
      September and 8 December 1998. Alfred Kolf, the political officer in the district of Galicia told
      Pankivsky that the Germans would campaign for volunteers for the Waffen-SS (with Germanic
      racial characteristics), especially in the regions of Podilla, Pokuttia, and the Carpathian Mountains.
      For the experiences of one such volunteer from Berezhany, Ternopil Oblast, see Melnyk, To Battle,
      op cit., pp. 9-10.

38   Within months of occupation young Ukrainians and Poles alike were selected for the infamous
      Ostarbeiter (eastern worker) programme. Initially introduced on a voluntary basis, the local
      German authorities under Lasch were increasingly forced to resort to systematic evacuations when
      news spread of the ill treatment of the workers who were forced to live in appalling conditions.

39   'Within the first few months of German occupation, the signs were visible all over, [in Galicia].
      When I went to town I noticed many signs, 'Nur fur Deutsche' ('Only for Germans') on trains,
      restaurants, hotels, theatres, movie-houses, barbers, stores and even on park benches'. Q15:
      Sokolsky.

40   Taras Bulba was the pseudonym of Taras Borovets born 9 March 1908, in Volhynia. Bulba was
      an excellent guerrilla leader who in 1941 organised the Polissian Sich, which was the first unit of
      the Ukrainian Insurgent Army. This formation originally operated in the Polissian swamps against
      Soviet military units which had been left behind following the German advance and having escaped,
      retreated into the treacherous and remote swamps where they mercilessly terrorised the local
      population unhindered by German security forces which avoided the area. For further details see
      An Army Without a State (Glory and Tragedy of the Ukrainian Insurrection Movement), Memoirs
      of Otaman T. Bulba-Borovets, Research Institute of Volyn Nr. 45, Society of Volyn, Winnipeg,
      Canada, 1981, pp. 319-321.

41   Roman Shukhevych was known by the pseudonym Taras Chuprynka.

42   The UPA was sustained above all by OUN-B and fought against Soviet Russia, Nazi Germany, the
      Poles and partly against the OUN-M.

43   Karl Lasch, born Kassel, 29 December 1904, was arrested by the Sicherheitspolizei, tried for
      'corruption and currency offences' and in June 1942, sentenced to death. A death certificate was
      found in Auschwitz concentration camp but it is still unclear whether he was shot on the orders of
      the Reichsführer-SS or committed suicide. See Document 3815-PS, Chef der Sicherheitspolizei, No.
      89/42. Geheim, Cracow, 25 April 1942, reproduced in The Trials of Major War Criminals before
      the International Military Tribunal, Nazi Conspiracy and Aggression, (The 'Red Series'), vol. VI, pp.
      745-752.

44   SS-Brigadeführer Otto Wächter: 8 July 1901–died 10 September 1949. SS Nr. 235,368. Married and father to six children. On 9 November 1939, Wächter was promoted to the purely SS rank of Brigadeführer and did not hold simultaneous rank in the *Polizei*. On 16 May 1944, he was promoted to SS-Gruppenführer und Generalleutnant der Polizei. He never held a rank in the Waffen-SS. See Personalakt Dr Otto Wächter NA A3343-SSO-213B.

45   Melitta Wiedemann, sound recording of Charlotte Wächter, Horst Wächter archive (hereafter abbreviated HWA).

46   Private correspondence from Wächter to his father dated 12 February 1942, HWA. The date of his appointment was previously incorrectly cited by the author as 1 January 1942. See Melnyk, To Battle, *op cit.*; p. 10.

47   Party No: 301093. Personalakt Dr Otto Wächter NA A3343-SSO-213B.

48   According to state requirements Wächter practised law for seven years between 1924–1931 in the Austrian courts and with local legal firms. He was in private practice in Vienna from 1 January1931, to 25 July 1934. See Lebenslauf, Personalakt Dr Otto Wächter NA A3343-SSO-213B. Also personal information from Horst Wächter, HWA.

49   Amongst the sports Wächter enjoyed swimming, rowing, climbing, fishing and skiing.

50   See Personal Bericht, *Ibid.*

51   Born 18 May 1898, died Hamburg 10 May 1977, Frauenfeld was a highly capable administrator and outspoken critic of the NAZI racial policies.

52   There is no conclusive evidence as to who was responsible for Dollfuss's death. He may have even been shot by his own deputy major Emil Fey.

53   He served in a regular Wehrmacht reserve infantry battalion (2 Company, (Infanterie) des Ersatzbataillions 40, Freising) from 17 March 1936–11 May 1936, as an ordinary soldier and from 4 June–29 July 1936, as an NCO.

54   There is ample evidence that Wächter did not condone Frank's administration policies. For example on 6 November 1939, the Gestapo chief in Cracow SS-Obersturmbannführer Bruno Müller implemented '*Sonderaktion Krakau*' (special action Cracow), without consulting the civil government. This resulted in the arrest of the entire staff of professors and academics of the Jagiellonian University and other academic institutions and their subsequent deportation to Sachsenhausen concentration camp. This caused widespread condemnation worldwide. Wächter publically criticised the action which took place without his knowledge and did everything in his power to free the academics. The action was disparagingly referred to by Wächter as 'smut', letter to his wife 17 December 1939. HWA. Although he exercised no direct executive authority in Police or security matters, in his capacity as Governor an execution warrant for 52 Poles in Bochnia was issued 18 December 1939 under Wächter's signature, as reprisal for killing two Viennese police officers. This is the only time Wächter is named in the Nuremberg Trial Proceedings: vol. 12, 112 day (April 23, 1946), p. 106. The circumstances of the execution naming Wächter's intervention are described by General Glaise von Horstenau in Broucek, p. 445. Also letter to his wife dated 18 December 1939. HWA. Likewise without his consent in December 1940, a decree organizing the expulsion of the city's 68,000 Jews also appeared under his name as did a further decree ordering the remaining 15,000 Jews to move into the newly created Ghetto ('Jewish Residence Zone') issued on 3 March 1941. Wächter, unlike his wife who was often in the company of the Franks, tried to keep his distance from them in private.

55   Memories Charlotte Wächter, HWA.

56   Private correspondence from Wächter to his father dated 12 February 1942, HWA.

57   According to his widow, when the Metropolitan greeted Dr Wächter and asked 'How may I serve you?' Dr Wächter responded by asking for his blessing and his benevolence. The Metropolitan who was

deeply moved said 'when I heard that you were coming, my first thought was that you wanted to arrest me, but like a miracle you asked for my support. How nice for me'. Charlotte Wächter 1977. HWA.

58   See Wächter's speech to the Governor and head of departments, 16:2:44, W. Prag and W, Jacobmeyer: Das Diensttagebuch des deutschen Generalgouverneurs in Polen 1939–1945, Deutsche Verlags Anstalt, Stuttgart, 1975, p. 800. (Hereafter Frank, Tagebuch).

59   Morality and Reality, The Life and Times of Andrei Sheptysky, Paul Robert Magocsi, Canadian Institute of Ukrainian Studies, University of Alberta, Edmonton, 1989, p. 132.

60   In doing so Wächter faced something of a dilemma. While he remained a firm believer in the principle 'Germany first', his administration often went further to accommodate the wishes of the population than it was required to and as often as not he was frequently obliged to use his influence and connections by first circumventing Frank and by exploiting the strained relations between Frank and Himmler in order to pursue his policy.

61   Otto Bauer was the Chief of Staff of Wächter's Galician administration and appointed minister of the interior responsible for internal security.

62   Dr Ludwig Losacker was Wächter's deputy (Director of internal affairs in the General Government and former Vice-Governor of Galicia). In 1943 Losacker was demoted by Himmler and on the verge of being shot because of his critical comments about German occupation policies, when by the intervention of Obergruppenführer Gottlob Berger Himmler's deputy in the RSHA in Berlin, to whom he fled, he was sent to a Waffen-SS penal battalion in Italy. He was captured by the Americans in 1945 and subsequently released. See Magocsi, Ibid. p. 142.

63   Ludwig Losacker: On the difficulties of being a German recollection from the Besieged Poland. p. 127. HWA.

64   Frank, Tagebuch, op cit.; p. 800.

65   SS-Gruppenführer und Generalleutnant der *Polizei* Friedrich Katzmann, born 6.5.1906 in Langendeer. SS Nr 3,065. From 18 May 1942 Katzmann held the post of SSPF in L'viv (Lemberg). He died under an assumed name in Darmstadt, 19.9.1957.

66   HSSPF Krüger gives vent to his frustrations with Wächter on this issue and on other maters in a five-page letter to him, see Abschrift! Der Höherer SS-und Polizeiführer Ost, Cracow, 24.II.1942 Regierungsgebaude, AZ. Kr/Fi - P.K. 14/42 Persönlich! Eigenhändig! Einschreiben! An den Gouverneur des Distrikts Galizien, SS-Brigadeführer Dr Wächter, Lemberg, in Wächter's personal file, NA T175, roll 32.

67   Der Dienstkalender Heinrich Himmler 1941–42, Christians, Hbg., 1999, p. 521, footnote 72.

68   Wächter's itinerary included visits to Kiev and Rivne.

69   Bormann was the head of the Party Chancery.

70   A large portion of this document is reproduced verbatim in Echo Der Woche, 16 October 1950.

71   On 1 March two hundred and sixty men were transferred in this way. See Fernschreiben, SSD/ HSSPF ost krk nr 1007, 25.2.43 1012, der Hoehere SS-und Polizeiführer ost.-az.:kr/fi-roem.zwei a/.-an den Reichsführer und chef der deutschen *polizei* Heinrich Himmler. See Wächter's personal file, NA T175, roll 32.

72   Gmund Nr.10 25.2.43. 1515 PO, An den Hoeheren SS-und Polizeiführer Ost SS-Obergruppenführer und General der Polizei Krueger, *Ibid.*

73   Anti-Communist sentiments and force of circumstance led many of these men to enlist in these formations although for some recruitment was the result of the offer of material benefits which would otherwise have been exceptionally difficult to obtain.

74   Berger to Himmler, 3 June 1943, Himmler File Document, HFD, H/10/34. Imperial War Museum, London (hereafter cited as HFD followed by index number). These units were under the jurisdiction

of the police authorities and utilised for auxiliary and security duties and generally not frontline combatant roles. Although heavily infiltrated by both factions of the OUN which ultimately intended to use them as the basis for a national revolutionary army, few had Ukrainian officers (one exception was Schutzmannschaft 201).

75   In his letter to Himmler dated 4 March 1943, Wächter states 'I am sending you further documentation regarding the setting up of the SS formation in Galicia' and must therefore have already broached the proposal with Himmler. See HFD, H/10/2.

76   Himmler to Wächter, Der Reichsführer-SS, Feld-kommandostelle, 18. January1943, Personalakt Dr Otto Wächter NA A3343-SSO-213B.

77   The first line of a secret letter from Wächter to Himmler dated 30 July 1943, suggests that the issue of the raising of a formation from Galician Ukrainians was actually discussed on 1 and not 2 March 1943, however the Vortragszettel (BA-KO, NS 19/1449, p. 38) refers only to a meeting between the two men on 2 March.

78   BA-KO, NS 19/1449, p. 38.

79   Besides the predicted simplification of the administration, the plan contained a political concept which would allow for the possibility of treating the Polish population in the new districts (especially in rural areas) according to their degree of loyalty. Simultaneously more freedom would be granted to those resident in Galicia. The objective here was to selectively apply the policy of suppression to the principal centres of resistance and unrest, and thereby achieve the disintegration of the solidarity of the Polish resistance movement. Letter from Der Gouverner des Distrikts Galizien v. 19. März 1943, - 3 Bl.Ph. an den SS-Gruf.Berger, zur Weiterleitung, Betrifft: Neue Distrikteinteilung im General Government. Nürnbg. Dok. NO-3225. Institut Für Zeitgeschichte Archiv, München.

80   Ironically, Generalgovernor Frank had already been forced to abandon a proposal to grant the Ukrainian population complete possession of the land they cultivated after protests from Berger and others that this would interfere with the German re-settlement programme. (See teleprinter message from Berger to Himmler 7 August 1942, NR.4510\7.8.42\16.20\SO) HFD, H/1/42.

81   Although Wächter's letter refers to a 'Division', from the available evidence it is likely that the original proposal included the concurrent formation of a separate unit of regimental strength intended for police duties.

82   Friedrich Wilhelm Krüger, born 08.05.1894, SS Nr. 6123: Party Nr. 171191. HSSPF in the General Government 1939–43.

83   See letter from Wächter to Himmler 4 March 1943. HFD, H/10/2.

84   Volodymyr Kubijovych: Meni 70, Munich 1970, p. 59.

85   From the documentation available to the author at the time of writing, it was not possible to determine the definitive origins of this 'Regiment'. Alexander Dallin accredits its inception to the manoeuvrings of Berger, with the support of two officials from Rosenberg's Ostministerium, Mende and Kinkelin, a logical and plausible explanation. Alternatively, it may have formed part of Wächter's original proposal, in which case it was possibly intended to be a separate entity from the 'Division', under the control of the Ordnungspolizei. Certainly from February 1943, various Polizei battalions were being grouped into German Polizei regiments. Under German decrees dated 29 March and 31 April Polizei Schützen Regimenter (Police Rifle Regiments) were to be raised from among the indigenous populations of the occupied eastern territories. These were to consist of three battalions, the first of which would be German, while the 2 and 3 would be Ostvolk, preferably Ukrainians, but with a cadre of 130 German officers and senior NCOs each. Six regiments were subsequently formed numbered 31–38. See D. Littlejohn, Foreign Legions of the Third Reich, vol.

4, James Bender Publishing 1987, p. 43. In this respect no doubt it reflected the growing trend to amalgamate *Polizei* battalions into larger units of regimental strength.

86 The term used in the original document 'vorausgebildete Ukraine' is somewhat ambiguous. The literal translation is 'pre-trained'. This would be applicable if it referred to the numerous Ukrainian men who had under taken Baudienst (construction service) which was restricted to the General Government and had a structure and function analogous to the Organisation Todt. Likewise it may have applied to those who during Soviet occupation had undergone military training which was compulsory in higher educational institutions.

87 See Berger to Brandt, Der Reichsführer SS Chef des SS-Hauptamtes, CdSSHA/Be/Vo. VS-Tgb,Nr.1689/43 geh., C.Adj. VS-Tgb.Nr. 923/43 geh. Berlin, den 20 Marz 1943. Betr.: Neue Distrikteinteilung im General Government. Nurnberg reference; unpublished series, record group 238, NO - 3172, NA.

88 In the letter dated 8 March 1943, Kubijovych requested the use of a variety of means to form a volunteer Ukrainian military unit on the territory of the General Government that would fight side by side with the Germans against the Soviets. On the same day Kubijovych conferred with Dr Ludwig Losacker in his capacity as Director of Internal Affairs in the General Governement and former vice-Governor of Galicia on the same subject.

89 See Hunczak, *In Enemy....*, *op cit.*; pp. 5-6.

90 Letter from Wächter to Himmler and Krüger 24 March 1943 with a proposal for a land reform entitled 'Verordnung uber die Beseitigung bolshewistischer Wirtschaftsformen auf dem Gebiete der Landwirtschaft'. HFD's, H/10/3 and H/10/4. Reference is made to this letter in Wächter's letter to Himmler of 3 April 1943. H/10/11.

91 The re-privatisation applied only to those farmers who were part of the Soviet style collective farms. The Germans renamed them 'Liegenschafen' and kept them intact.

92 Secret letter from Himmler to Wächter, Feldkommandostelle 28 March 1943. Tgb.Nr. 35/37/43g RF/Bn. HFD, H/10/5. For full text see Michael Melnyk, To Battle, The Formation and History of the 14th Galician Waffen SS Division, Helion and Co, Solihull, reprint 2007, p. 18.

93 Secret letter from Himmler to Wächter, Feldkommandostelle, 28 March 1943. Tgb.Nr. 47/82/43 RF/Bn. HFD, H/10/6.

94 '[...] The more generous our manner, the more effective [the reprivatisation] in terms of propaganda value [...]', Wächter's secret telegram to Himmler dated 3 April 1943, Governor Galicia, Lemberg, NR 76 2.4.43: 1725. HFD, H/10/9.

95 *Ibid.*

96 For example the Deputy leader Oleh Olshych opposed the Division. The fact that an Allied victory was in sight also undermined the willingness of OUN-M to support the idea of the Division. See Basil Dmytryshyn, Nationalities papers vol. XXI, No 2, Fall 1993, p. 72.

97 Kubijovych statement AA. In the statement Kubijovych maintains that he was willing to cooperate with the Germans to enable the Ukrainians to receive advanced military training, one of several basic prerequisites to gaining an independent statehood.

98 *Ibid.*

99 The meetings are mentioned in the secret teleprinter message from Wächter to Himmler, dated 12 April 1943, HFD. H/10/15.

100 Daluege was the head of the Ordnungspolizei (ORPO) Winklemann was the chief of his office.

101 Berger to Himmler 6 April 1943: cdSSHA/BE/Dr./VS-Tgb.Nr2239/43g. HFD, H/10/12.

102 Steiner was the commander of the European based '5.SS-Wiking Division'.

103 Felix Steiner, Die Armee der Geachteten, Plesse Verlag Gottingen 1963, p. 179.

104	In July 1942 Himmler had ordered the SS-FHA to make certain that men serving in the legions were wearing national emblems on their collar tabs in place of the SS runes. 'I want purely and simply for all time, to prevent the admission as the result of exigencies of war, of all men who are not from the strictest point of view qualified to be SS men'.

105	Himmler remained sensitive to the arguments of those who objected to the formation of the Division on racial grounds. When Kubijovych had approached Paul Dargel, Koch's assistant, with the suggestion of a separate Ukrainian armed unit he had received the reply 'There will be no arms for you Ukrainians, neither as *Polizei* or as an army. For you in the future Europe there will be only the broom and the hoe'. (Kubijovych statement, SA).

106	Teleprinter from Himmler's secretary SS Obersturmbannführer Dr Rudolf Brandt to Wächter Feld-kommandostelle 10 April 1943. Bra/V. HFD, H/10/13.

107	Those in attendance were: Gouverneur SS-Brigadeführer Dr Wächter, Generalleutnant der Polizei Pfeffer Wildenbruch, Chef des Amtes Otto Bauer, Vertreter des SS und Polizeiführers, SS-Brigadeführer und Generalmajor der Polizei Stroop, Oberstleutnant Wenerer, Major Walter Degener, SS Sturmbannführer Sielaff, Oberst Bisanz, Leiter der Unterabteilung Bevolkerungswesen u. Fursorge Pg Toscher, Stellvertreter des Leiters der Abteilung Propaganda, Dr Neuman Leiter des Prasidialamtes. See Niederschrift, HFD H/10/14.

108	*Ibid.*

109	This is the last reference to the 'Polizeiregiment' as a separate entity to be found which suggests that it was superseded by the formation of the Division which consequently absorbed all the personnel originally intended for it. *Ibid.*

110	*Ibid.*

111	*Ibid.*

112	Teleprinter message from Wächter to Himmler 12 April 1943. HFD, H/10/15.

113	See Teleprinter messages to Wächter and Krüger 13 April 1943: Bra/V. HFD, H/10/16.

114	Verbatim 'national-ukrainische Intelligenz-Gruppen'.

115	Himmler was evidently ignorant of Ukrainian history as in 1917, Bandera himself was an eight year old boy and therefore necessarily without influence.

116	Daluege to Winklemann z.Zt.Feld-kommandostelle, 14.4.43. Archives of the 'Brotherhood of Former Combatants'. (Hereafter abbreviated ABFC).

117	Krüger to Himmler, Der Höhere SS-und Polizeiführer Ost Kr/Fi- 560/43, geheim, 16.4.1943, HFD, H/10/18.

118	Teleprinter message Grothman to Wächter 16 April 1943, Gro/V. HFD, H/10/21. The prevalent opinion among the Nazi hierarchy including Hitler, Koch, Himmler and others, was that Eichhorn was murdered by a Ukrainian and this assumption was a major contributory factor which accounted for the anti-Ukrainian sentiment which permeated the upper echelons of the Nazi Party.

119	This date is probably a mistake on Berger's part and should have read 28.4.43.

120	See telegram from Berger to Himmler 16 April 1943, SSHA 4268. 16.4.43.1055. HFD, H/10/20.

121	In the teleprinter message Wächter actually states that '… I therefore intend to make the call to arms on 18.4.1943'. As this teleprinter message is dated 19.4.43, it would appear that Wächter quoted the wrong date. Teleprinter message no. 681 from Wächter to Grothmann, 19.4.43. HFD, H/10/22.

122	*Ibid.*

123	See From the Book of Lev, Ukrainian L'viv, 20–40 years, Memoirs, Schevchenko Scientific Society Memoir Library of SSS, Nr. 4, L'viv, 1998, pp. 132-133.

124	Kubijovych later said that the fact that Metropolitan Sheptysky had given his support to the formation of the Division was a major influence in his decision to cooperate.

125   From the Book of Lev, *op cit*.; pp. 132-133.

126   Kubijovych statement, SA.

127   *Ibid.*

128   There is some argument that in the latter part of the Division's existence, whilst deployed in an anti-partisan role in Slovakia and Slovenia, its soldiers did fight against American and British airmen, who were providing air-dropped supplies for the partisan movements in both countries. However it is important to note that when deployed in these two respective theatres the presence of the Allied air men was incidental. At no point during its history did the Galician Division or any of its affiliated units ever engage in combat with organised military forces of British or American origin.

129   Bisanz related this verbally to M. Dobrainsky. Interview, London, 15 March 1991.

130   A standing lion with a raised tail was the coat of arms for Galicia until 1772. In 1884 a crown was added as a symbol of statehood. Under Austrian rule a new coat of arms for the 'Kingdom of Galicia and Volodymyria' was created consisting of a lion with three crowns and a daw. The designer of the Divisional emblem retained the three crowns to allude to Galicia's Austrian heritage (gold, or yellow, and blue constitute the Ukrainian national colours).

131   The situation with the Latvian Self Administration, who were also negotiating the formation of a Latvian Legion (which later became the '15. Waffen-Grenadier Division der Waffen-SS' (Lettische Nr. 1) with the Germans at approximately the same time, is a case in point. Faced initially with the same uncompromising stance by the German authorities, the Latvians later obtained several significant concessions from the Germans. For example, the Latvians negotiated the appointment of a native Latvian - Rudolf Bangerskis - as 'Inspector General of the Latvian Legion'. This appointment gave a Latvian national simultaneous authority to supervise and inspect the Latvian Legion, a brigade and Polizei battalions made up of Latvians as well as the right to report his observations and suggestions directly to the High Command of the Army and to the Reichsführer-SS Heinrich Himmler himself. Other compromises reached with the German authorities included the institution of Lettish as the language of command for the legion.

132   Hunczak, In Enemy...., *op cit*.; p. 35.

133   See 'Der Gouverneur des Distrikt Galizien Tgb.N.104\43g, 28/4/1943, Betr: Aufstellung der SS-Schützen Division Galizien': ABFC.

134   This figure was given as an estimate of the number of men required to begin with.

135   See 'Der Gouverneur des Distrikt Galizien Tgb.N.104\43g, 28/4/1943, Betr: Aufstellung der SS-Schützen Division Galizien': ABFC. The document stated that '[...] the formation of the Division is to be utilised as much as possible in the sprit of an introduction of the Ukrainian population of Galicia to the concept of being Germanic'.

136   *Ibid.*

137   Directives for Recruitment Commissions for the SS-Schützen-Division Galizien. (In confidence! Only for the officials employed by members of the Recruitment Commissions), L'viv, 28.4.1943. SA.

138   Secret letter from Der Gouverneur des Distriks Galizien: zu Tgb.104\43g: Lemberg, den 28 April 43. ABFC. For full text of this document see Melnyk, To Battle, *op cit*.; p. 325.

139   For example see L'vivski Visti (L'viv news) [Nr. 93], Stanislavivske Slovo [18/83] among others. For propaganda purposes a cine film was also made on the occasion. An edited copy of the film is in the author's possession.

140   See Abschrift, Korrekturen der Reichsführer-SS bereits berucksichtigt annexed to Himmler's letter to Wächter of 28 March 1943, Tgb.Nr. 35/37/43g. HFD, H/10/5.

141   Instructions for Volunteers for the SS Riflemen Division Galicia. SA.

142   Later, Professor Kubijovych, in his capacity as head of the UCC sent a telegram to the General
      Gouverneur Frank in Cracow which read;   'I wish to express to the Government of the Reich my
      deepest thanks on behalf of the Ukrainian people of Galicia, for the opportunity for Ukrainians to join
      the battle against Bolshevism with weapon in hand. The entire Ukrainian people nurture feelings of
      upright gratitude to the Führer of the Grossdeutschen Reich, for the authorisation for the formation of
      the 'SS-Schützen-Division Galizien'. I request that your Excellency convey this gratitude to the Führer.
      We are especially grateful for your message to the Ukrainian people of Galicia and your best wishes for
      today's celebrations'. Kubijovych to Frank, 10 May 1943, HFD, H/10/26. The full text of his speech was
      later published in its entirety in the newspaper Krakivski Visti (Kracow News) 1 May 1943, Nr. 89.

143   For the full text in English see Melnyk, To Battle, *op cit.*; p. 27.

144   Khronoviat's function within the Military Board was head of recruitment.

145   For the text of Rev Laba's speech see HFD, H/10/47.

146   13 July 1943, Himmler's office (Brandt) to Berger see H\10\47.

147   Delivery of the recordings was delayed due to them being misdirected. Pöscher to Brandt, Lemberg,
      9 July 1943, Tgb.Nr. 35/96/43g. H\10\45.

148   22 July 1943, Berger to Brandt, CdSSHA/Be/Ra. See H\10\54.

149   Born 15.11.1890.

150   Prof. Kubijovych had hoped that he would be appointed to this post. General Victor Kurmanovych
      was appointed honorary leader of the Military Board.

151   Directives for Recruitment Commissions for the SS-Schützen-Division Galizien. L'viv, 28.4.1943.
      An original of this document is in the Shevchenko Archive in London. For details of the statutes see
      Minutes of the Meetings of the Military Board 'Galicia', edited by Roman Kolisnyk, Shevchenko
      Scientific Society of Canada, vol. 30, 1990, pp. 182-183.

152   *Ibid.* see also: An Den Wehrausschuss Galizien, Lemberg 28 April 1943. ABFC.

153   The document stated it was not necessary for them to have been born in Galicia but resident
      there for some time, confirmation of which was to be provided by the village head. Directives for
      Recruitment Commissions for the SS-Schützen-Division Galizien. L'viv, 28.4.1943. Schevchenko
      Archive, London, hereafter abbreviated SA.

154   Exceptions could be made where sentences had been pronounced under the Polish or Soviet
      authorities when a letter of permission could be sent to the Governor through the Military Board.

155   Directives for Recruitment Commissions for the SS-Schützen-Division Galizien. (In confidence!
      Only for the officials employed by members of the Recruitment Commissions), L'viv, 28.4.1943. SA.

156   For two examples see L'vivski Visti (L'viv news) [No. 93], and Stanislavivske Slovo (18/83).

157   See The Kracower Zeitung of 29 April 1943. The report on the formation of the Division appeared
      under the heading 'Formation of an 'SS Schützen Division Galizien' for the Ukrainian Youth'.
      The article also gave details about the Division's insignia and went on to say that the language of
      command would be German while the language for orders would be Ukrainian. It also announced
      that commissions would be given to former Ukrainian officers of the Austro-Hungarian Army. A
      copy of this cutting can also be found in the Himmler papers, HFD, H/10/24.

158   Alfred Bisanz and Jurij Krokhmaliuk travelled to Buchach, Stephan Volynets–Sambir and Turka,
      Mychailo Khronoviat visited Bibrka etc.

159   The Sich riflemen or 'Sichovi Striltsi' was a distinct unit of the Austro-Hungarian Army in the First
      World War which later became the nucleus of the Ukrainian Galician Army.

160   Q2: Havrych.

161   It seems likely that the German authorities were aware of, or at least suspected members of the
      Military Board of propagating nationalist opinions in their recruitment speeches for the Division.

However, so as not to hamper recruitment, no preventative action was taken until Dr Bauer issued a memorandum dated 18 August 1943 (by which time the first phase of recruitment was nearing its end), forbidding the Military Board from issuing any writings of a political nature without his consent or that of Alfred Bisanz. chef des Amtes, Lemberg, den 18. August 1943, ABFC.

162 At the same time a number of women volunteered for the hospital services.

163 In numerous personal interviews, questionnaires and letters to the author, from former veterans of the Division, in answer to the question 'Why did you volunteer'? the vast majority gave an answer which corresponded roughly with this statement.

164 Theo Andruszko letter to author, 6 July 2010.

165 Q6 Kolisnyk. There is some evidence that after the initial wave of enthusiasm had passed, in some cases pressure was exerted on school leavers who were told they had to sign these volunteer papers in order to get their last report: M. Klymchuk letter to author, 30 August 1990.

166 E. Shypailo letter to author, 2 November 1994.

167 AA.

168 For example; 'On the first day of recruitment, the principal of the trade school in Sanok, Mykhalevych enlisted with all his students' .... 'In Sambir, a large group of students from the local college arrived at the draft board led by their principal, Martynets'. Etc.

169 The name of the Plast organisation is derived from the Ukrainian word Plastun, a scout of the Zaporozhian Cossacks. Its main goals were to cultivate skills such as camping and outdoor activities, developing moral character and leadership qualities as well as fostering a sense of Ukrainian patriotism amongst its members.

170 Verbally to author M. Scharko, 9 March 1999.

171 It is impossible to put a figure on the number who joined purely because of anti-Communist sentiments as the overwhelming majority were. To give an indication of the strength of the anti-Russian sentiments of the population, Bender/Taylor make the unsupported claim that '[...] 20,000 are said to have volunteered at once as a result of the anti-Russian theme', Bender/Taylor, 'Uniforms...', vol. 4, *op cit.*; p. 22.

172 Rev. Dr Laba's sermon had included the phrase 'He who wants to be free must fight for it'. For the entire speech see HFD, H/10/47.

173 Of a random sample of fifty former Division members interviewed by the author, ten had served in other German formations prior to their service with the Division: three as auxiliary Polizei in various Shuma battalions; one in another Waffen-SS formation; one in the Brandenburg Division; one as a Luftwaffe auxiliary; three in regular Wehrmacht formations (i.e.: army) in non-combatant roles as Hilfswilliger (Hiwis) or helpers, and one as a former member of Nachtigall.

174 Interview I. Nyzka, Rushden, England, 6 January 1991.

175 R. Lazurko. Na Shliahah Evropy, Ukrainska Knyzhka, Toronto, 1985, p. 65

176 In his proclamation Wächter said 'Every member of this Freiwilligen-Division will be placed on an equal footing with the German soldier in equipment, pay, rations and maintenance arrangements for his family.' See Abschrift, Korrekturen der Reichsführer-SS bereits berucksichtigt annexed to Himmler's letter to Wächter of 28 March 1943, Tgb.Nr. 35/37/43g. HFD, H/10/5. In his address, Frank did likewise.

177 The literature issued to those who enrolled stated unequivocally that [...] '10. The volunteer receives the same uniform, equipment, food and pay as the German soldier. He receives the most fair and equal treatment. 11. After honorary service, he will be treated similarly in his social welfare, just as German soldiers after their discharge. A similar rule will be applied to those who in any way are wounded or affected by the war. 12. Members of the family which were supported by

the volunteer such as: 1. wife, 2. Family 3. children, will receive the same welfare as the families of German soldiers'. Instructions for Volunteers for the SS Riflemen Division Galicia. SA.

178   For the terms of the amnesty for escaped forced workers see 'Der Gouverneur des Distrikt Galizien Tgb.N.104\43g, 28/4/1943, Betr: Aufstellung der SS-Schützen Division Galizien'. SA.

179   For example in the Central State Archives of Supreme Bodies of Power and Government of Ukraine, hereafter abbreviated— TsDAVO of Ukraine, 2,185 names are listed for Kreishauptmannschaft Lemberg-Land, as of April 1944, whilst another dated 19 June 1944, lists 116 names for the Kreishauptmannschaft Brzezany. See TsDAVO of Ukraine. C(orpus). 3971. - E(ntry). 1. - F(older). 16. - 52 sh(eets).

180   A random sample of 50 families received on average approx 100 zlt each. *Ibid.*

181   Krakivski Visti, 16 May 1943, Nr. 20, reported Kubijovych's enlistment.

182   Taras Hunczak, In Enemy Uniforms, Time of Ukraine (Chas Ukrainy), Kiev, 1993 p. 35.

183   Volodymyr Keczun, unpublished memoir, p. 1.

184   Mychailo Kormylo, Memoirs of a Forgotten [Halychyna] Division Soldier, the autobiography of a young Ukrainian on the Eastern Front, unpublished memoir p. 2.

185   For the terms of the amnesty for escaped forced workers see 'Der Gouverneur des Distrikt Galizien Tgb.N.104\43g, 28/4/1943, Betr: Aufstellung der SS-Schützen Division Galizien'. SA.

186   *Ibid.*

187   The document also specified that non-commissioned officers of the former Polish Army who were in German prisoner of war camps in the Reich were to be placed at the disposal of the Division.

188   Bender/Taylor, Uniforms...., vol. 4, *op cit.*; p. 24, RF-SS, HA B1 Az 9a/Br.Galiz.Div./,v.1.7.1943.

189   At a meeting of the Military Board on 24 November 1943, there was difficulty in listing 50.

190   One example is Julian Temnyk. He was also a member of the Ukrainian Galician Army 1918–1920.

191   See personal-Akte NA A3343-SSO-145A.

192   Of those who enlisted 30 were dismissed because they were over 50. Most were aged between 45–55.

193   In addition nine veterinarians, two dentists, six dental technicians and two apothecaries had volunteered by November 1943.

194   Letter to author Dr W. Krywulak, 25 May 1994.

195   In a letter to author dated 20 October 1996, Dr Bohdan Rozdilsky, wrote; 'Some of us (doctors) in anticipation of a compulsory draft or (sooner rather than later) going underground and facing a total hopelessness in the Insurgents' Army, were more inclined to join the ranks of a regular military unit in which the chances of simple physical survival appeared to be somewhat better'.

196   Letter dated 28 June 1943, from Kaltenbrunner to Himmler, IV B3 - 416\43. HFD, H/10/38.

197   Brandt to Kaltenbrunner Feldkommandostelle, 16 July 1943, Tgb. Nr. 42/78/43. HFD, H/10/51. This was consistent with Himmler's previously expressed view towards the Church when he had written to Krüger advising him to endeavour to 'Make use of the vassalage of the Poles and Ukrainians to the Church and their love for their priests and other village notables, who should be made answerable for their good behaviour with their lives'. See Helmut Heiber, Reichsführer: Breife an und von Himmler, Deutsch Verlags Anstalt Stuttgart, 1968, p. 132-133.

198   Sennheim was a training camp established in Alsace where foreign troops underwent a six-eight week course to learn German as well as undergo basic military training. At the end of their training Laba received the rank of Waffen-Sturmbannführer, whilst the remainder were given the rank of Waffen-Untersturmführer, see I. Nahayewsky, Sprhady polovoho Duchovnyka: A Soldier Priest Remembers, Ukrainian Book Company, Toronto, 1985.

199   Letter from Berger to Himmler 26 July 1943, HFD, H/10/55.

200 Brandt to Berger Feld-kommandostelle, 31 July 1943: Tgb.Nr.36\178\43 g: HFD, H/10/58.

201 John A. Armstrong, Ukrainian Nationalism, 2nd Rev. ed. New York: Columbia University Press, 1963. p. 173.

202 Details of Koch's objections can be found in the so called 'Brandenburg memorandum', 16 September 1943, NA Document NO-3469. For Berger's attempt to refute some of Koch's criticisms of the Division, see his letter to Himmler dated 10.12.43. NS 19/2191 folder 1, BA-KO.

203 For an example of an anti-Divisional leaflet in both the Ukrainian and Polish languages see V. Veryha, Dorohamy druhoi svitovoi viiny, legendy pro uchast ukraintsiv u zdushuvanni varshavskoho povstannia v 1944 r.ta pro ukrainsku dyviziiu 'Halychyna'. Toronto: New Pathway, 1980. 2nd Rev. edn. Toronto: Bratstvo kolyshnikh voiakiv 1-oi ukrainskoi dyvizii UNA, 1984, pp. 216-220.

204 One veteran Mychailo Prymak, related an incident to the author whereby he returned to his home village of Lubachiv (close to the Polish/Ukrainian border) in uniform to spend a few days leave with his family. Having departed to rejoin the Division, his father was subsequently beaten up by local Polish civilians. Verbally to author M. Prymak, 8 November 1997.

205 For example see letter from Oberstleutnant B. Jewtymowytsch to the head of the historical section of the Military Board, Lemberg 3 July 1943, complaining about the behaviour of Polish civil servants and their disregard for documents issued by the Military Board. ABFC.

206 The OUN-M did not advocate a definite stand.

207 A further cause of their opposition stemmed from the fact that the Division provided competition for manpower-especially with regard to officers. For some of the arguments against the Division see Myroslav Prokop, 'U Sorokrichchia 3-oho Nadzvychainoho Velykoho Zboru OUN', in Suchasnist, 1987, nr. 3, p. 394.

208 Bulletin of the Organisation of Ukrainian Nationalists, Year III, 1943, nr. 11, AA. For full text see Melnyk, To Battle, op cit.; p. 34.

209 See 'Ukrainskyj Narode!' in Kravivski Visti, 2 November 1943 nr. 245 (983) and Hunczak 'The Ukrainian....', op cit.; p. 2.10.

210 The Ukrainian units of the Austro-Hungarian Army that were active during the First World War.

211 In his book Roman Krokhmaliuk describes how at a time when local UPA leaders who on their own initiative were actively hindering enlistment of volunteers, he met for thirty minutes with the UPA commander Roman Shukhevych, in a private residence in a suburb of L'viv. Following this meeting Shukhevych, agreed to allow UPA members to join the division to obtain proper training. Thereafter, the enlistment rate, especially in the L'viv region, showed a significant increase. See Roman Krokhmaliuk: The Glow in Eastern Europe, Toronto–New York: Bratstvo kolyshnikh voiakiv I-oi Ukrainskoi dyvizii UNA, 1978, pp. 40-41,

212 For a detailed discussion of the OUN/UPA's relationship with the Division see the article by Lev Shankovsky in America, July 12–16 1954, Philadelphia-reprinted in Ukrainska Dyvisia Halychyna, pp. 55-61, Kyiv, 1994.

213 See article by Bohdan Pidhayny entitled 'Two Paths One Aim', taken from the publication Brody: Zbirnyk stattei i narysiv (Brody: A collection of Articles and sketches), pp. 59-64, Oleh Lysiak, Munich, Bratstvo kol. Voiakiv Pershoi UD UNA, 1951. 1. p. 60.

214 This was later acknowledged by Fritz Arlt, a senior German official who dealt with the Ukrainian question. In a post war interview with Taras Hunczak, he stated that the Germans knew that the Ukrainians had their own agenda, but this did not matter so long as they would also serve German needs. Hunczak, In Enemy...., op cit.; p. 35.

215 'Der Gouverneur des Distrikt Galizien Betr:TGB.N.104\43G' Secret, Lemberg 28 April 1943, Betr.; Aufstellung der SS-Schützen Division Galizien', SA.

216   Krüger to Berger secret telegram dated May 11, 1943 HFD, H/10/27. The official recruitment figures of the Wehrausschuss Galicia quoted 31,034 as having enlisted by this date.

217   Enlistment report of the Wehrausschuss Galicia, ABFC.

218   In Wächter's secret circular letter dated 28 April 1943, to all local authorities concerning the ambitious recruitment programme which was about to commence, under section two he wrote; [...] '2) Canvassing... When one considers the large number of fully fit men who have already been drafted, it will not be easy to reach the numbers required for the formation of a division. A total of 20,000 men is needed to start with. Therefore every 100,000 inhabitants will provide, on average, 500 volunteers. I wish you to regard this number as an approximation only. As all use of coercion or even moral pressure is out of the question—these would only destroy the political aim of the undertaking—all our efforts will have to be concentrated on the area of canvassing if our goal is to be achieved'. See 'Der Gouverneur des Distrikt Galizien Betr:TGB.N.104\43G' Secret, Lemberg 28 April 1943, Betr.; Aufstellung der SS-Schützen Division Galizien'. SA.

219   Figure quoted in Himmler's reply to Wächter dated 17 May 1943. See tele-printer from Himmler to Wächter 544: HFD, H/10/29.

220   *Ibid.*

221   *Ibid.*

222   A detailed German account of the recruitment action in Kolomyia is given in an article entitled 'Ukrainische Freiwillige marschieren' in *Völkischer Beobachter* (Münchener Ausgabe), Nr. 151, 31 May 1943. AA.

223   A personal description of the events in Kolomyia was given in a letter to author dated 1 January1999, by I. Sadovey who was present throughout.

224   A copy of the film is in the author's possession. Wächter was so pleased with the success of recruitment in this region that he sent Himmler a photographic record of the formal announcement of the formation of the SS-Schützen-Division Galizien in Kolomyia. Brandt noted that the Reichsführer 'looked through the folder with interest'. Secret letter from Brandt to Wächter 29.6.43. HDF, H\10\39.

225   Kubijovych statement, see Heike, Eng. ed., *op cit.*; p. 145. Kubijovych maintains that this came about as the result of repeated petitioning by the MB and UCC. Later recruitment took place in the provinces of Cholm, and Hrubeshiv.

226   Enlistment report of the Wehrausschuss Galicia, ABFC.

227   *Ibid.* In Wächter's secret circular letter dated 28 April 1943, he had stated that as a matter of principle, enlistment into the Division was to be limited exclusively to Galician Ukrainians. It was however often virtually impossible to tell whether an individual originated from east or west Ukraine, in practice volunteers were recruited from both.

228   'Bericht uber die Werbeaktion bis 2 Juni 1943, einschliesslich' (see Appendix 1). ABFC.

229   Directives for Recruitment Commissions for the SS-Schützen-Division Galizien. (In confidence! Only for the officials employed by members of the Recruitment Commissions), L'viv, 28.4.1943. AA.

230   In the letter Berger referred to the proposed formation as the 'Galician Legion'. This was not however an accurate description as it had already been decided that the formation was to be a division.

231   Berger to Himmler 3 June 1943. HFD, H/10/34. In the Bender/Taylor publication: Uniforms..., vol. 4, *op cit.*; p. 22, the date of the order is incorrectly given as being 3 July 1943.

232   Secret interim report from Berger to Himmler dated 21.6.43 HFD, H/10/36.

233   Ironically, in view of the opening sentence, the figures in the document have erroneously been added together—the correct figure would be 23,518.

234 Berger to Himmler 2.7.1943, kr shas nr.8164 2.7.43 1400 =me= an den reichsfuehrer-ss und chef der deutschen polizei, Feld-kommandostelle, Urgent! Secret! NA, T175, roll 74, BA-KO, NS 19/1785 folder 1.

235 It is unclear exactly when the Ergänzungsamt der Waffen-SS, Ergänzungsstelle Warthe (XXi), Nebenstelle Lemberg came into being. It had 10–12 staff all of whom were German except Waffen-Obersturmführer Dr Stephan Molodawec, a general medical practitioner mobilised from Lodz who had served as a military doctor during the German/Polish war in the Polish Army.

236 From its inception the German authorities had done their best to limit the potential influence of the Military Board, which Wächter had refused to place under the control of a Ukrainian national. It did however continue to register the volunteers and maintain individual files as well as administer welfare facilities for the Ukrainian volunteers and also published a weekly newspaper (tabloid size with 6–8 pages) for the soldiers of the Division.

237 Of this number the commission also siphoned out those who were known or suspected of being politically unreliable.

238 Minutes of the Meetings of the Military Board 'Galicia', edited by Roman Kolisnyk, Shevchenko Scientific Society of Canada, Vol. 30, 1990, pp. 57-58. Dr Schulze also mentioned that 70 desertions had already occurred and that the *esprit de corps* varied between the different training camps in which the Ukrainian volunteers were undergoing their training. Former members of 11 armies had been identified and there are three divisions: trainees, reclaimants and deserters. In some areas of Galicia, as a solution to the problem of the 'draft dodgers' the German authorities resorted to holding the families of the so called 'deserters' responsible. In practical terms this amounted to German Polizei and security units arresting the fathers and brothers of those who had enlisted but failed to report, while in rural areas, to punish the 'deserters' livestock was seized and taken from the farms. Letter to author M. Klymchuk, 30 August 1990.

239 Leiter Ost Pöscher—Berlin 9 July 1943, to the Staatssecretaer. ABFC.

240 Letter dated 19 June 1943, from the Districtkommissar of Horochow Harter to the Generalkommissar for Volhynia und Podolien. HFD, H/10/35.

241 Fernschreib RFSS, RF/Br.- NA, T-175, roll 70, frame 2586531.

242 Hans Prützmann SS-Obergruppenführer und General der Polizei: born 31.08.1901: SS Nr. 3002: Party Nr. 142290.

243 Der Höheren SS und Polizeiführer Russland Sud, 8.7.43. Tgb. Nr. 145\43 (g) HFD, H/10/40.

244 Der Reichsführer SS Feldkommandostelle 14 July 1943, Tgb 48\10\43g. HFD, H/10/48.

245 See notes of the conference held on 12 April 1943, HFD, H/10/14.

246 Wächter's secret letter to Himmler 30 July 1943. DrWA/Ra ZL. 19/43 g: HFD, H/10/56. The report also contained two enclosures. For full text see Melnyk, To Battle, *op cit*.; pp. 326-327.

247 See letter to Himmler on dated 5 August 1943, 'Betr: SS Schützendivision Galizien', BA-KO NS 19\1785. This unsigned letter has been commonly and incorrectly attributed to Governor Wächter, however the very first line which begins 'I have been informed by the Governor of Galicia...', suggests that the letter was written by someone else, in all probability a high ranking party official who was senior in rank to Wächter (i.e.: Rosenberg). ABFC.

248 Himmler to Wächter 11 August 1943, Feldkommandostelle Tgb.Nr. 48/10/43g. HFD, H/10/59.

249 Wächter's secret letter to Himmler, 4 September 1943, ZI.19\43. HFD, H/10/63. In this letter Wächter said that 'these questions should be viewed in the context of a more long term development. The Austrian tradition was interrupted by twenty years of Polish rule and so was to a large extent lost among the younger generation who are providing the volunteers. In my opinion, the desired development requires influence to be applied step by step. This development can, I believe, be set in motion during the war, but cannot be completed until after the final victory'.

250   *Ibid.* After their meeting in March 1943, Wächter requested a personal audience with Himmler in writing on at least eight separate occasions.

251   The entry in the publication 'Verordnungsblatt der Waffen-SS', by the Verbindungsoffizier der SS beim OKH (SS Liaison Officer to the Army High Command) reads; 'Die wird unbekannt in 14.Waffen-Gren,Div. der SS (galizische Nr.1) [VOSS 1848g v. 4.8.44] Unbekannt in 14.Waffen-Gren. Div. der SS (ukrainsche Nr.1)' [VOSS 862g v. 12.11.44]. AA. A copy can be found in Document N 756/170 (Sammlung Vopersal), BA-MA.

252   HFD, H/10/42.

253   Der Reichsführer SS, Feldkommandostelle 5 July 1943, Tgb.Nr 35/88/43g RF/Bn. HFD, H/10/43. For the full text of the order see Melnyk, To Battle, *op cit.*; p. 50.

254   In his letter to Himmler dated 3.6.1943, Berger had said; 'The registered officers and NCOs will, after confirmation with the SS-Fuehrungshauptamt, be enlisted as soon as possible in retraining courses, and will form the foundation for the planned division'. cdSSHA/Be/Ra./VS-Tgb.Nr.3561/43g. HFD, H/10/34.

255   Prof. Kubijovych was to have addressed the volunteers but according to Pankivsky was forbidden to do so at the last moment by 'an order from above'. See Kost Pankivsky, Roky nimetskoi okupatsii. (Years of the German Occupation) New York: Kliuchi, 1965. 2nd ed. New York, Naukove tovarystvo im. Shevchenka, 1983, p. 241.

256   Email to author Jurij Ferencevych, 25 April 2010.

257   As reported in 'Krakivski visti', a translation of the speech was kindly provided to the author in a letter from Jurij Ferencevych dated 11 May 2010.

258   Roman Hawrylak, 'Memoirs of Bygone Years' (unpublished manuscript), p. 6.

259   Programme of the 'Festive Farewell of the first call up of officers, NCOs and riflemen to the SS-Rifle Division 'Galicia'' issued by the Military Board. An original example is in the author's possession.

260   The transport consisted of five II and III Class passenger wagons for officers and ten cattle wagons for recruits.

261   Zenon Kuk, unpublished memoirs, p. 1.

262   Amongst other things, volunteers were also advised to attend to all his outstanding matters both business and domestic as 'after recruitment you will have to wait a long time before you get your first leave to return home'. Instructions for Volunteers for the SS Riflemen Division Galicia. SA.

263   Kuk, op cit.; p. 1.

264   Identity tags were issued by the depot unit which received the soldier into the army and made out his Soldbuch (paybook). Consequently for administrative purposes the Ukrainian recruits were temporarily attached to this unit, whose designation subsequently appeared on their Erkennungsmarke (identity tags).

265   The information in the Lebenslauf included date and place of birth, parentage, schooling, employment and particulars of any previous military service.

266   Uniform was to be that of the Waffen-SS initially without the SS runes on the right lapel and with SS rank insignia on the left lapel. See Juttner's order dated 30 July 1943: Kdo.Amt d.Waffen-SS: Org.Tgb.Nr.982/43 g.Kdos. v. 30.7.1943 Aufstellung der SS-Frei.Division 'Galizien'. T175/108/2631292. The original document is held by the Imperial War Museum see also IWM H/1/249. According to official SS regulations, members of 'non-Germanic' divisions should not have worn the SS runes on the right lapel, however the first contingent who were inducted at Brno were issued uniforms with SS runes which they were apparently not required to remove.

267   Details regarding the recruits stay at Brno were provided in letters to the author E. Shypailo, 18 April 1995, 23 June 1995, and 27 August 1995, Roman Wysocky, 28 June 1995, and Roman Herasymowycz, 1 and 21 November 1995.

268 The figures are quoted from Ferkuniak, *Spomyny...*, *op cit*.; p. 6.

269 See 7.), 'Abschrift', (an eight page summary of the conference presided over by Wächter), HFD, H/10/14.

270 SS-FHA. Kdo. Amt d.Waffen-SS: Org.Tgb.Nr.982/43 g.Kdos.v. 30.7.1943 Aufstellung der SS-Frei. Division 'Galizien'. In July 1943 large parts of the camp were still under construction.

271 For example 35 officers chosen to serve in the artillery were sent directly to Beneschau near Prague. See memoirs of M. Dlaboha, Visti, nr.'s. 5-6 (43–44), May-June 1954.

272 Among the former officers who accompanied the recruits to Heidelager were Dmytro Ferkuniak, and Volodymyr Kosak (see Ferkuniak, *Spomyny...*, *op cit*.; p. 6). Kosak's Soldbuch (paybook/ identity papers) confirm that from 14 August 1943, - 28 August 1943, he was based at Heidelager as a member of the 12./Ausb.Btl z.b.V. AA.

273 Kormylo, *op cit*.; p. 3. After the first transport had left L'viv for Brno, the second and subsequent transports were sent directly to Heidelager.

2 Forging a Fighting Force

1 As of 27 August 1943, the German staff of the SS-Ausbildungs-Btl. z.b.V. included;
Btl. Kdr. SS-Sturmbannführer Bartelt (4.3.1901)
Btl. Adjutant; SS-Untersturmführer Artur Preuss (30.6.1907).
Verwaltungs-Fhr: SS-Obersturmführer Alfred Paul (7.12.1914).
Trp.Arzt: SS-Untersturmführer Erich Schmidt (11.11.1911).
Führer VI: SS-Untersturmführer Werner Urlen (23.11.1909).
For further details of the battalion's German staff, company and platoon (zug) commanders see 84/43 geh. SS-Ausbildungsbatl.z.b.V., IIa,Az.:21, Tgb.Nr.84/43 geh.27.8.43 betr.: Führerstellenbesetzungsliste an SS-FHA. RG-48.004m, Reel 6, SS-Ausbildungs battalion z.b.V., Karton 3, FILE 11, 1943, II, Holdings of the US Holocaust Memorial Museum Archives [Hereafter USHMM].

2 SS-Sturmbannführer Bernhard Bartelt: born 4 March 1901: Party Nr. 711242/SS Nr. 27759: Holder of EK I Class. Information about his career can be found in his Personal-Akte Bernhard Bartelt, NA, A3343-SSO-034 and his corresponding RuSHA file A3343-RS-A236.

3 The structure of a rifle company was as follows; one platoon = three squads, one company = three platoons. Selection was made basically by height - the tallest recruits were in the first platoon and the shortest in the fourth. Letter to author E. Shypailo, 2 November 1994.

4 The heavy companies had around 250 men each while each of the rifle companies had approximately 160.

5 An average daily strength report for the battalion for the month of August 1943, is given as follows: 177 Officers, 422 NCOs, 3,026 men, total 3,625. See 89/43 geh. SS-Ausbildungsbatl.z.b.V., (SS-Freiw.Div. 'Galizien'), SS-Tr.Ub.Pl.Heidelager, den 1.9.1943, IIb, Az.: 9w, Tgb.-Nr.89/43 geh.27.8.43 betr.: Monatliche stärkemeldung der Teilnehmer an der Feldpost-bezw. SS-Feldpost, RG-48.004m, Reel 6, SS-Ausbildungsbattalion z.b.V., Karton 3, FILE 11, 1943, II, USHMM.

6 Der Reichsführer SS, Feldkommandostelle 5 July 1943, Tgb.Nr 35/88/43g RF/Bn. HFD, H/10/43.

7 Letter to author R. Kolisnyk, 6 June 1995.

8 This was Schützmannschafts-Batl. 204, which was 'Wachbattalion' responsible for security at Heidelager.

9 Keczun, unpublished memoirs, pp. 5-6.

10 Kormylo, *op cit*.; p. 4.

11   Keczun, *op cit*.; p. 7.

12   See Geheim, August 1943, Nr. 4, Nachrichtendienst fur die Leiter der Abteilung VI, I. Führer and
      Autoritat and II. Schulung oder Erziehung, pp. 1-6. RG 48.004m, Reel 5, SS-Ausbildungsbattalion
      z.b.V., Karton 3, FILE II, 1943, II, USHMM.

13   Kormylo, *op cit*.; p. 4.

14   Lafettes were specialist carriages for the machine guns.

15   Keczun, *op cit*.; p. 8.

16   Letter to author Theo Andruszko, 3 March 2012.

17   Ferkuniak, 'Spomyny...', *op cit*.; p. 8. Ferkuniak and 8 others were assigned to the 10th training
      company.

18   SS-FHA. Kdo. Ant d.Waffen-SS: Org.Tgb.Nr.982/43 g.Kdos.v. 30.7.1943 Aufstellung der SS-Freiw.
      Division 'Galizien'.

19   *Ibid*. The document actually read: 'Language to be used for commands: 'Galician'[*sic*]: language to
      be used for orders: German'.

20   Heike, Eng. ed., *op cit*.; p. 9.

21   For example the Ukrainians were described by their SS-instructors as being 'open minded and eager
      to learn', 'Pioniereinheiten der 14 Waffen-Gren Div der SS (Ukrain.Nr 1)', U-6, Dr H. Schmitt -
      unpublished manuscript.

22   Kormylo, *op cit*.; p. 7.

23   In an interview with the author, Stephan Sadiwsky, who had previously served with the Red Army,
      before being captured by the Germans, escaping and joining the Ukrainian partisan movement,
      commented: 'Before we joined the Division we had heard about 'SS training' and we were
      terrified....it wasn't easy - but we got almost every Sunday off, we had warm comfortable barracks,
      hot food and ample weapons and equipment. When we were in the UPA we lived in the forest, using
      any weapons we could find, always short of food and always on the move day and night with no
      time to rest'. Diss, England, 27th February 1989.

24   Interview S. Dmytryk, Rushden, England, 21 October 1990. Injuries included splinters from shells,
      bullet wounds and occasional stab wounds. Verbally to author M. Prymak, 3 November 1997.

25   Chornij, *op cit*.; p. 46.

26   Kormylo, *op cit*.; p. 9.

27   Heike, Eng ed., *op cit*.; pp. 18-19.

28   Nachrichtendienst fur die Leiter der Abteilung VI, II. Schulung oder Erziehung, p. 5, RG 48.004m,
      Reel 5, SS-Ausbildungsbattalion z.b.V., Karton 3, FILE II, 1943, II. USHMM.

29   All regular SS recruits underwent ideological training, however the influx of non-Germanic personnel
      into the Waffen-SS forced the SS-Hauptamt to give up its uniform ideological indoctrination and
      prepare a specially tailored program for each national or ethnic group. As the Galician Ukrainians
      were of Slavic origin the lectures deliberately avoided mentioning the inferiority of the Slav race,
      which was the very essence of the Nazi ideological doctrine. Further details can be found in the
      Bundesarchiv in Berlin reference BA-R NS 31/450.

30   Letter to author Theo Andruszko, 18 January 2010.

31   Kormylo, *op cit*.; p. 2.

32   Verbally to author R. Drazniowsky, 13 March 1997 and Heike, Eng. ed., *op cit*.; p. 70.

33   Verbally to author M. Prymak, 8 November 1997, Kormylo, *op cit*.; p. 10.

34   Kormylo, *op cit*.; p. 5.

35   According to Ferkuniak the officers had taken the oath the day before on 28 August Ferkuniak,
      'Spomyny...', *op cit*.; pp. 8-9.

36   SS-Sturmbannführer Bernhard Bartelt: born 4 March 1901: Party Nr. 711242/SS Nr. 27759: Holder of EK I Class. Information about his career can be found in his Personal-Akte Bernhard Bartelt, NA, A3343-SSO-034 and his corresponding RuSHA file A3343-RS-A236.

37   The choir was conducted by Vasyl Ostashevsky.

38   The text of the officially prescribed oath for foreign troops is given in Juttner's circular dated 30 July 1943, Kdo.Amt d.Waffen-SS: Org.Tgb.Nr 982/43 g Kdos. v. 30.7.1943 Aufstellung der SS-Frei. Division 'Galizien'.

39   'My idemo v biy', Nr. 38 (39). AA. For further information about this special edition see 'Do Peremohy - Tyzhnevyk Dyviziyi' (To Victory - The Weekly of the Division), Visti Kombatanta, Nr.2, 1972, p. 41.

40   This visit was arranged by the Military Board which was responsible for administering welfare and recreational facilities for the recruits.

41   SS-Ausbildungsbatl.z.b.V., (SS-Freiw.Div. 'Galizien'), Heidelager, Post Pustkow.Dist.Krak. II b Az.: 12d Tgb.-Nr.130/43 geh. 19.10.43. betr.: Stärkemeldung, Bezug: Besprechung RF-SS mit SS-Stubaf.Bartelt. RG-48.004m, Reel 6, SS-Ausbildungsbattalion z.b.V., Karton 3, FILE 11, 1943, II, USHMM.

42   According to Ferkuniak the verification commission was established on 20 August 1943, and consisted of Col. Agathon Dobriansky, Lt. Col. Barvinsky, Major Kastel and Cpt. Uhryn Bezhrishnyi. It recommended that sixteen officers be discharged as unsuitable. See Ferkuniak, 'Spomyny...', *op cit.*; p. 8.

43   *Ibid.*

44   Inter-company football matches were sometimes played. It should however be noted that no sports equipment or clothing was available for matches and games had to be played in army issue shoes. The only recreational facilities available for the camp were a canteen (where beer could be purchased) and a bordello called 'Haus Waldeslust' (House of Joy in the woods). Roman Hawrylak, 'Memoirs...', *op cit.*; p. 9.

45   Keczun, *op cit.*; p. 7.

46   By 30 October 1943, there were 70 known deserters, see Minutes of the Military Board 30 October 1943, ABFC. The OUN leadership did not encourage these desertions and therefore Roman Shukhevych (aka Gen. Chuprynka) issued instructions that volunteer members of the OUN could only leave the Division as the direct result of an order from the OUN commander. The result was a significant reduction in the desertion rate. See 'UPA and the Division 'Halychyna'', Lev Shankovsky, published in 'America', July 12-16, Philadelphia, 1954.

47   Dmytryshyn, 'SS Division Galicia...', *op cit.*; p. 64. *op cit.*; see also Kost Pankivsky 'Roky nimetskoi okupatsii', 1941–1944 (New York, Toronto, 1965), *op cit.*; pp. 244-247.

48   Mykola Fylypovych, 'Dobrovoltsi', unpublished manuscript, p. 23. These recruits were sworn in on 17 October 1943.

49   SS-Haupsturmfuhrer Johannes Kleinow, born 10 February 1901, Party Nr. 112, 214: SS-Nr. 28,740. Former member of 'Schutzmannschaft 207. See Personal-Akte NA A3343-SSO-178A.

50   This staff list includes some zug commanders, see 105/43 geh. SS-Ausbildungsbatl.z.b.V., IIa,Az.:21, Tgb.Nr.105/43 geh v.27.9.43 betr.: Führerstellenbesetzungsliste an SS-FHA. RG 48.004m, Reel 5, SS-Ausbildungsbattalion z.b.V., Karton 3, FILE 11, 1943, II, USHMM. The list including staff appointments is reproduced in full in Melnyk, To Battle, *op cit.*; pp. 58-59.

51   Figure given in the 'Minutes of the Military Board', 30 October 1943, ABFC.

52   Of this number 3,140 (13 officers and 3127 recruits) were based at Heidelager while the remainder were attending training courses elsewhere. See SS-Ausbildungs Batl.z.b.V. SS-Freiw.Div

'Galizien', Heidelager, Post Pustkow. Dist.Krak, II b Az.: 12 d Tgb.Nr, 130/43 geh. H Geheim!, Betr.: Stärkemeldung. Bezug: Besprechung RF-SS mit SS-Stubaf. Bartelt, RG 48.004m, Reel 5, SS-Ausbildungsbattalion z.b.V, Karton 3, FILE II, 1943, II,. USHMM. For the month of September 1943, the average daily strength for the SS-Ausbildungs-Batl. z.b.V. (SS-Freiw.Div. 'Galizien'), was 3,842. The specific figures for the three categories were: 28 German and 20 Ukrainian officers, 410 German NCOs and 382 German and 3220 Ukrainian men. See *Ibid.*, SS-Ausbildungs-Batl. z.b.V. (SS-Freiw.Div. 'Galizien'), SS-Tr.Ub.Pl. Heidelager, den 1.10.1943, IIb, Az.: 9w, Tgb.Nr. 109/43 geh. H/Kr, Betr.: Monatliche stärkemeldung der Teilnehmer an der Feldpost bezw. SS-Feldpost. *Ibid.*

53   See Der Gouverneur des Distrikts Galizien, An den Reichsführer-SS und Chef der Deutschen Polizei Heinrich Himmler, Lemberg den, 30 Oktober, 1943, DrWa/Ra, 263, HFD, H/10/67.

54   SS-Panzer-Grenadier-Schule Galiz.Offz.Lehrgang, Leschan, den 30.10.1943, Betr.: Galiz.Offz. Lehrgang, Bezug: Schr.Wehrkanzlei Nr. 4/48/943 v.20.10.43. Schevchenko Archive hereafter abbreviated SA.

55   In his memoirs Ferkuniak states that the vast majority of those given the highest rank of Waffen-Hauptsturmführer including Barvinsky, Uhryn-Bezhrishnyi, Dawybida, Kotyl and Wasylew were dismissed within months on one pretext or another following Pobihushtschyi's machinations to remove Dawybida which Freitag used as an excuse commenting 'As I see it there is no solidarity among you Ukrainians'. Dmytro Ferkuniak, 'Spomyny....', *op cit.*, p. 12.

56   *Ibid.* pp. 10-11. Some arrived with the rank of Standartenoberjunker (officer cadets with substantive rank of warrant officer) and were commissioned shortly after their arrival at Heidelager.

57   In his memoirs one of their number wrote: 'Men came to the Division Galicia as officers of various former armies. Not only did they forget their military profession but they had changed in charter. They had forgotten the behaviour of an officer, the camaraderie and the obligation of duties. It was no wonder that in such a gathering of various men, you could always find those who wished they were not there at all. As soon as the screw had tightened one could see the reluctance of some to accept their new environment. Now they used all kinds of excuses just to avoid their duties'. Ferkuniak, 'Spomyny...', *op cit.*; p. 10.

58   There are many recorded instances of complaints by these older officers to the Military Board, about their treatment at the hands of the German NCO instructors. Several of their letters of complaint have been persevered and copies of some are in the author's possession. Three officers, P. Holoyda, M. Konkol and V. Poniatyshyn later signed a declaration to this effect dated 31 October 1944, which was verified by Osyp Navrotsky in his capacity as an executive officer of the Military Board. AA.

59   Kuk, *op cit.*; p. 5.

60   Evhen Pobihushtschyi, born 15 November 1901, in Postoliwka. He saw active service with the Ukrainian Army from 1 November 1918 until May 1920 and then from 15 July 1928 until 19 March 1935 he served in the Polish Army with the 57 Infantry Regiment, rising to the equivalent rank of Captain. With the German invasion of Poland in September 1939, he was captured and held by the Germans as a prisoner of war until his release on May 1940. On 15 May 1941, he joined *Roland*. He attended the Heersschule für Btl.Abt. Führer, Antwerpen from 17 April - 13 May 1944, and was described by his course commanders as 'a passionate soldier'. On 15 November 1943, he was confirmed in the rank of Waffen-Sturmbannführer. Personal-Akte, NA, A3343-SSO-384A.

61   Hawrylak, 'Memoirs...', *op cit.*; p. 12.

62   Only the Germans from the 11 and 2 companies remained to finish the training of 2 additional companies which arrived later. These Germans were eventually remained with the Division in various positions and functions. Kuk, unpublished memoirs *op cit.*; p. 5.

63   Heike, Eng. ed., *op cit*.; p. 14.

64   Ferkuniak, *op cit*.; p. 14.

65   The 12 MG-Lehrkompanie was commanded by SS-Obersturmführer Herbert Schneller.

66   'Anschhriften'; SA. Additional camps at which Ukrainians underwent training included: Amsterdam, Arolsen, Bielefeld, Brno, Cannstatt, Graz, Hamburg-Rahlst, Hamm, Karlsruhe, Kensberg, Koblenz, Leshany, Lübeck, Maastricht, Mielefeld, Moerchingen, Oldenburg, Orthez, Osnabrück, Radom, Rallstedt, Strassburg, Sennheim and Verdun.

67   'Pioneer Battalion of the Galician Division, Bohdan Kutny and Taras Katzchmarchuk, unpublished paper, p. 1. Interview S. Dmytryk, Rushden, England, 21 October 1990.

68   Kormylo, *op cit*.; p. 12.

69   Hawrylak, 'Memoir....', *op cit*.; p. 9. The regime at Lauenburg was the inspiration behind a song which the Ukrainians sang which went: 'From Lauenburg we want out, from this crazy house, we've had it up to here, yes sir! yes sir! yes sir! Theo Andruszko email to author, 18 January2010.

70   Keczun, *op cit*.; p. 15.

71   Kuk, *op cit*.; p. 9.

72   Letter to the author Roman Herasymowycz, 21 November 1995.

73   SS-Führungshauptamt Amt XI, Abt.2/I, Az:22b16, Amt V Abt IIa. 10. Dez.1944, Betr.: 16 Kriegs-Junkerlehrgang as der SS-und Waffen-Junkerschule Braunschweig. SA.

74   'Minutes of the Meetings of the Military Board 'Galicia'', edited by Roman Kolisnyk, Shevchenko Scientific Society of Canada, vol.30, 1990, pp. 57-58. Dr Schulze also mentioned that 70 desertions had already occurred and that the esprit de corps varied between the different training camps in which the Ukrainian volunteers were undergoing their training. Former members of 11 armies had been identified and there are three divisions: trainees, reclaimants and deserters. In some areas of Galicia, as a solution to the problem of the 'draft dodgers' the German authorities resorted to holding the families of the so called 'deserters' responsible. In practical terms this amounted to German Polizei and security units arresting the fathers and brothers of those who had enlisted but failed to report, while in rural areas, to punish the 'deserters' livestock was seized and taken from the farms. Letter to author M. Klymchuk, 30 August 1990.

75   'Bericht für die Zeit vom 28.IV-24,IX.1943' also 'Bericht über die Werbeaktion für SS-Schützen Division Galizien' 1.8.1943. SA.

76   In November 1943, Alfred Bisanz repeated that the Baudienst was ready to release some 5,000 men who had completed their term of service to the Division. 2 days later the matter was discussed again and the suggestion made that these men be denied home leave to which they were entitled in order to prevent many from failing to report for duty. 'Minutes of the Meetings of the Military Board 'Galicia'', edited by Roman Kolisnyk, Shevchenko Scientific Society of Canada, vol.30, 1990, pp. 57-58.

77   Jaroslav Wenger, From Baudienst to the Division 'Galicia'. Veterans' News, # 4, 2012, pp. 111-113.

78   By preventing the consolidation of these forces in one location the Germans intentionally or otherwise, mitigated their potential threat in the event of a large scale mutiny.

79   See message to Gren. Ers. Regt. 34 KOBLENZ, from Galizien SS. Volunteer Div. SS. Troop Training Area HEIDELAGER, signed BARTELT, SS. Stubaf, 26/11, HW16/101, CX/MSS/Q.24, 6/12/43, Public Records Office, Kew, London, (hereafter abbreviated NA, PRO, Kew).

80   Heike, Eng. ed., *op cit*.; p. 17.

81   SS-Brigadeführer Walter Schimana: born 12:3:1898 in Troppau Czechoslovakia—committed suicide in Salzburg prison on 12.9.1948. SS Nr. 337,753/Party Nr. 49,042. Holder of Iron Cross I and II Class awarded for anti-partisan actions). Commander of 'Kampfgruppe Schimana'. He was

an anti-partisan specialist and is shown as being responsible for the formation of the 14. Division in the SS-FHA. Kdo. Ant d.Waffen-SS: Org.Tgb.Nr.982/43 g.Kdos.v. 30.7.1943 Aufstellung der SS-Frei.Division 'Galizien'. For further details of career see Personal-Akte Walter Schimana NA, A3343-SSO-078B and his RuSHA file NA, A3343-RS-F0316.

82   See Interrogation report Walter Schimana, 3 February 1947, p. 7. http://www.ifz-muenchen.de/archiv/zs/zs-1420.pdf.

83   SS-Führungshauptamt, Berlin Wilmersdorf, den 22.Sept.1943, Amt II Org.Abt.1a/II, Betr.: Neugliederung der SS-Freiw.Div.'Galizien', SA.

84   These units were finally completed in January 1944.

85   The Fusilier Battalion of the Ukrainian Division, p. 1, J. Hnatkiw (unpublished paper).

86   Prior to this change both individuals and departments within the SS establishment continued to use their own terminology when referring to the Division. Thus at different times it was variously referred to as; 'SS-Freiwilligen-Division 'Galizien'' (by Himmler in his letter to Wächter dated 28 March 1943 HFD, H/10/5); the 'Ukrainische-SS-Polizei-Schützen Division' (by Berger in a letter to Himmler dated 6 April 1943, HFD, H/10/12); the 'Galizische Division' (in a teleprinter message from Daluege to Winklemann of 14 April 1943); 'SS-Schützen Division Galizien' (both in Wächter's proclamation dated 28 April - and in Berger's letter to Himmler of 21 August 43); and the 'Legion Galizien' (In Berger's letter to Himmler dated 3 June 43 HFD, H/10/34). After June 1943 the confusion abated.

87   This order was dated 22 October 1943, see Bender Taylor, 'Uniforms...' vol. 4, *op cit.*; pp. 28-29. It appears that the actual renumbering of the infantry regiments did not however take place for several weeks.

88   Born 28.10.1888.

89   Born 30.01.1887, died 17.12.1954. Both Barvinsky and Kotyl were later dismissed from the Division.

90   Born 01.01.1893, died 27.11.1968.

91   It should be noted that these men all attended an officer retraining course at Leschan which ran from 30 August 1943 - to 30 October 1943 and were not confirmed in their officer ranks until 1 November when they returned to the Division. Ferkuniak, *op cit.*; p. 11.

92   See Daluege to Winklemann z.Zt.Feld-kommandostelle, 14.4.43. ABFC. See also secret letter from Kruger to Himmler 16 April 1943, H/10/18.

93   Berger's letter to Himmler 3 June 1943, CdSSHA/Be/Ra./VS-Tgb.Nr. 3561/43g. HFD, H/10/34.

94   *Ibid.*

95   *Ibid.*

96   Himmler's circular to all officers: Der Reichsführer SS Tgb.Nr. 35\88\43g Feld-Kommandostelle 24 June 1943. HFD, H/10/37.

97   The original circular which was issued by Oberst Hans Flade, a senior official within the head office of the *Ordnungspolizei*, bears no heading and is dated June 1943 (the day is missing). ABFC. Hans Flade born 27.10.1898, SS Nr. 393 251, NS Nr. 8,185 303. On 9 November 1944, Flade was promoted to Chef Kommando Amt, Hauptamt Ordnungspolizei.

98   See Himmler's circular dated 5 July 1943, Feldkommandostelle Tgb.Nr. 35/88/43g. HFD, H/10/43.

99   Each company had a strength of about 110 soldiers and was comprised of three infantry platoons, a communications section and various support services such as cooks, tailors, etc.

100   Earlier when Berger had warned that the SS main office had neither the necessary weapons nor training cadres to accommodate the formation of a new Waffen-SS division, he also stated that the proposed training cadres (i.e.; *Ordnungspolizei* personnel) should be incorporated if only

temporarily into the Waffen-SS. This would explain a number of anomalies such as the confusion over the issue of various types of insignia to the volunteers who were sent to these regiments. See Berger to Himmler Feldkommandostelle, SSHA 4268 16.4.43. 1055. HFD, H/10/20.

101 Verbally to author V. Skilnyk, 10 February 2013.

102 The Ukrainians enlisted into these regiments initially blank collar patches. German officers and NCOs of these units wore Polizei uniforms which carried appropriate ranks. With the exception of helmets bearing Polizei markings, no other Polizei uniforms or insignia were worn by the Ukrainian volunteers at any time (although the Ukrainian recruits were issued with some Polizei stamped equipment such as rucksacks and blankets).

103 A number of pre-worn uniforms (complete with the SS lightning rune collar patches) were issued to the Ukrainians soldiers which would account for this anomaly. Letter to author I. Sadovey, 22 August 2000.

104 Figure provided in a recruitment report at a meeting of the Military Board on 30 October 1943.

105 Born 12 March 1898, Party Nr. 2,639,652, holder of the Baltenkreuz, EK 1 and II Class, Verwundetenabzeichen in Schwarz and the Deutsches Kreuz in Gold. Information taken from his service record See Personal-Akte NA A3343-SSO-071.

106 *Ibid.* These included operations 'Hamburg', 'Altona', 'Franz', 'Erntefest I', 'Erntfest II', 'Hornung' and 'Föhn'. See Der SS-und Polizeiführer in Weissruthenien, Minsk, den 30.März 143, 00061, an den Reichsführer SS und Chef der Deutschen Polizei im Reichsministerium des Innern, Betr.: Vorzugsweise Beförderung des Majors d.Sch.Siegfried Binz, geb. am 12.3.1898 in Ostseebad Binz a/Rügen, Kommandeur des I./23, Heimatstandort: Recklinghausen. Bezug: O-Kdo. II P.I (1a) 37/43 vom 13.3.43.

107 By order of the Chef der Ordnungspolizei in Berlin dated 25 January1944, the 4 Regiments' III battalion was transferred by train from Fernschweiler to Maastricht in the Nederlands where it was temporarily accommodated in the Tapijin barracks. However the same order stated unequivocally that 'It [III Batl] remains attached (and subordinate) in every respect to the Regiment'.' Der Chief der Ordnungspolizei Kdo, g.I-Ia(I) Nr. 983/43(g), Berlin den 25 Januar 1944, Betr.: Verlegung des III./Galizischen SS-Freiwilligen - Rgt.4'. SA.

108 Telegram Der Chef der Ordnungspolizei, Berlin, den 5. Juli 1943, Kdo, I O (3) 1 Nr. 378/43, ABFC.

109 Recruitment report at a meeting of the Military Board on 30 October 1943.

110 See telegram Der Chef der Ordnungspolizei, Berlin, den 5.Juli 1943, Kdo, I O (3) 1 Nr. 378/43. ABFC. Polizeibataillon 11, to which Oberst der Sicherheitpolizei Franz Lechthaler belonged prior to serving with the 5 Regiment, operated in the Kauen/Sluzk region. Here on 27 October 1941, a two day operation was carried out against the entire Jewish population. In the early 1960's Lechthaler and a Polizeimajor named Willi Papenkort who also participated in the action, were brought to trial before the Schwurgericht Kassel, twice. The charges on both occasions were 'Beihilfe zum Totschlag an 550 Menschen im Smolensk and Sluzk', where according to the report 'Lechthaler war der Kommandeur des Exekutions-Bataillon 1941–1942'. While Papenkort was freed, Lechthaler was subsequently convicted and sentenced to a 3 1/2 year and an additional 2 year term of imprisonment. A full description of the action in question (omitting the actual numbers of victims) appears in Nurnberg Documents PS-1104.

111 Telegram Der Chef der Ordnungspolizei, Berlin, den 5.Juli 1943, Kdo, I O (3) 1 Nr. 378/43. ABFC.

112 Report given at a general meeting of the Military Board October 1943, at which Dr Schulze incorrectly gave the strength of this unit as being 1,293.

113 See Der Chef der Ordnungspolizei, 6 August 1943. Kdo. I 0 (3) 1 Nr. 469/43. SA.

114 For further details relating to the formation, organisation and structure of this regiment including the names, ranks and positions to which they were posted of many of the German command

personnel see a four page document, Erlass des Chef der Orpo (Kdo. I 0 (3) 1 Nr. 526/43 v 7.9.1943 Betr.; Aufstellung des Gal.SS-Freiw.Rgts.7. BA-KO, R 19/1 106.

115   Born 29 April 1895, Party Nr. 7, 238, 661, SS Nr. 442, 406.

116   Recruitment report of the Military Board on 30 October 1943. See also memoirs of Rev D. Kowaluk, Visti, Nr. 118, 1965, pp. 36-39. Initially there were problems with a training facilities for the 7 Regiment in Salies de Bearn and it appears that some recruits had to be temporarily housed in hotels and boarding houses.

117   Born 13 July 1895, Party Nr. 4, 663, 977.

118   See The Reichsrangliste der Offiziere der Schutzpolizei und Gendarmerie,1. Teil, Generale und Stabsoffiziere, Berlin, Reichsdruckerei, 1941.

119   For a list of the proposed appointments see Gal. SS-Freiw. Rgt. 8, Maastricht, den 25.Oktober 1943, Fernschrift, an den chef des Aufstellungsstabes der Gal.SS-Freiw. Regimenter 4-8. Berlin, Betr.; Offizierstellenbesetzung. Bezug; Verfg. vom 12.10.1943. BA-KO, R 20/66.

120   Oberstleutnant, 2 Hauptmann, 3 Oberleutnante, 2 Leutnante, 1 Leutnante d.Res.,3 Rev-Leutnante 118 Unterführer (of which 12 gvH suitable), 1 German doctor, 2 Galician doctors. See SS-Freiw. Rgt. 8, Maastricht, den 28.Oktober 1943, Fernschrift, (Oberstleutnant d.SchP.u.Kommandeur Gal. SS-Freiw.Rgt.8. Schwertschlager) an den Befehlshaber der Ordnungspolizei in Nimwegen. Betr.; Vorhandene Offiziere und Unterführer bei der aufgelösten Pol.- Waffenschule IV, Aufstellung des Gal.SSFreiw.Rgt.8. Bezug; FS. Nr.616 vom 27.10.1943. BA-KO, R 20/66.

121   A document dated 12 August 1943 states that some NCOs and men of the 1 battalion of the 8 Regiment stationed in Märisch-Ostrau, were transferred to Pol.Schützen-Rgt.36, whilst the remaining men were formed into two companies which were to remain with the battalion staff at Märisch-Ostrau until their probable assignment to the 7 Regiment and other Galician reserve units. See Der Chef der Ordnungspolizei, Berlin, den 12. August 1943, Kdo. I 0 (3) 1 Nr. 484/43, Schnellbrief, Betr.: I./SS-Pol.8, Bezug: Erlass vom 6.8.1943 - Kdo I 0 (3) 1 Nr. 466/43, R 19/104, BA-KO.

122   For further details including staff appointments etc see Schnellbrief Chef der Ordnungspolizei/kdo. I 0 (3) Nr. 455 II/43 v 20.8.1943 Betr.; Aufstellung des Gal. SS-Freiw. Ersatz-Batl. Heidenheim, R 19/103), BA-KO.

123   R. Chomickyj, unpublished memoirs, p. 1.

124   Josaphat Konchak, Visti Kombatanta, Nr.3, 1996, pp. 83-88.

125   Letter to author I. Sadovey, 27 February 1999.

126   *Ibid.*

127   Der Reichsführer SS und Chef der Deutschen Polizei, O-W IV (c) 4614/2/XII, Berlin NW7, den 21 Dez.1943, Landesarchiv Saarbrücken, Bestand Md1, Nr.81.

128   Schimana received a telegram from Himmler dated 22 October 1943, notifying him that he was to leave his appointment as the commander of the SS-Freiwilligen-Division 'Galizien' and with effect from 9 November 1943, assume the post of the Höheren SS-und Polizeiführer as the replacement for Jürgen Stroop. BA-KO, NS 19/2191 folder 1.

129   Fritz Freitag: Born 28 April 1894, in Allenstein east Prussia; Party Nr. 3,052,501 \ SS Nr. 393,266. Married with two children, Freitag served in the German armed forces in World War 1 from 1.4.1914 until 17.12.1918 and the Freikorps from 15.1.1919 until 15.4.1919. On 3.2.1920 he joined the Schutzpolizei (security police) and rose to the rank of Oberführer (colonel). Freitag transferred to the 4 SS-Polizei Panzergrenadier Division at the outbreak of World War II. See Personalverfügung Der SS-Oberführer Fritz Freitag, Personal File NA, A3343 SSO-220.

130 Schimana did not take up his new appointment in Greece until 19 November 1943, and according to his service record Freitag's appointment was effective as of 20.10.1943. There must therefore have been an overlap between Schimana's departure and Freitag's arrival. *Ibid.*

131 These units were placed under Himmler's direct command as of 27 June 1941, See 'Unsere Ehre Heisst Treue, Kreigstagebuch des Kommandostabes Reichsführer SS. Tatigkeitsberichte der 1 und 2 SS-Inf.Brigade, der 1. SS-Kav.-Brigade und von Sonderkommandos der SS'. Vienna, Frankfurt, Zürich: Europa, 1965, pp. 15-23. Charged with similar 'special tasks', they were used for the pacification of rear areas of the rapidly advancing German Army.

132 The term 'pacification' was merely a euphemism for the killing of suspected partisans and innocent civilians (ie Jews).

133 In a typical entry dated 24.8.1941, Freitag diligently reported 114 prisoners taken, 283 Jews shot, and a haul of captured booty amounting to only 2 guns, 3 heavy and 6 light machine guns. See 'Brigadegefechtsstand, den 29.8.1941, Tatigkeitsbericht fur die Zeit vom 24.8.1941/1200 Uhr - 29.8.1941/1200 Ukr', 'Unsere Ehre...', *op cit.*; pp. 122-123.

134 From 4 January1943 - 20 April 1943.

135 For details of Freitag's career, appointment dates, positions see his personal file - NA, A3343 SSO-220.

136 At time of his appointment as Divisional commander Freitag held both the Iron Cross I. and II. Class, (clasp for EK II.KL awarded 5.2.1942, clasp for EK.I. Class awarded 6.3.1942) the German Cross in Gold (awarded 30.4.1943), the Ostmedaille and the wound badge in both silver and gold. For details of his service record prior to joining the Galician Division see 'Personalverfügung der SS-Oberführer Fritz Freitag', SS-Führungshauptamt Amt V/Abt.IIa/Ref 2, Az.:21c 24 Fu.P. PZ, Gren, 29.1.1944. PersonalAkte - NA, A3343 SSO-220. ff 584-695.

137 Freitag does however appear to have had some indirect contact with local Ukrainian militia units whose co-operation he acknowledges in the secret daily activity reports of the 1.SS Infanterie Brigade and who are described as having 'done a very valuable job as regards clearing the partisans and paratroops from the army rear area'. In the same reports he criticises conduct of the local Ukrainian population for being 'two faced' as it was known to be assisting the Jews hiding in the woods' and supplying the partisans with food and information. See 1.SS Brigade IIa/449/41, Abt,Ic.27/41 geh.E/Schu. Brig.St.Qu.20.8.194, Betr.: Tatigkeitsberichter v.20.8.41/1200 Uhrs bis 24.8.41/1200 'Unsere, Ehre Heisst Treue', *op cit.*: p. 118. See also '1.SS Brigade IIa/449/41, Abt,Ic.26/41 geh.E/Schu. Brig.St.Qu.20.8.1941, Betr.: Tatigkeitsberichter v.17.8.41/1200 Uhrs bis 20.8.41/1200, *Ibid.* p. 110.

138 Heike, Eng. ed., *op cit.*; p. 6.

139 *Ibid.*, p. 7.

140 Ferkuniak, *Ibid.* p. 9.

141 Heike, Eng. ed., *op cit.*; p. 7.

142 *Ibid.* For a discussion of Freitag's character and personality see pp. 6-7.

143 *Ibid.*, p. 9.

144 Kormylo, *op cit.*; p. 13.

145 Heike states that originally the German political authorities had contemplated filling only the Division staff with Germans but the requisite number of Ukrainian officers were simply not available. Of those who did undergo training, many proved to be unsuitable because of out moded experience in modern warfare and had to be dismissed. Heike, Eng. ed., *op cit.*; p. 15. In marked contrast in his unpublished memoirs Waffen-Haupsturmfuhrer Ferkuniak one of the very few Ukrainians to serve on the Division's general staff, states that this was because 'Ukrainian

officers were obstacles for the Germans which prevented them from taking complete control over Ukrainian soldiers'. Ferkuniak, 'Spomyny....', *op cit.*; p. 12.

146   The itinerary for the visit included a tour of the sights of the city and an evening visit to the opera house to watch two acts of the play Hamlet by Schekspir![*sic*]. See programme for the visit by the Kommandeur of the SS-Schützen Division Galizien SS-Oberführer Freitag on 19./20. November 1943. SA.

147   See Roman Kolisnyk, The Military Board and the Ukrainian Division, Shevchenko Scientific Society of Canada vol.30: 1993. p. 32.

148   SS-Sturmbannführer Johannes Georgi: born 17 August 1912. See Personal-Akte NA A3343-SSO-008A.

149   Rudolph Michel, born 28 December 1920, Osnabrück: SS-Nr.466 716.

150   SS- Obersturmführer Herbert Schaaf: born 4 March 1908. SS-Nr. 465057. See Personal-Akte NA A3343-SSO-063B.

151   SS-Hauptsturmführer Erich Finder SS Nr. 16, 939, was transferred from the 8 SS Kav. Div. to the 14 Galician Division with effect from 20 April 1944, as IIA. See message to 8. SS Kav. Div. from SS. Ops. H.Q. IIA Katz; dated 15/4/1944, Top Secret Copy No.13 CX/MSS, Q.53, 24/4/44, HW 16/101 NA, PRO, Kew and Personal-Akte NA A3343-SSO-008A.

152   SS-Obersturmführer Herbert Oskar Hanel: born 18 July 1912. SS-Nr. 121, 523. See Personal-Akte NA A3343-SSO-060A.

153   SS-Sturmbannführer Hans-Georg Ziegler: born 31 August 1912, SS-Nr. 254 020. See Personal-Akte NA A3343-SSO-021C.

154   SS-Sturmbannführer Otto Sulzbach: born 18 May 1909. SS-Nr. 1,364/Party Nr. 61,317. His appointment with the SS-Freiwilligen-Division 'Galizien' was effective as of 16 September 1943. See Personal-Akte NA A3343-SSO-170B.

155   SS-Obersturmbannführer Dr Max Specht: born 8 November 1898, SS-Nr. 118,403/Party Nr. 2,725,210. See Personal-Akte NA A3343-SSO-145B.

156   SS-Hauptsturmführer Werner Beneke: born 14 July 1911, SS-Nr. 211 942. See Personal-Akte NA A3343-SSO-056.

157   SS-Sturmbannführer Dr Oskar Kopp: born 30 May 1910. See Personal-Akte NA A3343-SSO-199A.

158   SS-Sturmbannführer Heinz Behrendt: born 20 July 1904. SS-Nr. 243,666. See Personal-Akte NA A3343-SSO-052.

159   Karl-Robert Zoglauer: born 3 July 1907, SS-Nr. 46 147. See Personal-Akte NA A3343-SSO-025c.

160   In his memoirs Heike states that Freitag's desire to appoint commanders with recent frontline experience (and thus maintain a 'margin of certainty') was partly defensible in view of the need to prepare the Division for battle in the shortest possible time.

161   In 'My Life's Mosaic' Pobihushtschyi states 'Nobody from the Division's staff had informed me that a new commander had arrived to take over command of WGR 29, which I was commanding.' 'My Life's Mosaic', The Association of Ukrainians in Great Britain, 1982, p. 126.

162   Hans Forstreuter: born 1 November 1912, SS-Nr. 422,180/Party Nr. 3,324,777. Holder of German Cross in Gold, EK I. and II Class, Infantrei Sturmabzeichen and Nahkampfspange in bronze. In his Lebenslauf dated 20 March 1943, Forstreuter gives his party number as being 3,744,129. See NA, A3342-SSO-215.

163   See SS-Führungshauptamt, Amt V/IIa.Iof.1, 16/SSO.Ho. 11.11.1943 Personalverfugung Der SS-Sturmbannführer Forstreuter, NA, A3342-SSO-215.

164   SS-Obersturmbannführer Friedrich Dern: born 5 March 1896, SS-Nr. 38,707/Party Nr. 1,202,729. Holder of EK I. and II. Class. For details see his Personal-Akte NA, A3343-SSO-143.

165 SS-Obersturmbannführer Paul Herms: born 29 September 1903, SS-Nr. 129,135/Party Nr. 5,274,317. Holder of EK I. Class, saw active service with the SS-V.T.-Division (mot) (with both the 'Germania' and 'Der Führer' regiments) and then from February 1942 until April 1943 with the 6th SS-Gebrigsdivision 'Nord'. For further details of his career see his Personal-Akte, NA, A3343-SSO-091a.

166 SS-Standartenführer Friedrich Beyersdorff: born 9 August 1892, in Kiel, SS-Nr. 405,820/Party Nr. 4,738,054. Holder of EK I. and II. Class.

167 For the appointment see his service record, SS-Führungshauptamt Berlin Wilmersdorf, 1.12.43, IIa/Az 21c 16 Lg,-/Ge, Personalverfung Der SS-Obersturmbannführer Friedrich Beyersdorff. NA, A3343-550-220.

168 Born 10.11.1911. SS-Nr. 490,441. Personal-Akte NA A3343-SSO-181A.

169 SS-Sturmbannführer Josef Remberger: born 9 June 1903, in Steinweg nr Regensburg, SS-Nr. 267,977/Party Nr. 1,929,332. Holder of EK I. Class. He transferred from the 4.SS-Polizei Div. Personal-Akte NA, A3343-SSO-023B.

170 SS-Hauptsturmführer Wolfgang Wuttig: born 22 October 1915, SS Nr. 423,123. See Personal-Akte NA A3343-SSO-017C.

171 SS-Hauptsturmführer Karl Bristot: born 12 September 1915, SS-Nr. 202,908/Party Nr. 4,887,138. Formerly member of the '4.SS-Polizei Panzergrenadier Division'. Holder of Deutsches Kreuz in Gold, EKI. Class, KVK with Swords, Verwundetenabzeichen in Silber. Personal-Akte NA, A3343-SSO-107.

172 SS-Sturmbannführer Hermann Kaschner: born 7 November 1914, Party Nr. 5,177,822: SS Nr. 317,675. See Personal-Akte NA A3343-SSO-155A.

173 SS-Obersturmbannführer Franz Magill: born 22 August 1900, SS Nr. 132,620/Party Nr. 4,137171. Holder of EK I. and II. Class. See Personal-Akte Franz Magill, NA, A3343-SSO-288A.

174 For a staff listing as of 22 October 1943, see Die Waffen-SS und Polizei 1939–45 (Führung und Truppe) Kurt Mehner, Militär-Verlag, Klaus D. Patzwall, Norderstedt, 1995, p. 225.

175 Born 24 September 1902, in Malaschiwzi (Ternopil Oblast). In 1924 Michael Brygidyr completed high school and served in the Polish Army in which he graduated from a non commissioned officers school. From 15 July 1940, - 19 August 1942, he served in the Wehrmacht and from 20 August 1942 - 5 March 1943, in Schutzmannschaft 201 as commander of 2 company with the rank of SS-Hauptsturmführer before enlisting in the 14 Gal. Div. on 17 July 1943. He attended a retraining course at SS-Pz.Gren.Sch. Prosetschnitz - Galiz. Offz. Lehrgang in Leschan. His appointment with the '14 Gal. Div.' with the rank of SS-Hauptsturmführer was confirmed 1 November 1943. His retraining was completed after attending the 15 Batl. Führer Lehrgang at Antwerpen from 3-29 January1944, after which he was appointed as commander of I./WGR 29. For details see his SS-Officer file, NA, A3343-SSO-112.

176 Mykola Palienko: born 12 September 1896, Besidkor, Ukraine. He enlisted in the Galician Div. on 17 May 1943.

177 SS-Hauptsturmführer Wilhelm Allerkamp: born 21.9.1913 in Wehsede an der Weser, SS Nr. 357,155, Party Nr. 1429 593. Former member of the 4.SS-Pol.Pz.Gren.Div. See Personal-Akte, NA, A3343-SSO-008.

178 Heike states whenever possible Freitag even reserved company and platoon commands for Germans. Heike, Eng. ed., *op cit.*; p. 15.

179 Those marked with * exact birthdates unknown but likely to have been around 25 years old.

180 Email to author Myron Radzykewycz, 27 March 2010.

181 Beyersdorff had commanded a regiment in the *Polizei* Division while Forstreuter had previously commanded a battalion.

182   Wittenmeyer, Allerkamp, and Kurzbach, were amongst the most prominent of the German battalion commanders as were Sparsam, and Gläss who were battery commanders all of whom had previously served with the 4 *Polizei* Panzer Grenadier Division. Other former members of this division who served on the Galician Division's staff included Schaaf, Kopp, Georgi, and Schmitt.

183   This formation was comprised of three companies which were subsequently split up and assigned to the infamous Einsatzgruppes' A, B and C'. Dern's activities during his tour of duty with this unit were sufficient to ensure that he faced allegations of war crimes for which he was subsequently tried and sentenced in the early nineteen sixties. See Das Sonderkommando 4a der Einsatzgruppe C und die mit diesem kommando eingesetzten Einheiten wahrend des Russland - Feldzuges in der Zeit vom 22.6.1941 bis zum Sommer 1943, Zentrale Stelle der Landesjustizverwaltungen, Ludwigsburg, den 30.12.1964. pp. 43-44. At the time Dern held the rank SS-Sturmbannführer.

184   Personal-Akte NA A3343-SSO-181A.

185   See Beurteilung für den SS-Obersturmbannführer Friedrich Dern, geb.am: 5.3.96, dated 20.4.1944 Personal-Akte NA A3343-SSO-181A.

186   Personal-Akte NA, A3342-SSO-215.

187   See Beurteilung für den SS-Sturmbannführer Hans-Boto Emil Forstreuter, geb. 1.11.1912, SS Nr. 422 180 v RDA: 9.11.1942. dated 28 April 1944, Personal-Akte NA, A3342-SSO-215.

188   Personal-Akte, NA, A3343-SSO-091a.

189   See Beurteilung für den SS-Obersturmbannführer Paul Herms, geb. 29.9.03, SS Nr. 422 180 v R.D.A.: 20.4.43. Personal-Akte, NA, A3343-SSO-091a.

190   See Beurteilung für den SS-Obersturmbannführer Friedrich Beyersdorff, geb. 9.8.92, R.D.A.: 30.1.43. dated 22. Juni 1944. Personal-Akte NA, A3343-550-220.

191   Magill graduated from the post of riding instructor at the SS-academy at Braunschweig, to command a squadron of cavalry in the SS-Totenkopfverbände. In September 1939 he was assigned to SS-Cavalry Regiment 1, and later was commander of SS-Cavalry Regiment 2 which undertook anti-partisan operations in the remote swamps of the Pripyat marshes. For details of this particular action see 'Unsere Ehre Heisst Treue, (Bericht uber den Verlauf der Pripjet-Aktion', 12 August 1941) *op cit*.; pp. 227-30, and Ruth-Bettina Birn; 'Zweierlei Wirklichkeit. Fallbeispiele zur Partisanbekampfung im Osten' in Wegner (ed) Zwei Wege, p. 275. Confirmation of Magill's appointments can be found in his service record (Personal-Akte Franz Magill) NA, A3343-SSO-288A. After the war Magill was tried in Braunschweig (20.04.1964) and found guilty of complicity in murder of at least 5254 cases and at least 100 cases of attempted murder for which he was sentenced to five years imprisonment. See SKs 1/63 - in JuNSV Lfd Nr. 570 - vol. 20. On 15th November 1941, Magill was re-assigned to the staff of the HSSPF in White Russia with the rank of SS-Sturmbannführer.

192   SS-Hauptsturmführer Karl Bristot: born 12 September 1915, Fohnsdorf (Steiermark), SS-Nr. 202,908/Party Nr. 4,887,138. Personal-Akte NA, A3343-SSO-107.

193   See Beurteilung für SS-Hauptsturmführer Karl Bristot, den 22. Juni 1944, *Ibid*.

194   The SS-Führungshauptamt was the operations headquarters of the whole SS, responsible for training, organisation and employment with the exception of tactical deployment of the Waffen-SS field divisions.

195   Papers from his personal file confirm that SS-Untersturmführer Hanel (born 18.07.1912, Schlettau/Anaberg), served with 1./SS-Totenkopf-Reiterstandarte and at Majdanek. AA.

196   Grigorij Osowoy, born 12.10.1923 in Liman/Kharkiv, Ukraine had previously served with the 44.Inf.Div. at Stalingrad where he was wounded. After recovering from his wounds he was sent to the Trawniki camp in October 1942 before requesting a transfer to the SS-Freiwilligen-Division

'Galizien' at Heidelager which was approved on 11 August 1943. Details of Osowoy's service record and transfer are well chronicled in a series of documents for example, SS-Standortkommandantur Lublin der Waffen-SS, Lublin, den 11. August 1943, Az.: 23/43/Vo/Hg, Betr.; Versetzungsgsuch des SS-Wachmann Georg Ossowoy,[*sic*] geb. 12.10.1923, Bezug: Gesuch des Osowoy v.1.8.43. SA.

197   There are several such examples of non-Ukrainian individuals who were transferred to the 14 Galician Division because they were bilingual in Russian or Polish, such as Jakob Wiens (born 21.09.1901), a German born in Muntau, Ukraine. Wiens who spoke both, was a former member of the *Allgemeine SS* who transferred to the Waffen-SS in January 1940. In September 1941, his knowledge of the Russian language was sufficient to earn him a posting to *Der Wirtschafter Russland-Süd* (SS economic and administrative Department) in Kiev. In November 1943, Wiens transferred for service with the Galician Division with the commissioned rank of SS-Obersturmführer in the Division's Nachschub-Truppen (supply section), in all probability because of his fluency in both Russian and Polish. Personal statement, Jakob Wiens, München 8.2.1962. SA.

198   In extreme cases individuals were openly arrogant and contemptuous toward the Ukrainians 'boasting of their German superiority'. The commander of the 30th Regiment SS-Obersturmbannführer Hans Boto Forstreuter and his adjutant SS-Hauptsturmführer Kurkowski were among the worst culprits for displaying this kind of behaviour (letter to author E. Shypailo, 20 September 1994). The assertion that some of the senior German officers displayed something akin to Ukrainophobia is confirmed by the Division's Operations Officer W.D Heike whose memoir gives a balanced view of the German officer personnel assigned to the unit. Heike, Eng ed., *op cit*.; pp. 12-15.

199   For further details see Personal-Akte Wolf Dietrich Heike, NA, A3343-SSO-76A. Heike's claim that he remained a member of, and was paid by the General Staff up until the end of the war (hence retaining his Wehrmacht rank) is substantiated by his Soldbuch, a copy of which is in the author's possession. His rank was therefore converted to that of SS-Sturmbannführer. Heike was appointed to the post from 1 January1944, although he actually arrived at Heidelager on 10 January1944.

200   On 1.4.1934, Heike enlisted as an officer cadet in the 2, Artillery Regiment at Schwerin, before going on to attend the Kriegsschule in München. He served as a battery officer in the Artillery Regiment at Rendsburg and on 1.4.1936, was commissioned as a 2nd Lieutenant. At the outbreak of World War II, Heike was serving as battery chief with 2. Artillery Regiment in the 30 Infantry Division and took part in both the Polish and western campaigns winning the Iron Cross II. Class on 4.11.1939. The Iron Cross I. Class followed soon after on 6.11.1940. On 1.12.1940, he was posted with his battery to the newly formed 110 Infantry Division with which he later fought against the Soviet Union becoming on 1 October 1941, first aide-de-camp (01) on the Division's staff. From 1 September 1942, Heike took part in general staff training with the 5. Pz. Division in the heavy defensive fighting in the sector to the north east of Vyazma. From 1.3.- 30.5.1943, he attended the *Kriegsakademie* in Berlin and from 25.6.1943, served as 2 general staff officer (1b) with the 122. Infantry Division in the Staraya Russa sector. On 1.8.1943 he was promoted to the rank of Major. Heike was also the recipient of Sturmabzeichen, and the Ostmedaille. See Personal-Akte Wolf Dietrich Heike, Lebenslauf and Personalangaben, NA, A3343-SSO-76A, and Soldbuch, AA.

201   Heike himself describes his position as '1. *Führungsgehilfe des Div.Kdr.*' - i.e.; first assistant to the Divisional commander. His main duties were as Operations Officer. As a major on the General Staff of the German Army, Heike was assigned by the then Chief of Staff of the OKH Generaloberst Zeitzler, to temporary service with the Waffen-SS because of the severe shortage within the Waffen-SS of 1a's.

202   Freitag's evaluation which is dated 1 July 1944, concludes with the statement 'H[eike] stands firm on the grounds of nationalsozialistischen ideology', although it is hard to see how this could be the case especially as he was never a member of the Nazi Party. See Galizische SS-Freiw.Div, div.Gef. St., den 1. Juli 1944, Kommandeur, Beurteilung für den SS-Sturmbannführer Wolf-Dietrich Heike, Geb.am:27.6.13, R.D.A.:1.8.43 1 Generalstabsoffizier. Personal-Akte Wolf Dietrich Heike, NA, A3343-SSO-76A.

203   Richard Landwehr, Fighting For Freedom, Bibliophile Legion Books, Silver Spring, Maryland, 1985, p. 204.

204   Born 19 April 1914, Zweibrücken, SS-Nr. 422,124. Party member who served in the SA from 5 March 1933 - 1 April 1935. Prior to joining the 14 Gal. Div, Wittenmeyer joined the 4.Polizei Div., 30 January1940, and was later attached to 'Kampfgruppe Fegelein' from 1 December 1942, to 1 February 1943. See Personal-Akte Friedrich Wittenmeyer, NA, A3343-SSO-002C.

205   Heike, Eng ed., *op cit.*; p. 6.

206   There is evidence that German commanding officers at regimental, battalion, company and platoon level escaped punishment for blunders or mistakes for which they were fully responsible as will be seen in later chapters.

207   Born 17 May 1896, Perevozets, Kalush Oblast, Paliiv was a member of the Polish parliament (Sejm) from 1928-30. He enlisted into the Galician Division on 17 July 1943. (Information taken from his service record, SA).

208   Hunczak, 'The Ukrainian...', *op cit.*; p. 4. 6.

209   The account continues 'The following day Hauptsturmführer Paliiv came to my room and asked me 'What sort of discussion did you have with the Germans last night? Your discussion was reported to the Divisional commander in the presence of a Divisional judge and they were having discussions about your statements'. Paliiv told the commander that my remarks were correct. That people did not wish to be called Galicians. Paliiv stated that German officers wish to continue this discussion with me if I wished to come to the officer's lounge. I told Paliiv that today was my Christmas and so was tomorrow, but that after that I could talk to them as much as they wished. The Divisional commander sent my case to Berlin. Two or three weeks later the commander declared that name Galician would be changed to Ukrainian. Regarding the Trident, he said the military commission stood by the coat of arms of L'viv. The reasons given were that Galicia was the most enlightened part of Ukraine and that the coat of arms of Galicia should remain as the coat of arms of the Division'. Dmytro Ferkuniak, Spomyny z Zhyttia Dywiziji Halychyna (Memoirs from Life in the Division 'Galicia') unpublished manuscript. p. 18.

210   Letter to author Theo Andruszko, 20 April 2010.

211   Jaroslav Owad, Bo viyna viynoiu, L'viv, 1999. p. 86.

212   In his memoirs Heike acknowledges that the Division's command was aware of this problem but unable to take effective preventative action as long as it was based at Heidelager. Heike, Eng. ed., *op cit.*; p. 25.

213   Freiw.SS-Schütze Nikolaus Skyba, born 20.02.1916 in Selyska, Pidhorodyscha, he had previously served with the Wehrmacht as an interpreter.

214   Freiw.SS-Schütze Serhi Surkiv, born 22.2.1913.

215   Fernschreiben 35984 Au Gericht der 14 Galizischen SS-Freiw.Division and Urteil zur Bestätigung und Gnadensashen 35988. AA. In his memoirs Nahayevsky relates: 'One day I was visiting the prison, where I saw W.Obstuf. Baranenko, commander of the 6 company of the 30 Regiment, who was from Greater Ukraine. He volunteered for the Division from a German POW camp. Some maintain that the Gestapo arrested him for his hatred of the Germans. I was told Baranenko was

a capable officer and popular among his soldiers. W-Uscha. Yasinsky from the same company was arrested together with him. I had a conversation with them from which I learned that they both were charged with cooperation with the UPA, specifically that they were issuing falsified furlough documents and railway passes for personnel who travelled home but never came back to Neuhammer. The Gestapo said that the printed forms and the stamp were authentic, but the signatures were forged. Both prisoners pleaded not guilty. They remained in jail when the Division was departing to the front, [...] I could not visit them and do not know what happened to them after my departure to Wandern'. Dr Izydor Nahayewsky, Memoirs of a Field Chaplin, p. 72.

216　Even after receiving a death sentence Baranenko continued to write letters pleading for clemency. The sentence all the time being set aside pending an examination of these letters. Until the end of the war he was incarcerated in Dachau from where he was eventually liberated by the Americans. He returned to the USSR, where he was also convicted of being a former member of the Galician Division and died in November 1991 in the village Dobromil (Starosambirsky district of L'viv.)

217　Born 19 September 1914. Graduated from Berlin technical University as an aero engineer just before the war, and held a flying license. As a member of OUN he was a liaison messenger charged with various assignments and directly reporting to Riko Jary, one of the OUN leaders in Ukraine. He took part in the Beyersdorff campaign as Adjutant to Bristot, and later adjutant to Forstreuter who commanded WGR 30. In June 1944 he was transferred to the artillery regiment as the commander of the 2 battery of the II./battalion. On 25 July he was wounded in the leg and taken prisoner. He was in a POW hospital in Atkarsk Saratov County until September 1946, following whivch he worked in an airplane plant in Zagorsk. In December 1946 he received Soviet citizenship but remainder as a special settler (with several restrictions). He held the position of director of the technical section and later chief engineer of the plant. He married there and had 2 children. In 1954 he was freed from his special settler status and went to L'viv but unable to find employment, returned to his old place of work. In 1966 he got a job in a plant run by the Academy of sciences in L'viv. Letter to author R. Kolisnyk, 9 April 1996.

218　Basic Guidelines for Field Chaplains of the Division issued by Father Mychailo Levenets (undated), SA.

219　*Ibid.* For full text see Melnyk, To Battle, *op cit.*; p. 328.

220　Nahayewsky, *op cit.*; p. 72-73.

221　Having a civilian organisation directly attached to the Galician Division was a unique distinction within the German military establishment.

222　A list of Ukrainian candidates for the propaganda-Zug den SS-Schützendivision Galizien dated 13 July 1943, gave the following names:
Wortberichters (journalists): Ivan Martschuk, Ivan Durbak, Stephan Konrad, Lev Schankiwskyj. Filmberichters (film reporters): Jaroslav Kezalo, Volodymyr Ratysch, Vladimir Dawydok, Roman Pryjma, Rabij Ewstachij. Rundfunksprecher (radio broadcasters): Stanislav Krawlschyschyn, Wasyl Bavuza, Demijan Lischlschynskyi. Zeichner (illustrators): Mychajlo Mychalewytsch, Bohdan Makohin, Julian Woljanjuk, Andrij Lepkyj. Rundfünktechniken (radio technician): Lev Tschotyzbak, Mykhailo Tzezkiwnyk, Jurij Holobradskyj. Bildberichter (photo-reporters): Eugen Brykowytsch, Ivan Danyschtschuk, Ing. Kurylowytsch, Ivan Kowalskyj. Lemberg den 13.Juli 1943, Verzeichniss der Kandidaten für den Propaganda-Sug den SS-Schützendivision Galizien, ABFC.

223　Letter to author O. Lysiak, 19 March 1996.

224　Memoirs of M. Ostroverkha, Visti Kombatanta No's. 2,3,4,5,6, (1972).

225　A good example of previous successful activities of this nature was the entertainment programme entitled the 'Great Concert of Selected Songs' performed by Ukrainian artists, at the L'viv Opera

House on 15 September 1943. Individuals were able to pick their favourite song and dedicate it to friends or family members serving in the Division, in return for a contribution being made to the welfare fund for Riflemen of the Galician Division, whereupon those traditional songs attracting the most donations were performed. The largest donations from single Galician families were also announced during the concert when the entire amount raised was presented to the Ukrainian Military Board. See flyer dated 10 August 1943, issued under the names of Dr Kost Pankivsky and Mychailo Kushnir in his capacity of Head of the Cultural Section of the L'viv branch of the Ukrainian Central Committee. SA.

226   Each parcel contained sugar, honey, baked goods, dry fruits, apples, cigarettes, nuts, shoe polish, toothpaste, shoe laces, a pencil, a Christmas card with greetings, a notebook and 10 postcards.

227   See Message to SS Ustuf SZILLAT, Liaison Officer of SS Ops HQ. in Wehrkreis X, Hamburg, from 14 Galician SS Volunteer Div. Abt. VI, SS Troop Training Area HEIDELAGER, signed pp. ZOGLAUER, SS Hstuf, and Cdr Abt, 6, on 17/12, HW 16/100 Copy No. 13 12/1/44, CX/MSS/Q.32. NA, PRO, Kew. In fact the delivery of the packages to Galicians in the named locations caused those within the British intelligence who were responsible for analysing the decrypted enigma messages to draw this amusing and entirely erroneous conclusion in their Top Secret Report which read;

'Top Secret, covering information received between 0800 hrs. 21/12 and 1800 hrs. 11/1/44. General.

1. Three documents, two of 17/12, and one of 29/12, dealing with Christmas comforts for Galician volunteers of the SS appear to throw some interesting light on the internal affairs of Germany. Comforts were being sent to 'volunteers of SS volunteer Division Galizien' in a number of places including: OSNABRUECK, HAMM, VERDUN, LUEBECK, HILVERSUM, KARLSTADT, RADOLFZELL, HAMBURG, MOERCHINGEN and MUENSTER; moreover this list is not complete. Four points should be noticed: (a) with the exception of HILVERSUM and MOERCHINGEN, no SS training units are known in these places. (b) In MUENSTER the information regarding the comforts was sent to [the] Liaison Officer of the SS Ops. HQ in Wehrkreis VI. (c) Most of the towns names are towns with fairly large populations, many of them bombed by the Allies. (d) SS Division Galizien is in training at HEIDELAGER.

It will be remembered that when volunteers for the SS from GALICIA were called for, the Germans announced that they had sufficient volunteers for six divisions [*sic*]: so far as is known to the present, however, only one division and five independent regiments have been formed. Also in the past, there have been several cases of Polish and White Russian Schützmannschaft battalions being sent in to keep order in GERMANY after air-raids. I[t] would, therefore, seem that these 'Galizien Volunteers' who received Christmas comforts are attached to the SS Div. Galizien for administrative purposes, but are being used in large towns for police and guard duties: that, in fact, **the Master Race is being kept in order by 'sub-men"** (author's emphasis). See SS REPORT NO. 12. Copy No.12 HW16/83, NA, PRO, Kew.

228   The Military Board simultaneously delivered 20 x 100kg of wheat, 4 x 100 kg of poppy seeds and 4 x 100 kg of honey for the preparation of the traditional sweet 'Kutya' and spent the sum of 100,000 Zloty on Christmas events and entertainment for the recruits.

229   NS 19/1785: Der Höhere SS-und Polizeiführer Ost Koppe to Dr Brandt, Cracow 8 Jan. 1944, 'Spenden der Bevölkerung des Districts Galizien für die 'SS-Freiwilligen-Division Galizien". HFD, H/10/75. The letter read 'I would ask you to inform the Reichsführer about this exemplary donation which bears witness to a considerable capacity for sacrifice in the Galician people'.

230   The Bandura is a Ukrainian musical instrument similar in construction and appearance to a Lute.

231   Ferkuniak, 'Spomyny....', *op cit.*; p. 17. Ferkuniak ascribes hardship of the families of Division members and the failure of the German authorities to provide the promised relief as the main cause.

232   *Ibid.*

233   The visits took place in late November/early December 1943. On his return, Dr Makarushka gave a very positive account to the Military Board on the conditions and training of these volunteers in France and their high morale. During the visit to the 4 Regiment, the German training instructors are said to have remarked to Wächter that the Ukrainians should be sent to fight only on the eastern front, and warned of a catastrophe if they should deployed anywhere else. On the whole Wächter was pleased with the visit and viewed the Ukrainian soldiers as intelligent and enthusiastic. For details of the report see 'Minutes of the Military Board', 14 December 1943, ABFC.

234   Himmler refers to this report in his letter to Wächter of 31 December 1943, See RF/M, 263, Field command. HFD, H/10/73.

235   To 14 Galician SS. Volunteer Infantry Division, from [Orpo] Chief of Staff, signed RODE, SS. Oberführer, on 11/12/43, Subject: Disbanding of Galician Polizei Regiments 6 and 7. HW16/100, Most Secret, Copy No. 13, CX/MSS/Q.41, 22/2/44, NA, PRO, Kew.

236   Teleprinter, Der Chef der Ordnungspolizei, Berlin, den 23 Dezember 1943, Kdo. g I (Org.3) Nr. 282/43 (g). Betr.; Abgabe von 2.000 Freiwilligen der 14. Gal. SS-Freiw.Regiment. BA-KO, R 19/326. The document specified these soldiers were to only bring with them their uniforms and personal kit and not their weaponry.

237   For further information relating to this unit see Schnellbrief Chef der Ordnungspolizei/kdo. I 0 (3) Nr. 455 II/43 v 20.8.1943 Betr.; Aufstellung des Gal. SS-Freiw. Ersatz-Batls. Heidenheim, R 19/103, BA-KO.

238   Letters to author I. Sadovey, 17 January1999 and 9 February 1999.

239   Letter to author I. Sadovey, 9 February 1999.

240   On 31 January1944, a second instruction was issued giving further explicit details of their disbandment. See Schnellbrief Der Chef der Ordnungspolizei, Berlin den 31. Januar 1944, O-Kdo.g I Org. (3) Nr.305/43 (g.). Betr.: Auflösung der Gal.SS-Freiw.Regimenter 6 u. 7, R 19/304, BA-KO.

241   Letters to author, I. Sadovey 17 January1999 and 9 February 1999.

242   See NA, T175 roll 141, frame 2668945.

243   Feld-Kommandostelle, 22 January1944: RF/N.36/141/44. HFD, H/10/76. Schützmannschafts-Bataillon 204 comprised of three companies of Ukrainians with a combined strength of around 500 men, predominantly from Galicia.

244   Der Reichsführer SS, Feldkommandostelle 5 July 1943, Tgb.Nr 35/88/43g RF/Bn. HFD, H/10/43.

245   It should be noted that a telegram concerning the transfer of the battalion dated 8 February 1944, sent to the Chef der Ordnungspolizei indicated that the final arrangements for the transfer had not yet been made when it asked; 'Please let us know at what time the Galician SS Volunteer Division will take over the battalion and when we can anticipate the return of the German personnel, who are presently attached to the battalion and also uniforms, equipment and motor-pool which is owned by the *Polizei* .....' See Der Chef der Ordnungspolizei Berlin NW7, den 8 Februar 1944, Kdo. g I Org.(11) Nr.96/43 (g). An SS-Führungshauptamt in Berlin-Wilmersdorf, Betr,: Übernahme des Schützmannschafts batl. 204 in die Galizische SS-Freiwilligen-Division, R 19/326, BA-KO.

246   Letter to author O. Horodysky, 26 February 1999.

247   *Ibid.*

248   Along with Governor Wächter, Dr Otto Bauer (Deputy Governor of Galicia), had devoted considerable effort to improving the attitude of the German administration towards the local residents, both Ukrainian and Polish, as well as to the organisation of the Galician Division.

249   The chief of the office of the Governor.

250   Originally the German *Sicherheitsdienst* were thought to have been behind the killings. Bauer, who was married to a Swiss national was unpopular with them because of his frequent interventions on behalf of interned or arrested Ukrainians. Had also resided in the USA immediately prior to World War II, which was enough in itself to alert the suspicions of the xenophobic German security services and fuel rumours that they were responsible for his death. The actual assassin Kuznetsov was captured by the UPA and executed by them on 2, March 1944 in Volyhnia.

251   On this occasion forty five members of the Divisional band travelled to L'viv. In its entirety the band consisted of seventy eight musicians. Initially it was led by Kapelmeister Andrij Krawchuk. Later this position was held by SS-Oberscharführer Johannes Thiessen. All musicians were trained as front line medics and were pre-assigned to the three infantry regiments. The Tennermarsch a traditional arrangement from the old Austro-Hungarian Army was chosen as the Divisional march.

252   This included greatcoats (ubermantel), woollen toques (a circular knitted pull over scarf).

253   The first public appearance of soldiers of the Division, albeit for entertainment purposes, was on Wednesday 15 September 1943, when the Divisional choir under Vasyl Ostashevskyj made a highly successful public appearance together with other Ukrainian artists, at the Wünsch Konzert held in the L'viv Opera House. The 'Great Concert of Selected Songs' was dedicated to the soldiers of the Galician Division and was broadcast on the radio on 21 September 1943 at 1900. Hrs. Flyer dated 10 August 1943, issued under the names of Dr Kost Panskivsky and Mychailo Kushnir in his capacity of Head of the Cultural Section of the L'viv branch of the Ukrainian Central Committee. AA. Also letter from Bohdan Kutny, 27 July 1999 who took part in the event several photographs of which later appeared in the Divisional newspaper Do Peremohy.

254   Letters to author W. Motyka, 15 April 1993, and M. Holowaty 30 October 1999.

255   Keczun, *op cit.*; p. 11.

3   First Combat Assignments

1   'Kovpak's' partisans' was the general designation of all Soviet partisans which fought in the north-western districts of Ukraine even though Major General Sydir Kovpak was only active in this area of Galicia during summer and autumn of 1943. Kovpak who was himself a Ukrainian Communist, had previously directed operations in the Sumy region using a mixture of Ukrainian and Russian Communist partisans.

2   Although ordinarily regular Wehrmacht or Waffen-SS combat formations stationed in the General Government were not subjected to the authority of the HSSPF, in exceptional cases individual frontline units were temporarily seconded for the execution of special assignments.

3   Wilhelm Koppe: SS-Obergruppenführer und General der Polizei: born 15 June 1896, SS-Nr. 25,955/Party Nr. 305,584.

4   It should be noted that both the 4 and 5 regiments were at this time temporarily seconded to the Ordungspolizei (ORPO) which greatly facilitated their deployment in this capacity.

5   See 'Personalverfugung der SS-Oberführer Fritz Freitag', SS-Führungshauptamt Amt V/Abt.IIa/Ref 2, Az.:21c 24 Fu.P. PZ, Gren, 29.1.1944. See Personal-Akte NA, A3343 SSO-220.

6   Beyersdorff's service record shows his appointment was effective as of 1 January 1944, see Personalverfugung, SS-Führungshauptamt, Amt V IIa/Az.; 21c 16 Lg,-/Ge. 1.12.43. Personal-Akte NA, A3343-SSO-066, although M. Dliaboha, states that he did not actually arrive at Heidelager until 7 January 1944. Visti Nr. 5-6 (43–44), May-June 1954.

7   A decrypted enigma message refers to a communication dated 13/2 addressed to Amt X, from 14 SS Freiw. Div, requesting urgent allocation of 45 cbm. 'O' ['Otto'] (ie Petrol) fuel as replacement

for fuel consumed in setting up 'Battle Group' on 9/2. See HW16/100, Most Secret, CX/MSS/Q.41, 22/2/44, NA, PRO, Kew.

8   Heike states that Himmler did not issue the order but had merely mentioned the possibility of using elements of the Division to fight the Soviet partisans active in western Ukraine. Koppe then conveyed the order on the basis of these discussions. See Heike, Eng ed., *op cit.*; pp. 20-21.

9   HW16/100, Most Secret, CX/MSS/Q.46, 16/3/44. NA, PRO, Kew.

10   Heike Eng ed., *op cit.*; p. 20.

11   M. Dlaboha, gives the date of the second order as being 15 February 1944, see Visti Nr. 131, 1969, pp. 101-103.

12   HW16/83, CX/MSS/SS Report 16. 24/2/44. NA, PRO, Kew.

13   *Ibid.*, p. 21. Roman Dolynsky, 'Boieva hrupa Bayersdorffa', Visti, Nr.'s. 3-6 (77-80), pp. 10-11: also Nr.'s. 7-10 (78-80), pp. 6-9. There is some discrepancy over the eventual size of the battle group. According to Dolynsky it consisted of two infantry battalions (the second being commanded by Waffen-Hauptsturmführer Rembalovych). For his part Heike omits the cavalry reconnaissance unit. Waffen-Obstuf. M. Malecky who took part in the organisation of both groups was originally assigned as the commander of one of the two infantry battalions, but remained in Heidelager when the order was revised omitting the second battalion. Letter to author R. Kolisnyk, 11 December 1997.

14   Other Ukrainian officers assigned to the artillery were: Waffen-Untersturmführer Mychailo Dliaboha, Waffen-Untersturmführer Krajczyk, and Waffen-Untersturmführer Roslak.

15   No exact date is available from surviving documentary records thus far found however 13 February seems likely as according to one participant 'Almost simultaneous with the return of the Honour Company we got our marching orders - to the Kochanivka railway station', email to author Theo Andruszko, 7 April 2012.

16   Immediately before departure the personnel selected to be part of KGr. Beyersdorff were hurriedly issued with arm shields and collar patches bearing the Galician lion emblem. In the absence of any instructions to the contrary the soldiers were directed incorrectly to attach the armshield to the lower right sleeve. Later this was changed to the correct position of the upper left sleeve.

17   M. Dlaboha, 'Boiova hrupa Bayersdorff ', Visti, Nr. 131, 1969, pp. 101-103.

18   Email to author Volodymyr Keczun, 30 December 2011.

19   Letter to author R. Kolisnyk, 2 January1998.

20   Altogether some 2,000 packages were distributed to the soldiers of Kampfgruppe Beyersdorff containing baked goods, meat and cigarettes, and copies of local newspapers and Do Peremohy were also distributed.

21   Letter to author M. Holowaty, 13 July 2000.

22   For further details see M. Dlaboha, 'Boiova hrupa...', *op cit.*

23   Chornij, unpublished memoirs, pp. 46-47.

24   *Ibid.*, p. 48.

25   Central State Archives of Supreme Body and Government of Ukraine. - Fund 3971. - Catalogue 1. - Folder 5. - Sheet 37.

26   Dlaboha, 'Boiova hrupa', *op cit.*

27   Letter to author J. Kunycky, 10 March 1993.

28   The 'Winter Campaigns' were offensives undertaken by troops of the Army of the Ukrainian National Republic against the White Russian and Bolshevik armies in 1919-20 and 1921, conducted as partisan warfare behind enemy lines.

29   M. Dlaboha, 'Boiova hrupa...', *op cit.*

30   518 Ortskommandantur I/524, 518/22 (Polizei-Lagemeldungen: February 1944) 'Der Kommandeur der Ordnungspolizei im District Lublin 1a, Lublin, den 25. Februar 1944, Tägliche Lagemeldung, (22/133) and) 'Der Kommandeur der Ordnungspolizei im District Lublin 1a, Lublin, den 29. Februar 1944, Tägliche Lagemeldung, (22/157), Lublin, Archiwum Panstwowe w Lublinie. (Hereafter cited as APL).

31   *Ibid.*, Der Kommandeur der Ordnungspolizei im District Lublin 1a, Lublin, den 5. März 1944, Tägliche Lagemeldung, (23/34-35), APL.

32   *Ibid.*

33   Der Kommandeur der Ordnungspolizei im District Lublin 1a, Lublin, den 7. März, 1944, Tägliche Lagemeldung, (23/47), APL.

34   Waffen-Hauptsturmführer Roman Dolynsky produced a comprehensive report on the activities of the Kampfgruppe. He wrote that in the third and final stage of the operation, elements of it took part in the assault on the bulk of the partisans which had been surrounded, inflicting significant casualties. However, a large group of around one hundred and fifty managed to escape to the north where the terrain was boggy. For further details of the operation see Dolynsky 'Boieva hrupa Bayersdorffa', Visti, Nr.'s. 3-6, 7-9, Munich, 1957.

35   Keczun, *op cit.*; pp. 11-13.

36   Letter to author R. Kolisnyk, 2 January 1998. Other elements entrained on 20 March 1944, Dolynsky, 'Boieva...', *op cit.*; Nr.'s. 7-10 (78-81), p. 8.

37   On the same day II./Gal.SS-Freiw. Rgt 5 received the order to return to its parent regiment on foot to Zwierzyniec and then by rail to Biala Podlaska.

38   Letter to author R. Kolisnyk, 2 January 1998.

39   An unconfirmed figure of ten killed and thirteen wounded is given as the number of casualties by V.Styrkul in 'We accuse', Kyiv, Dnipro Publishers 1984, p. 169.

40   Letter to author R. Kolisnyk, 2 January 1998.

41   'It was in the town (or village) of Ulanow. It was not exactly clear what had happened. Some said that he was shot through the window by the Soviet partisans, others claimed that he was not careful with his machine pistol and accidentally shot himself. The latter was most probable. At the time of the shooting I was in the next room, so I did not witness it, but myself and three friends took his body to the morgue at the cemetery. We buried him with the military honours the next day at the town of Krasnik'. Walter Motyka email to author, 12 January 2011.

42   Dolynsky gives a figure of approximately one hundred and fifty men who received decorations for their part in the campaign - Germans such as SS-Hauptsturmführer Kleinow, SS-Hauptsturmführer Bristot and SS-Obersturmführer Schneller, received the Kriegsverdienstkreuz (War Service Cross) I./Class while Ukrainians including Waffen-Hauptsturmführer Rembalovych Waffen-Hauptsturmführer Palijenko and Waffen-Hauptsturmführer Dolynsky received the Kriegsverdienstkreuz II./Class. See Dolynsky, 'Boieva...'.*op cit.*; Visti Nr.'s. 3-6, 7-9, 1957.

43   Heike, Eng. ed., *op cit.*; p. 22.

44   Dolynsky, 'Boieva...', *op cit.*; Visti, Nr.'s. 3-6, 77-80, p. 12.

45   Heike, Eng. ed., *op cit.*; p. 22.

46   This account as related by M. Malecky letter to author, 12 May 1995.

47   Email to author Theo Andruszko, 28 April 2011.

48   Chornij, *op cit.*; p. 47.

49   BdO Stuttgart.

50   An der Chef der Ordnungspolizei Berlin, Geheim, Kdo I Org (3) I Nr. 78/44, v 3.2.44 Nr. 552, Betr.: Marsch und Einsatzfähigkeit des Gal SS-Freiw. Rgt 4. SA.

51   BdO.Dag.Nr. 154 8/2 0855. An den RFSS und ChdDtPol. Chef der Ordnungspolizei in Berlin NW7, Betr.: Einsatzbereitschaft des Gal.SS-Freiw.Rgt.5, 3.2.1944. SA.

52   Der Chief der Ordnungspolizei, Abschrift, Berlin, den 9 Februar, 1944. Kdo.g I-Ia (i) Nr. 1020 11/43 (g), Fernschreiben, An die BdO in Stuttgart, Danzig, Nimwegen und Cracow, Betr,: Verlegung der Gal. SS-Freiw.Rgtr.4 und 5. BA-KO, R 19/326. The III battalion did not leave from Maastricht to which it had been temporally transferred, until 19 February. See KTB OB West v 1.2.-28.2.1944, RH 19 IV/22 and RH 19 IV/23, BA-MA.

53   At a session of the Governor and department chief in Cracow on 16 February 1944, Wächter explained:

'The population, in particular the general farming population, is as yet still anti-Bolshevik in its feelings. Should the Bolsheviks succeed in further pursuing their propaganda and in setting up a liberation army (Befreiungsarmee), then it would become impossible to discount the concern that they could make rapid gains in terms of influence. The nationalist youth of Ukraine is ready and willing to march. German propaganda should adopt a unified and consistent approach. Many of those Ukrainians who are friendly towards the Reich and allied to us have turned to the German leadership and declared 'Give us an opportunity. Show us that you have plans for us; perhaps self-administration as is the case in *Estland*'. The situation is ripe and cries out for political measures. A gesture must be made towards the wavering Ukrainians. This would enable us to take the wind out of the sails of the nationalist Ukrainian youth and turn it into an active component of German interests. The German political approach towards the Ukrainians is extraordinarily confused. A German radio station in Königsberg ended each transmission with the cry 'Hail, free Ukraine'. Should a Ukrainian say this openly in Lemberg then he would be arrested. This utter confusion in the official German approach, is intolerable. The drafting of young people from the R.K.U. and their deployment as FLAK soldiers in the Reich does not make sense in their eyes. It is contrary to the Reich's Ukrainian political policy. If an absolutely consistent and positive position regarding Ukraine is not taken soon, dire consequences will result. The only basis (for this) is represented by the SS-Schützendivision Galizien. This has succeeded in catching for German interests, a section of the active Ukrainian youth who want to march. There are still many Ukrainians who are convinced that while no future could be expected under Stalin, prospects (of a future) are still being offered by the Germans. It is requested that a decisive emphasis is given to the political factors, when deploying the first formations of the SS-Freiwilligen-Division Galizien. The force is initially, to be valued in terms of propaganda rather than militarily, being poorly armed, not possessing heavy weapons and Paks (anti-tank guns) etc. Every thing depends upon how it performs in its first active deployment. The political element should not be neglected. It may be a good idea to make among its ranks political arrangements in our direction, by giving it politically well disposed Ukrainian officers. The volunteers would then receive constant propaganda influence via these officers'. Frank, Tagebuch, *op cit.*; p. 800.

54   The detachment from the 12 MG-Lehrkompanie and the Divisional band.

55   Wächter suggested that the II./4 Rgt be used.

56   Teleprinter message from Berger to Himmler, shas nr. 1049 14/2/44 2130, H/10/77. For full text see Melnyk, To Battle *op cit.*; p. 101.

57   Himmler to HSSPF Ost SS-Obergruppenführer Koppe, 16 February 1944, H/10/78.

58   The III battalion went via Maastricht in the Netherlands. It arrived here on 8th February 1944, and was temporarily subordinated to the commander of the Wehrmacht in the Netherlands (Gen.Kdo. LHHHVIII.AK). The next day on 9 February 1944, Himmler ordered the transfer of the battalion to rejoin its parent regiment under the command of the *Ordnungspolizei* in Krakow, however departure was delayed until 19 February.

59   The entry dated 7 March 1944, in 'Minutes of the Meetings of the Military Board 'Galicia' Shevchenko Scientific Society of Canada vol. 30: 1993, pp. 91-93, refers to the warm welcome received by 4 Regiment in Galicia.

60   A full list of attendees as well as the text of the speeches made on this occasion were published in 'Das Generalgouvernement', 25 February, 1944. A copy can be found in the Schevchenko Archive, London.

61   For the full text see Melnyk, To Battle *op cit*.; p. 101. The text of the speech made by Pyndus was quoted verbatim in an article in the Lemberger Zeitung of 25 February 1944, entitled 'Marsch in ein neue glückliche Zukunft' (March to a New, Successful Future). SA.

62   Speech of Governor Wächter to 1./4th Regiment. L'viv, 25 February 1944. SA.

63   While the higher German authorities actively opposed any association with the UPA, in at least one instance (i.e. 6./II), contact was instigated by the German company commanders who instructed the Ukrainian soldiers to give the daily password to the local UPA units in order to avoid any unnecessary conflict. Later, this co-operation was further extended when one UPA unit acted as an escort for the company. Verbally to author I. Maksymiw, 27 November 1995.

64   Lemberger Zeitung, *op cit*.

65   In the Cracow area some elements of this regiment were reported to have been assigned to Kampfgruppe Rheingold to fight against the partisan brigade Naumow, in the forests of Bilgoraj - 100 km south of Lublin.

66   Reisebericht u. Bericht über die Besprechung mit dem Kommandeur des Gal. SS-Freiw.Rgt.4, Major der Schutzpolizei Binz, R19/333, Bundesarchiv.

67   Hence a German medical officer was requested as a replacement. *Ibid*.

68   According to the account of M.Khronviat the HQ of the II battalion should have been in the village of Berlyn but was moved to Koniushkiv. See Tys-Krokhmaliuk 'U Zbarazi', Visti, Munich, #15, 1952, pp. 18-19.

69   Verbally to author W. Skilnyk, 23 December 2012.

70   Verbally to author W. Skilnyk, 23 and 26 December 2012.

71   See this account and other related documents see NA, T354, roll 177, frame no's 3828925 to 3828938.

72   See Tys-Krokhmaliuk 'U Zbarazi' *op cit*.; pp. 18-19.

73   Positive verification of Soviet collaboration with the Poles in Huta Pieniacka can be found in Mieczyslaw Juchniewicz, 'Z dzialalnosci organizacyjno-bojowej gwardii ludowej w obwodzie lwowskim ppr-gl,' in Wojskowy Przeglad Historyczny, (Warsaw), Nr. 4 (48), pp. 153-154.

74   The first two casualties were Roman Andriichuk and Oleksa Bobak, lavish funerals for whom took place at the Heldenfriedhoff, Brody, on 2 March 1944, accompanied by a Luftwaffe band. Alfred Bisanz was present as was Governor Wächter who laid a wreath. The third soldier Yurii Hanusiak, was wounded and died a few days later in hospital in L'viv. He was buried in the city on 7 March. Gal. SS Freiw. Regt. 4, O.U., den 3.3.1944, Regiments Tagesbefehl Nr. 10. SA.

75   The other two members of the Military Board were Jurij Krokhmaliuk and Dr Liubomyr Makarushka.

76   For details of the action in which Khronoviat himself took part see the 'Minutes of the Military Board' *op cit*.; 7 March 1944, pp. 91-92.

77   See for example Antoni B. Szczesniak and Wieslaw Z. Szota, Droga do nikad (Warsaw, 1973), p. 127. This account as well as those of other Polish or Soviet authors is largely based on the report on the action sent less than a month later by the underground Polish Armia Krajowa to the Polish Government in exile in London which states; 'On February 27, 44 [sic] at 5.00 am the 14th

Division of the Ukrainian SS [*sic*] surrounded the village Huta Pieniacka from three sides, shooting from a distance at houses, set some buildings on fire and then entered the village, plundering all the belongings of the inhabitants. The people were gathered in the church or shot in the houses. Those gathered in the church, men women and children were taken outside in groups, children killed in front of their parents, their heads smashed on tree trunks or buildings then thrown into the burning houses. Men and women were partially shot in the cemetery, partially gathered in barns, where they were shot at and then set on fire with a grenade. The village was completely burned down. The only people who saved themselves were those who on finding out about the approaching Ukrainian SS, managed to hide in the forests (only men) or those who pretended to be dead or managed to hide in potato holes in the basements. Right now it is difficult to establish how many survived as they spread themselves around the area. Many injured with burned arms and legs are being treated, impossible to say how many since people from surrounding villages took them to their homes after the SS left. Not a single shot was fired on the SS division on the part of the inhabitants since they were considered part of the German Army.'

Reported by Uta WSK Huta Pieniacke who survived badly burned. The action of the SS was to be a revenge killing for 4 SS men on Feb 23 who in the number of about 60 entered the village in the evening and begun to plunder the houses. Since they wore German uniforms and spoke Ukrainian, they were taken for a disguised band. Thus the local defense action started killing 2 for sure and wounding several. Since the Ukrainian SS came to the area such cases may repeat themselves in every Polish village.' A copy of this report can be found in the Huta Peniatska case files at the Cracow Regional Office of the Polish Main Commission [for the investigation of crimes against the Polish nation]. This version of the events and subsequent witness statements by survivors relate the event in graphic and dramatic detail but contain several significant discrepancies. For example some statements refer to 'Ukrainian Nationalists' (i.e. partisans) who accompanied the pacifying force.

78   The only non Polish evidence thus far which states the Ukrainians were responsible for the pacification can be found in the Reports of the Representatives of the Ukrainian aid Committee (subordinated to the Ukrainian Central Committee) currently located in the Michael Chomiak Collection in the Provincial Archives of Alberta 85,191, folder 59 sheet 358 under item 55/3. This mentions the incident at Huta and states unequivocally that the 'pacification' was conducted by Galician soldiers in retaliation for the death of their two comrades on the outskirts of the village. However even this report begins by quoting an incorrect date of 'On 29 February 1944'. At the time of writing the author has found no evidence which is sufficient to substantiate either sides contention beyond all reasonable doubt.

79   Mitscherling held the rank of Hauptmann der Schutzpolizei.

80   Gert Frick, 'Fester Platz Tarnopol 1944', Verlag Rombach Freiburg, 1969, pp. 26-27.

81   For details see Vasyl Petrovskyj, Visti, Nr. 6-7, 1952, Munich.

82   Frick, 'Fester...", *op cit.*; p. 31.

83   *Ibid.*, p. 44.

84   Anlagen zum KTB Pz.AOK 4, RH 21-4/201, BA-MA.

85   Frick, 'Fester....', *op cit.*; p. 68.

86   In 'Berezhany' Visti, No's. 4-5, Munich, 1952, Jurij Krokhmaliuk, states that only two men returned while other sources give a figure of four. For the personal account of one survivor see Vasyl Petrovskyj, Visti, Nr.'s. 6-7, Munich, 1952.

87   The photographer was Karl Weyer and the reporter was Oleh Lysiak. Two of the Ukrainian recipients were Wasyl Wykluk and Wasyl Bilecky who was recommend for the award after

capturing and recovering a Soviet light anti-tank gun during a combat action in the locality. Letter to author O. Lysiak, 14 June 1996.

88   518 Ortskommandantur I/524, 518/22 (Polizei-Lagemeldungen: March 1944) 'Der Kommandeur der Ordnungspolizei im District Lublin 1a, Lublin, den 28. März 1944, Tägliche Lagemeldung', (23/183) and) 518/24, Polizei-Lagemeldungen: April 1944) 'Der Kommandeur der Ordnungspolizei im District Lublin 1a, Lublin, den 6. April 1944, Tägliche Lagemeldung', (24/37).APL.

89   For further details of the activities of the 5 Regiment see unpublished memoirs of Josaphat Konchak, Visti Kombatanta, Nr.3, 1996, pp. 83-88.

90   Ukrainian sources give a total figure of around one hundred men from the Regiment having successfully deserted to the UPA, while it was stationed in the vicinity of Zamosc, see Shankovsky 'UPA and the Division...', reprinted in Visti, July-August 1954, # 7-8 (45-46), p. 10. In the article the author describes in some detail the UPA units in which former Divisional soldiers excelled.

91   518 Ortskommandantur I/524, 518/23 (Polizei-Lagemeldungen: March 1944) 'Der Kommandeur der Ordnungspolizei im District Lublin 1a, Lublin, den 9. März 1944, Tägliche Lagemeldung, (23/59), Lublin, APL.

92   *Ibid.*, Der Kommandeur der Ordnungspolizei im District Lublin 1a, Lublin, den 16. März 1944, Tägliche Lagemeldung, (23/109), APL.

93   *Ibid.*, 518/24 (Polizei-Lagemeldungen: April 1944) 'Der Kommandeur der Ordnungspolizei im District Lublin 1a, Lublin, den 20 April 1944, Tägliche Lagemeldung, (24/127), APL.

94   Two such instances have been verified by former members of the Regiment; the first in a squad of about 50 men stationed in the village of Stryzhiv, (Oleksandr Kozak, letter to the author dated 22 March 1993) and the second involving a company stationed in the village of Bilapidlaska. (Verbally, to author S. Reskovitch, 27 November 1995). In all probability the plans were discovered by Polish speaking Germans in the units. Additionally, in his memoirs Josaphat Konchak mentions the desertion of the 1 platoon, 2 company 1 battalion to the UPA. ABFC.

95   Easter Monday. The term 'Wet Monday' originating from a pagan custom representing the cleansing of the soul when males chase after girls and splash them with water.

96   Letters to author Roman Bilohan, 26 December 2012 and 6 February 2013.

97   Roman Chomickyj, unpublished memoirs, pp. 1-3.

98   For full text see Melnyk, To Battle, *op cit.*; p. 104. Fernschreiben, + kdr LbL nr 298 16/5/1530, an den höheren SS-u. pol.führer ost - führungsstab roem. eins a - Cracow, betr.: roem.eins a banden meldung. geheim. AA.

99   SS-Oberscharführer Rudolf Baronyay and SS-Untersturmführer Emil Weis both members of 3./ Gal.SS-Freiw.Regt.5, (Kriegsverdienstkreuzes II.Klasse mit Schwerter,) also took part in defensive actions against partisan attacks in Kosin on 26 April 1944 and Zabuze on 13 May 1944. Another example, SS-Oberwachtmeister d.Sch. Wilhelm Glück 1./Gal.SS-Freiw.Regt.5, was decorated with the (*Kriegsverdienstkreuzes II.Klasse mit Schwerter,*) for bravery under enemy fire during a heavy partisan attack in the forests south of Lublin in Zwierzenie and Susic (district of Bilgoraj); I./Gal. SS-Freiw.Rgt.5, Dresden, den 6.12.1944, An den Höheren SS-und Polizeiführer in Cracow, Betr.; Anträge auf Verleihung des Kriegsverdienstkreuzes II.Klasse mit und ohne Schwerter. SA.

100   Frank, Tagebuch, *op cit.*; p. 828.

101   Der Chef der Ordnungspolizei Berlin 22.4.44 Tgb Nr. Ia/1269/44 geh Betr. SS-Freiw. 4 und 5. SS-Oberführer Rode. Abschrift von Fernschrift NS 19/1785, BA-KO.

102   On one occasion, in a speech in Cracow on 12 May 1944, Wächter declared 'The commander of the 'Galician' Division was thoroughly satisfied with his troops'. Frank Tagebuch, *op cit.*; pp. 847-848.

4 Final Preparations

1 This was facilitated by the departure of the approx 21,000 men of the 13. SS-Freiwilligen b.h. Division (Kroatien) from Neuhammer to Croatia in mid-February 1944 which left sufficient space for the 14 Galician Division.

2 Notification of the impending move was duly sent to the appropriate authorities such as the Field Equipment Inspectorate in Berlin and the Transport Officer of the SS by various departments of the Division's staff including the second general stabsoffz. from Section Ib (Quartermaster supply - weapons and ammunitions) SS-Obersturmführer Schaaf as early as 13 February. For further details see, HW16/100, Most Secret, CX/MSS/Q.41, 22/2/44, NA, PRO, Kew.

3 The 14.Galiz.SS-Frew.Div. is listed as being based at Neuhammer as of 20 February 1944.

4 Large parts of Heidelager were still under construction.

5 Letter to author Orest Slupchynskyj, 4 January 2013.

6 Letter to author Theo Andruszko, 3 January 2011.

7 Keczun, *op cit.*; p. 13.

8 Born 12.11.87 at Eberswalde, CO I R 372 1.9.39. Kdt Tr. Ub.Pl Neuhammer 15.11.43 until it was captured by the Red Army.

9 See message to SS Ops. HQ II, Org. Abt. from 14 Gal. SS. Volunteer Div., signed pp. Div. Kdo, Second General Staff Officer SCHAAF, SS Oberstuf., CX/MSS/Q.36, HW16/100, NA, PRO, Kew.

10 SS-Sturmbannführer Sepp Syr, born 18 October 1903, SS-Nr. 283, 029. See Personal-Akte NA A3343-SSO-171B.

11 See Personalverfügung Der SS Sturmbannführer S.Syr SS-Führungshauptamt Amt V/Abt.IIa 25.2.44. *Ibid.*

12 See Dienstlaufbahn des Syr Sepp, *Ibid.*

13 See message to SS Transport Officer West, UNNA, signed STEIGLITZ on 8/3/44, HW 16/100, CX/MSS/Q.52, 16/4/44., NA, PRO, Kew.

14 The original cadre for the SS-Flak Ausb.u.Ers.Btl were selected in August 1943 and sent to the SS school in München for appropriate instruction. Unable to fulfil the necessary requirements most were returned to Heidelager where SS-Sturmbannführer Viters had begun organising and *Flak-Abteilung* primarily from personnel from the 2, 11 and 12 training companies. The largest contingent came from the 2 company and comprised mainly of students. On completion of their basic training, in December 1943, those selected for service with the *Flak-Abteilung* command of which had now passed to SS-Sturmbannführer von Kuester, were sent to München for a three month training course conducted by SS instructors and which by all accounts did not include any form of 'political' education. Throughout this period, every Sunday the trainees were able to attend Mass which was held for the Ukrainian workers in the area. On completion of the course in March 1944, the soldiers returned to Neuhammer. Letters to author, Roman Hayetsky 1 January1993, and Myron Pasij 10 January1994. See also message to 14 Galician SS Volunteer Division, from Ops. H.Q. signed Gutberlet, SS Staf., 18/1, HW16/100, Most Secret, CX/MSS/Q.37, 31.1.44, NA, PRO, Kew.

15 I.T, Visti, 1984, Nr.3, p. 74.

16 SS-Sturmbannführer Serge von Kuester, born 12 December 1896, SS-Nr. 314,013. See Personalakt NA A3343-SSO-227A.

17 The battery of 2 cm guns had a strength of 200 personnel and consisted of four squadrons each consisting of three canons, plus six MG 42 heavy machine guns used in an anti-aircraft role.

18 The battery of 3.7 cm guns had a strength of 200 personnel and consisted of three squadrons each consisting of three canons, plus six MG 42 heavy machine guns used in an anti-aircraft role.

19   One squadron of four 88 mm guns, one squadron of two 20mm anti-aircraft guns.

20   Heike, Eng ed.; *op cit.*; p. 25.

21   *Ibid.*, p. 13. Heike goes on to state that Freitag kept him on because of his ability to organise courses of study and training.

22   For full text see Melnyk, To Battle, *op cit.*; p. 106. See Abschrift, Meldung vom 15.3.1943. Verband: 14. Galizische SS-Frw.Div. Unterstellungsverhaltnis. AA. A copy of this document can be found in Document N 756/170 (Sammlung Vopersal), BA-MA.

23   *Ibid.*

24   Born in 22.3.1906 in Muntau by Halbstadt, Ukraine. SS-Nr. 22,984. Party Nr. 663,222.

25   Ferkuniak; 'Spomyny.....' *op cit.*; p. 13.

26   Einsatzgruppen D was an operational task force of the Sicherheitspolizei and Sicherheitdienst charged with special missions (i.e.; liquidations) in occupied territory of opponents and enemies of the Nazi regime.

27   According to his personal file, in June 1941 Wiens was appointed to serve with Einsatzgruppen D as a Dolmetscher (interpreter) with Sonderkommando 10a under SS-Sturmbannführer Heinz Seetzen. Within weeks of the German invasion of the Soviet Union Wiens was appointed a Teilkommandoführer (section leader) and together with his group of ten men actively participated in executions. In spring 1942, Wiens transferred to Einsatzkommando 12 in the Stalino area and once again personally took part in mass liquidations. All four Einsatzgruppen were turned into static Sicherheitspolizei command posts and he was still serving with Einsatzgruppen D in January 1943, after its conversion to KdS (Kommandeure) Simferopol. In March 1944 after attending a short training course, he was appointed to the '14 Division's' staff as Ic/a, and in doing so joined his younger brother Jakob who was also serving with the Division in the Nachschub-Truppen as an SS-Obersturmführer.

28   Beurteilung fur den SS-Haupsturmführer Wiens, Div.St.Qu., 15.11.44 Nr. 1, 376

29   Born 19 September 1914, prior to the outbreak of the Second World War Kaczmar had studied and graduated from the Berlin Technical University as an aeronautical engineer. As a member of the OUN he was a liaison-messenger charged with various assignments and reporting directly to Riko Jary (an OUN leader based in Berlin). In September 1941 Kaczmar was arrested by the Gestapo because of his affiliation with the OUN-B, but later released on the grounds of ill health. He was directed to join the Division by M. Lebed of the OUN in Ukraine. He served with Kampfgruppe Beyersdorff as adjutant to Bristot, and later became adjutant to the commander of WGR 30, Hans-Boto Forstreuter. Wiens sought to arrest him and was only prevented from doing so by the direct intervention of Waffen-Hauptsturmführer Dmytro Paliiv. Although he was a first rate officer he was subsequently denied the promotions that he deserved. Wounded in the leg and captured at Brody, he was subsequently sent to work in an aircraft plant at Zagorsk. In December 1946 he received Soviet citizenship but remained as a 'Special settler' (with restrictions). In 1954 he was freed from his 'Special settler' status and eventually settled in L'viv in 1966 where he resided until his death on 8 January 1999.

30   Ferkuniak, 'Spomyny ...', *op cit.*; pp. 19-20.

31   See 17, April 1944, Auszug aus der Stärkemeldung des SS-FHA, 14.Galiz.SS-Freiw.Division. The respective strengths given in the table below clearly demonstrate that at this point the Division suffered from a crippling lack of officers and NCOs, with a shortfall of 1765 NCOs alone.

32   The I./Btl. was comprised of companies 1-4; II./Btl. 5-8, III./Btl. 9-12.

33   SS-Grenadier-Ausbildungs-und Ersatz-Regiment 14 (ukrain. Ausbildungs-Regiment 1), AA.

34   *Ibid.* Usually such a regiment would be responsible to a reserve commander in the rear. Its independent status is confirmed by the fact that it was explicitly forbidden to transfer any cadre personnel from it to the Galician Division.

35 Heike, Eng. ed., *op cit.*; p. 26. A copy of this document can be found reference document N 756/170 in the Sammlung Vopersal, BA-MA

36 Personal file - NA, A3343 SSO-220, f 619.

37 Hawrylak, 'Memoirs...', *op cit.*; p. 12, also letter to author Roman Herasymowycz, 1 November 1995.

38 Holos Ukrainski Visti, 22 June 1944.

39 Wächter's attitude towards the Galician Division's first combat deployment is adequately summarised by his comments during a session of the Governor and head department leaders in Cracow on 16 February 1944; '[...] the troops [those of the Galician division] are primarily more propagandistically than militarily to be valued, [as they are] not in possession of heavy weaponry and Paks etc. Everything depends on how they are at the first deployment. The political moment cannot be neglected with them'. Frank: Tagebuch, *op cit.*; p. 800.

40 By doing so Wächter showed considerable acumen as Model not only had a reputation as an extremely talented military commander but as an inspired improviser, renowned for employing unorthodox methods to get the required results.

41 Heike, Eng. ed., *op cit.*; p. 27.

42 Wächter was probably referring to bestowal of twenty four Iron Crosses II. Class to members of the 4 Regiment - four of them Ukrainian - for their bravery (see section on deployment of 4 Regiment).

43 Der Gouverneur des Distrikts Galizien, Lemberg, 3 Mai, 1944, Dr Wa/Ra An den Reichsführer-SS und Chef der Deutschen Polizei, Reischinnenminister Heinrich Himmler, H/10/80.

44 Himmler's schedule is set out in his diary of official appointments, AL1862/4 Imperial War Museum.

45 A copy of the audio recording can be found in National Archives Washington DC, Record Group 242- Item 206.

46 For example see Himmler's speech on the principles of the SS order to the generals of the SS at Poznan, 4 October 1943, selected extracts of which appear in translated form in 'The Order of the SS', Frederic Reider, W. Foulsham and Co, Berks, England, 1981, pp. 205-215.

47 Rede des Reichsführer-SS auf dem Appell des Führerkorps der Galizischen SS-Freiw-Infanterie-Division in Neuhammer am 16. Mai 1944. R 52 III/3c, BA-KO, and audio recording, AA. For an English translation of the full text of the speech see Melnyk, To Battle, *op cit.*; pp. 329-330.

48 Affidavit of J Temnyk dated 1 August 1989, AA. This account was subsequently corroborated by Waffen-Obersturmführer Bohdan Pidhayny.

49 Although there is no record of Himmler's reaction, in the article 'Dmytro Paliiv - Soldier and Patriot', Vasyl Veryha writes 'After the officers had been dismissed, a German staff officer approached Paliiv, shook hands with him and said 'I congratulate you', See Veryha, Visti Kombatanta, 5-6, 1968.

50 Der Reichsführer-SS, Field-Command, 28.5.1944, Bra\H. G.b.Nr.39\37\44, AA.

51 Several publications such as 'Die Woche' and 'Signal' published reports and pictures of the visit as recorded by SS- *Kriegsberichters'* Markert and Loos.

52 The album survived the war and was looted by an American GI, from Himmler's residence in Bavaria. At the time of writing it is currently available for purchase at Gary Hendershott.net.

53 Kormylo, *op cit.*; p. 16.

54 Heike, Eng. ed., *op cit.*; p. 28.

55 Wächter's promotion was effective as of 16 May 1944, which coincided with the date of Himmler's arrival for his inspection of the Division. See Personalakt Dr Otto Wächter NA, A3343-SSO-213B.

56 See Der Reichsführer-SS Feld-kommandostelle, den 21.5.1944 Tgb.Nr.: 1537/44 Gro/Dr. See NA, A3342-SSO-215.

57   For exact times see Himmler's diary of official appointments 17 May 1944, AL1862/4, IWM.

58   *Ibid.*, frame 7311020.

59   For the original order (effective 11 May) to report to the 3. Totenkopf Division, and subsequently countermanding instruction see SS-Führungshauptamt Berlin-Wilmersdorf, Kaiserallee 188, den 15.5.1944, Amt V/Abt.IIa/Ref. 2 Az.: 21c 16/Fu/31 Personalverfügung SS-Sturmbannführer Heike, Wolf. Personalakt Wolf Dietrich Heike, and SS-Führungshauptamt Berlin-Wilmersdorf, Kaiserallee 188, den 22.5.1944, W II Abt. 2 z.: 21clc./RS./illegible, Bert.: Versatzung SS-Stubaf. Heike, Wolf Bezug: Pers, -Verfüg. FHA/IIa V. 15.5.44. Personal-Akte NA, A3343-SSO-76A.

60   Heike, Eng. ed., *op cit*; p. 28, R. Krokhmaliuk, 'Zahrava na skhodi: spohady i dokumenty z pratsi u viiskovii upravi 'Halychyna' y 1943–1945 rokakh'. (The Glow in Eastern Europe), Toronto-New York: Bratstvo kolyshnikh voiakiv I-oi Ukrainskoi dyvizii UNA, 1978, pp. 81-82. Members of the MB and UCC were also invited to Neuhammer to inspect the Division during May 1944.

61   Although according to the organisational chart dated 30 July 1943, it was originally intended to have three battalions for each of its infantry regiments, the Galician Division was formed with only two battalions per regiment (see organisational chart dated 22 September 1943, SA). The entry in the publication Verordnungsblatt der Waffen-SS, by the Verbindungsoffizier der SS beim OKH (SS Liaison Officer to the Army High Command) records the order dated 1 June 1944 for the SS-Gren.Ausb.u.Ers Rgt 14/galiz Nr.1) at Wandern to provide the manpower for the III battalions for the Galician Division. [Tg.Buch-Nr VOSS 1606g v.11.6.44]. AA. This document can be found in the BA-MA in document N 756/170 (Sammlung Vopersal). Reference to the same order (SS-FHA, Amt II Org.Abt. Ia/II, Tgb. Nr II/8602/44) is also made in a document issued by the SS-Führungshauptamt, dated 5 Sept 1944; Amt II Org.Abt.Ia/II Tgb.Nr.2880/44 g. Kdos., v.5.9.1944, Betr: Neuaufstellung der 14. Waffen-Gren.Div. der SS (galizische Nr. 1). (ABFC). It wasn't until 5 September 1944 when the completed battalions were actually transferred to the 29, 30 and 31 Regiments.

62   During their stay in southern France, one group of Ukrainians who had formerly belonged to the 6 Regiment, and the Galizisches SS-Freiwilligen-Ersatz-Bataillon Tarbes, made plans to desert to the Maquis. During transfer the train came under attack by Allied aircraft in the vicinity of the city of Tours. In the resulting confusion the group led by Osyp Krukovsky deserted to the Maquis taking with them 4 horses, 4 machine guns, 25 rifles, 10 sub-machine guns and other matériel. As members of the resistance, the Ukrainians who were ultimately incorporated into the French Foreign Legion, fought with some success against the Germans until the end of the war. For details see Myroslav Nebeliuk, Under Foreign Flags, Piuf Editions, SCIP, Paris, 1951, pp. 195-201.

63   Letters to author I. Sadovey, 17 January and 9 February 1999.

64   Abschrift von Fernschrift 22.4.1944, Betr.Galiz.SS-Freiw.Rgt.4 und 5, Der RFSS hat gem.FS Kdo.-Stab RFSS. Nr.570 v. 22.4.1944 -Tgb.Nr.Ia/1269/44 geh.-die Abgabe der Gal. SS-Freiw.-Rgt. 4 und 5 an 14. Gal. SS-Freiw.-Div befohlen. SA.

65   See 'Uberführung der Gal. SS-Freiw.-Rgt. 4 und 5 in die Waffen-SS'. Der Chef der Ordnungspolizei, Kdo.g.1 Org.(3) Nr.104/44(g), Schnellbrief., Berlin, den 9 June 1944, R 19/326, BA-KO.

66   'Uberführung der Gal. SS-Freiw.-Rgt. 4 und 5 in die Waffen-SS'. Der Chef der Ordnungspolizei, Kdo.g.1 Org.(3) Nr.104II/44, Berlin, den 17.June 1944, R 19/105, BA-KO. As of 18 May 1944, the regiment was officially disbanded in Strassburg.

67   The incorporation of soldiers of both units into the Division's three infantry regiments just before they left for the front was confirmed verbally to the author by members of both regiments; I. Maksymiw 27 November 1995, and S. Reskovitch, 15 January1996.

68   Verbally to author S. Reskovitch, 15 January1996.

69 Abschrift! Der Höhere SS-und Polizeiführer im General Government Befehlshaber der Ordnungspolizei, Cracow, den 29. Juni 1944, Akt.Z.: Abt. III b (1) 2795 d - Tgb.Nr. 1441/44 (g.) -Geheim, Betr.; Übernahme des Schutzmannschafts-Batl.204 in die Galizische SS-Freiwilligen-Division. R 19/326, BA-KO.

70 The order for transfer followed a message to the commander of Heidelager from SS Ops H.Q. Amt. II Org. Abt. IE, I (1) on 1/3, which reads; 'After the arrival of Guard Bn. 5 or of the men transferred from SS. Geb. Jaeger Bn. 7 to relive Shuma Bn. 204, 200 German speaking men are to be despatched to the 14. Gal. SS Volunteer Division'. See HW 16/101, CX/MSS/Q.48, 21/3/44, NA, PRO, Kew.

71 This battalion was comprised of Ukrainians from Eastern Ukraine. The chaplain assigned to it was Rev Markevych.

72 Private letter from Otto Wächter to his wife Charlotte Wächter, Lemberg, 20 June 1944. HWA.

73 *Ibid.*

74 At a meeting with Dr Fritz Arlt on 17 June 1944, Wächter complained about the command deficiencies in the Division. He stated that he felt as a former *Polizei* general Freitag's psychological leadership qualities for a Ukrainian Division were inadequate, compared to the Division's 1a (first assistant to the Divisional commander) Major Heike who was understanding and sympathetic towards the Ukrainians and a good Gesprächspartner (literally 'speaking partner'). See Fritz Arlt, 'Polen Ukrainer Juden Politik', Wissenschaftlicher Buchdienst, Herbert Taege, 31694 Lindhorst, 1995, p. 105.

75 Private letter from Otto Wächter to his wife Charlotte Wächter, Lemberg, 20 June 1944. HWA.

76 d'Alquen was the editor of the weekly SS journal 'Das Schwarze Corps' (The Black Corps), and commander of the SS war correspondents regiment known as 'Kurt Eggers'. Once he had converted to opposing the 'Untermensch' (sub-human) doctrine, his influence played a pivotal part in ultimately persuading Himmler to revise his views on the utilisation of former Soviet nationals in the service of the German armed forces. See Thorwald, 'The Illusion...', pp. 196-207.

77 In a letter to his wife dated 20 June 1944, Wächter confirmed that d'Alquen was in attendance when he wrote; 'Yesterday I had guests, Brigadeführer Freytag [sic] visited. Also Gunther d'Alquen the chief editor of *Das Schwarze Korps* and head of the large propaganda apparatus of the Waffen-SS has also visited me several times - an interesting guy'. Letter from Otto Wächter to Charlotte Wächter, 20/6/44, HWA.

78 Heike, Eng. ed., *op cit.*; p. 28. Thorwald writes that the results of Skorpion exceeded all expectations, encouraging approximately 4,500 desertions in the area in 18 days. Thorwald, 'The Illusion...', pp. 202-203.

79 Heike, Eng. ed. *op cit.*; p. 117.

80 In all probability, the favourable disposition adopted by General Raus towards the Division, stemmed from his previous experiences with the Ukrainians as a former officer in the Austro Hungarian Army.

81 By 31 May 1944, the 'Galizische SS-Div.' was mentioned be being used together with 1 or 2 Hungarian reserve divisions, to relieve the 1. and 371 Infantry Divisions. For further details see Panzerarmee-Oberkommando 1 Abt. 1a Nr. 17/44 g. kdos. Chefs. A.H.Qu., den 31.5.1944. An Oberkommando H.Gr. Nordukraine, Studie 'Schild und Schwert'. (Fall a), T313 roll 73, frames 7311028 and 7311030.

82 See Panzerarmee-Oberkommando 1 A.H.Qu., den 9.6.1944. Abt. 1a Nr.21/44 g.k. Chefs. Bez. H.Gr. Nordukraine, Ia Nr.0802/44 g.k.Chefs, An Oberkommando H.Gr. Nordukraine, Studie 'Schild und Schwert' (Fall b), T313 roll 73, frame 7311006. The same document also allowed for the possibility of 1 or 2 Hungarian reserve Divisions and the 'Galizische SS-Div.' relieving 1. and 371 Infantry Divisions. For further details see *Ibid.*, frame 7311003.

83   Letter to author R. Wysocky, 23 May 1996.

84   The details of one such manoeuvre are given by Liubomyr Ortynsky in his account entitled 'Polkovi Vpravy' (Regimental Manoeuvres) Visti, 1951, June Nr. 6 (8).

85   Heike, Eng. ed., *op cit*.; p. 29.

86   Letter to author R. Drazniowsky, 11 March 1996.

87   This included anti-tank weaponry and new automatic weapons. Letter to author R. Drazniowsky, 11 March 1996.

88   According to Waffen-Obstuf. M. Malecky, an announcement regarding the Division's destination was made to the officers at a meeting shortly before departure. Letter to author 7 March 1996. The proposed area for deployment was confirmed verbally to author by V. Veryha, 19 February 1996. Also Kormylo, *op cit*.; p. 16.

89   Heike, Eng. ed., *op cit*; p. 36. In his memoirs Ferkuniak writes that the explanation for the change as given to him by Dmytro Paliiv was that the orders for the Division's original deployment in the Kolomyia region had been revoked because 'it could have led to conflict with the Hungarians'. Ferkuniak, 'Spomyny ...', *op cit*.; pp. 24-25.

90   The operation was named after Prince Peter Bagration an Imperial Russian Army officer who had fought Napoleon in 1812.

91   The Allied invasion of Europe codenamed Operation Overlord was launched on 6 June 1944.

92   For an account of the collapse of Army Group Centre, see Earl F Ziemke, 'Stalingrad to Berlin: The German Defeat in the East', Military Heritage Press, New York, 1985, pp. 313 - 325 and Alex Buchner, 'Ostfront 1944, The German Defensive Battles On The Eastern Front', 1944, Schiffer Publishing, USA, 1991, pp. 143-218. The German armies were in a hopeless position because Hitler's rigid hold on orders were depriving them of all strategic latitude and seriously impeded even their tactical operations.

93   Ziemke, 'Stalingrad...' *op cit*.; p. 325. For further details see Buchner 'Ostfront...', *op cit*; p. 213.

94   The 47 Rifle Corps was also in front reserve. Further details of the distribution of rifle divisions in the 1 Ukrainian Front can be found in 'L'vov - Sandomierz 1944', The Soviet General Staff Study, (translated and edited by David M Glantz and Harold S Orenstein from the Directorate For The Exploitation Of War Experience Of The USSR Armed Forces' General Staff, secret, copy 6191, Collection of War Materials for the Study of War Experience No. 22, January-February 1946) Military Publishing House of the People's Commissariat of Defense, Moscow, 1946, 'L'vov, pp. 26-29. In addition the 1 Czechoslovak Army Corps was subordinated to this front. For a full Soviet Order of Battle and unit and formation cadre of 1 Ukrainian Front on 13 July 1944, Melnyk, To Battle, *op cit*., pp. 330-334.

95   *Ibid.*, p. 29.

96   The Front also had 11 anti-aircraft divisions and 17 anti-aircraft regiments.

97   *Ibid.*, p. 33.

98   *Ibid.*, pp. 36-37.

99   This figure which includes rear service and support personnel is the same as that quoted as the total strength of the 1 Ukrainian Front as of 13 August 1944, *Ibid.*, Appendix 4, table p. 192. Appendix 2, on p. 190, quotes the following strength returns for the 1 Ukrainian Front at the beginning of the operation; 843,000 men, 13, 825 guns and mortars, 2432 anti-tank guns, 1222 anti-aircraft guns 2206 self-propelled guns. Other figures provided by Konev are 13,079 mortar and artillery pieces, 2,200 tanks, and self-propelled guns, and 3,000 planes. See Marshal I Konev. 'Zavershenie osvobozhdenia sovetskoi Ukrainy i vykhod na Vyslu, in Voienno-istoricheskii zhurnal', Moscow, July 1964.

100 Harpe took over from Model who was transferred to Army Group Centre 28 June Buchner 'Ostfront.', *op cit*; p. 222.

101 Fourth Panzer Army (Harpe) was comprised of 8 Corps, 56 Panzer Corps, 42 Corps and 46 Panzer Corps (16/17 Pz. Divs) plus rear reserve Corps.

102 First Panzer Army: (Raus) consisted of 13 Corps, 48 Panzer Corps, 24 Panzer Corps, 59 Corps, 3 Panzer Reserve (1/8 Pz. Divs).

103 On page 62 of his book 'The Russo-German War, Summer, 1944', (Destruction of the Eastern Front) Penn: Valour Publishing Co 1987, p. 62. V. Madej, gives the numbers of tanks available to the panzer divisions as follows; 16 Pz: 22, 17 Pz: 21 + ('+' indicating reinforcements were expected), 1 Pz: 61 and 8 Pz: 77. This information is partly corroborated by Heike who states in his memoirs that the 4 Panzer Army (that is the 16 and 17 Pz.Div.s) had approximately 40-50 tanks in total, Eng. ed., *op cit*.; p. 37.

104 On page 128 of the previously cited 'L'vov, Sandomierz' report it states that 'opposite 60 Army's sector the enemy had around 230 tanks and self-propelled guns which belonged to the 8 Panzer Division, 506 Separate Panzer Battalion and the 311th Assault Gun Battalion'. If the known figures for the 1 Panzer Division (61) and those of the 16 and 17 Pz. Div.'s (43 in total), are added to this the overall figure is around 334 operational tanks and self-propelled guns.

105 This source states that at the time of the commencement of their offensive, aligned against 1 Ukrainian Front were 32 German infantry divisions, plus 5 panzer and 1 panzer grenadier divisions, which amounted to around 300,000 men, equipped with 800 tanks, 230 self-propelled guns, 3,500 guns of various calibres, 1,900 mortars and supported by 700 aircraft (440 bombers, 150 fighters and 60 assault aircraft and 50 reconnaissance planes). 'L'vov, Sandomierz' 1944', *op cit*.; p. 18.

Confusion over the number of German divisions and consequent total of manpower may have been caused by the late redeployment of some of the German units. However despite this discrepancy, Soviet estimates in respect of the strength of German armour and aircraft are almost certainly exaggerated. For example, contrary to their claims, the number of operational tanks available to the four main panzer divisions involved amounted to approximately one hundred and eighty one. Taking into consideration additional self-propelled guns belonging to smaller units, this would still be significantly short of the Soviet figure of 800, which appears to have been computed on the assumption that five armoured divisions were present (and not four) and that each was at its full authorised strength of 165 tanks per division, which was certainly not the case. Similarly, it is doubtful as to whether their estimate of Luftwaffe strength is accurate as the numbers of aircraft quoted above are more likely to have represented 'paper authorisations'.

106 For an insight into the concerns of the German command regarding the disturbance of troop and equipment transports to the front see 'Bandenlage im Monat April 1944', 'Bandenlage im Monat Mai 1944', 'Bandenlage im Monat Juni 1944', NA, T313, roll 406, frames 8697467-8697477.

107 The transfer from AGNU of these units to Army Group Centre was in response to the Soviet offensive in Belorussia, See Ziemke 'Stalingrad...', *op cit*.; p. 330.

108 Heike mentions the failure of the efforts to rescind the new standing orders in his memoirs although he does not specify who made the representations, or to whom they were subsequently made. See Heike, Eng. ed., *op cit*.; p. 36. As Wächter was largely responsible for engineering the Division's deployment in the first place, it is likely that he lead the opposition to the change of plans.

109 *Ibid.*, p. 36.

110 Abschrift, Der Reichsführer-SS Feld-kommandostelle den 27 Juni, 1944, H/10/81. The re-designation was in accordance with an order issued by Himmler that the racial characteristics of Waffen-SS

divisions should be included in their titles. The Galician Ukrainians were given the lowest form of title, that of 'Waffen' or non Germanic. Thus from 27 June 1944, the Division was re-titled once again. As a rule, the style of title conferred on any Waffen-SS division fell into three categories and varied depending on its racial composition; Units composed of German volunteers were styled 'SS-Division'; Units containing a high percentage of 'racial' Germans and Germanic volunteers (i.e.; Scandinavians, Dutch, Flemings, Walloons, and Frenchmen) carried the designation 'Freiwilligen' e.g.: 11. SS-Freiwilligen-Panzer-Grenadier-Division 'Nordland'; Units containing a preponderance of 'non Germanic' personnel especially members of the Slavic and Baltic peoples carried the designation 'Waffen' as part of their names, and where necessary, a national description was appended in brackets at the end e.g.: 15. Waffen-Grenadier-Division der SS (Lett. Nr.1). In the same way officers of non Germanic origin could not become fully fledged members of the SS corps and were therefore designated accordingly as Waffen-Führer der SS. Individual rank was given in the same way i.e.; Waffen-Untersturmführer.

111   Among its quota of horses, the Division received several hundred directly from the eastern front, a large percentage of which were sick, wounded or had simply been starved to such an extent that they ate everything in sight, even trying to gnaw on the iron chains in the stables and tents. As a result of their generally poor condition many subsequently had to be destroyed. I. Nakonechny, 'From the Veterinary Company into the Bolshevik Camp', Visti Kombatanta, Nr. 5-6, 1994, pp. 118-120.

112   Details of the first transport to leave Neuhammer were provided by I. Nakonechny letters to the author dated 6 March 1993 and 17 April 1996.

113   Thirty eight transports were required to transport the entire Division to the front.

114   Kormylo, *op cit.*; p. 31.

115   SS-Grenadier-Ausbildungs-und Ersatz-Regiment 14 (ukrain. Ausbildungs-Regiment 1), AA.

116   *Ibid.*

117   Verbally to author V. Tomkiw, 23 December 1996. Within two weeks about one third of this group had failed the course mainly because of language difficulties.

118   V. Veryha letter to author, 29 April 1993.

119   For further details of the defence of the Division's disembarkation zone by the anti-aircraft detachment see B. Nebozhuk, 'Brody' Visti Kombatanta 1992, Nr. 2, p. 72.

120   Heike refers to the meeting in his memoirs. (Eng. ed., *op cit.*; p. 38) Although no record of the meeting exists, Heike mentions that upon rejoining the Division at the front, Freitag filed a special request with XIII Army Corps that the Division be committed as a whole and not as individual regiments, and that it should always remain under its own command. It would seem likely that the origins of the request were directly attributable to the discussion between Wächter and Freitag on that occasion.

121   Born 20.12.1891 in Wittgendorf, in July 1944 Hauffe was a highly decorated officer holding both the German Cross in Gold (awarded 25.7.43) and the Ritterkreuz (Knights Cross) conferred on him as commander the 46 Infantry Division.

122   Heike, Eng. ed., *op cit.*; p. 37.

123   To cite as an example the Pioneer Battalion was equipped with liberal quantities of close support weapons such as the formidable 8.1 cm mortar, both the *Panzerschreck* and the Panzerfaust (infantry weapons similar to a bazooka designed for anti-tank combat), and flame-throwers. It also had at its disposal some of the very latest weaponry including the most recent models of machine guns and the new Goliath, a small radio controlled device resembling a miniature tank of the type used during World War 1 which carried an explosive charge used for the destruction of tanks.

(See Schmitt; 'Pioniereinheiten...', *op cit.*; U.7.) Personal weaponry was also generally of a higher standard with a high proportion of automatic and semi automatic weapons being issued.

124   To ensure a rapid advance for their armoured and motorised forces, the capture of the main road to L'viv which ran through Zolochiv was of primary importance.

125   Heike, Eng. ed., *op cit.*; p. 38.

126   For a comprehensive account (with situation maps) of the encirclement of XIII AK which took place from the end of March until mid-April 1944 and the subsequent piercing of the encirclement by Panzerverband Friebe (a unit from 8 Panzer Division) see NA, T313, roll 73, also T315, roll 2152 for an account of the 361 Infantry Division's part and T315, roll 2147 for the rôle of the 349 Infantry Division.

127   'L'vov - Sandomierz 1944', *op cit.*; p. 128.

128   Heike, Eng. ed., *op cit.*; p. 38. See also the secret twenty seven page after action report by General Lange entitled 'Korpsabteilung 'C' in der Kesselschlacht des XIII AK sudwestlich Brody vom 13-22 Juli 1944'. IC Nr. 12/44/Geh, vom 2.11.44, 171/44 Geh, Geheim, p. 2, NA, T78 roll Nr. 139-H 41/2. In his after action report General Lange claims that the 'Korpsabteilung C 'had by itself also nearly completed preparation of the Prinz Eugen Stellung, including the positions for the artillery and the heavy infantry weapons' [and other secondary positions], (Lange, p. 1) a claim that many Ukrainian veterans angrily refute. They contend that for the most part the trenches were largely on paper and had to be built from scratch, for example in a letter to author dated 3 February 1998, Waffen-Unterscharführer Roman Drazniowsky a platoon leader serving with the 3/I/30, stated unequivocally 'The trenches were only on paper, we had to build those trenches when we arrived'.

129   An organisational chart gives the following disposition of the Corps HQ at the beginning of the battle:
Stab Gen Kdo XIII AK
Korpskartenstelle (mot) 413
Feldgen.Trupp (mot) 413
Kraftf.Komp. 413
Kraftf.Inst.Zug 413
Pi-Regts.Stab 516 (ko.Pi.Fhr)
Art.Kdr. 413
Korps Jagd-Kdo.XIII
Panz.Zerst.Kp.XIII
Nachr.Abt. 53 mit 1,3,4.Kp und Versorg.Staffel
Feldpostamt 413
See OKH/Abwicklungsstab, Sachgebiet: E XIII, Rudolstadt/Th.,den 29.Okt.1944, NA, T78, roll 139 frame no: 6067693.

130   The following Heerstruppen are listed as being attached to the Army Corps:
Art. Regt. z.b.V. 617
s.Art.Abt. 842
le.Beob.Abt. 35
Sturm Geschutz-Brigade 249
Pi-Batl. 672
Heers Art.Abt II/70
Heers Art.Abt 841
Ibid.

131   This figure for '*Gesamtstärke des Verbandes*' (total number in unit) for K.Tr.XIII A.K., and the subsequent strengths of the corps' other units quoted, (with the exception of the Galician Division)

are taken from the final report dated 1 March 1945, of the liquidation commission activated to establish the losses of the XIII Corp's army units. (See NA, T78 roll 142 frame 6072050). These figures however in all probability represent each units overall total strength and not the respective actual battle strengths or 'kampfstarke'. A more accurate assessment of the number of men each of the corp's army units could deploy in the field can be calculated by reducing the quoted total strength of each of the army units by around 20 per cent.

132   *Ibid.*

133   See NA, T78 roll 142 frame 6072050. By calculating the various figures cited in Gefechtsbericht der 361. Inf.Div., the 'battle strength' of this unit is estimated at 9,000. NA T315 roll 2152, frames 000002 - 22.

134   A Korpsabteilung was equivalent to one infantry division. It consisted of three weakened divisions each with the approximate strength of one infantry regiment.

135   Figure taken from report dated 1 March 1945, NA, T78 roll 142 frame 6072050. Lange, 'Korpsabteilung 'C' in der Kesselschlacht, *op cit.*; pp. 26-27 gives the strength of the unit (ie; probable 'combat strength') as being 9059.

136   Lange, 'Korpsabteilung 'C' in der Kesselschlacht, *op cit.*; p. 2.

137   According to a strength return dated 30 June 1944, these troops consisted of; 725th Battalion (8 officers, 62 NCOs, 338 men; total 408); the 502 Battalion (5 officers, 34 NCOs and 191 men: total 230) and the 327th Battalion (2 officers, 15 NCOs and 88 men; total 105) See NA T313, roll 73, frames 7310732-73310733.

138   This unit was comprised of 5 officers, 38 NCOs and 220 men: total 263 men. *Ibid.*

139   Consisting of 9 officers, 57 NCOs and 251 men plus 29 men of the Pz.Jag.Zug: total 346. *Ibid.*

140   Heike gives a figure of 11,000 (see Eng. ed., op. cit.; p. 53). As has already been noted the third battalion of each of the three infantry regiments were still in the process of being formed and the personnel assigned to them remained at Neuhammer. Other absentees included those attending training courses and those who were sick.

141   The figure of 41,000 would be the maximum corps strength. The actual 'fighting strength' would have been reduced. It is worth noting that the figures provided by the report of the liquidation commission also includes a further 9,362 men for the 340.Inf.Div, part of which was also later surrounded with XIII AK, See NA T78 roll 142 frame 6072050. Buchner gives an estimate of XIII.A.K's strength as 65,000, Buchner 'Ostfront....', *op cit.*; p. 228, but this would be taking into account the strengths of the 340.I.D. and the 349 I.D.'s which although trapped with XIII AK's were not originally part of it. In my previous book I cited a total pre-battle strength for XIII AK, as being 55,100 (see Melnyk, To Battle, *op cit.*, p. 118), having erroneously added the strength of the 349 I.D. to the total. This unit was not initially part of the corps.

142   Figure taken from report dated 1 March 1945, NA T78 roll 142 frame 6072050.

143   Heike, Eng. ed., *op cit.*; p. 37.

144   *Ibid.*

5   On the Eastern Front

1   Bender/Taylor, 'Uniforms....', *op cit.*; vol. 4, p. 48. The strength return referred to is as of 30 June 1944. It does not include those in the Reserve Regiment which was in the process of relocation to Neuhammer or those on leave.

2   A document in the author's archive dated 3 July 1944, lists 136 Ukrainian officers, the vast majority of whom were present at Brody. For full list see Melnyk, to battle *op cit.*; p. 356.

3 WGR 31 was under the command of SS-Obersturmbannführer Paul Herms. SS-Hauptsturmführer Heinz Kurzbach commanded the I battalion.

4 Jurij Ferencevych email to author, 1 July 2010.

5 SS-Obersturmbannführer Forstreuter commanded WGR 30. SS-Hauptsturmführer Siegfried Klocker and SS-Hauptsturmführer Friedrich Wittenmeyer commanded the I and II battalions respectively.

6 At the time of the battle of Brody WGR 29 was commanded by SS-Standartenführer (as of 1/7/44) Friedrich Dern. Waffen-Hauptsturmführer Mychailo Brygidyr commanded the I battalion and SS-Hauptsturmführer Wilhelm Allerkamp the II battalion.

7 Interview W. Molodecky, Toronto, 2 June 1993.

8 1 comp. W.Ostuf. Mykola Horodysky, 2 W.Ostuf. Stephan Hulak, 3 comp. W.Ustuf. Roman Duda, each company was supported by one platoon of the 4 comp. W.Ostuf. Roman Bojcun. Battalion command was in Hlushyn and the supply section in Hayi Dubecki. Roman Bojcun, 'Kurin fiuzyliriv I. UD UNA pid Brodamy', Visti, Nov. - Dec 1953, Nr.s 11-12 (37-38), pp. 5-6.

9 Stepan Hulak, 'Fiuzylirskyi Kurin', Visti, February-March 1952, Nr.'s 2-3 (16-17) p. 6 and Roman Bojcun, 'Kurin fiuzyliriv I. UD UNA pid Brodamy', Visti, Nov.—Dec. 1953, Nr.s 11-12 (37-38), pp. 5-6.

10 Interview Julian Wilshynsky, Toronto, 6 June 1993.

11 Unlike all the other units of the Division, the 14.Feld Ersatz Battalion was billeted in public buildings and houses in the villages in which the respective companies were stationed, 'The medical Service of the Field Reserve Battalion of the 1 Ukrainian Division 1944–45' an unpublished manuscript, Dr W. Krywulak, AA. Also interview Petro Maslij, Scunthorpe, 8 February 1992, and Jurij Krokhmaliuk, 'Polevyi Zapasnyi Kurin Pid Brodamy' (Field Replacement Battalion at Brody) Visti, 952, Nr. 2-3 p. 12.

12 In his article 'The UPA and The Division', Lev Shankovsky goes as far as to say that the mere presence of strong UPA units was enough to convince the Germans to redeploy the Division; 'Initially the Germans planned to deploy the Division in the regions of Kolomyia and Horodenka. The German command subsequently changed these plans because it seemed inadvisable to place the Division in regions where the UPA had a very strong presence. Therefore the Division was transferred to the region of Brody where only one company of UPA ('Druzhynnyky') was active'. See Shankovsky 'The UPA...' *op cit.*; pp. 55-61, Kyiv, 1994. English translation by Ostap Sokolsky, p. 4. While the Germans were undoubtedly concerned about the influence of the UPA on the Ukrainian soldiers in the Division, it would appear that Shankovsky has exaggerated the extent of the concern.

13 Kormylo, *op cit.*; p. 32.

14 Letter to author V. Veryha, 10 January 1994.

15 Letter to author W. Sirsky, 22 March 1993.

16 One such instance was related to the author by a former member of the WGR 31, who together with three other Ukrainian soldiers rescued several cows that had been taken by Germans soldiers of another Division from Ukrainian villagers near Brody. Letter to the author Oleh Ostrowsky, 19 January 1997.

17 W. Lange, The Second Encirclement at Brody, unpublished manuscript, NA, D-300, pp. 3-4.

18 Heike, Eng. ed., *op cit.*; p. 39.

19 A number of desertions did take place from the Division, for example one soldier from 7/II/WGR 30, deserted to the UPA with a machine gun and ammunition. This was reported to the company commander Waffen-Obersturmführer M. Malecky who asked the UPA to make arrangements for

the return of the soldier to the Division. This subsequently took place and no further action was taken against the soldier. Letter to author 17 April 1996.

20   An UPA group known as 'Druzhynnyky' (Comrades in arms) operated in the Brody region under the command of Lieutenant 'Chernyk' See Pobihushtschyi, 'My Lifes...', *op cit.*; p. 165, and Shankovsky, 'UPA...', *op cit.*; pp. 55-61.

21   The training of recruits and the provision of supplies to the UPA was confirmed by former members of the Division in numerous interviews and letters to the author. For example the 3 company of the Pioneer Battalion was instrumental in providing the UPA with medical supplies. Interview Julian Wilshynskyj, Toronto, 6 June 1993.

22   Letters to author R. Drazniowsky, 11 March 1996 and 1 April 1996.

23   Interview Julian Wilshynsky, Toronto, 6 June 1993.

24   Letter to author Jurij Ferencevych, 1 July 2010.

25   See Galizische SS-Freiw.Div. Div.Gef.St., 9.7.44, Freiwillige SS-Fuhrer der Division. BA-MA RS4/40 SS-Kriegsberichter-abteilung. Verwaltung. Personalwesen. Band 3. Oktober 1941-Dezember 1944.

26   Bohdan Pidhayny refers to the instruction by the OUN to young men to join the Division in the article 'UPA- Dyviziia-Halychyna-Nimtsi', Visti Kombatanta, 1990, Nr. 3, p. 65. It is worth noting that the number of men enlisted in this way was limited because the Division did not have the capacity to accommodate them in large numbers.

27   Interview W. Sirsky, Toronto, 5 June 1993.

28   Heike, Eng. ed., *op cit.*; p. 39.

29   *Ibid.*

30   W. Lange, The Second Encirclement at Brody, unpublished manuscript, NA, D-300, p. 4.

31   Lange, 'Korpsabteilung 'C' in der Kesselschlacht, *op cit.*; p. 4.

32   Letter to author W. Sirsky, 26 January 1992.

33   Verbally to author Volodymyr Yankivsky, 18 February 2013.

34   Lange, 'Korpsabteilung 'C' in der Kesselschlacht, *op cit.*; p. 3.

35   NA, T314 roll 1186 frame 0025.

36   'L'vov - Sandomierz 1944', *op cit.*; p. 64.

37   *Ibid.*; pp. 63-64.

38   For details of the Soviet strike on XIII AK's left flank, *Ibid.*, pp. 165-168.

39   As part of 4. Panzer Army, the 16 and 17 Panzer Divisions were known as 46 Panzer Corps. Both units had recently been involved in heavy fighting at Cherkassy and Ternopil which accounted for their lack of useable armour. V. Madeja, Russo-German War Summer 1944, (Destruction of the Eastern Front) Penn: Valour Publishing Co, 1987, p. 62.

40   See Konev's memoirs http://militera.lib.ru/memo/russian/konev

41   Between 13-15 July 3 Guards and 13 Armies' shock groups penetrated the German defensive to a depth of between 15-30 kms. In this period, 13 Army alone destroyed 2450 officers and men, 25 guns, 25 tanks and self-propelled guns and 18 armoured transports. 'L'vov - Sandomierz 1944', *op cit.*; p. 67.

42   *Ibid.*, pp. 70-73.

43   See Konev's memoirs http://militera.lib.ru/memo/russian/konev

44   'L'vov - Sandomierz 1944', *op cit.*; p. 68.

45   W. Lange 'Korpsabteilung 'C' in der Kesselschlacht des XIII AK südwestlich Brody vom 13-22 Juli 1944'. IC Nr. 12/44/Geh, vom 2.11.44, 171/44 Geheim, NA T78, roll 139-H 41/2, pp. 4-5.

46   Lange, 'Korpsabteilung 'C' in der Kesselschlacht', *op cit.*; p. 4. Also see Heike, Eng. ed., *op cit.*; p. 41.

47 See 'Überblick uber den Werdegang der Aufstellung bis zum Tag der Auflösung'. (Review Over the Development of 349 Infantry Division From the Day of Formation to the Day of Disbandment), p. 9, NA T315, roll 2152.

48 *Ibid.* p. 9.

49 10 Artillery battery was destroyed, 11 and 4 were captured intact. *Ibid.* pp. 8-9.

50 *Ibid.* p. 10.

51 See Konev's memoirs http://militera.lib.ru/memo/russian/konev

52 The original directive suggested that one regiment [i.e. WGR 29], was to occupy Pieniaki and 1625 hrs on 13 July it had 3 Pak guns in place in the village, see NA, T314 roll 1186 frame 0160. Following this, the rest of the 14 Galician Division was to redeploy into XXXXVIII Pz.K.'s sector to which it would then be subordinated. It planned to deploy 2 of the Galician Division's regiments (WGR 39 and WGR 30) in the zone from the forest east of Kruhiv over Pieniaki, as far as the left border of the Corps and a third (WGR 31) behind in reserve. NA, T314 roll 1186 frame 0037. However by 2035 hrs that same evening the earlier directive was countermanded and the 14 SS-Galician Division was to remain in place under XIII.A.K and I reinforced regiment was due to take up position between Pieniaki to Krukow, see NA, T314, roll 1186 frame 0161.

53 Heike, Eng. ed. *op cit.*; p. 38.

54 The strength of WGR 30 including staff, staff company, line companies 1-8 and 13 company (excluding 14 company) was recorded in a post battle casualty report as produced by V. Veryha as being 1,903 men (34 Officers, 116 NCOs and 1753 enlisted men). Of this number 54 were German (14 officers, 35 NCOs and 5 men). See 30 SS Freiw. Gren. Regt. Abwicklungstelle O.U., den 22.9.44. SA.

55 In 'Pershyi Den' Boiv Pid Brodamy' (The First Day of the Battle at Brody) Toronto, Kalendar-Almanakh Novoho Shliakhu, 1984), p. 103. V. Veryha, a former member of WGR-30, states that it received the order to move into this area in the late evening of 13 July. This is confirmed in the accounts of Waffen-Untersturmführer Bohdan Pidhayny 'Dva Shliakhy - Odna Meta', in Brody: Zbirnyk Stattei i Naryciv, edited by O. Lysiak, p. 115 and Pavlo Sumarokiv, in 'V Otochenni Pid Brodamy. Proryv 2-ho Kurinnia 30-ho Polky UD Halychyna', Visti, 1961, Nr. 103, pp. 70-74.

56 Heike, Eng. ed., *op cit.*; p. 43.

57 *Ibid.*

58 Email to author O. Slupchynsky, 17 January 2014.

59 'L'vov - Sandomierz 1944', *op cit.*; p. 67.

60 Email to author O. Slupchynsky, 17 January 2014.

61 Letter to author O. Slupchynsky, 1 November 1998.

62 Heike, Eng. ed., *op cit.*; p. 43.

63 Veryha, 'Pershyi Den' *op cit.*; pp. 104-105.

64 R. Drazniowsky verbally to the author, 26 February 1996.

65 All the Ukrainians who were present have commented on the sorry state of the withdrawing German units and that they urged them not to engage the enemy but retreat because of their overwhelming superiority. For example verbally to author Drazniowsky, 22 November 1993, and 26 February 1996, letter to author O. Slupchynsky, 1 November 1998, letter to author Vasyl Veryha, 4 June 1996.

66 See Veryha, http://web.archive.org/web/20100811193903/http://lib.galiciadivision.com/brody/brody13.html.

67 Letter to author R. Drazniowsky, 3 February 1998.

68 Kormylo, *op cit.*; p. 33, also audio tape 3.

69   NA T314, roll 1186 frame, document No: 0507.

70   The original commander of 14./WGR 30 was Waffen-Obersturmführer Ivan Strutynsky who was arrested by Gestapo in June 1944.

71   Both 13./and 14./companies which were directly under Divisional command were known to have been deployed at Brody as is evidenced by both the post battle casualty reports and awards lists. For example Staff.-Gren.Div.der SS\gal Nr.I.\Einsatz: Ostfront, Sudabschnitt Verleihungsliste Nr.I., fur Eiserne Kreuze 2.Klasse, which lists SS-Unterscharführer Helmut Heis (14./30) as being a recipient of the Iron Cross II Class for his bravery during the battle. For the full list see Melnyk, To Battle, *op cit.*; pp. 334-335.

72   The strength of WGR-30 was recorded in a post battle casualty report as being 1,903 men—for companies numbered 1-8 and 13. See 30 SS Freiw.Gren.Regt. O.U. den 22.9.44, Abwicklungsstelle Feldp.Nr. 05-330. SA. To this figure must be added the personnel of the 14 and the II artillery battalion plus the attached supply and support personnel. The overall figure is therefore likely to have been closer to 2,500 men.

73   'Überblick, *op cit.*; p. 11.

74   The after action report of 349.I.D. Acknowledges that because of the nature of the terrain in the area of operations and repeated Soviet attacks, contact was lost between its 912 Regiment and the remainder of the 349.I.D. See 'Überblick *op cit.*; p. 13. Under these circumstances there was no possibility of communication between WGR 30 and the 349.I.D. In his memoir Heike states 'the greatest drawback of fighting in that encirclement was the fact that communication with our right flank [i.e. 349.I.D.] was impossible'. Heike, Eng. ed. *op cit.*; p. 46.

75   V. Veryha, 'Pershyi...', *op cit.*; p. 106.

76   'Überblick, *op cit.*; p. 11.

77   A radio message at 1210 hrs on 15 July stated that 'Regiment 30 needs to be subordinated to a higher command', possibly because it was in danger of being cut off. T314 roll 1186, frame 0180.

78   See the report by SS-Obscha. Mekat, Waffen-SS SS-Standarte 'Kurt Eggers' 14.Gal.SS-KB.Zug, Berlin-Zehlendorf, den 1.8.1944, An die Standarte 'Kurt Eggers' Stellvertreter i.K., Sturmbannführer Kriegbaum, Geheim! Betr.: SS-KB-Zug 'Galizien'. RS16/6 BA-MA.

79   Heike, Eng. ed., *op cit.*, p. 44.

80   *Ibid.*

81   Email to author O. Slupchynsky, 11 January 2015.

82   This was the Russian made machine pistol PPSh-41 (Pistolet-Pulemyot Shpagina)

83   Kormylo, audio tape 3.

84   For example in a letter to the author Waffen-Unterscharführer Roman Drazniowsky was given command of 3 company when its commander W.Obstuf. Bohdan Pidhayny was injured. Letter to the author 1 April 1996.

85   'Überblick...', *op cit.*; p. 13.

86   Heike, Eng. ed.; *op cit.*; p. 43.

87   *Ibid.*, p. 44.

88   'Überblick...', *op cit.*; pp. 11-12.

89   'L'vov - Sandomierz 1944', *op cit.*; p. 66.

90   'Ibid., p. 68.

91   *Ibid.*

92   In his book Alex Buchner, states the 8 Panzer Division's counterattack was led by the 10 Panzer Regiment's 1 battalion (which had only one full strength panzer company), the 4 and the 301 Panzer Battalion, Ostfront 1944, *op cit.*; p. 224.

93 'L'vov - Sandomierz 1944', *op cit.*; p. 69.

94 *Ibid.*

95 For details see 'Panzer Battles', Major General F.W Von Mellenthin, Futura Publications, London, 1984, pp. 340-341.

96 The Soviet General Staff Report states that 60 Army's 23 Rifle Corps, 15 and 28 Rifle Corps, advancing with a tank and a mechanised brigade (from 3rd Guards Tank Army) continued the offensive on the morning of 15 July supported by artillery fire and massive air strikes, 'Overcoming heavy resistance and repelling counterattacks by the 8 PZ Div. and the SS 'Galicia' Division which were approaching from the depths...', [author's emphasis]. ' L'vov - Sandomierz 1944', *op cit.*; p. 169.

97 The infantry reached the line Werkhobuzh-Iwaczow, Lange, 'Korpsabteilung 'C' in der Kesselschlacht,, *op cit.*; p. 5.

98 'Überblick...', *op cit.*; p. 10.

99 The 349 Infantry Division had previously been attached to XXXXVIII Panzer Korps of the 4 Panzer Army. Thereafter it was subordinated directly to the command of XIII AK 'Überblick...', *op cit.*; p. 10.

100 'L'vov - Sandomierz 1944', *op cit.*; p. 70. The Soviet attack on the L'viv axis (i.e.; the southern pincer), was more difficult than had been anticipated as 38 Army's attack had faltered on the German tactical defenses and 60 Army had opened only a small gap through the main German defenses east of the village of Koltiv. Marshal Konev's decisive response was to thoroughly analyse all the circumstances surrounding 38 Army's failure to fulfil the mission assigned to it, following which he ordered Rybalko's 3 Guards Tank Army and Lelyushenko's 4 Tank Army to thrust their armies successively into the 'Koltiv corridor', on 60 Army's front in order to hold and widen the corridor, accompanied by 31 and 4 Guards Tank Corps whose missions were to hold open the shoulders of the penetration. See David M. Glantz and Jonathan M. House, When Titans Clashed, How the Red Army Stopped Hitler, University Press of Kansas, 1995. pp. 210-211. See also Erickson 'The Road...', *op cit.*; pp. 235 and 695-697.

101 The first elements of these reinforcements were committed during the night of the 15/16 July.

102 In the latter part of the war the prefix Guards signified a first rate Soviet unit.

103 Veryha, 'Pershyi..', *op cit.*; p. 113.

104 Heike, Eng. ed., *op cit.*; p. 40.

105 *Ibid.*, p. 44.

106 *Ibid.*

107 It comprised of Kdr. III./A.R.219, with Rgt.gr. 691, Stab Pi. Btl. 219 with 2 companies and 8./A.R.219. Lange, 'Korpsabteilung 'C' in der Kesselschlacht, *op cit.*; p. 6.

108 *Ibid.*

109 Lange, 'Korpsabteilung 'C' in der Kesselschlacht, *op cit.*; p. 7.

110 B. Levitsky, http://web.archive.org/web/20091213064507/http://lib.galiciadivision.com/brody/brody11.html.

111 Lange, 'Korpsabteilung 'C' in der Kesselschlacht, *op cit.*; p. 6.

112 The early withdrawal of German units and the lack of prepared positions were confirmed to the author by several veterans of the battle during interviews conducted between 1989–1996, including former members of the Fusilier Battalion interview O. Wawryk, Fakenham, England 22 March 1990, WGR 29, interview I. Nyzka, Rushden, England, 6 January1991, and the supply unit, letter to author S. Wasylko, 11 March 1998.

113 B. Levitsky, http://web.archive.org/web/20091213064507/http://lib.galiciadivision.com/brody/brody11.html.

114   Infanterie Geschütz was an infantry support unit equipped with 7.5 cm cannon.

115   Email to author J. Ferencevych, 11 July, 2010.

116   Apart from being the only infantry regiment with a Ukrainian battalion commander, in July 1944 all WGR 29's infantry, artillery, and anti-tank companies were commanded by Ukrainians. Of the total number of forty two officers serving with the regiment, thirty four were Ukrainian and eight were German. See Lubomyr Ortynsky 'Pikhotnyi polk UD' (An Infantry Regiment of the Ukrainian Division,) Visti, pp. 13-14.

117   For example the staff company of WGR 31 suffered killed and wounded after being attacked by aircraft on this day, see Bohdan Levitsky, The 30 Anniversary of the Battles at Brody, (Commemoration of Sunday 16 July 1944). http://web.archive.org/web/20091213064507/http://lib.galiciadivision.com/brody/brody11.html

118   Lange, 'Korpsabteilung 'C' in der Kesselschlacht, *op cit*.; p. 6.

119   *Ibid.*, p. 7.

120   *Ibid.*, pp. 6-7. These precise instructions as issued to the 361 Infantry Division are confirmed in 'Gefechtsbericht der 361 Inf.Div.', NA T315, roll 2152, p. 7, frame 000009.

121   'Überblick...', *op cit*.; p. 12. Its forward units were placed in front of this line.

122   'Gefechtsbericht der 361', *op cit*.; p. 8 - frame 000010, also Lange 'Korpsabteilung 'C', *op cit*.; p. 7.

123   L. Ortynsky, eb.archive.org/web/20091216190449/http://lib.galiciadivision.com/brody/brody20.html.

124   Kampfgruppe Haid was commanded by Obstlt. Haid Kdr Gren.Rgt.953 of the 361 Infantry Division. For its subsequent orders and deployment see 'Gefechtsbericht der 361', *op cit*.; p. 7, frame 000009.

125   *Ibid.*

126   'Überblick...', *op cit*.; p. 12.

127   *Ibid.*

128   B. Levitsky, http://web.archive.org/web/20091213064507/http://lib.galiciadivision.com/brody/brody11.html.

129   *Ibid.*

130   The estimation of the regiment's losses was provided by Roman Drazniowsky, who took command of 3 company after its commander was wounded, verbally to the author 26 February 1996.

131   Pobihushtschyi, 'My Lifes...', *op cit*.; 1982, p. 173. By the end of 16 July all eight of the regiments Ukrainian company commanders were killed, wounded, or missing; I./Btl. W-Obstuf. Rozanetz (1 co) missing, W-Ustuf. Berezowsky (2 co) killed, W-Obstuf. Pidhayny (3 co) wounded, W-Obstuf. Pospilovsky (4 co) killed. II./Btl. W-Obstuf. Jurniuk (5 co) missing, W-Obstuf. Sumarokiv (6 co) wounded, W-Obstuf. Malecky (7 co) wounded, W-Obstuf. Makarevych (8 co) captured. The Ordonnanz Offizier of the 1 battalion W-Ustuf.' Andrij Borynetz also perished.

132   Kormylo, audio tape file 8. AA.

133   Heike, Eng. ed., *op cit*.; p. 45.

134   Lange, 'Korpsabteilung 'C' in der Kesselschlacht, *op cit*.; p. 7.

135   This was III./AR 219.

136   Lange, 'Korpsabteilung 'C' in der Kesselschlacht, *op cit*.; p. 8.

137   'L'vov - Sandomierz 1944', *op cit*.; p. 171. 23 Rifle Corps was assigned the sector Zharkiv–Maidan Pieniacky–Opaky to a point north east of Koltiv.

138   M. Dlaboha, http://web.archive.org/web/20091217235006/http://lib.galiciadivision.com/brody/brody17.html.

139   'L'vov–Sandomierz 1944', *op cit.*; p. 171. 23rd Rifle Corps was assigned the sector Zharkiv–
       Maidan Pieniacky–Opaky to a point north east of Koltiv.

140   M. Dlaboha, http://web.archive.org/web/20091217235006/http://lib.galiciadivision.com/brody/
       brody17.html.

141   L. Ortynsky, eb.archive.org/web/20091216190449/http://lib.galiciadivision.com/brody/brody20.
       html.

142   *Ibid.*

143   Interview W. Molodecky, Toronto, 2 June 1993.

144   During the battle W. Molodecky received a field promotion to the rank of Waffen-Unterscharführer.
       Interview W. Molodecky Toronto, 2 June 1993.

145   The company had four platoons - two commanded by Germans and two by Ukrainians. Each
       platoon was comprised of four squads of eleven men. One squad consisted of: one gun with a five
       man crew: one machine gun (MG 42 with two men): a *Panzerschreck** with two men, a driver and
       the Geschützführer or Squad Leader. * The Panzerschreck otherwise known as the Ofenrohr was a
       rocket launcher, similar to the Bazooka which fired a 7 pound hollow-charge rocket projectile.

146   For a full account of his experiences based on an interview conducted in Toronto on 2 June 1993
       see Melnyk, To Battle *op cit.*; pp. 155-156.

147   Memoirs of Myron Radzykewych, 'Svoboda' Almanac, 1999, pp 119-132.

148   *Ibid.*

149   Ferkuniak; 'Spomyny.....' *op cit.*; p. 28.

150   Heike, Eng. ed., *op cit.*; p. 45.

151   R. Bojcun, 'Kurin fiuzeliriv 1.UD UNA pid Brodamy', Visti, November-December1953, Nos.11-12;
       37-38. Interview W. Molodecky, Toronto, 2 June 1993.

152   Interview Julian Wilshynsky, Toronto, 6 June 1993.

153   Felix Korduba 'Brody', 'Dyvision tiazhkoi artylerii pid Brodamy' (Detachment of Heavy Artillery
       at Brody), pp. 96-102.

154   Lange, 'Korpsabteilung 'C' in der Kesselschlacht, *op cit.*; pp. 8-9.

155   *Ibid.*, p. 9.

156   L'vov - Sandomierz 1944', *op cit.*; p. 171.

157   *Ibid.*, p. 175.

158   In his report General Lange seeks to apportion the blame for the failure of this attack squarely on
       the '14.SS-Freiw-Div.Galizien' when he writes 'The SS [i.e.; 14 Galician Division] had been unable
       to overcome the stronger enemy resistance it had faced and came flooding back in a state of total
       disorder. As a result the Fusilier Battalion came under most heavy fire on both flanks. The attack
       was thus halted'. Lange, 'Korpsabteilung 'C', *op cit.*; p. 9.

159   W. Lange, 'Korpsabteilung 'C' in der Kesselschlacht, *op cit.*; p. 9.

160   In his report Lange wrote 346 I.D. in error.

161   W. Lange, The Second Encirclement at Brody, unpublished manuscript, NA, D-300, p. 8.

162   The presence of the heavy 'Joseph Stalin' type tanks is confirmed in 'Überblick, *op cit.*; p. 11.

163   The tanks were captured Soviet T34's.

164   The attack was delayed from the start after the preparatory artillery fire fell short amongst German
       troops. 'Überblick...', *op cit.*; pp. 12-13.

165   Lange, 'Korpsabteilung 'C' in der Kesselschlacht, *op cit.*; p. 9.

166   Major General Von Mellenthin offers the following account of the failed attack by the 8 Panzer Division.
       'On the evening of 17 July tried to make contact with XIII Army Corps, in order to arrange for
       them to attack southwards on the 18, while 8 Panzer Division struck north, but communications

failed. I assembled the regimental commanders and explained my plan, in particular I stressed the moral significance of the attack on which depended the salvation of 40,000 of our encircled comrades...In order that there should be no confusion over command, I placed the infantry units holding our front line under the command of the panzer regiment for the duration of the night. At dawn on 18 I went to the battle HQ of the Panzer Regiment... and found to my astonishment that our infantry-due to attack in an hours time-were withdrawing southwards... the commander of the Panzer Regiment confessed that he had ordered this withdrawal as he wished to re-group before launching the attack. I immediately relieved him of his command, but once again the disobedience of this division had done irreparable harm. In the circumstances I had no choice but to cancel the attack'. Mellenthin, 'Panzer...', *op cit*.; pp. 342-43.

167   Heike, Eng. ed., *op cit*.; p. 45.

168   'L'vov - Sandomierz 1944', *op cit*.; p. 173.

169   Interview Petro Cisarsky, Norwich, England, 14 November 1999.

170   See Memoirs of Roman Lazurko, http://web.archive.org/web/20100717122059/http://lib. galiciadivision.com/lazurko/r04.html

171   Interview Petro Maslij, Scunthorpe, England, 8 February 1992.

172   For an account of the escape of the supply units of the 361 Infantry Division see Hauptfeldwebel W.Mehlhorn, Im Felde, den 10 Febr.45, Bezug; Abw.-Stab OKH/361 v.16.11.44, Betr.: Erlebnisbericht. NA T78, roll 139-H 41/2.

173   Lange, 'Korpsabteilung 'C' in der Kesselschlacht, *op cit*.; p. 10.

174   This unit was part of the 9 Mechanised Corps. 'L'vov - Sandomierz 1944', *op cit*.; p. 74.

175   At the time of its encirclement, in addition to the five divisions which made up XIII AK, small parts of other formations which had been broken off from their parent formations at the beginning of the Soviet offensive or during the counterattacks, were also surrounded. These included small contingents of the 1 and 8 Panzer Divisions, the 357 Infantry Division, the 20 Pz. Gren. Division, and the garrison forces within Brody itself (725, 502, 327 Infantry Battalions).

176   The most recent Soviet sources cite the following formations as having been amongst the surrounded forces; the 361 and 340 Infantry Divisions, the 454 Security Division, the SS Infantry Division 'Galicia', and the remnants of the 349 Infantry Division along with detachments of the 505 and 507 separate panzer battalions. 'L'vov - Sandomierz 1944', *op cit*.; p. 143. In fact, in mid-July 1944, Panzer Abteilung 506 was attached to 8 Panzer Division (see TIGER The History of a Legendary Weapon 1942–45, Egon Kleine and Volkmar Kühn, Translated by David Johnston, J.J. Fedorowicz, Winnipeg, Manitoba, Canada, 1989, p. 114), however there is no evidence to suggest that Pz.Abt. 505 was present. Moreover, Korps Abteilung 'C' has been omitted as has Pz. Abt.509 which was known to have been deployed around Sokal in mid-July 1944.

177   'L'vov - Sandomierz 1944', *op cit*.; p. 74.

178   Izvestia Nr. 170, 19 July 1944, p. 1, col. 6-7.

179   Konev hoped to outflank and capture L'viv off the march before the Germans had time to bring up their reinforcement.

180   'L'vov - Sandomierz 1944', *op cit*.; p. 76.

181   That is 3 Guards Tank and 4 Tank Armies, 60 and 38 Armies and General Sokolov's Cavalry Mechanised Group. *Ibid*.

182   *Ibid*., p. 175.

183   *Ibid*., p. 179.

184   Communications difficulties was one of the main contributory factors which prevented the corps from conducting a successful breakout.

185 Lange, 'Korpsabteilung 'C' in der Kesselschlacht, *op cit.*; p. 10.

186 *Ibid.*; pp. 10-11.

187 Heike, Eng. ed., *op cit.*; p. 44.

188 This made the Galician Division easily distinguishable from the regular army units operating alongside it and also served to identify individual soldiers as being Waffen-SS personnel.

189 M. Dlaboha, http://web.archive.org/web/20091217235006/http://lib.galiciadivision.com/brody/brody17.html.

190 *Ibid.*

191 Interview W. Sirsky, Toronto, 3 June 1993. See also L. Ortynsky, eb.archive.org/web/20091216190449/http://lib.galiciadivision.com/brody/brody20.html.

192 Regarding the issue of alcohol to the Red Army men, in his account W. Sirsky who took part in the counterattack wrote 'By now the sun had set and the evening air was heavy with the smell of alcohol from the dead Soviets'. Interview W. Sirsky, Toronto, 3 June 1993 and letter to author 24 October 1992.

193 L. Ortynsky, eb.archive.org/web/20091216190449/http://lib.galiciadivision.com/brody/brody20.html.

194 M. Dlaboha, http://web.archive.org/web/20091217235006/http://lib.galiciadivision.com/brody/brody17.html.

195 W. Sirsky letters to author 26 January 1992, 22 March 1992, 24 October 1992 and interview, Toronto, 3 June 1993.

196 Ferkuniak, 'Spomyny...', *op cit.*; p. 26.

197 L. Ortynsky, eb.archive.org/web/20091216190449/http://lib.galiciadivision.com/brody/brody20.html.

198 'Überblick...', *op cit.*; p. 13.

199 These were 359 and 99 Rifle and 68 Guards Rifle Division's.

200 This was the 336 Rifle Division.

201 'L'vov - Sandomierz 1944', *op cit.*; pp. 171-175.

202 Interview W. Molodecky, Toronto, 2 June 1993 and letter to author 15 July 1996.

203 See the report by the adjutant of the 349.I.D, von Meyerinek, Div.Gef,St., den 28.7.44, An den Adjutanten des XXXXVIII.Pz.Korps Herrn Major Prahmann. NA T315, roll 2147, frame 000052. These were most likely to have been elements of the 237 tank brigade which had been left behind at Koltiv see 'L'vov - Sandomierz 1944', *op cit.*; p. 172.

204 *Ibid.*, frames 000052-53.

205 'L'vov - Sandomierz 1944', *op cit.*; p. 75.

206 'Breakout at Brody', Visti Kombatanta, #1, 1994, pp. 94-103.

207 In a letter to the author dated 6 September 1996, a former member of the II./WGR 31 confirmed that during the battle his company took several prisoners whom they transferred to the Division's military police unit which was composed predominantly of Germans. One of the prisoners met his son who was fighting in the Galician Division and together they both tried to escape from the encirclement. The son was killed and the father remained behind. See also LZ 'Remembrances, 38 years' Visti 1982, Nr. 5-6, pp. 54-55.

208 Interview I. Nyzka, Rushden, England, 6 January1991.

209 To make up for the high losses suffered by all Red Army units, local commanders mobilised vast numbers of the local male population aged between 18-50 and sent them into battle as infantry, untrained, and poorly armed and equipped, 'Take rifles from fallen comrades'. This is confirmed in the previously cited Soviet General Staff Study of the L'vov - Sandomierz Operation which states

'During the preparations for the operation, the 1 Ukrainian Front's formations and units received considerable personnel replacements that were drafted from the right bank of the Ukraine region. A great deal of work on combat and political training was done with these men'. *op cit.*; pp. 51-52. In March 1944, 'Booty Ukrainians' are said to have constituted 40 per cent of the 38 Army under General Moskalenko, which was one of Red Army units that took part in the encirclement and destruction of XIII AK in July 1944. Earl. F: Zeimke, 'Stalingrad to Berlin: The German Defeat in the East', Military Heritage Press, New York, 1985, p. 279.

210   The good treatment of Red Army prisoners as long as they remained under the direct supervision of the Division's Ukrainian soldiers has been verified by several veterans, R. Wysocky letter to author, 23 May 1996. See also 'SM', 'Spomyny, Horiachi Dni Pid Brodamy' (Remembrances; The Hot Days at Brody). Visti, 1979, Nr. 3, pp. 43-44. A Ukrainian veteran of the battle told how during the breakout, himself and another member of his company were voluntarily joined by a group of about ten Soviet POW's who were also trying to escape from the encirclement. The entire group rested in a barn overnight. Both men felt uneasy with the prisoners and in the early hours of the morning simply 'ran away' from them. B. Jasinsky letter to author, 6 September 1996.

211   Letter to author R. Drazniowsky, 1 April 1996.

212   V. Veryha, 'Breakout of the Encirclement', Visti Kombatanta, Nr. 3-4, 1971, p. 28 and email to author Jurij Ferencevych, 11 June 2010.

213   R. Bojcun, 'Kurin fiuzeliriv 1.UD UNA pid Brodamy', Visti, November-December 1953, Nos.11-12; 37-38.

214   *Ibid.*

215   L. Ortynsky, eb.archive.org/web/20091216190449/http://lib.galiciadivision.com/brody/brody20. html.

216   Lange, 'Korpsabteilung 'C' in der Kesselschlacht, *op cit.*; p. 12.

217   To increase its effectiveness, for the breakout attempt a group from the 361 Infantry Division and the 249 Assault Gun Brigade were temporarily subordinated to KAC For details of the plan see Lange, *op cit.*; pp. 12-13.

218   Heike, Eng. ed., *op cit.*; p. 47.

219   *Ibid.*, p. 48.

220   According to Lange's testimony, during the briefing Curt Von-Hammerstein informed the assembled commanders incorrectly that not only that a successful drive was underway by the 1 and 8 Panzer Divisions of XXXXVIII Panzer Corps but that there were only enemy security forces between its positions and the main L'viv - Zolochiv road to a depth of five kilometres. Lange, 'Korpsabteilung 'C' in der Kesselschlacht, *op cit.*; pp. 12-13.

221   *Ibid.*, p. 11.

222   Heike, Eng. ed., *op cit.*; p. 47.

223   During the battle several of the Division's soldiers encountered females in combatant roles, especially as members of tank crews. In an interview which took place on 6 January 1991, in Rushden, England, I. Nyzka of 8./II./WGR 29 related to the author how during the breakout he found the body of a young woman in a destroyed Soviet tank. Likewise W. Molodecky described a similar incident during an interview on 2 June 1993, in Toronto. For details of his account see Melnyk, to Battle, *op cit.*; p. 172. In a letter to the author dated 23 May 1996, Roman Wysocky confirmed that early in the battle his (artillery) unit downed a Soviet biplane which had two crew, one was which was a young woman.

224   Heike, Eng. ed., *op cit.*; p. 47.

225   Memoirs of Myron Radzykewych, 'Svoboda' Almanac, 1999, pp. 119-132.

226 Email to author J. Ferencevych, 1 July 2010.

227 Heike, Eng. ed., *op cit.*; p. 45.

228 To prevent its destruction, on 18 July the Division's medical section was relocated from Potutory to Pochapy. For further details see 'Surgeon Volodymyr Prokopovych', Visti, 1981, Nr. 1, pp. 65-66.

229 Soviet records indicate that on 18 July the Germans in Pidhirtsi launched counterattacks 3 times against the right flank of 60 Army, 'L'vov - Sandomierz 1944', *op cit.*; p. 171.

230 R. Bojcun, 'Kurin fiuzeliriv 1.UD UNA pid Brodamy', Visti, November-December1953, Nos.11-12; 37-38.

231 Lange, 'Korpsabteilung 'C' in der Kesselschlacht, *op cit.*; pp. 11-12.

232 R. Bojcun, 'Kurin fiuzeliriv 1.UD UNA pid Brodamy', Visti, November-December1953, Nos.11-12; 37-38.

233 Interview J. Wilshynsky, Toronto, 6 June 1993.

234 'Gefechtsbericht...', *op cit.*; p. 10.

235 Interview W. Molodecky, Toronto, 2 June 1993.

236 *Ibid.*

237 Interview J. Wilshynskyj, Toronto, 6 June1993.

238 Letter to author W. Sirsky, 22 March 1993. Soviet sources confirm that the Germans succeeded in dropping only 8 tons of fuel, by parachute during the period of the encirclement. 'L'vov - Sandomierz 1944', *op cit.*; p. 177.

239 Heike, Eng. ed., *op cit.*; p. 47.

240 *Ibid.*, pp. 46-47.

241 For a full account of one such occurrence where a group set out on bicycles to contact their regimental HQ only to discover that Soviet tanks and infantry had got there first, see W. Sirsky; The Staff Company WGR 29 at Brody', Visti Kombatanta; Nr. 4, 7-8, 1953, pp. 33-34. Two other such instances were also related to the author; A member of the Pioneer Battalion returned to the Divisional command post during the battle to find that it had been abandoned in such haste that a great many items and personal effects had been left behind. Julian Wilshynsky letter to author, 27 May 1996; A Ukrainian grenadier serving with 8./II./WGR 29 recounted that two men had been sent to the battalion HQ to get orders but found no one there. Interview I. Nyzka, Rushden, England, 6 January1991.

242 Heike, Eng. ed., *op cit.*; p. 47. The actual date of Herms' death as stated in his service record is given as being 22 July 1944, and this appeared in the subsequent obituary published in Das Schwartz Korps. However, this date which is generally taken as the end of organised resistance by the remnants of XIII AK which were still trapped, is approximate. See his service record NA A3343-SSO-091A.

243 The *Katyusha* (Little Katie) was one of the most formidable and effective weapons in the Soviet armoury. Christened by the Germans 'Stalin's Organs' because of the peculiar noise of the rocket in flight, the Katyusha was an 82 mm solid fuel rocket carrying a 6.5lb high explosive warhead with a maximum range of about 6,000 yards. The weapon could be launched from an open frame mounted on the back of a 2.5 ton truck which carried 36 rockets. A heavier model of 132 mm calibre and carrying a 40lb warhead was also introduced. To preserve secrecy this weapon was always manned by NKVD troops.

244 Letter to author I. Nakonechny, 6 March 1993. Interview I. Nyzka, Rushden, England, 6 January1991.

245 Ferkuniak, 'Spomyny...', *op cit.*; p. 26. In his memoirs Ferkuniak states that during the battle he met two Ukrainian officers, Waffen-Untersturmführer Volodymyr Kosak and Waffen-Hauptsturmführer

Mychailo Brygidyr who stated that without their officers in command the Ukrainian units panicked. Heike confirms that German units had also panicked, see Heike, Eng. ed., *op cit*.; p. 47.

246   See the report by SS-Obscha. Mekat, Waffen-SS SS-Standarte 'Kurt Eggers' 14.Gal.SS-KB.Zug, Berlin-Zehlendorf, den 1.8.1944, An die Standarte 'Kurt Eggers' Stellvertreter i.K., Sturmbannführer Kriegbaum, Geheim! Betr.: SS-KB-Zug 'Galizien'. RS16/6 BA-MA.

247   Heike, Eng. ed., *op cit*.; p. 47.

248   *Ibid*. Heike states that the decision to reject the offer of assistance was based on the fact that the soldiers of the UPA were mainly youths lacking military training and uniforms.

249   W. Lange, The Second Encirclement at Brody, unpublished manuscript, NA, D-300, p. 10.

250   Heike, Eng. ed., *op cit*.; p. 48.

251   361 Division's signals detachment (Nachrichten Abt). reported that at 0220hrs on 20 July the 14./ SS.Freiw.Div. 'Galizien' had been subordinated to the 361 Division. See from 'Überblick uber den Werdegang der Aufstellung bis zum Tag der Auflösung', Nachrichten Abt. 361. p. 2 under entry for 20.7.1944. NA, T315, roll 2152.

252   Every Ofenrohr was manned by two soldiers.

253   'Brody': zbirnyk stattei I narysiv (Brody; A Collection of Articles and Memoirs), Edited by Oleh Lysiak, Munich: Bratstvo kol. Voiakiv Pershoi UD UNA, 1951.

254   Lange, 'Korpsabteilung 'C' in der Kesselschlacht, *op cit*.; p. 14.

255   For a detailed but somewhat embellished blow by blow account of the breakout see *Ibid*., pp. 14-27.

256   'L'vov - Sandomierz 1944', *op cit*.; p. 78.

257   Interview I. Nyzka, Rushden, England, 6 January1991. It should be noted that several veterans elaborated on the movement difficulties caused by the effect of the rain on the poor quality roads.

258   Lange, 'Korpsabteilung 'C' in der Kesselschlacht, *op cit*.; p. 11.

259   Letter to the author S. Wasylko, 11 March 1998.

260   Most of the trucks were Renault with a few Opel Blitz. Email to author Z.Wrublevsky via A. Zhukevych, 1 June 2012.

261   Ferkuniak, 'Spomyny...', *op cit*.; p. 16.

262   W. Lange, The Second Encirclement at Brody, unpublished manuscript, NA, D-300, pp. 10-11.

263   Virtually all the memoirs of the veterans of the battle emphasis the complete Soviet air superiority. Reference to the particularly devastating air-attacks which took place on the 20 July is made by Ferkuniak, 'Spomyny...', *op cit*.; p. 20.

264   'L'vov - Sandomierz 1944', *op cit*.; p. 79.

265   In a letter to author dated 10th January1994, V. Veryha, wrote that 'Soviet planes appeared in such profusion that they even shot at individuals and single vehicles'.

266   Ferkuniak, 'Spomyny...', *op cit*.; p. 26.

267   *Ibid*. In his report General Lange falsely states 'The anti-aircraft guns of the 14.SS-Freiwi. Div-Galizien had been abandoned by their crews and no longer took part in the fighting'. Lange, *op cit*.; pp. 16-17.

268   To cite as an example the I./A.R 217 shot down one enemy aircraft with carbines. Lange, *op cit*.; pp. 16-17.

269   In a letter to the author dated 11 March 1998, S. Wasylko described how he went to assist the injured troops when one of two Soviet aircraft was brought down in Bilyi Kamin on 20 July by rifles and flak guns of the Galician Division, when it crashed amongst the troops.

270   Wolfgang Lange: 'Korpsabteilung C; Vom Dnjeper bis nach Polen' (November 1943 bis Juli 1944) Scharnhorst-Buchkameradschaft, Neckargemund, 1961, p. 106.

Endnotes   393

271   See Mykola Fylypovych, 'Z fiuziliramy pid Brodamy', Visti, November 1964, Nr. 115, pp. 84-85.

272   'L'vov - Sandomierz 1944', *op cit*.; p. 78.

273   *Ibid.*

274   *Ibid.*

275   Memoirs of Myron Radzykewych, 'Svoboda' Almanac, 1999, pp. 119-132.

276   Lange 'Korpsabteilung 'C' in der Kesselschlacht....', *op cit*; p. 17.

277   In his unpublished paper entitled 'The Second Encirclement of Brody, July 1944, Generalleutnant Wolfgang Lange wrote; 'The assault gun battalion had started to destroy its guns before the attack got underway without waiting for orders. Thus it not only deserted the infantry units in their most difficult battle, but also endangered them by demolishing the guns near the approach road to the infantry assembly area and by starting large fires in parts of Bonyshyn which illuminated the infantry units, making them visible to the Russian defenders'. W. Lange, 'The Second Encirclement..' *op cit*.; p. 15.

278   In an interview with the author Waffen-Unterscharführer Julian Wilshynsky recalled how the Germans had to destroy one tank because it ran out of fuel. Interview, Toronto, 6 June 1993.

279   Interview Ivan Nyzka, Rushden, England, 6 January1991

280   Schmitt, 'Pioniereinheiten...', *op cit*.; p. 7.

281   In his account, Jurij Kopystansky who was attached to the Galician Division's Kriegsberichter unit states that he learned of the event via a special radio bulletin, see Visti Kombatanta 1994, Nr. 1. pp. 94-95, as did other groups which still had access to working radios.

282   It is difficult to access the full extent of the impact of the news of the attempt on Hitler's life on the German soldiers as evidence is often contradictory and conflicting. Some Ukrainian veterans contend German morale collapsed when news reached them while others assert that they took it very calmly and that any noticeable decline in morale came about as a result of a feeling of utter hopelessness against such overwhelming Soviet superiority; Letter to author, Roman Wysocky, 23 May 1996. The truth would seem to lie somewhere in between.

283   R. Drazniowsky verbally to author, 4 May 1996.

284   Interview I. Nyzka, Rushden, England, 6 January1991.

285   Email to author J. Ferencevych, 1 July 2010.

286   Although one mixed group had successfully broken out, at 2215 hrs on 20 July 1944, 1 Panzer Army recorded incorrectly 'radio message from IIa, KAC and 44. SS-Galizien [*sic*] have broken out of the pocket'. NA T314, roll 1186, frame 0221.

287   Lange 'Korpsabteilung 'C' in der Kesselschlacht...' *op cit*.; p. 18.

288   Heike, Eng. ed., *op cit*.; p. 47.

289   The failure of the relief attempt by elements of 8 Panzer Division and an armoured battlegroup from 1 Panzer Division, was caused by a combination of factors including a failed radio link between LVIII Panzer Corps and XIII AK, and the disobedience of the commander of the 8 Panzer Divisions' Panzer Regiment. For a full explanation see Mellenthin, 'Panzer...', *op cit*.; p. 342.

290   Buchner, Ostfront 1944, *op cit*.; p. 231.

291   The first group which broke out at 0400 hrs on 21 July near Iasenivtsi consisted mostly of elements of 217 Division reinforced by stragglers and the 249 Assault Gun Brigade (less armour).

292   Ferkuniak, 'Spomyny...', *op cit*.; pp. 26-27.

293   Letters to author W. Sirsky, 22 March 1993 and 26 January 1992 and interview Toronto, 3 June 1993.

294   Ferkuniak, 'Spomyny....', *op cit*.; p. 27.

295   Heike, Eng. ed., *op cit*.; p. 50.

296   M. A. Polushkin, 'Na sandomirskom napravlenii', *op cit.*; pp. 73-77 and 79-80.

297   'L'vov - Sandomierz 1944', *op cit.*; p. 176.

298   According to Buchner, the commander of the 349.I.D, was notified at 2100hrs on 21 July that he had complete freedom of action. Buchner, Ostfront 1944, *op cit.*; p. 231.

299   Email to author J. Ferencevych, 1 July 2010.

300   See GPD (German Police Decrypt) 2874 No. 1 Traffic: 21.7.44, EE, LYZ de SPY 1519 SSD ESG7 Nr.10 1445 472 DQH 6890, An SS Führungshauptamt Berlin, von Kdr. Felders.batl.14. To SSFHA Berlin, HW 16/70, NA, PRO, Kew. Because of the known provenance of this message (that is a decrypted enigma radio transmission), it is exceptionally unlikely that the figures quoted could be wrong. The number quoted as being 'members of the Feld Ersatz Battalion' would still seem to be too high unless for example this is a generic term referring to all those from the Division (other than those included in the separate figures for the support and supply units) who had gathered in the Sambir area on that particular day. Alternatively, the reason for the artificial inflation of the strength of this unit could be explained by the rapid influx of personnel who enlisted in July 1944, en-masse, in preference to being drafted into the Red Army, and who were promptly sent to the FEB.

301   These were comprised of the remaining elements of the KAC and the 349 Infantry Division along with the attached Divisional Gruppe 339.

302   Several of the wounded were gathered in barracks in Zolochiv. I. Nakonechny, letter to author, 6 March 1993.

303   Heike, Eng. ed., *op cit.*; p. 50.

304   *Ibid.*, p. 58.

305   *Ibid.*, p. 50.

306   In his account General Lange recounts these events sparing no epithet when describing his own 'heroism' and that of the German soldiers who took part in grandiloquent terms. See Lange 'Korpsabteilung 'C' in der Kesselschlacht...' *op cit.*; p. 23-24.

307   Email to author J. Ferencevych, 1 July 2010.

308   Jurij Kopystansky, Visti Kombatanta 1994, Nr. 1. pp. 94-103.

309   Among the XIII AKs' senior officers and commanders of breakout units, Oberstleutnant Simons (Kdr.Div.Gr. 183), Major von Bonin, Fhr.Div.Gr.217, Hauptmann Zingl Kdr.Fus.Btl.KAC, were posted as 'Missing'. Lange, 'Korpsabteilung 'C', *op cit.*; p. 27.

310   Heike, Eng. ed., *op cit.*; p. 58.

311   M. Kormylo, *op cit.*; pp. 38-39.

312   Interview I. Nyzka, Rushden, England, 6 January1991.

313   Interview J. Wilshynsky, Toronto, 6 June 1993.

314   From the memoirs of survivors it seems that the treatment of Ukrainians who fell into enemy hands varied considerably and was dependent on the individual from the Soviet military counter-intelligence (SMERSH) who conducted the interrogation immediately after capture. Some of those who were captured changed into army uniforms or discarded their Ukrainian/Waffen-SS insignia as quickly as possible to avoid detection. However, it was still possible to identify the Ukrainian soldiers since unlike their army counterparts, each one was indelibly tattooed under his left armpit with his blood group. Often identifiable Ukrainian officers were shot immediately. The experiences of Andrej Veremenchuk, a Ukrainian who was captured and witnessed the execution of Division members were related to the author in a letter from R. Kolisnyk dated 22 March 1993.

315   Close to Kniaze in the Bonyshyn forest, Waffen-Grenadier Wrublevsky was with a group of 8 men from his unit when one was wounded in the spine. Despite the obvious encumbrance, his friends refused

to leave him and between them they managed to carry him hoping to get him medical attention. At approximately 0500 hrs on 21 July the group reached the main Zolochiv/L'viv road when in the dark they saw the headlights of two trucks moving in their direction. Believing them to be German Opel Blitz trucks, one of the group flagged them down as they wanted to help their wounded friend get to a field hospital. Unfortunately they turned out to be Soviet trucks full of soldiers who immediately took them prisoner. Upon so doing the captain approached Zenon, took a knife and said to him in good Ukrainian 'Are you crazy ? Do you want to be shot?' and then proceeded to take his knife and cut off all Zenon's insignia, before taking him prisoner. Email to author Z.Wrublevsky via A. Zhukevych, 31 May 2012.

316   Ivan Polulach's German mother registered him as volunteer for the Division. During the battle of Brody he noticed the heels of the shoes of a soldier who was hiding. He pulled him out and asked him what he was doing. The soldier answered, 'What should I be fighting for?' That prompted him to desert, obtain civilian clothes and eventually work in Germany under alias.

317   Letter to author R. Kolisnyk, 5 August 1996.

318   'During the breakout from Brody I did not see one single German carrying a weapon. In contrast every Ukrainian (even the mortally wounded) had a weapon of some sort – be it a rifle, machine gun or pistol'. Verbally to author S. Wasylko, 19 November 1997.

319   In his book 'The Russian German War, 1941–45', London, The War Office, 1956, p. 99, General A Guillaume states that by the evening of 22 July some German units were telephoning the Soviet command for instructions as to how to reach the points of assembly for prisoners.

320   'L'viv-Sandomierz 1944', *op cit.*; p. 177.

321   Guillaume quotes from the interrogation report of an officer on Hauffe's staff as follows 'Knowing that the Soviet air force was engaged in White Russia, we never could have imagined that it could intervene against us with such resources. It has ceaselessly bombed us so that we could not even raise our heads. Even the old officers who had fought in the 1914–1918 war were morally shaken'. Guillaume, 'The German...', *op cit.*; pp. 99-100.

322   'Istoriia Velikoi Otechestvennoi Voiny Sovetskogo Soiuza', vol. 4, p. 214. Other commanders of the 217 battlegroup and 183 battlegroup were classified as missing.

323   Returning to the locality in the early 1990's, Roman Drazniowsky who had successfully broken out of the pocket was informed of this by local inhabitants. Verbally to author 27 November 1993.

6   The Final Reckoning

1   Emails to author J. Ferencevych, 11 June 2010 and 25 September 2010.

2   Heike, Eng. ed., *op cit.*; p. 51.

3   *Ibid.*

4   The meeting with a mechanised infantry group accompanied by tanks was confirmed by several veterans of the battle who took the same route including Heike, Eng. ed., *op cit.*; p. 51, W. Sirsky letter to author, 20 October 1992, and B. Jasinsky verbally to author, 18 June 1996.

5   Interview J. Wilshynsky, Toronto, 6 June 1993.

6   See entry for 23.7.1944, 0826hrs: Chef-Armeechef. NA T314, roll 1186, frame 0222.

7   Heike incorrectly states that in one such battle in the town of Holohory the Corps' commander Hauffe was killed. *Ibid.*, p. 50. Hauffe was in fact captured without a fight on 22 July and died the following day. 'L'viv-Sandomierz 1944', *op cit.*; p. 79.

8   M. Kormylo, *op cit.*; pp. 39-40.

9   Several memoirs describe attacks by Soviet air craft during this period, for example Ferkuniak, 'Spomyny...', *op cit.*; p. 28.

10   Email to author J. Ferencevych, 25 September 2010.

11   For example see report dated 28.7.1944, morning report of Pz.A.O.K.1. as of 0600 hrs, indicates that there was a battle involving elements of the Galician Division. It reads; '18. SS-Galizien. Enemy advance through ford 2 kms north of Zhuravno was repelled after bloody fighting. NA T314, roll 1186, frame 1341.

12   Letters to author W. Sirsky, 22 March 1993 and 26 January1992 and interview Toronto, 3 June 1993.

13   See '...im Letzten Aufgebot, 1944–45', Die Geschichte der 18.SS-Freiwilligen-Panzergrenadier-Division Horst Wessel; Wilhelm Tieke and Friedrich Rebstock, pp. 18-29.

14   Ferkuniak, *op cit*.; p. 29.

15   *Ibid*. From the moment they reached Staryi Sambir, the survivors of the Galician Division encountered refugees heading west to escape the advancing Red Army, whom they often assisted as best they could.

16   In his memoirs Heike writes that during an evening meal given for the surviving commanders of XIII AK units, Raus expressed his gratification to Freitag for having extricated at least part of the division from the encirclement. The credit should not however have gone to Freitag as by this time he already resigned command of the Division. Heike, Eng. ed., *op cit*.; p. 52.

17   Kormylo, *op cit*.; pp. 40-41.

18   See comments by Oberst Wilck in endnote 80.

19   Email to author J. Ferencevych, 25 September 2010.

20   When asked why he didn't abscond Waffen-Unterscharführer Wasyl Sirsky commented because 'I was determined to fight against the Soviets as a soldier of the Division'. Letter to author W. Sirsky, 22 March 1993.

21   Similarly survivors from the entrapped German units also frequently encountered UPA bands at this time. For example in an after action report dated 15th February 1945, entitled 'Gefechtsbericht fur die Zeit vom 22.7. - 4.8.44, Lt Domschke, (Ausb.Komp. Gren.Ers.u.Ausb.Batl.58, 361.Inf.Div.) writes; '27.7.44. We marched about 30 kms. In the evening we had a short rest in the forester's station near Kopky. Here we encountered a partisan group of 80-100 persons [these must have been UPA]. They wanted us to march with them in the direction of Kiev. After the theft of a map and one light machine gun (MG 42), which were seized from us, we managed to disengage from them....', NA, T313, roll 73 frame no's: 6067671-1- 6067671-2.

22   Erich Kernmayr who had recently been posted to the Galician division described a meeting with a detachment of Ukrainians en route to the foothills of the Carpathians, who suddenly found themselves selves face to face with a group of heavily armed irregulars. He goes on to say that the partisan leader was completely taken aback to find himself talking to his own countrymen and tried in a torrent of words to persuade the Ukrainian SS men to join him, but they refused. In the end the partisans simply let them go on. Erich Kern, 'The Dance Of Death', Collins Clear-Type Press, London, 1951. p. 195.

23   Email to author Bohdan Chambul, 1 February 2010.

24   Drazniowsky verbally to author 4 May 1996. For a description of a similar meeting between UPA members and soldiers of the Division from a German perspective see Erich Kern, 'Der Grosse Rausch, Russlandfeldzug', 1941–1945, Zuerich, 1948, p. 148.

25   Letter from Otto Wächter to Charlotte Wächter, 25/7/44, HWA.

26   Letter from Otto Wächter to Charlotte Wächter, 27/7/44, HWA.

27   Ferkuniak wrote 25 July in his memoirs but this date is incorrect. Ferkuniak, 'Spomyny...', *op cit*.; p. 29.

28 *Ibid.* The Ukrainian officers included; Brygidyr, Ferkuniak, Kosak, Czuczkewycz, Ortynsky, Chaplain Levenetz, Dr Panasiuk, Honcharenko, Bayborak, Sylenko, Bojcun, Dolynsky, Yaskevych and Karantnyzky.

29 Heike, Eng. ed., *op cit.*; p. 52.

30 For example a report by Luftflotte 6 (Air-Fleet 6) to the OKH General Staff Operations Department commander Generalfeldmarschall Model (Army Group Centre) dated 15 July 1944, entitled Beurteilung des Lage am 15.7.1944 (Review of the Situation on 15.7.1944), gives an excellent and accurate analysis of the situation facing the Army Group on this date. It reads; Review of the Situation on 15.7.1944

'The enemy commenced the expected attack operations in sharply concentrated spearheads, along the lines [directions] expected from this Army Group in accordance with its structure and the regional [geographical] conditions—North-westwards Ternopil and south-westwards Luzk. At the former point the involvement of the 4.Pz.Army has been confirmed and at the latter point the 1.Pz. Army.

All indications are that [the enemy] will shortly also attack at Kovel with very considerable forces. It is uncertain whether the enemy will also commence an appropriately timed [lit. temporally stepped] approach southwards of the Dniester in order to attack in the direction of Stanislav.

The strength of the enemy is unchanged with 99 infantry divisions and with 3900 tanks and self-propelled guns mostly attached to three Panzer Armies.[The enemy] has the freedom to sharply concentrate their forces at weakening points during the attack along the line/region defined by them.

The Army Group North-Ukraine faces this enemy with 37 divisions (of which 7 are Hungarian) along the front. At the beginning of the attack the Army Group North-Ukraine had 6 light Divisions (of which one was Hungarian), and 4 infantry Divisions (of which 3 were Hungarian) in reserve.

Decisive is:

The allocation of forces for the Army Group at the end of June was tailored to having just sufficient forces to allow a good prospect of success in countering the enemy attack at all points, making use of reserves in particular Panzer units. Since that time the Army Group has given away (taking into account the addition of the 17.Pz.Div) 6 Panzer-Divisions, 3 Panzer-Abteilungen, and 3 Infantry Divisions. This amounts to nearly all of the reserve, as the Hungarian divisions are of minimal value. The 14. SS.Freiw.Div.'Galizien' and the newly arrived combat group of the 18.SS.Freiw. Div. are only to a small extent ready for deployment. The consequences of this reduction in forces have been reported by the Army Group in the past two weeks'. See Geheime Kommandosache, Fernschreiben. 15.7.1944, Zeit: an O.K.H./GenstdH/Op.Abt. KR Generalfeldmarschall Model H.Gr.Mitte, g.Kdos. nachr.: Luftflotte 6, Beurteilung des Lage am 15.7.1944, RH 19 VI/19, BA-MA.

31 Heike, Eng. ed., *op cit.*; p. 52.

32 In so doing, he joined others such as Fritz Arlt who headed the Eastern Volunteers Desk (a special advisory agency within the SS-FHA which sought to mobilise the support of the hitherto subjugated eastern peoples en masse in the defence of the collapsing Reich. Himmler approved the formation of the *Leitstelle Ost* in June 1944 to gain formal jurisdiction over the eastern volunteers already fighting on the German side. Berger subsequently appointed Dr Arlt as its head and charged him with the task of raising and organising volunteer formations composed of eastern nationals within SS formations. Arlt accepted the position with the proviso that he was 'authorised to concede national autonomy to the same extent to both those formations made up of the outlying nationalities and those made up of Soviets'. Without the authority to make such far reaching

concessions, Berger nevertheless permitted Arlt to pursue his own course without interference. Arlt promptly created a number of separate bureau's within his organisation for Belorussia, Latvia, Lithuania, Estonia, Russia, and the Caucasian countries (thus upholding the principal of political separateness). See Thorwald, 'The Illusion...', *op cit*.; p. 189.

33   Letter from Otto Wächter to Charlotte Wächter, 20/6/44, HWA.

34   28 Juli, 1944 dzt Kracow, Gouverneur des Distrikt Galizien, An den Reichsführer-SS und Chef der Deutschen Polizei Reichsinnenminister Heinrich Himmler, NA T175, roll 32.

35   Fernschreiben 344/64 Geheim, 1 Aug 1944 An den Gouverneur SS-Gruppenführer Wächter, Kracow. NA T175, roll 32.

36   According to Ferkuniak, Freitag actually said 'Your battalion fought bravely. Your only mistake was when the enemy started to encircle your individual companies. Instead of pulling them back you rushed all your reserves into the battle. This was the reason that your battalion collapsed'. Ferkuniak, 'Spomyny...', *op cit*.; p. 29.

37   *Ibid.*

38   'There could be no mistake' wrote Ferkuniak 'In order to hide their misdeeds and inefficiencies in command, they covered it with an imagined unwillingness to fight'. *Ibid.*

39   Waffen-Obersturmführer Roman Bojcun. Related orally to R. Kolisnyk. Freitag was also known to suffer from a heart condition.

40   Kormylo, *op cit*.; p. 37.

41   Ferkuniak, 'Spomyny...', *op cit*.; p. 30. Among the German officers who exhibited this type of behaviour was the commander of the staff company WGR 29, SS-Untersturmführer Weiss, who 'upon reaching the safety of Trans-Carpathia, refused even to stay under the same roof with the seven remaining men from the staff company, calling them cowards'. Interview W. Sirsky, Toronto, 5 June 1993.

42   The Hunyadi Stellung was a German defensive line protecting the mountain passes into Hungary.

43   In 1938 Uzhorod was detached from Galicia and incorporated into Hungarian territory.

44   After action reports by former members of the 361.I.D, 'Korpsabteilung C' and the 349.I.D., and a map showing the locations of the assembly areas of all XIII AKs' units, indicate that for the most part they withdrew along the same route passing through Khodoriv and Stryi, to their designated assembly area of Mukachiv. Further information and extensive post-Brody reports for both units can be found in their entirety on NA microfilm no's T315, roll 2152 (361.I.D.) and T315, roll 2147 (349.I.D.) respectively.

45   Ferkuniak quotes this figure in 'Spomyny...', *op cit*.; p. 30.

46   Verbally to author R. Drazniowsky, 4 May 1996, letter to author, B. Kalba, 24 June 1996.

47   Erich Kern, 'The Dance Of Death', Collins Clear-Type Press, London, 1951. p. 195.

48   Alexander Lutsky, Ukrainian War Reporters at Brody, 'Brody': zbirnyk stattei I narysiv (Brody; A Collection of Articles and Memoirs), Edited by Oleh Lysiak, Munich: Bratstvo kol. Voiakiv Pershoi UD UNA, 1951.

49   Email to author J. Ferencevych, 25 September 2010.

50   Keczun, *op cit*.; p. 17.

51   Email to author Theo Andruszko, 25 June 2010.

52   Email to author J. Ferencevych, 25 September 2010.

53   Letter to the author, W. Sirsky 20 October 1992.

54   No individual unit escaped without any casualties, either killed or wounded. For example in July 1944 the 3 company of the 14.Feld Ersatz Bataillon had a strength of 250 men of which

approximately 80 returned to Neuhammer after Brody. Of the remainder, some deserted to the UPA, some were wounded and sent to German hospitals, around a dozen were killed and the rest deserted and remained in Galicia. Letter to author Ostap Sokolsky, 9 September 1996. The battalion also lost one of its doctors. 'The Medical Service of the Field Reserve Battalion of the 1 Ukrainian Division 1944–45' unpublished manuscript, Dr W. Krywulak, p. 3, AA. From the 780 men who deployed with the Division's supply troops, 78 gathered in Serednje. Verbally to author, S. Wasylko, 19 November 1997.

55   Heike cites that enquiries with the '18. SS-Freiwilligen-Panzergrenadier-Division Horst Wessel' which was in the Iaslo district revealed that a number of the Division's soldiers had been assigned to it.

56   Oleh Puszkar Lagernyi Tryptykh, Ukrainskyi Arkhiv, Warszawa, 1994, p. 272. Puszkar was the commander of the 1 squad, 1 platoon, 1./I./WGR 31 who was himself taken prisoner, states that in the first camp he read in a Moscow newspaper that 2,000 soldiers of the Galician Division were captured by the Soviets. Many of the officers and the badly wounded were shot on the spot and the majority of the rest given sentences of ten years hard labour.

57   For full text of such a notice see Melnyk, 'To Battle *op cit.*; Appendix 10, p. 334.

58   The strength of WGR-30 was recorded as being 1,903 men—for Rgt. Stab. Stabskp. Stab I./30, companies numbered 1-4, Stab II./30 companies numbered 5-8 and 13. See 30 SS Freiw.Gren. Regt. O.U. den 22.9.44, Abwicklungsstelle Feldp.Nr. 05-330. SA. This figure does not include the personnel of the 14 company. SA.

59   R. Bojcun, 'Kurin fuzeliriv I. UD YNA pid Brodamy', in Visti, November-December 1953, Nos.11-12 (37-38), P.6. Slightly different figures are given by Mykola Fylypovich who gives a figure of 40 from 1,000 in Visti, November 1964, Nr.115, pp. 85.

60   W. Sirsky, 'Molod Druhoii Svitovoi Viyny' [The Youth of the Second World War] Visti Kombatanta 198, Nr. 1, p. 79.

61   Email to author Jurij Ferencevych, 6 July 2010.

62   Julian Wilshynsky Interview, Toronto, 6 June 1993. In fact none of the Ukrainian officers serving with the 14 Pioneer Battalion returned to the Division, 'Pioneer Battalion of the 14 Galician Division Bohdan Kutny and Taras Katzchmarchuk unpublished paper p. 3 and letter to author B. Kutny, 24 November 1997.

63   Verbally to author S. Wasylko, 19 November 1997.

64   NA T70, roll 106 frames 3630210 and 3630211.

65   Ferkuniak, 'Spomyny...', *op cit.*; p. 13.

66   On 25 July 1944, Kaczmar was wounded and taken prisoner. He was a POW hospital in Atkarsk Saratov County until September 1946. Then he worked in an airplane plant in Zagorsk. In December 1946 he received Soviet citizenship but remainder as a special settler (with several restrictions). He held the position of director of the technical section and later chief engineer of the plant. He married there and had 2 children. In 1954 he was freed from his special settler status and went to L'viv but could not find employment, so he returned to his old place of work. In 1966 he got a job in a plant run by the Academy of sciences in L'viv. Letter to author R. Kolisnyk, 9 April 1996.

67   Schmitt, 'Pioniereinheiten..', *op cit.*; p. 8.

68   Later, when the survivors had returned to Neuhammer a special 'Abwicklungstelle' ('liquidation office') was established to verify all the information about returnees. The statistics were forwarded to the Divisional headquarters. In order to certify the death of a soldier in action verification was required by two or more independent witnesses. For the results from WGR-30 see '30 SS Freiw.

Gren. Regt. Abwicklungstelle O.U., den 22.9.44. SA. The figures for the Ivano-Frankivsk branch of the Brotherhood of Former Members of the 1 Ukrainian Division as of 15th April 1993 are as follows;

Former members of the Division:	190
Were at Brody:	141
Successfully broke out of the encirclement:	10
Taken prisoner by the Soviets:	92
Joined the UPA:	33

69 Verifying the actual figure is impossible partly because there are no complete UPA records to refer to and many served under pseudonyms.

70 Waffen Unterscharführer Evhen Smyk, led one of the larger groups which deserted from the staff company of WGR 29, letter to author W. Sirsky, 22 March 1993. The figure of 3,000 was mentioned at a UPA conference in 1992, but again this is only an approximation, see 'America', July 12-16 1954, Philadelphia - reprinted in 'Ukrainska Dyvisia Halychyna' pp. 55-61, Kyiv, 1994. English translation by Ostap Sokolsky, pp. 4-6. A more realistic number would have been one thousand given the situation, the circumstances, possibilities and the terrain and its size. The author shares the view of some veterans who feel that it is unlikely that 3,000 men could have been absorbed into reliable units of the UPA which had neither the necessary organisational nor technical capacity to accommodate such a large influx in such a short space of time. The UPA operated principally with small mobile units as large groups would have attracted too much attention and for those who failed to break out, their chances of reaching a reliable UPA unit were slim.

71 For example, a first rate officer Waffen-Hauptsturmführer Ivan Semenovych Rembalovych, the former commander of the 1 company of the Pioneer Battalion, born 1897 in Horodnia, joined the UPA after having been wounded during the fighting at Brody. Under the alias 'Kropyva' he subsequently went on to organise an officer school in the Carpathian Mountains for the UPA which held three or four courses, lasting 3–4 months each. He was eventually captured on 17 May 1950, and convicted by the Carpathian War Zone, according to the Criminal Code of the USSR, 54-1a:54-11, and subsequently executed on 8 September 1950. This information is confirmed in a document from the Security Service of Ukraine, Nr. 13729, dated 14 October 1998. AA.

72 This figure included the sections of the supply troops which found themselves outside the encirclement and thus escaped almost entirely unharmed. Lange 'Korpsabteilung 'C' in der Kesselschlacht...' *op cit.*; p. 27.

73 *Ibid.*

74 28 officers, 62 NCOs and 199 men were certified as killed, while 112 officers, 18 officials, 1008 NCOs and 4883 men were classified as 'missing' See 'Gefechtsbericht...', *op cit.*; frame 000022.

75 See NA T78, roll 142 frame 6072050.

76 Wolfgang Lange: 'Korpsabteilung C Vom Dnjeper...', *op cit.*; p. 116.

77 The Soviet figures for killed and captured personnel incorporate all those from the 'Brody Grouping', including a force of around 3,000 infantry from the 454 Security Division and the 340 Infantry Division which penetrated into the woods east of Kaminka Strumilova where they were surrounded and liquidated by 112 Rifle Division on 19 July. They are however in all probability still exaggerated.

78 'L'vov - Sandomierz 1944', *op cit.*; p. 178.

79 Div.Gef,St., den 28.7.44 An den Adjutanten des XXXXVIII.Pz.Korps Herrn Major Prahmann. NA T315, roll 2147 frames 000052-53.

80 During a secretly monitored conversation between three captured German generals, Oberst

Reimann, Gen.Lt. Elfeldt, and Oberst Wilck (commander of the 913GR of the 349.I.D.) on 27 October 1944, Wilck made reference to the casualty figures for XIII AK and reiterated his previous comments regarding the Galician Division's performance (see his statement cited earlier in relation to the fighting on 15 July in which his unit was involved). The conversation went as follows:

ELFELDT: 'Those are all desperate measures because everything else has failed'.

WILCK: 'Yes. Then there is actually an SS GALICIA 'Division', which was perfectly equipped and consisted of Galician volunteers. They were in the so-called 'Rudolf' position, which had been constructed about 10 or 12 km behind the front line. This was the last line which should have been held at any cost according to Model's theories. It was lost even before the Soviets approached. They made off as soon as they noticed that things were starting. Afterwards we disarmed the remnants of them'.

ELFELDT: 'How many of your Division got out of the pocket?'

WILCK: 'Only about 12,000 out of 65,000 men in the 'Korps' got out. But without—there were assault guns there in great quantities—it was pitiful; all new artillery, new guns and all the wounded were lost'.

[asked where the 12,000 men re-assembled:] 'Far behind the lines; I believe only after they'd got beyond the CARPATHIANS. The Russian had learnt all that from us. First of all, they formed an inner circle; there was still plenty of time. Two days later they had strengthened it to such an extent that an actual hard fight was necessary to get through there at all; besides which they had formed an outer circle. We got out 40 or 50 km to the south of L'WOW. We got through in the neighbourhood of STRIJ. There was another small position behind the River STRIJ, which forms a perfect obstacle, as it is marshy, secure against tanks and all that'. See CSDIC (UK) S.R. REPORT—S.R.G.G. 1068, WO 208-4169, NA, PRO, Kew.

Appendix 1

'Bericht uber die Werbeaktion bis 2.Juni. 1943 einschliesslich'. ABFC.

District	Volunteered	Accepted	Rejected
Berezhany	3,567	2,731	836
Drohobych	2,195	2,085	110
Zolochiv	2,476	2,312	164
Kaminka Sturmilova	2,112	2,012	100
Rava Ruska	2,579	1,777	802
Kolomyia	11,325	8,537	2,788
Sambir	2,094	1,840	454
Stanyslaviv	8,827	6,276	2,551
Chortkiv	7,343	5,078	2,265
Ternopil	3,118	1,749	1,369
Kalush	850	623	227
Stryi	2,690	1,604	1,086
L'viv (city)	2,915	2,802	113
L'viv (district)	10,909	8,710	2,199
Strength in Dist. Galicia 2:6:43	63,000	47,935	15,064

Peremyshl	1,821	1,429	392
Iaroslav	2,732	1,502	1,230
Sianok	14,446	2,008	12,438
Strength in Dist.	18,999	4,939	14,060
Cracow 2:6:43			
	Total in both		
Districts	81,999	52,875	29,124

Appendix 2

Letter from OUN to Governor Wächter, HW Archive.

Copy

Organisation of Ukrainian Nationalists

                    (: O.U.N. :)

                    Unabhängigkeitsbewegung

                    Landesexecutive: West

                    SIII 454-13 A 43 -Bd

To Herrn Governor

Des Distrikts Galizien

Dr Otto Wächter in Lemberg

Regarding: Prevention of a planned murder by the Bolsheviks

    Reference; Our report S I A

    Attachments: temporarily not available

Our organization is in possession of a document which can prove the planned murder of the person of the Governor of Galicia. At the command from Moscow, the plan is for the Bolshevik agents in Galicia to carry out an assassination of the Governor in his apartment in L'viv.

    The Bolshevik murderers are waiting for their planned signal from Moscow. The target for their assassination is perfectly clear.

    At the crucial moment of a large-scale offensive in the east, Moscow wants to forcibly 'remove' in such a manner the members of the German administration who have found a common language with the local population.

    Germans who behave in such manner with the indigenous population are particularly dangerous for Moscow, who know the German political targets in the occupied east territories.

So it was for example with Gauleiter Kube in White Russia who mastered White Russian problems very skilfully. Now comes the time of the Galician Governor whose meaning of cooperation work is not negligent.

On the contrary kommissar Erich Koch need not worry about any threats against his 'esteemed' person as Moscow values him, and he will certainly by rewarded by Stalin for his hard work in Ukraine after the war with the order of Lenin with swords and diamonds.

We are not in favour of the German policy in the east. We believe that very little good will come of this policy, but we do care about the fate of the German official in our area Dr Waechter who is very understanding and humane. But we have no intention of letting Bolshevik murders into our land.

Bolshevism is our Enemy No. 1 and the free movement of the Bolshevik 'men' in nationalist west Ukraine cannot be permitted by our organization.

We know that it is also apparent that Moscow's act would cause strong pressure for German retribution against the native Ukrainian population (i.e. Bilyi Oslavy, Stanyslav district). Therefore our boys will remain on their heels and will inform you accordingly.

We will also ensure that our members undertake to watch over your personal security.

But we ask you Herr Governor to exercise proper caution and not move freely in L'viv.

We also ask you to take proper measures for the security of your wife and children.

Beware the enemy. You know how malicious he is, and who takes care of himself, good God will take care of him.

Further information will be forthcoming.

With our best wishes your Honour Herr Governor

Organisation of Ukrainian Nationalists
FREEDOM MOVEMENT

Archive Sources and Select Bibliography

Unpublished papers, manuscripts and memoirs of veterans of the 14 Galician Division

CHORNIJ, Julian: unpublished memoir.

CHOMICKYJ, Roman: unpublished memoir.

DRAZNIOWSKY, Roman: Kampfgruppe Wildner, (unpublished paper).

FERKUNIAK, Dmytro: Spomyny z Zhyttia Dywiziji Halychyna (Memoirs from Life in the Division 'Galicia') unpublished manuscript.

FYLYPOWYCH, Mykola: Masheruyut Dobrovoltsi (The Volunteers Are Marching) unpublished manuscript.

HAWIRKO, Andrej: The Structure-Organisation and Command of the 14 Artillery Regiment of 1 Ukrainian Division UNA in Slovakia, September–November 1944, unpublished paper.

HAWRYLAK, Roman: Memoirs of Bygone Years unpublished manuscript.

HERASYMOWYCZ, Roman: (A history of) The 1 Company, I Battalion, 30 Regiment/1 Ukrainian Division (14 Galizien) (unpublished paper).

HNATKIW, Jaroslav: The Fusilier Battalion of the Ukrainian Division, (unpublished paper).

HRYCYSZYN, Michael: Smert Podolav (I Overcame Death) (Unpublished memoirs of Ukrainian who served with the '5 Wiking Division').

HORODYSKYJ, Orest: 'The Organisation, Formation and History of 'The Volhynian Self-Defence Legion' 1943–45 (unpublished paper).

KECZUN, Wolodymyr, unpublished memoir.

KORMYLO, Mychailo, Memoirs of a Forgotten [Halychyna] Division Soldier, the autobiography of a young Ukrainian on the Eastern Front, unpublished memoir.

KRYWULAK, Dr W: The Medical Service of the Field Reserve Battalion of the 1 Ukrainian Division 1944–45, (unpublished paper).

KUK, Zenon: The 5./II./WGR 30 (unpublished memoir).

KUTNY, Bohdan and KATZCHMARCHUK Taras: The Pioneer Battalion of the '14 Galician Division, (Eng. trans. unpublished paper - originally published in edited form in *Visti Kombatanta*).

MOTYKA, Walter: unpublished memoirs.

MYKULA, Volodymyr: unpublished memoirs.

SCHMITT, DR Helmut: Pioniereinheiten Der 14. Waffen-Grenadier-Division, (ukrainische Nr. 1), April 1987, (unpublished manuscript).

VERYHA, Vasyl: Ukrainian Division 'Galicia' (Unpublished manuscript).

WENGER, Jaroslav, 'Form Baudienst to the Division 'Galicia': unpublished memoir.

Unpublished papers, manuscripts and memoirs (other)

GRAF, von NOSTITZ Eberhard Die 2.PZ.Armee (Von der Monatswande April/Mai 1945 bis zu Kapitulation), unpublished paper.

HARTENECK, Gustav: (commander 1 Kav.Korps.) Das Deutsche Kavallerie-Korps, Bundesarchiv-Militararchiv, February 1963, unpublished manuscript.

HILLS, Dennis: Bellaria/Moscow Mission/Repatriation Problems [in connection with the Ukrainian Division] (unpublished paper).

LANGE, Wolfgang: 'The Second Encirclement at Brody'.

LOSACKER, Ludwig: 'On the difficulties of being a German—Recollection from a Besieged Poland'.

LUCIUK, Lubomyr Y.: Divisia Halychyna (unpublished manuscript).

Newspapers and periodicals

Das Schwarze Korps (The Black Corps) 1935–45. (The official newspaper of the SS).

Der Freiwillige–Kameradschaftsblatt der Hilfsgemeinschaft der Soldaten der ehemaligen Waffen-SS, Munin Verlag GmbH, Osnabruck, 1955–1977.

Do Peremohy (To Victory), the weekly newspaper published by the Military Board for the soldiers of the division.

Do Boyu [Zum Kampf] (To Battle), Divisional newspaper (January 1945–May 1945).

Krakivski visti (Cracow News).

Lemberger Zeitung.

The Spectator.

Visti (Veterans News) published in Munich.

Visti Kombatanta (Veterans News) published in Toronto.

Books and Articles

ANDREYEV, Catherine: *Vlasov and the Russian Liberation Movement; Soviet Reality and Émigré Theories.* Cambridge, Cambridge University Press, 1987.

ARLT, Fritz: *Polen Ukrainer Juden Politik*, Wissenschaftlicher Buchdienst Herbert Taege 31694 Lindhorst, 1995.

ARMSTRONG, John A: *Ukrainian Nationalism 1939–45*, 2nd revised edition, Littleton, Colo: Ukrainian Academic Press, 1980.

BEITZELL, Robert: *Tehran Yalta Potsdam, The Soviet Protocols*, Academic International, 1970.

BETHELL, Nicholas: *The Last Secret*, Coronet Books, 1987.

BIHL, Wolfdieter: *Ukrainer als Teil der Streitkräfte des Deutschen Reiches im Zweiten Weltkrieg*, Osterreichisches Ost–und Sudosteuropainstitut, Jahrgang 29, Wien, 1987.

BIRN, Ruth Bettina: *Die Höheren SS-und Polizeiführer: Himmler's Vertreter im Reich und in den besetzten Gebieten*, Droste Verlag GmbH, Düsseldorf, 1986.

BROSZAT Martin: *Nationalsozialistische Polen Politik 1939–45*, Schriftenreihe Der Vierteljahrshefte für Zeitgeschichte Nr.2, Stuttgart, 1961.

BUCHHEIT Gert: *Der Deutsche Geheim Dienst*, (Abwehr), München, 1966.

BUDNYI, Vsevelod B.: Rimini 1945–47, Symposium 1, Persha Ukrainska Dyviziia Ukrainskoi Natsionalnoi Armii u britanskomu poloni v Italii (Ukrainian National Army, First Ukrainian Division in British Internment in Italy), Veterans of the Ukrainian National Army, First Ukrainian Division, Toronto, 1979.

BULBA-BOROVETS *Taras: An Army Without a State, (Glory and Tragedy of the Ukrainian Insurrection Movement)*, Memoirs of Otaman T.Bulba-Borovets, Research Institute of Volyn No. 45, Society of Volyn, Winnipeg, Canada, 1981.

BURTYK Ivan: *Ternystyi Shlakh 2-i Dyvizii UNA (The Thorny Road of the 2 Division of the UNA)*, Published by United Soldiers and Friends of the 2 Division of the UNA, New York, 1994 Clifton (Obeyednannia Voyakiv i Pryiateliv 2-i Dyvisii UNA).

BUSCH Erich: *Die Fallschirmjäger-Chronik 1935–1945: Die Geschichte der Deutschen Fallschrimtruppe*, Podzun-Pallas-Verlag, 1983.

CHILD, Cliffton J.: *The Ukraine under German Occupation 1941–44: Survey of international affairs 39–46, Hitler's Europe*, Edited by T. and V. Toynbee, Oxford University press, 1954.

CHIROVSKY, Nicholas L.: *An Introduction to Ukrainian History* vol. 3, Philosophical library, New York, 1986.

COWGILL, Anthony, Lord Brimelow, Christopher Booker: *The Repatriations From Austria in 1945, The Report of an Inquiry*, 2 volumes, Sinclair-Stevenson Ltd, London, 1990.

DALLIN, Alexander: *German Rule in Russia, 1941–1945: A Study of Occupation Policies*, London: Macmillan, 1957. 2d Rev. ed. Boulder, Colo: Westview press, 1981.

Das Sonderkommando 4a der Einsatzgruppe C und die mit diesem Kommando eingestzten Einheiten während des Russland–Feldzuges in der Zeit vom 22.6.1941 bis zum Sommer 1943, Zentrale Stelle der Landesjustizverwaltungen, Ludwigsburg, den 30.12.1964.

Dienstaltersliste der Schuzstaffel der NSDAP: (SS-Obersturmbannführer und SS-Sturmbannführer), Stand vom 1.Oktober 1944, Herausgegeben vom SS-Personalhauptampt, Berlin, 1944.

Dienstaltersliste der Schuzstaffel der NSDAP: (SS-Obersturmbannführer und SS-Sturmbannführer), Stand vom 9.November 1944, Herausgegeben vom SS-Personalhauptampt, Berlin, 1944.

Dienstaltersliste der Waffen-SS: (SS-Obergruppenführer—SS-Hauptsturmführer), Stand vom 1.July 1944, Neu herausgegeben von Brun Meyer, Biblio Verlag, Osnabrück, 1987.

Der Dienstkalender Heinrich Himmler 1941/42, Christians, Hbg., 1999.

DMYTRYSHYN, Basil: The Nazis and the SS Volunteer Division 'Galicia', *American Slavic and East European Review* 15, No:1 (February 1956), 1-10.

The SS Division Galicia: Its Genesis, Training, Deployment, Nationalities Papers vol. XXI, No. 2 Fall, 1993.

DORRIL, Stephen: *MI6, Fifty Years of Special Operations*, Fourth Estate, London, 2000.

Druzhyny ukrainskykh natsionalistiv u 1941–1942 rokakh, München, Nasha knyhozbirnia, 1953.

EDENSOR, Tim and Kelly MIJ: (editors) *Moving Worlds, Personal Recollections of Twenty One Immigrants to Edinburgh*, Polygon, Edinburgh, 1989.

ERICKSON, John: *The Road to Berlin, Stalin's War with Germany*, vol. 2, Weidenfield and Nicholson, London, 1983.

FAJDIGA, Mirko: *Braciceva brigada na Štajerskem, Koroškem in Gorenjskem*, 2. knjiga, Zalozba Obzorja Maribor, 1994.

Feldbacher Beitrage zur Heimatkunde der Südoststeiermark, Heft 4 (1989) 1945: Kriegsende in der Sudoststeiermark, Feldbach, 1989.

FISCHER, George: *Soviet Opposition to Stalin*, Harvard University Press, Cambridge, Mass, 1952.

FRICKE, Gert: *Fester Platz Tarnopol 1944*, Verlag Rombach Freiburg, 1969.

GLANTZ, David M, and HOUSE, Jonathan M., *When Titans Clashed, How the Red Army Stopped Hitler*, University Press of Kansas, 1995.

The Battle of L'vov, July 1944, The Soviet General Staff Study, Routledge, Great Britain, 2002.

GUILLAUME, General A.: *The German Russian War 1941–1945*, London, The War Office, 1956.

Handbook on German Military Forces: (United States War Department technical manual, TM-E 30-451), 15 March 1943. Washington D.C.

HEIBER, Helmut: *Reichsführer: Briefe an und von Himmler*, Deutsch Verlags Anstalt, Stuttgart, 1968.

HEIKE, Wolf Dietrich: *Ukrainaka dyviziia 'Halychyna': Istoriia formuvannia i boiovykh dii u 1943–45 rokakh. (The Ukrainian Division Galicia, the History of its Formation and Military Operations 1941–45)*, Translated by Roman Kolisnyk, Toronto, Bratstvo Kolyshnikh voiakiv 1-oi ukrainskoi dyvizii UNA, 1970.

Sie Wollten die Freiheit: Die Geschichte der Ukrainischen Division 1943–1945. Dorheim: Podzun Verlag, n.d., 1973.

The Ukrainian Division 'Galicia', 1943–45, A Memoir, Shevchenko Scientific Society, Toronto–Paris–Munich, 1988.

HILLS, Dennis: *Tyrants and Mountains: A Reckless Life*, John Murray, London, 1992.

HIRNIAK, Kost: *Ukrainskyj legion samooborony: prychynky do istorii. (Ukrainian Self Defence Legion)* Toronto: Nakladom starshyn i voiakiv legionu, 1977.

HÖHNE, Heinz: *The Order of the Deaths Head*, Pan Books Ltd, 1972.

HORODYSKY, Orest: *Dva dni v partyzantsi, (Two Days Among Partisans)* Samostiina Ukraina (Chicago-New York), No. 7 (161), July 1962.

HRYTSAK, Pavlo: *Vezhi i Kulemety (Spohady z Dyvizii bolshevytskoho polonu); (Towers and Machine-guns, Memoirs from the Division and Bolshevik prisons)*, Brotherhood of Veterans of the 1 Ukrainian Division of the UNA, Munich, 1959.

HUNCZAK, Taras: *In Enemy Uniforms, Kiev, Time of Ukraine* (Chas Ukrainy), 1993.

On the Horns of a Dilemma, The Story of the Ukrainian Division Halychyna, University Press of America, 4720 Boston Way, Lanham, MD 20706, 2000.

IL'NYTSKYJ, Roman: *Deutschland und die Ukraine, 1934–45: Tatsachen europaischer Ostpolitik, ein Vorbericht*. 2 vols., Munich: Osteuropa Institut, 1955.

Istoriia Velikoi Otechestvennoi Voiny Sovetskogo Soiuza 1941–1945, Moscow 1960–1963, vol 4.

KALBA, Myroslav: *U lavakh Druzhynnykiv*, Denver, USA, 1982.

'Nachtigall' A Battalion of the Ukrainian Nationalists (Facts and Documents), Denver, USA, 1984.

Druzhyny Ukrainskyh Nationalistiv u 1941–1942, rocac, München, 1953.

KAMENETSKYJ, Ihor: *Hitler's Occupation of Ukraine (1941–44), A Study of Totalitarian Imperialism*, Marquette Slavic Studies II, 1956.

KECZUN, Volodymyr: *Memoirs of a Soldier Our Community*, Adelaide, Australia, 2013.

KERN, Erich: *Der Grosse Rausch, Russlandfeldzug, 1941–1945*. Zurich, 1948.

The Dance Of Death, Collins Clear-Type Press, London, 1951.

KLANJSCEK, Zdravko: *Deveti korpus slovenske narodnoosvobodilne vojske 1943–1945*, Drustvo piscev zgodovine NOB Slovenije, Ljubljana, 1999.

KLIETMAN, K. G.: *Die Waffen SS. Eine Dokumentation*, Osnabrük: Verlag 'Der Freiwillige', 1965.

KLUBERT, Tomáš: *Obrnené jednotky v Slovenskom národnom povstaní*, self-published in Nové Mesto nad Váhom, 2007.

KNOBELSDORFF, Otto von: *Geschichte der niedersachsischen 19.Panzer-Division (Bis 31.10.1940, 19 Infanterie-Division)*, Verlag Hans Henning Podzun, Bad Nauheim, 1958.

KOLISNYK, Roman: 'The Military Board and the Ukrainian Division', *Shevchenko Scientific Society of Canada* vol. 30: 1990.

Minutes of the Meetings of the Military Board 'Galicia', *Shevchenko Scientific Society of Canada* vol. 30: 1993, (supplement to the above).

KOSYK, Volodymyr: *The Third Reich and the Ukrainian Question, Documents 1934–1944*, Ukrainian Central Information Service, London, 1991.

L'Allemagne national-socialiste et L'Ukraine, Publications de l'est Européen, Paris, 1986.

KOVAC, A: *Ukrainska vyzvol'na borot'bai 'VLASOVSCYNA'*, Deutschland, 1948.

KOVAL, Roman: Ivan Rembolovych, Historical Club 'Kholodny Yar', 2012.

KRÄTSCHMER, Ernst-Günther: *Der Ritterkreuztrager der Waffen-SS*, Plesse Verlag, Gottingen, 1957.

KROKHMALIUK, Roman: *Zahrava na skhodi: spohady i dokumenty z pratsi u viiskovii upravi 'Halychyna' y 1943–1945 rokakh*. (*The Glow in Eastern Europe*), Toronto-New York: Bratstvo kolyshnikh voiakiv I-oi Ukrainskoi dyvizii UNA, 1978.

KROKHMALIUK, Jurij-Tys: *Guerra Y Liberatd. Historia De La Division 'Halychyna' (D.U.I) Del Ejercito Nacional Ucranio (43–45)*, Biblioteca del Instituto informativo, Buenos Aires, 1961.

KUBIJOVYCH, Volodymyr: *Meni 70* (*I am 70*), Paris-Munich: Naukove tovarystvo im. Shevchenka, 1970.

Meni 85 (*I am 85*), Paris-Munich: Molode zhyttia, 1985.

KUCHER, Mykhailo Stanyslaw, *For Ukraine, for her Freedom*, Minotaur', Novovolynsk, Ukraine, 2003.

KUZIO, Taras: U.S. support for Ukraine's liberation during the Cold War: A study of Prolog Research and Publishing Corporation, Communist and Post-Communist Studies (2012), oi:10.1016/j. postcomstud.2012.02.007. Article in *Communist and Post-Communist Studies*, March 2012.

LACKO, Martin: *Slovenské narodné povstanie 1944*, Slovart, Bratislava, 2008.

LANDWEHR, Richard: *Fighting For Freedom*, Bibliophile Legion Books, Silver Spring, Maryland, 1985.

LANGE, Wolfgang: *Korpsabteilung C; Vom Dnjeper bis nach Polen, (November 1943 bis Juli 1944)*, Neckargemund, 1961.

LAZURKO, Roman: *On Europe's Crossroads, Memoirs*, Published by the Brotherhood of Former Soldiers of the 1 Ukrainian Division of the Ukrainian National Army, Chicago, 1971.

LEDERREY, Colonel E: *Germany's Defeat in the East*, (The Soviet Armies at War 1941–45), London, The War Office, 1955.

LEWYCKYJ, Bohdan: *Ukraincy a likwidacja Powstania Warszawskiego*, Paris: Kultura, Nr.6, 1952.

LITTLEJOHN, David: *The Patriotic Traitors*, William Heinemann Ltd, London, 1972.

Foreign Legions of the Third Reich, vol. IV, R. James Bender Publishing, California, 1987.

LOGUSZ, Michael O.: *Galicia Division, The Waffen-SS 14 Grenadier Division, 1943–1945*, Schiffer Military History, Atglen, PA, 1997.

LUCIUK, Lubomyr Y.: *Searching For Place: Ukrainian Displaced Persons, Canada, and the Migration of Memory* (Toronto, University of Toronto Press, 2000.

LYSIAK, Oleh: Brody: Zbirnyk stattei i narysiv (Brody: A collection of Articles and sketches), Munich, Bratstvo kol. Voiakiv Pershoi UD UNA, 1951.

MACIW, Bohdan: *A Photographic History of the Ukrainian Galician Division; from its Founding in 1943 to its Release from Captivity in 1949*, (Eng. Edition) L'viv, ZUKC, 2012.

MAGOCSI, Paul Robert: *Morality and Reality, The Life and Times of Andrei Sheptytskyi*, Canadian Institute of Ukrainian studies, University of Alberta, Edmonton, 1989.

MAROLT, Joze: *Šercerjeva brigada na Štajerskem*, Zalocba Obzorja Maribor, 1993.

MATLA, Zynovii: *Pivdenna pokhidna hrupa, Nasha knyhozbirnia*, München, 1952.

MEDYNSKY, Stephan: *The Trials of the Ukrainian Division*, (Dyvisiynymy stezhkamy), private publication, Toronto, 1991.

MEHNER, Kurt: *Die Waffen-SS und Polizei 1939–45*, (*Führung und Truppe*) Militair-Verlag, Klaus D. Patzwall Norderstedt, 1995.

Die Geheimen Tagesberichte der Deutschen Wehrmachtführung im Zweiten Weltkrieg 1939–1945, (vols. 1-12) Biblio Verlag, Osnabrück, 1985.

MELLENTHIN, F. W.: *Panzer Battles*, Futura, Macdonald and Co. Ltd, London, 1984.

MELNYK, Michael James: *Alphabetical Listing of Former Officers from* the '14. *Waffen-Grenadier-Division der SS (galizische Nr. 1)*, Private publication, August 2001.

Alphabetical Listing of Former Officers from the '14. Waffen-Grenadier-Division der SS (galizische Nr. 1) revised, private publication, October 2010.

To Battle, the Formation and History of the 14 Galician Waffen-SS Division, Helion and Co., Solihull, England, 2002.

To Battle, the Formation and History of the 14 Galician Waffen-SS Division, Helion and Co., Solihull, England, corrected reprint 2007.

MOLAU, Andreas: *Alfred Rosenberg—Der Ideologe des Nationalsozialismus—Eine politische Biografie*, Verlag Siegfried Bublies, Koblenz, 1993.

MOORE, John P.: *Offiziereliste Der Waffen-SS*, J. P.Moore Publishing 2001.

NAHAYEWSKY, Rev Isidor: *Spohady poliovoho dukhovnyka*, Toronto, Ukrainian Book Co., 1985.

NEBELIUK, Myroslav: *Under Foreign Flags*, Piuf Editions, SCIP, Paris, 1951.

NEUFELDT, H. J., HUCK, J., TESSIN, G.: *Zur Geschichte der Ordnungspolizei 1936–1945*. Als Manuskript gedruckt, Koblenz, 1957.

NEULEN, Hans Werner: *An deutscher Seite, Internationale Freiwillige von Wehrmacht und Waffen-SS*, München, 1985.

ORTYNSKYJ, Lubomyr: Prawda o Ukrainskiej Dywizji. Paris: *Kultura*, Nr.11, 1952, 109-116.

OSTROWSKY, Oleh: *Vodyla molodistj*, (*Led by Youth*) R.V.O, (Osnova Foundation) L'viv, 1996.

OWAD, Jaroslav: *Bo viyna viynoiu*, L'viv, 1999.

PAZIUK, Michael: *Victim of Circumstance*, (*A Ukrainian in the Army of the Third Reich*) Bridge Books, Wrexham, Clwyd, 1995.

PANCHUK, Gordon R. Bohdan: *Heroes of Their Day: The Memoirs of Bohdan Panchuk* (Toronto, Multicultural History Society, 1983.

PANKIVSKY, Kost: *Roky nimetskoi okupatsii.* (*Years of the German Occupation*) New York: Kliuchi, 1965. 2nd ed. New York, Naukove tovarystvo im. Shevchenka, 1983.

PIDHAYNY, Bohdan: *Two Paths One Aim*, article translated from the Ukrainian by J. Hnatkiw.

PRAG, Werner and JACOBMEYER Wolfgang: *Das Diensttagebuch des deutschen Generalgouverneurs in Polen 1939–1945*, Deutsche Verlags-Anstalt, Stuttgart, 1975.

POBIHUSHTCHYI-REN, Evhen: *My Life's Mosaic*, Association of Ukrainians in Great Britain, 1982.

POHL, Dieter: *Nationalsozialistische Judenverfolgung in Ostien 1941–1944*, Organisation und Durchführung eines staatlichen Massenverbrechens, (Publikation des Insituts für Zeitgeschichte), R. Oldenbourg Verlag GmbH München, 1997.

POLUSHKIN, M.: *Na Sandomirskom napravlenii Lvovsko–Sandomirskaya Operatsiya* (*July–August 1944*). Moscow, Voenizdat, 1969.

PUNTIGAM, Oberstleutnant Josef-Paul: *Ortskampf-am Beispiel der Stadt Feldbach im Jahr 1945*, Truppendienst 1/1989.

Vom Plattensee Bis Zur Mur, Die Kampfe 1945 im Dreilandereck, Hannes Krois, Feldbach, Österreich.

PUSZKAR, Oleh: Lagernyi Tryptykh, Ukrainskyi Arkhiv, Warszawa, 1994.

REBET Lev: *Svitla I tini OUN*. München; Ukrainskyi samostiinyk, 1964.

Reichsrangliste der Offiziere der Schutzpolizei und Gendarmerie, 1. Teil, Generale und Stabsoffiziere, Berlin, Reichsdruckerei, 1941.

Reichsrangliste der Offiziere der Schutzpolizei und Gendarmerie, 2. Teil, Hauptleute, Berlin, Reichsdruckerei, 1941.

Reichsrangliste der Offiziere der Schutzpolizei und Gendarmerie, 3. Teil, Oberleutnante und Leutnante, Berlin, Reichsdruckerei, 1941.

SEMOTIUK, Jaroslav: *Ukrainian Military Medals*, Shevchenko Scientific Society in Canada, Toronto, Canada, 1991.

SEMCHYSHYN Myroslav: 'From the Book of Lev', Ukrainian L'viv, 20–40 years', *Memoirs*, Schevchenko Scientific Society Memoir Library of SSS, No. 4, L'viv, 1998.

SHANDRUK, Pavlo: *Arms of Valour*, (Trans by O. Olesnicki), New York, Robert Speller and Sons, 1959.

SHANKOVSKY, Lev: UPA and the Division 'Halychyna, published in *America*, July 12–16, 1954, Philadelphia.

Pokhidni hrupy OUN; prychynky do istorii pokhidnykh hrup OUN na tsentralnykh I skhidnikh zemliakh Ukrainy v 1941–1943 rr. Ukrainskyi samostiinyk, München, 1958.

SKORUPSKYI, Maksym: U nastupakh i vidstupakh: Spohady, Chicago, 1961.

SLABOSHPYTSKYI, Mykhaylo and STETSENKO Valerii: Ukrainian Division 'Galicia', Association 'Negociant-Plus', Brotherhood of Former Soldiers of the 1 Ukrainian Division on the UNA, Editorial Board of the newspaper *News from Ukraine*, Kiev, Toronto, 1994.

STETKEWYCH, L.: Jak z Berezhan do Kadry. Spogady z dyvizii. Ternopil: Dhzura, 1998.

STIMPEL, Hans-Martin: *Die Deutsche Fallschirmtruppe 1942–1945 Einsätze auf Kriegsschauplätzen im Osten und Westen*, E.S. Mittler, 2001.

STRLE, Franci: *Veliki finale na Koroškem*, Ljubljana 1976.

STIPLOVSEK, Dr Miroslav: *Šlandrova brigada, Knjižnica NOV in POS 10*, Ljubljana, Maribor 1971

STRIK-STRIKFELDT, Wilfred: *Against Stalin and Hitler*, Macmillan and Co., 1970.

STERCHO, Petro: *Karpato-ukrainska derzhava: do istorii vyzvolnoi borotby karpatskykh ukraintsiv u 1919–1939, rokakh*, Toronto, 1965.

Spysok Polyahlych v WII-hiy Svitoviy Viyni v Boyakh proty CCCR (Obyednannya Buvshykh Voyakiv u Velykiy Brytaniyi, London 1953 (Listing of the killed soldiers of the '1 Ukrainian Division' and other Military Formations in World War II in the Battles Against the USSR) published the *Association of Former Combatants in Great Britain*, London, 1953.

SZEZESNIAK, Antoni B. and WIESLAW Z.: *Szota, Droga do nikad*, Warsaw, 1973.

TATARSKYJ, Volodymyr: Pid Chotyrma Praporamy (Under Four Flags), Buchdruckerei u. Verlag, München 1983.

TESSIN, Georg and NEUFELDT H. J.: *Zur Geschichte Der Ordunungspolizei 1936–1945*, Schriften des Bundesarchivs vol. 3, Koblenz, 1957.

THOMAS, N. and MIKULAN, K.: *Axis Forces in Yugoslavia 1941–45*, Osprey publications, London, 1995.

THORWALD, Jurgen: *The Illusion (Soviet Soldiers in Hitler's Armies)*, Harcourt Brace Jovanovich, New York, 1975.

TIEKE, Wilhelm, and REBSTOCK, Friedrich: '...im Letzten Aufgebot, 1944–45' Die Geschichte der 18.SS-Freiwilligen-Panzergrenadier-Division Horst Wessel', Truppenkameradschaft 18/33, Regensburg, 1995.

TOLSTOY, Nikolai: *Victims of Yalta*, Corgi Books, 1971.

The Minister and the Massacres, Century Hutchinson Ltd, London, 1986.

TORKE, Hans-Joachim HIMKA John-Paul: *German–Ukrainian Relations in Historical Perspective*, Canadian Institute of Ukrainian Studies Press, Edmonton, 1994.

Unsere Ehre Heisst Treue, Kriegstagebuch des Kommandostabes Reichsführer SS. Tätigkeitsberichte der 1. und 2. SS-Inf.Brigade, der 1. SS-Kav.-Brigade und von Sonderkommandos der SS. Vienna, Frankfurt, Zurich: Europa, 1965.

UKRAINE: Encyclopaedia of, vols. 1–5, University of Toronto Press, 1985, Edited by Volodymyr Kubijovych.

VASHKOVYCH, Vasyl: *The First Ukrainian Division at Gleichenberg, Styria*, Veterans News No. 1, 1972, pp. 41-47.

The Ukrainian Independent, 1972, pp. 567-568.

VENOHR, Wolfgang: *Aufstand in der Tatra (Der Kampf um die Slowakei) 1939–44*, Athenaum, 1979.

VERYHA, Vasyl: Dorohamy druhoi svitovoi viiny: legendy pro uchast ukraintsiv u zdushuvanni varshavskoho povstannia v 1944r.ta pro ukrainsku dyviziiu 'Halychyna'. Toronto: New Pathway, 1980.2d Reved. Toronto: Bratstvo kolyshnikh voiakiv 1-oi ukrainskoi dyvizii UNA, 1984.

Pid sontsem Italii: voiaky dyvizii 'Halychyna'-pershoi ukrainskoi dyvizii Ukrainskoi Natsionalnoi Armii v brytiiskomu tabori polonenykh '5ts' u Belliarii, Italiia, cherven-zhovten 1945. Toronto, Shevchenko Society, 1984.

'General Pavlo Shandruk and the Ukrainian National Army' 1945–1985. *Article in Visti Kombatanta*, 1985, Nr. 2. pp. 42-45.

'Slidamy bat'kiv' (L'viv, 2002).

VINTER, E,: Vizantija ta Rym v Borot'bi Za Ukrainu, Vydavnytstvo Jurija Tyschenka, Prague, 1944.

WALKER, Jonathan: Operation Unthinkable, The Third World War: British Plans to Attack the Soviet Empire, The History Press, 2013.

ZAHACHEVSKYI, Evstakhii: Beliariia, Rimini, Anhliia, Chicago-München, 1968.

ZELENKO, Constantine: Shche pro dyviziiu 'Halychyna. Ukrainskyj samostiinyk (Munich) 23, No's. 11–12 (November - December 1972),: 26-32; 24, No. 1 (January 1973): 25-32; 24. No.2, (February 1973): 30-41.

ZELENY, Zenon: *Ukrainske iunatstvo v vyri druhoii svitovoi vinny (Ukrainian Youth in the Turmoil of World War II)*. Toronto; Bratstvo kolyshnikh voiakiv 1-oi ukrainskoi dyvizii UNA, 1965.

ZIEMKE, Earl F. and BAUER Magna E.: *Moscow to Stalingrad: Decision in the East*, Military Heritage Press, New York, 1988.

ZIEMKE, Earl F.: *Stalingrad to Berlin: The German Defeat in the East*, Military Heritage Press, New York, 1985.